D1243816

THE LIBRARY OF
RHODE ISLAND
SCHOOL OF
DESIGN

WITHDRAWN
FROM THE
RHODE ISLAND SCHOOL
OF DESIGN

Raymond Unwin:
Garden Cities and Town Planning

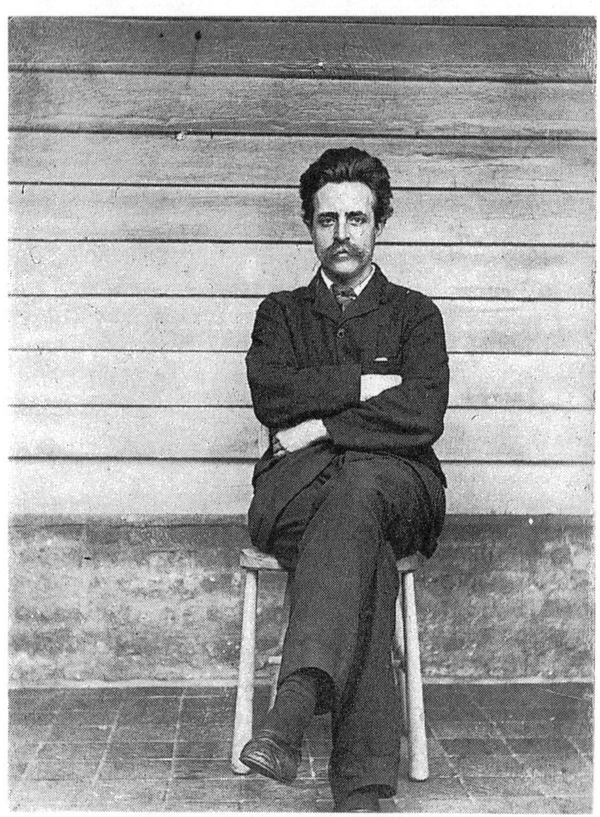

Frontispiece Raymond Unwin, *c.* 1895. The sense of purpose of the young architect and engineer is evident in this photograph taken shortly before the formation of the Parker and Unwin partnership

Raymond Unwin: Garden Cities and Town Planning

MERVYN MILLER

Leicester University Press
Leicester, London and New York

NA
997
.U59
M55
1992

To my parents

© Mervyn Miller, 1992

First published in Great Britain in 1992 by Leicester University Press
(a division of Pinter Publishers)

All rights reserved. No part of this publication may be reproduced, stored in a retrieval system, or transmitted in any form or by any means, electronic, mechanical, photocopying, recording or otherwise, without the prior permission of the Leicester University Press.

Editorial offices
Fielding Johnson Building, University of Leicester, University Road, Leicester, LE1 7RH, England

Trade and other enquiries
25 Floral Street, London, WC2E 9DS, England

British Library Cataloguing in Publication Data
A CIP catalogue record for this book is available from the British Library
ISBN 0-7185-1363-0

For enquiries in North America please contact
PO Box 197, Irvington, NY10533

Library of Congress Cataloging-in-Publication Data
A CIP catalog record for this book is available
from the Library of Congress

Typeset by Mayhew Typesetting, Rhayader, Powys
Printed and bound in Great Britain by
Billing & Sons Ltd, Worcester

4.28.92

Contents

List of Figures

Unless otherwise stated the illustrations are from the author's collection, or the author was the photographer.

Acknowledgements

My detailed acquaintance with the life and work of Raymond Unwin, and his cousin and partner Barry Parker, dates back to 1974, when I discovered the wealth of information on the development of Letchworth, while I was working in the North Hertfordshire District Council Planning Department. The First Garden City Heritage Museum at Letchworth, and the Letchworth Garden City Corporation, provided further material; the assistance of John Moss Eccardt and the late Horace Plinston during the early stages of my research is gratefully acknowledged.

Extending further afield, the help of Brigid Grafton Green, Hampstead Garden Suburb Archivist, was invaluable in broadening the context of my work. Access to Unwin papers deposited in the British Architectural Library at the Royal Institute of British Architects, and in the Departmental Library of Architecture and Town Planning at Manchester University, helped me to approach Unwin's public career. Although not as comprehensive as expected, the Public Record Office material shed light on Unwin's wartime activities and his close involvement with the Tudor Walters Committee – though regrettably much relating to its detailed work has disappeared. Michael Hughes of Welwyn Garden City Library made available correspondence between Unwin, Parker and Osborn.

Surviving members of the Unwin and Parker families helped to define the personality behind the planner. The late Peggy Curtice Hitchcock corresponded regularly and lent me a fascinating file of correspondence between her father and Ethel Parker, prior to their marriage, which brought the zealous Socialist League convert vividly to life. Likewise, the late Christy Booth patiently recalled vivid memories of her cousin, supplemented by letters covering the last fifteen years of his life, in which his mature wisdom illuminates references to his Greater London work and American journeys. The late Geoffrey Barry Parker, and his wife Barbara, added further detail to the detailed account left by Mabel Parker of the Parker aspects of the partnership.

I am grateful for valuable comments and encouragement during the early stages of research from the late Sir Frederick Osborn, the late Sir Nikolaus Pevsner, the late Steen Eiler Rasmunsen and the late Lewis

Mumford. I shall never forget the afternoon spent with Mumford at Amenia, his home in upstate New York in 1978. Carl Feiss provided a vivid account of Unwin's teaching at Columbia University. I readily acknowledge the varied contributions made in published and unpublished work by, among others, Michael Day, Dean Hawkes, Frank Jackson, Keiji Makino, Mark Pritchard, Mark Swenarton and Nicholas Taylor. Through the Planning History Group I have made fruitful contact with Christine C. Collins, Gerhard Fehl, Michael Harrison, Michael Simpson and Tony Sutcliffe.

It was in 1978, through the Planning History Group, that I first met Gordon Cherry who suggested that I broaden the scope of my research to embrace the full range of Unwin's work, to be set in the context of his contribution to the evolution of British Town Planning. I was delighted to complete this as a Ph.D. Thesis at the Centre for Urban and Regional Studies, Birmingham University, under Professor Cherry's wise and kindly guidance, in September 1981. He has been tireless in his encouragement and conviction over the past decade, that a revised version should be prepared for publication. This has entailed much work and I am particularly grateful to Mrs Sheila Murray for her labours on the chaotic printout.

Finally, this book is dedicated to my parents, who have provided encouragement and generous support for my education over many years.

Mervyn Miller
Ashwell
April 1991

The author gratefully acknowledges the contribution made by the following organisations to publication costs:

Ashdale Land and Property Co. Ltd.
The Edward Harvist Charity
The Joseph Rowntree Memorial Trust

1

To Speak of Planning is to Speak of Unwin

On 23 November 1938, at a dinner at Grosvenor House, London, the Garden Cities and Town Planning Association presented the Ebenezer Howard Memorial Medal to Sir Raymond Unwin. He had served as President of the Royal Institute of British Architects in 1931–3, had been knighted in 1932 and had received the Royal Gold Medal in Architecture in 1937. Honorary degrees had been conferred by Prague, Manchester, Trondheim and Harvard Universities, underlining his acceptance as *the* elder statesman of town planning. Frederick Osborn, himself a protégé of Ebenezer Howard, had invited fellow planning pioneers – G. L. Pepler, Patrick Abercrombie and W. R. Davidge. Walter Elliot, Minister of Health, appropriately paid tribute to Unwin's tireless public work under his distinguished predecessors Christopher Addison, John Wheatley and Neville Chamberlain (Howard Medal Presentation, 1939).

Elliot emphasized the fusion of 'the memory of the theorist' (Howard) with 'the work of the practical planner (Unwin) . . . universally acclaimed . . . as the foremost exponent'. The Garden City experiment had been a model for the pioneering 1909 legislation, but Unwin had continued to press 'towards the final goal, and prescription and precept do not carry us very far until they are translated into practice'. So completely identified was he 'with planning of the past and present and with visions of the planning of the future, that to speak of planning was to speak of Unwin too'.

Almost thirty years before the Garden Cities and Town Planning Association itself had prophesied such acclaim:

> It is impossible to estimate rightly Mr Unwin's work for Garden Cities and town planning, but when the history of the movement comes to be written . . . it will be seen how great a share he has had in moulding not only public but professional opinions, and the vast amount of work he has done. (*Garden Cities and Town Planning*, 1911)

The guest of honour, a slight, elderly man, attired, no doubt to his chagrin, in formal white tie and tails rose to speak. Characteristically, he declared that he had already received abundant honours, and singled out his brother-in-law and former partner, Barry Parker, to whom his 'debt . . . for help in aspects for which my early training had not prepared me is greater than any acknowledgement here appropriately could discharge'. He dwelt upon Howard's contribution to planning:

> Howard realised that the true purpose of planning . . . is to afford greater and wider opportunities for securing the right location of human activities, and for creating . . . an environment more appropriate than haphazard development . . . Howard's conception [*sic*] of a new planned order . . . was foreign to the economic and social ideas of his day. We can hardly be surprised therefore, though we may well be disappointed, that thirty years have been needed for us to learn and to become accustomed to . . . planning; and that we are only now seeking through Royal Commissions to base our planning on the firm foundation which Howard laid.

Unwin speculated on the complexities of planning for the future. The chaos of metropolitan congestion, the waste of suburban sprawl, the Achilles' heel of land values and compensation provided fundamental challenges. He turned to Elliot with a personal plea:

> If you, Sir . . . could establish a national board or commission to study this problem of distribution and to embody their findings in a master plan to serve as a guiding basis – not a straightjacket – and if you could establish for this vast city [Greater London] a regional board . . . and to give guidance and support to the hundred or more local planning authorities who are trying in vain to make a coherent plan out of the crazy patchwork . . . you would have earned the gift of this medal far better than I have.

Unwin had served the advisory Greater London Regional Planning Committee during 1929–33 and appreciated its limitations. The Royal Commission, under the Chairmanship of Sir Montague Barlow, which examined the Distribution of the Industrial Population, would take Unwin's evidence advocating the strategy of planned dispersal (HMSO, 1940). Abercrombie later presented this with compelling conviction in his *Greater London Plan* (Abercrombie, 1945).

Unwin's career paralleled the evolution of British town planning. The turn of the century marked both the mid-point in his life and the emergence of town planning as a recognized means of controlling the use and development of land. Before 1900 Unwin had been an engineer and had served his socialist apprenticeship. He had become interested in the design of working-class housing and its societal context. Unwin emerged from provincial obscurity to become a respected authority on questions relating to housing and town planning. He joined the Garden City Association in 1901 and planned three of the most influential schemes which incorporated the new standards of community design – New Earswick (1902), Letchworth Garden City (1904) and Hampstead Garden Suburb (1905).

Following his organization of the 1910 Town Planning Exhibition, Unwin was unanimously elected a Fellow of the Royal Institute of British Architects. In 1914 he was a founder of the Town Planning

Institute. Recruited to the Local Government Board in 1914, his public career involved the development of wartime munitions communities and membership of the Tudor Walters Committee on working-class housing through which Garden City standards became the model for post-1919 local authority housing. He served as Chief Housing Architect in the newly formed Ministry of Health and, following his 'retirement' in 1928, grappled with the planning of the Greater London Region until 1933. He served on or gave evidence to key governmental inquiries into housing and planning. He had succeeded Howard as President of the International Housing and Town Planning Federation in 1928, had influenced the adoption of public housing in the United States, under Roosevelt's 'New Deal', and had been Visiting Professor of Town Planning at Columbia University, New York.

The diverse antecedents of planning in Britain

Raymond Unwin himself related planning to his overall concern for social welfare and his rejection of *laissez-faire*. In an introduction to a procedural manual on the 1909 Housing and Town Planning Act he wrote:

> 'Town Planning' has a prosaic sound, but the words stand for a movement which has, perhaps, a more direct bearing on the life and happiness of great masses of the people than any other single movement of our time. The relative proportion of people who dwell in cities to those who dwell in country villages has been rapidly growing and while . . . much of the beauty of our old towns has been destroyed, little has been done to secure even a decent standard of health and comfort, much less to create beauty in the new urban areas which have been developed to accommodate this rapidly increasing population. Town Planning simply represents the attempts of a community to control town development with a view to providing health, convenience and beauty. (Bentley and Pointon Taylor, 1911, p. v)

Unwin focused on the industrial city as the prime evil to be refuted through management of development, berating the fact that the urbanization process that had assisted the accumulation of national wealth had left a trail of environmental and social problems. The 1851 census recorded that more than 50 per cent of the population of England and Wales were town dwellers, rising to 72 per cent in 1891 and 80 per cent in 1911. Between 1801 and 1901 the total population rose from 8.9 million to 32.6 million, and that of London from 864,000 to 4.5 million, with a rapid spread of the suburban fringe beyond the London County Council (LCC) area created in 1889. By 1901, there were 75 towns, excluding London, each with more than 50,000 inhabitants and a total population of 10 million. The fastest growth had occurred when controls were minimal (Ashworth, 1954).

The consequences of cholera epidemics in the 1830s, an outcome of the appalling housing conditions, had stimulated the concern of Edwin

Chadwick and J. P. Kay. The 1848 Public Health Act, although permissive, established a strong link between health and housing, which culminated seventy years later in the formation of the Ministry of Health. By 1875 legislation enabled the closure of unfit housing and slum clearance, while model bye-laws set constructional and development standards. Yet the 'Bye-law Suburbs' became the bane of such commentators as John Ruskin, William Morris and, subsequently, Unwin himself, who recorded stultifying compliance with prescribed minimum standards. Allied to public health were social problems. Novelists such as Charles Dickens and Mrs Gaskell assisted the awakening of the public conscience. In 1889 Charles Booth's *Life and Labour of the People of London* recorded that 35 per cent of the east London population of 900,000 were in the lowest three classes of poverty and inhabited the worst housing. Seebohm Rowntree's *Poverty: A study of town life* (1901) revealed a similar situation in York, and was instrumental in his father's decision to develop the model settlement at New Earswick, outside the city. The Victorians became fascinated by statistics – mortality rates, occupancy rates and population density – which enabled a more precise quantification of the problems.

Advances in housing design were achieved by housing trusts combining moral fervour, altruism and capitalism in their 'Five per cent philanthropy'. The high cost of urban land generally necessitated tenement schemes, particularly in London. The Society for the Improvement of the Labouring Classes (1844) employed Henry Roberts as their architect. He evolved plans that could be combined vertically or laterally and designed a block of four flats sponsored by Albert, Prince Consort, at the Great Exhibition of 1851 (Curl, 1983). The Peabody Trust (1862) and the Improved Industrial Dwellings Company (1863) were among the nine major trusts that by 1905 had housed 123,000 people. Industrialists learned the economic, social and advertising value of model housing. The dour utopian rectitude of Robert Owen's New Lanark (begun in 1798) had few literal successors, but by the 1860s a mainstream of industrial model villages had emerged, particularly in West Yorkshire, with Saltaire (1853–63), Copley (1847–53) and Ackroydon (1859) (Creese, 1966). The retention of Gilbert Scott, one of the most eminent of the mid-Victorian Gothic revivalists, as consultant architect for the latter indicated the rising importance of aesthetic considerations. Thirty years on, William Lever's development of Port Sunlight, Cheshire (1888 onwards) (Hubbard and Shippobottom, 1988) and George Cadbury's promotion of Bournville, four miles from the centre of Birmingham (1894 onwards), (Harvey, 1906) represented the zenith of model industrial villages. New Earswick (1902 onwards), designed by Barry Parker and Raymond Unwin, was a prototype for the First Garden City at Letchworth (1904) (Tarn, 1973). Public authorities had made a rather poor showing, although council-built housing had appeared from the 1840s. Not until 1890 did national legislation, the Housing of the Working Classes Act, generally permit local authority initiative, but this was mainly confined to the LCC (Beattie, 1980).

The transition from limited, regulatory intervention in urban crises, to more broadly based legislation was complex; progress was halting and incremental. The public-health approach helped to promote public interest in housing issues. Beyond that lay the vision of what might be, shaped by Hegelian confidence in progress, the Benthamite maxim of the greatest good for the greatest number, Christian and Fabian Socialism, Utopianism, the Garden City and the Arts and Crafts movement. Several of these diverse strands were found in Unwin's approach to town planning. Although the practical outlook of the Victorians tended to favour the doers, the thinkers provided the creative spark that fired Unwin and his fellow planning pioneers to seek the synthesis of sound practicality, leavened with a marginal but indispensable concern for aesthetic satisfaction (Cherry, 1970, 1974, 1988; Miller, 1984).

The Garden City sprang from both visionary and practical antecedents. Ruskin and Morris inveighed against the consequences of the industrial revolution and vividly anticipated the community of the future (Swenarton, 1989).

> Providing lodgements [for working people] . . . means a great deal of vigorous legislation and cutting down of vested interests . . .; thorough sanitary and remedial action in the houses that we have, and then the building of more, strongly, beautifully, and in groups of limited extent, kept in proportion and walled round, so that there may be no wretched and festering suburb anywhere, but clean and busy streets within and open country without, with a belt of beautiful garden and orchard round the walls, so that from any part of the city perfectly fresh air and grass and sight of far horizon might be reachable in a few minutes walk. This is the final aim. (Howard, 1946, p. 50)[1]

'Art and Socialism', a lecture given by Morris in Leicester in January 1884, hinted at the ideal synthesis. The requisites of the 'fuller life' were 'honourable and fitting work', 'decency of surroundings' and 'leisure'. The first was a fundamental concern of the guild-socialists, and 'decency of surroundings' was elaborated to an environmental agenda, anticipating comprehensive planning:

> 1) Good lodging; 2) Ample space; 3) General order and beauty. That is: 1) Our houses must be well-built, clean and healthy. 2) There must be abundant garden space in our towns, and our towns must not eat up the fields and natural features of the country. 3) Order and beauty means that not only our houses must be stoutly and properly built, but also that they be ornamented duly: that the fields be not only left for cultivation, but also that they be not spoilt: no one for instance be allowed to cut down, for mere profit, trees whose loss would spoil a landscape: neither on any pretext should people be allowed to darken the daylight with smoke, to befoul rivers, or to degrade any spot of earth with squalid litter and brutal wasteful disorder. (Morris, 1884, p. 127)

Morris looked to socialism to bring this vision into being. It seemed simultaneously far distant yet tantalizingly almost within grasp. It was thus with many other utopian experiments. James Silk Buckingham's 'Victoria' (1849), a model town a mile square, with a population of 10,000, was now an acknowledged source for Ebenezer Howard's Garden City. Edward Bellamy's vision of Boston 2000 AD transformed by consumerism allied to cooperation, published in *Looking Backward* (1888), brought contrasted reactions from Morris and Howard. The latter was determined on 'helping to bring the new civilisation into being', but Morris was goaded into writing *News from Nowhere*, which appeared during 1890 in instalments in *Commonweal*, the Socialist League's weekly newspaper. He vividly evoked a craft-based socialist society modelled on the mediaeval guild system, suffused with the roseate hue of retrospect. In place of the capitalist metropolis there would be a federation of interdependent villages, with a barter exchange as substitute for entrepreneurship. Here was the source for the 'natural groupings' and 'agents of crystallisation', as *leitmotivs* in Unwin's writing.

Howard's *Tomorrow: A Peaceful Path to Real Reform* finally appeared in 1898. Howard stressed consensus and chose a title in tune both with his philosophy and the times. Unwin also looked towards pragmatic consensus as the platform for advance, which ultimately proved him to be the ideal architect to assist in the translation to material form of the Garden City. The concept stretched the enabling mechanism of 'Five Per Cent Philanthropy' to assist the development of a complete town, on one sixth of a 6,000 acre estate, with the remainder preserved as a permanent agricultural belt, stressing the interdependence of town and country. Land values enhanced by development were to be safeguarded for the benefit of the whole community. The demarcation of different land uses in Howard's diagrams anticipated the introduction of primary land-use zoning. Although initially a single Garden City would be developed, Howard envisaged that an eventual cluster of six, surrounding a slightly larger 'Central City', with a total population of 250,000, forming a 'Social City' would result. Initially dismissed, Howard's concept proved to be one of the key features of planned urban development, particularly as modified by Unwin, and the basis for British housing and town-planning policy during the twentieth century (Howard, 1898).

Civic design in Victorian Britain generally lagged behind Continental Europe notwithstanding the precedents of Bath, Edinburgh New Town and Regent's Park, London. The art had to be learned anew: Haussmann's Parisian *grands boulevards* were acclaimed though little emulated. The more intimate approach to townscape design found in Camillo Sitte's *Der Stadtebau nach seinen kunstlerischen Grundsatzen* (*City Planning according to Artistic Principles*, 1889) based upon his analysis of mediaeval Italian and German towns, was in harmony with Ruskin's and Morris' panegyrics of mediaevalism. These coloured Unwin's early phase of housing design and town planning, adapted to the open layout of the Garden City (Collins, 1965). His *Town Planning in Practice* (1909) represented the summit of his enthusiasm for the Sittesque approach (Unwin, 1909).

Formal design was exemplified by Sir Aston Webb's remodelling of The Mall and Admiralty Arch as a formal axial approach to the Victoria Memorial and Buckingham Palace, a set piece of imperial London. In 1910 the Royal Institute of British Architects hosted a comprehensive international Town Planning Conference and Exhibition in which civic design and the American 'City Beautiful' movement attracted wide attention (RIBA, 1910, 1911). Unwin organized the exhibition and he acquired a greater appreciation of formal designs, consolidated by his first visit to the United States in 1911. The broadest approach – that of Patrick Geddes – brought in social and economic aspects of the City Region in addition to physical factors. His emphasis on the relationship between society and environment assisted the emergence of the process of survey-analysis-plan (Geddes, 1949). Geddes' material made a strong impression at the 1910 exhibition. His holistic vision lay beyond the narrow confines of early statutory town planning, but it was reflected in the London Society regional survey from 1912 and later in the informal regional plans. Unwin was conversant with Geddes' work from the early 1900s, and his involvement with the London Society, and subsequently the Greater London Regional Planning Committee, brought experience of the broader scale.

The professions and planning

The varied antecedents of town planning created uncertainty about its professional framework. The formation of the Town Planning Institute in 1914 arose from a desire to bring the different professions together to share their individual contributions to the discipline. The major land-based professions – architecture, civil engineering and surveying – each possessed related expertise but none encompassed the full range (Cherry, 1974; Hawtree, 1975). Architects were associated with the design of prestigious buildings and had undertaken civic design. Before professional ethics had been codified, they had often acted in an entrepreneurial role as developer. The Royal Institute of British Architects, founded in 1834, emphasized the architect's role as a professional gentleman and vetoed his developmental activities. Architects had little experience of the design of working-class housing, but Henry Roberts' prolific work for housing trusts in the 1840s and 1850s was a notable exception (Curl, 1983). Architects were involved with all major model industrial villages from Saltaire (1851) onwards, and their roles at Port Sunlight and Bournville, allied to the Arts and Crafts movement's emphasis on the smaller house, helped to establish architectural primacy in innovative housing design, which the Garden City Movement consolidated. In the local authority field, the LCC, with its housing division (1893), provided virtually the only large-scale public practice.

The engineer was the Victorian local authority 'jack of all trades', coping with public health, housing and building construction; provision of services and infrastructure, notably sewerage, highways and bridges;

laying-out public parks; and designing municipal buildings. Civil engineers, whose Institute dated from 1818, were largely involved with structural design and transport infrastructure. The foundation of the Incorporated Association of Municipal and County Engineers in 1873 brought professional status to local-authority officers. Surveyors, whose Institution dated from 1868, were found in rural county districts and the estate offices of the landed gentry for whom they often developed building estates. The Grosvenor and Bedford Estates in London made two of the most significant contributions towards controlling the urbanization of the capital city in a manner that anticipated town planning. Nor was such activity confined to the metropolis. Professional boundaries were fluid, and many in any case emerged from a background of 'self-help' with little formal training. One of the most notable, Sir Joseph Paxton, was initially engaged by the Duke of Devonshire as a gardener on his estate at Chatsworth, Derbyshire, but later designed a model estate village at Edensor, prepared a layout for the suburban development of Buxton, designed public parks at Birkenhead and Halifax, advised the Midland Railway on its buildings and designed and supervised construction of the Crystal Palace for the 1851 Great Exhibition (Chadwick, 1961, 1966).

Approaching consensus

Around the turn of the century the diverse professional approaches merged in the common cause of housing. The LCC used the powers of the Housing of the Working Classes Act of 1890, with flatted developments at Boundary Street and Millbank. The 1900 amendment to the legislation, which enabled local authorities to develop housing schemes outside their boundaries, was used for the LCC cottage schemes at Totterdown Fields, Tooting (from 1902) and at White Hart Lane, Tottenham, (1904) (Beattie, 1980). Several observers hailed the plans for the latter as the coming of the Garden City.

Propagandists gathered strength. The Workmen's Housing Council (1893) pressed for municipal action to relieve the housing shortage. In 1900 the National Housing Reform Council, created by Henry Aldridge and William Thompson, two notable advocates of the case for town planning, began its campaign for legislation. The rival Garden City Association had been formed in 1899 (Beevers, 1988; Miller, 1989). Under the secretaryship of Thomas Adams, later estate manager at Letchworth and the first President of the Town Planning Institute, it embraced housing and town planning. Municipal housing was a major theme at the Association's first conference, held at Bournville on 21–2 September 1901, with 250 delegates. Unwin moved the first resolution which urged local authorities 'to set a good example by building cottages outside [their areas]; only then will pressure be relieved at the centre'. His meeting with Seebohm Rowntree led directly to the commission for New Earswick, while his paper 'On the building of houses in the Garden City' became, in essence, the design brief for Letchworth. Unwin's presence exemplified his ability to be in the right place at the right time with the right people, with significant consequences both for his own career and for the evolution and advancement of town planning.

There was also a growing awareness of continental advances in town management. One of the most influential commentators was T. C. Horsfall (1841–1932), who from the 1890s visited German cities and reported enthusiastically on their control of town expansion through binding plans, sometimes allied to powers of compulsory acquisition and redistribution of land, and the differential zoning of land use (Reynolds, 1952). Horsfall's *Improvement of the Dwellings and Surroundings of the People: The Example of Germany* (1904) pressed for public intervention to control private-sector decisions:

> without control and guidance . . . from Town Councils, private enterprise does not, and cannot, provide enough new houses; (and) does not place them in right relation to other buildings. (Horsfall, 1904, p. 7)

This formed the basis for legislation of 1909, which followed the German model of planned suburban expansion, but with local authority regulating rather than promoting development. From 1904, the building of the First Garden City at Letchworth provided a well-publicized example of a qualitative approach to town design, with a functional basis very close to that of German extension plans, albeit exercised through ground-landlord control (Miller, 1989). This was soon followed by Hampstead Garden Suburb, much closer to the political power base of Whitehall (Grafton Green, 1977). The time was ripe for legislation to assist the creation of an urban form appropriate to twentieth-century life. As early as June 1903 the Garden City Association had resolved to press for legislation to promote 'the scientific development' of towns, and in 1904 the National Housing Reform Council followed suit. In 1906, Councillor J. S. Nettlefold successfully urged Birmingham City Council to approve town planning and municipal land assembly, the first local authority so to do. In December 1906 (Cherry, 1975) Nettlefold joined a deputation from the National Housing Reform Council to the Prime Minister, Sir Henry Campbell Bannerman, and the President of the Local Government Board, John Burns. Unwin and Geddes were among those who took up the matter directly with Burns. The Housing and Town Planning Bill was introduced in the 1908 Parliamentary Session and enacted in December 1909 (Minett, 1974).

2
'Prentice Period

Unwin's formative period spanned the 1880s to the turn of the century. His personal beliefs represent the key to his career (Creese, 1966, 1967; Swenarton, 1989). His outlook during adolescence was shaped by the self-contained life of Oxford, when initially he seemed to be on the point of entering the Church, following his elder brother. A crisis occurred and he questioned fundamentally both his own motivation and the relevance of the established Church as a spiritual, moral and social guardian of society. Naturally eclectic, his view of the ideal society was shaped by John Ruskin (1819–1900), William Morris (1834–96), Edward Carpenter (1844–1929) and James Hinton (1822–75). The first two remained dominant into the twentieth century and their view of society and art remains open to reinterpretation. Carpenter's advocacy of the simplicity of life remains a minority cult, while Hinton, who attempted to reinterpret religion in a late-nineteenth century context, is all but forgotten. Yet Hinton's work, which Unwin painstakingly analysed, perhaps exerted the closest personal appeal during his period of doubt and uncertainty.

Unwin was a natural convert to socialism during its fluid formative period in the 1880s. An early member of Morris' Socialist League, he was later involved with the Social Democratic Federation, the Labour Church and, ultimately, the Fabian Society. Socialism became a surrogate gospel and it underlay his work. The League initially gave him a platform for evangelism: his overtly didactic approach, with its attitude of professional superiority, is now difficult to countenance.

Unwin's concern for society began with the general malaise of industrial life and materialism, expressed at length in his *Commonweal* articles which appeared between 1887 and 1891. His ultimate focus on housing and community design was not initially apparent. More often it is the futility of work and the inadequacy of reward that stand out. Concern for housing emerged in the mid-1890s, which saw both his marriage and the partnership with his brother-in-law, Barry Parker (1867–1947). Parker's papers on house design appeared from 1895 and were certainly discussed with Unwin. Direct experience of land acquisition and housing development came during his final years with the Staveley Coal and Iron Company and, subsequently, with Parker when he evolved design prototypes, conceived as the setting for a fulfilled family life. At the same time he worked outwards to fit the individual family into its communal context, through techniques of grouping that emerged as a methodology of site layout at the turn of the century. *The Art of Building a Home* (Parker and Unwin, 1901) brought his and Parker's work to a wide audience. Unwin's contributions, which dealt almost entirely with a communal view of housing, were arguably its most influential aspect. The Fabian Society Tract *Cottage Plans and Common Sense* followed in 1902: it was a landmark in the literature of housing design.

Unwin and Parker both passed through a lengthy formative period. Contemporaries were far more precocious in establishing themselves in practice. C. F. A. Voysey (1857–1941), C. R. Ashbee (1863–1942), Edwin Lutyens (1869–1944) and M. H. Baillie Scott (1865–1945) were well-established by the early 1890s. However, the provincial obscurity of Parker and Unwin in Buxton, Derbyshire, seems to have provided the latter with the opportunity to analyse the social basis of their work in depth. This long period of acculturation paid dividends shortly after 1900, when the architect was challenged to extend his sphere of concern from the individual building to whole communities. Unwin, in particular, was amply equipped to rise to the demands of New Earswick, Letchworth Garden City and Hampstead Garden Suburb.

Family background and Oxford adolescence

In the early 1800s the Unwins opened a small tannery in Rotherham, Yorkshire.[2] By mid-century, William Unwin (1827–1900), Raymond Unwin's father, had inherited the business, but found entrepreneurial cut-and-thrust distasteful. His mother, Fanny Unwin, had had a keen intellect. Widowed, she had married John Booth, by whom she had two daughters and a son. The younger daughter, Frances (1835–1922), subsequently married Robert Parker (1828–1901), linking the Parker and Unwin families. William Unwin married Elizabeth Sully, of Bridgwater, Somerset, whose family had shipping interests in the South Wales coal trade. They had two sons: William, born 27 July 1862, and Raymond, born 2 November 1863, at Whiston, near Rotherham. William Unwin kept control of the business until the early 1870s when his step-brother took over. In 1874 the family moved to Oxford. William Unwin enrolled at Balliol College, taking his BA in 1877 and his MA in 1881. He became an extra-collegiate tutor and frequented progressive intellectual circles. Poverty and property were of prime concern. Henry George's *Poverty and Progress* (1880) was eagerly studied; Raymond and his father attended the first meeting of the Land Nationalisation Society – Alfred Russell Wallace's *Land Nationalisation* had appeared in 1882.

The city of Oxford exerted a profound influence on Raymond Unwin. The quiet collegiate quadrangles, the noble sweep of the High Street and the then unspoilt water meadows of the Isis were recalled time and again. Furthermore, Ruskin and Morris were frequent visitors. However, the family legend that Ruskin corrected Unwin's boyhood drawings is surely apocryphal, for his draughtsmanship remained stilted, a medium to convey information rather than a pleasurable pursuit in itself. In 1937, after receiving the Royal Gold Medal in Architecture, Unwin gratefully remembered the 'liberal education' acquired in Oxford:

> One who was privileged to hear the beautiful voice of John Ruskin declaiming against the degradation of *laissez-faire* theories of life, to know William Morris and his work; to imbibe in his impressionable years the thoughts and writings of men like James Hinton and Edward Carpenter, could hardly fail to follow after the ideals of a more ordered form of society, and a better planned environment for it than that which he saw around him in the 'seventies and 'eighties. (Unwin, 1937a)

Raymond Unwin attended Magdalen College School. He was expected to follow his brother to Magdalen College to read Divinity and to take Holy Orders. The Unwins had been acquainted with the distinguished historian Arnold Toynbee (1852–83). Unwin consulted a close associate of Toynbee's, Samuel Barnett, Vicar of St Jude's in Whitechapel, in the East End of London, who periodically returned to Oxford to recruit graduates for community service. In 1884 he had founded Toynbee Hall, Whitechapel, the pioneer University Settlement. Barnett asked Unwin whether he was more troubled by man's unhappiness or his wickedness. On receiving the reply 'unhappiness' he advised Unwin against entering the Church. Many years later, after Henrietta Barnett had engaged him to plan Hampstead Garden Suburb, Unwin reminded her husband of the incident. In the early 1880s Unwin felt incapable of resolving his doubts by remaining in Oxford. He was always conscious that his actions had deeply disappointed his father, who did not live to witness his son's ultimate success. His return northwards was a decisive factor in assisting his conversion to socialism and his discovery of a practical means for expressing his social concerns. Before leaving Oxford, Unwin met Edward Carpenter, who had himself recently broken with the Church, who would shortly found a small commune at Millthorpe, a few miles south of Sheffield. An intimate friendship developed over the next decade (Unwin, 1931b).

Return northwards

In 1881 Raymond Unwin moved to Chesterfield, an historic market town fifteen miles south of Sheffield. He began an engineering apprenticeship at Oliver's Lodge, an offshoot of the Staveley Coal and Iron Company. He developed a close friendship with his cousins, Barry and Ethel Parker (1865–1949). Robert Parker, their father, had prospered as Chesterfield manager of the Sheffield Banking Company and presided over a sizeable family as the archetypal Victorian *paterfamilias*

Figure 1 The Parker family with Raymond Unwin, *c.* 1898 (FGC Mus.). Photographed in the garden of 'Moorlands', the Buxton family home: Unwin stands on the left, Barry Parker on the right; Ethel Unwin sits at her father's feet, with Edward Unwin, centre, clad in flannel smock and sandals

(Figure 1). Unwin was at first admitted to the family circle, but his growing attachment to Ethel Parker, which coincided with his conversion to socialism, was soon viewed with disdain. Plans for an engagement were vetoed for many years. Unwin was forced to commit his aspirations to letters and diaries, the surviving of which are highly informative about his personal development.[3]

While his relationship with Ethel Parker was frustrated, that with Carpenter deepened. Almost twenty years older than Unwin, Carpenter's break with convention was viewed by the younger man as a fresh, revolutionary gesture he might emulate (Carpenter, 1916; Tsuzuki, 1989). Naturally gregarious, yet ascetic, vegetarian and homosexual, Carpenter had dismissed the Church as irrelevant to contemporary society and had attained intellectual liberation from the study of the literature of the American pastoral school, notably Emerson, Whitman and Thoreau. He had visited the United States in 1877; in 1880 he had lodged with a working-class family at Totley, on the southern fringes of Sheffield, working on his own 'song of Freedom', *Towards Democracy*. Nearby was St George's Farm, an abortive communal experiment founded by Ruskin; influenced by this, Carpenter acquired a tract of land at Millthorpe, an unspoilt hamlet in the Cordwell valley, three miles south of Totley, in the foothills of the moors. Following Thoreau's advocacy of the simple life, Carpenter and his followers became virtually self-sufficient, selling surplus produce at local markets.

Homespun clothes and sandals (the latter made by George Adams, who later moved to Letchworth) became virtually a uniform among the camp followers, Unwin included.

Unwin impressed Carpenter as 'a young man of cultured antecedents . . . healthy, democratic, vegetarian', (Carpenter, 1916, pp. 131–2), in many respects a younger version of himself. Unwin remained personally attracted to Carpenter even after his own marriage in 1893. Unwin's son, born in 1894, was named Edward, after Carpenter, who stood as godfather, 'if', he declared, 'an atheist is capable of being a godfather'. Yet Unwin was not an uncritical admirer, as he wrote to Ethel Parker in 1883:

> Mr Carpenter struck me as being inclined to think too little of Christianity as a means of Socialism. I'm not inclined to teach Socialism and keep Christianity to myself. The two must go together and though the matter of first importance just now is one of social justice, yet this need not be separate from the religious side.[4]

Already Unwin can be seen as striving for the reconciliation of conflicting viewpoints – perhaps the reason why Christian Socialism and the Labour Church made such a profound impact on his outlook. He was most impressed by *Towards Democracy* which 'brought a bewildering revelation':

> During 1883 and 1884 I spent happy weekends with him [Carpenter] and his companions . . . In October [1884] . . . on the occasion of my leaving the district, he gave me the first edition of *Towards Democracy*. The feelings compounded in mystification, escape and joy with which I read it through on the journey to Oxford are still in memory . . . the sense of escape from an intolerable sheath of unreality and social superstition which the first reading . . . brought to me is still fresh. It helped me to realise, too, the effort which it cost the writer himself to break through. (Unwin, 1931, p. 234)

Millthorpe perhaps represented an idyllic respite from Unwin's concern for 'the overwhelming complexity and urgency of the social problem', but seems to have been too self-contained to provide the answer he sought. Nevertheless, the influence of Millthorpe on Unwin's mode of life was profound and he turned to Carpenter again in 1887 to seek solace during enforced isolation from Ethel Parker.

Manchester and the Socialist League

Early in 1885 Unwin became an engineering draughtsman in Manchester. He was drawn into the vortex of the Industrial Revolution, to a city whose development and prosperity was regarded as a triumph of mercantile capitalism. By the mid-1880s, however, Manchester suffered from industrial stagnation and unemployment; efforts were made to complete the Manchester Ship Canal in an attempt to restore trading prosperity (Briggs, 1968). Manchester was regarded as a key recruitment area for socialism. As Unwin recalled in 1935, when receiving an honorary Doctorate from Manchester University:

> At the time, 1885, for a young man who had acquired from Ruskin a considerable taste for economic theories sometimes associated with the name of Manchester . . . to come to Manchester was a liberal education. At that time Ford Madox Brown was painting two of his frescoes . . . in the Manchester Town Hall. Charles Rowley was at the height of his activity in spreading culture and education in Ancoats, veterans of the Chartist and other movements frequented the County Forum and there was much discussion of social problems. It was a red letter-day when William Morris took him [Unwin] to supper with Ford Madox Brown, and he 'readily took up the more hopeful view of Life' William Morris propounded and served an apprenticeship in founding the Manchester Branch of the William Morris Socialist League. (Unwin, 1935a)

Morris played a central role in the formation of British socialism, even though his rejection of Parliamentary and democratic tactics ultimately isolated him. His path led from his revival of the decorative arts and crafts, beginning with his furnishing of 'The Red House' that Philip Webb (1831–1915) had designed for him. Morris founded 'The Firm' in 1861, which was responsible for the production of his textile, wallpaper and furniture designs. His studies of mediaeval literature and Icelandic sagas led to his concern for the survival and protection of mediaeval buildings and artefacts. In 1877 he founded the Society for the Protection of Ancient Buildings, was involved with the Art Workers Guild (1884) and the Arts and Crafts Exhibition Society (1887). He saw the revival of the guild system as the means of improving both the standard of design and quality of everyday objects, and, moreover, the work satisfaction of the craftsman. Morris' vision, depicted through his lectures and articles, was far removed from the dialectical polemic of *Das Kapital*. Morris presented a transformation of society and environment, built, however, upon the Marxist prerequisites of communal ownership and utilization of resources, for all its Utopist mediaeval imagery (Glasier, 1921; Henderson, 1967; Thompson, 1977).

In January 1883 Morris had joined the Social–Democratic Federation, led by H. M. Hyndman (1842–1921), a Parliamentarian; but frustration and impatience with gradualism led to a schism in December 1884. The Morris faction formed the Socialist League, which advocated 'the principles of Revolutionary International Socialism'. Raymond Unwin wrote excitedly about 'the split' to Ethel Parker in February 1885, on the eve of publication of the first issue of *Commonweal*, the League's broadsheet. The League organized offshoots in major cities and Unwin became Secretary of the Manchester branch. His reports published in *Commonweal* described Sunday morning open-air meetings in Ashton Old Road, occasionally dispersed by the police, and the earnest atmosphere of temperance in the club room. Unwin broadened his knowledge by study of Marx. He defended Morris':

> preaching a new order of things . . . leaving it to others to show how it is to be done . . . Nationalisation of land and capital are the first two great steps, but it is useless to find a definite means until there is power enough to bring it to a question of means at all, at present it is only a question of agitating, educating and organising.[5]

Herein lay a fundamental weakness. The indefinite period of waiting dissipated revolutionary fervour and disillusioned supporters.

Unwin also attended meetings of the Social–Democratic Federation (SDF) and the Ancoats Brotherhood, which sought to bring eminent lecturers to a working-class area. T. C. Horsfall, the enthusiast for German town-planning, was closely involved with Ancoats; speakers included Morris, Carpenter, the socialist artist Walter Crane and, later, the anarchist Peter Kropotkin. Unwin also met Bruce Glasier (1859–1920), a fellow acolyte of Morris (Day and Garstang, 1975). A Scot who had failed as an architect through lack of finance and social connections, Glasier had become an engineering draughtsman in Glasgow (Thompson, 1971). Both he and Unwin were aware of the peripheral role of the architectural profession with the design of mass-housing: 'society needs . . . many bricklayers for one architect' (Unwin, 1887c) was Unwin's verdict. Glasier's intuitive approach to socialism, built upon an assumed innate goodness of mankind, drew a ready response from Unwin and they remained close friends until Glasier's death in 1920.

Throughout 1885 and 1886 Unwin worked hard to organize an active cadre of Manchester socialists. He was a delegate at the League's summer conference in June 1886, meeting May Morris, with whom he maintained an acquaintance for twenty-five years. The League was unable to sustain its membership in the face of the Parliamentarians, but Unwin felt a personal responsibility for the failure of the Manchester branch. He resigned as secretary in November 1886 and returned briefly to Oxford.

Commonweal polemic

Unwin wrote extensively for *Commonweal* between 1886 and 1890. The content was culled from his omnivorous reading. The tone was polemical as a political manifesto and paralleled his involvement with the League's meetings and lectures. A major formative influence was the writing of James Hinton, a distinguished aural surgeon who had pondered deeply on the ethical and moral dimensions of Christianity. Hinton's widow had collaborated with Havelock Ellis over the posthumous publication of *The Lawbreaker* in 1884. In it Hinton portrayed Christ as 'the lawbreaker', thrusting aside convention, paving the way for 'the play of natural law' within which the mature individual would strike a balance between self-interest and selflessness. Hinton believed that atheism, through its focus on man rather than a personified God, would paradoxically emerge as the true Christianity. And 'if man ceased to make disorder, service and pleasure would correspond' (Hinton, 1884, p. 216). Morris' socialist concept that honourable, fitting work underlay the ideal society was elevated to a spiritual plane. Unwin sought permission from Margaret Hinton to prepare a study of her husband's work for a wider audience. Extensive drafts, some copied out by Ethel Parker, survive as testimony to a task that seemed important but remained incomplete.[6]

A few passages possessed a vividness that illuminates Unwin's subsequent career. In choosing a parable to illustrate Hinton's proposition of a progression from licence, through imposed restraint, to true, selfless freedom, he took the image of a house, firstly as drawn by a child: 'the result has a certain general resemblance to the cottage, the prominent features . . . are there but it is wrong in all its proportions and detail'.[7] Education in perspective, proportion, shape and colour would produce 'a picture with much greater accuracy of detail . . . in fact the details would probably obtrude themselves . . . and the whole production would appear stiff and conventional'. The mature artist would revert to a sketch technique through his understanding 'that this restraint has been an education providing him with a trained eye and hand and greatly developed ideas'. A decade later he and Parker would formulate an understanding of the detailed aspects of the home and subsequently broaden their horizons to the community scale with the broad-brush confidence of mature social artists.

The *Commonweal* articles were derivative and immature. Several were obviously based upon lectures; 'The Dawn of a Happier Day', given in Manchester in January 1886, survives written out in a cheap school exercise book.[8] Later Unwin would become proficient at improvising from cryptic notes. A recurrent theme was the perceived falseness of capitalist materialism, rewarding 'a few with enormous wealth, living in idleness, while the mass of the people have to toil hard to live at all'. Beyond the Marxist thesis of surplus value lay a concern for the quality of life.

> At present we are in such a fearful hurry to get rich that we entirely lose sight of the fact that our riches are only useful insofar as they contribute to the happiness of our lives.

The prescription involved communal ownership of land and the means of production; the enlightened lifestyle owed more than a little to Carpenter.

> The wants and comforts conducive to a happy life are comparatively few. A home to live in, furniture, clothes, food, books and a few works of art about comprise the list.

Here was the origin of the marginal but vital element of beauty that Unwin argued was inseparable from the true solution to any design problem. And the phrase stands as a description of his own lifestyle.

The *Commonweal* articles mark Unwin's transition from revolutionary to pragmatist. In 'The Axe is Laid unto the Root' (Unwin, August 1886), he considered 'nothing short of revolution will do'. In March 1887, 'Social Experiments' commended efforts to establish communal cells, based on cooperative societies or 'associated homes', for training 'valuable allies . . . [which] will help to prepare for a more complete change when we are in a position to make one' (Unwin, 1887d). 'Broken Cisterns', November–December 1887, emphasized the lack of theoretical rigour in existing political institutions (Unwin, 1887a).

Unwin was unwilling to trust 'political economy' to provide the final solution. His advocacy of 'the abolition of private property in the means of production' indicates his commitment to Marxism, but he now hoped that the change might come 'through conversion of the majority to our views instead of coming violently'. The elimination of unnecessary competition would enable the progressive reduction of working hours, full employment, greater job satisfaction, rising quality of products and leisure time in which to enjoy a fuller, more satisfying life. Flexibility and local initiative would follow the regulation of the transitional period. Unwin applied the Hinton model, with a progression from licence – characterized by *laissez-faire* capitalism, through the regulation and restraint to the true freedom accorded to the mature society. Later he would argue that planning itself was an agent of increasing the individual's freedom and range of choice.

Studies of historical pre-capitalist communities were an important influence. In 'Early Communal Life and What it Teaches', April–May 1887 (Unwin, 1887b), he drew extensively on the Belgian socialist Emile de Laveleye. Primitive societies had, he argued, evolved a high degree of communal property and cooperation, out of which the feudal system had emerged. The recent (1861) emancipation of the Russian serfs had strengthened the 'constitutional atoms', community groupings that Unwin later regarded as basic planning units. Such organizations brought out the interrelationship between the individual and social elements in human nature. He concluded that:

> it is in the society which shall give the fullest scope to what is best in both these sides, and maintain the best balance between them, that we must look to find the greatest happiness and the greatest goodness.

Unwin's anthropological studies overlapped with those of Patrick Geddes; they recognized each other as kindred spirits when they met about eighteen years later. Their studies of Auguste Compte's philosophy of positivism drew divergent reactions, however. For Geddes it formed the inspiration for his 'thinking machines' to encapsulate human knowledge and experience within a single system. Unwin looked to the élitist assumptions and in 'Positivism and Socialism', July–August 1887, he spelled out his contention that a society ruled by the combination of a spiritual authority – the intellectuals – and a temporal authority – bankers, merchants and manufacturers – even if using their wealth as trustees for the common good, would bring nothing more than a reinforcement of capitalism (Unwin, 1887c).

Unwin's search for a *via media* was stated in 'Socialist Tactics – A Third Course', published in *Today* (Unwin, 1887e). A previous article by Percival Chubb, of the Fellowship of the New Life, acted as a catalyst. Chubb commended 'the ethical claims of socialism and its incomparable powers as a moral and religious gospel'. Integral were 'a deeper sense of human dignity, a more exacting demand for freedom, a keener susceptibility to beauty and recoil from ugliness' (Chubb, 1887), aspects that Unwin made material at New Earswick, Letchworth and Hampstead. In his rejoinder Unwin advocated 'education towards enlightenment' as a way of resolving the conflict between the revolutionary and the Parliamentarian. As with many contemporaries, his faith in the power of education was unshakeable. Education was not viewed as the agent of negative compromise; rather it would enable either side to appreciate the other's strengths and weaknesses, leading ultimately to conciliation.

Barrow Hill

In the spring of 1887 Unwin became chief draughtsman at the Staveley Coal and Iron Company of Barrow Hill, at £150 a year. Its founder, Richard Barrow (1787–1865) had by 1860 built up a business with 4,000 employees and a company village of 600 stone-built cottages, between Chesterfield and Staveley. His successor, Charles Markham (1823–88) negotiated new colliery leases from the Duke of Devonshire and built up a large combine based on mining, iron and steel.[9] Following his sudden death, his son Charles Paxton Markham (1864–1926) took control. He had served his apprenticeship in the 'curiosity shop' at Oliver's Lodge, alongside Unwin, and sympathized with socialism to the extent of contributing to *Commonweal*. His initial actions after taking the helm appear to have been hostile to trade unions. Unwin regarded the appointment as nepotism and distrusted his impetuous self-confidence.[10] Yet Markham appears to have respected Unwin, taking him to newly opened pits and on surveys. Unwin's *Commonweal* article 'Down a Coal Pit', (Unwin, 1890), presented a vivid picture of the immigrant Irish miners taking a long, slow railway journey before dawn to work the pits at Warsop Vale, Nottinghamshire.

Unwin's post with its prospect of promotion might have seemed a means of overcoming Robert Parker's opposition to his attachment to his daughter. The response was an embargo on contact that lasted until September 1887, when the Parkers moved to Buxton. He poured out his frustration in a diary in the form of a long letter to Ethel Parker.[11] The daily round was described in detail. Unwin worked under George Bond, the general manager, and was responsible for designing and supervising the manufacture of mining equipment. In *Commonweal* he recorded his unease at being 'set to design machinery for the express purpose of displacing labour' and used as an example a hydraulic crane, which the diary reveals was his first design work (Unwin, 1888).[12] Another *Commonweal* contribution, 'Diary of a Tramp', recorded anguish at witnessing an unemployed hand turned brusquely away from the factory gates:

> But that man's face! I have more than once wished that it would go away from my memory! He stood for a moment and as that ray of hope died from his face there settled on it such a look of utter misery and despair as I hope it may not often fall to my lot to see again. (Unwin, 1889b)

'Sympathy with everyone in trouble and with the underdog'[13] were to remain enduring personal traits.

Mechanical engineering did not provide much career satisfaction and in August 1891 he applied for the post of Borough Engineer to the Bridgwater Urban District Council, possibly hoping that his mother's local connections might assist him. He was unsuccessful. At this time he and Parker first discussed partnership as architects.[14] Further expansion of the Staveley Company brought work relevant to that long-term objective, involving the laying-out of colliery villages.

A noteworthy local precedent was New Bolsover, a model village built between 1888 and 1892 by the Bolsover and Cresswell Colliery Company. The settlement nestled on the open slopes below Bolsover Castle and consisted of a double quadrangle of well-designed terraced housing facing a school, shops and a large institute. By contrast the Staveley Company schemes remained severely utilitarian.[15] Typical was Poolsbrook (*see* Figure 2), built 1892–3 a mile south of Staveley: 216 cottages in terraces of twelve in an unrelieved rectangle, divided by cobbled streets and back alleys bordered with privies and outhouses. Unwin reacted against such parsimony, which he berated in *Nothing Gained by Overcrowding* twenty years later. Poolsbrook was flanked by a branch-colliery railway, while its surroundings were pock-marked by pit banks. Unwin pressed Markham to provide a hot-water supply and baths in the houses, but to no avail. The public buildings – two Chapels, a mission room, an hotel and a school – fared a little better. Within stringent cost limits Unwin provided a school with well-lit, functional classrooms, a design repeated at Arkwright Town and Warsop Vale, two more company settlements. Unwin also designed the single-storey Infants School at Barrow Hill in 1893, a modest structure with large windows pointing forward to his radical design for the New Earswick School of 1912. Extensive housing development also took place at Brimington, Barlborough, Markham Colliery and Warsop Vale. The last, built 1893–1900 was of considerable size; its nucleus was a large double quadrangle of terraced housing that surrounded the cricket ground. Nearby stood a rugged stone-built block of mechanics' houses that were among Unwin's earliest housing designs.[16]

The broadening stream of socialism

Extramural political activities continued. Unwin lodged with the Crees in Spital, a working-class district east of Chesterfield. Joe Cree, his

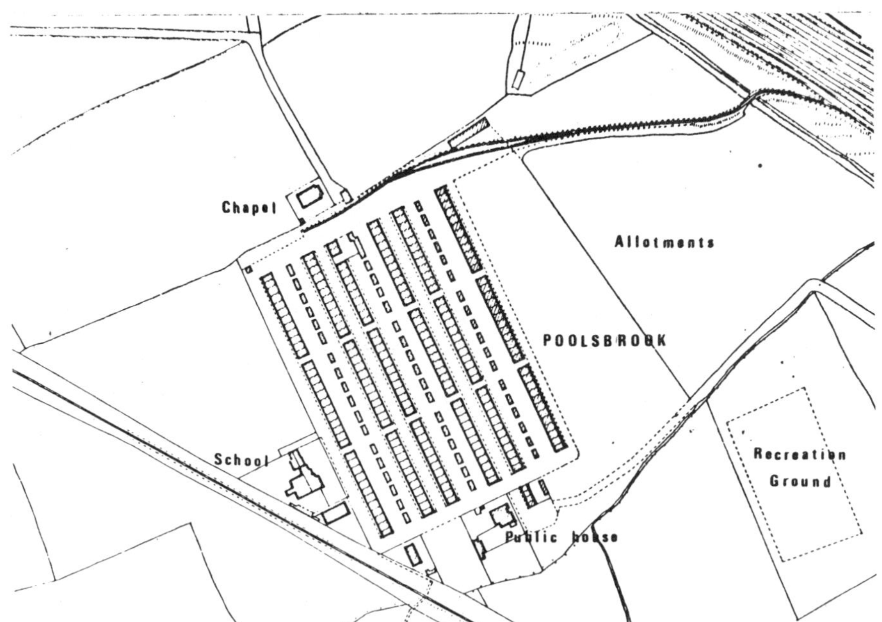

Figure 2 Poolsbrook, 1891–4. The ubiquitous bye-law layout of street and alleys which Unwin successfully strove to eliminate in his subsequent work

contemporary, accompanied him to many of the local socialist events. The Socialist League was a waning star, and in the summer of 1887, Unwin became involved with North of England Socialist Federation meetings held at Clay Cross, six miles south of Chesterfield. Its leader, J. L. Mahon, was attempting to build a solid political base in the north around the Northumberland pit strike. The Federation's espousal of Parliamentarianism represented a significant landmark in progress towards the formation of the Independent Labour Party in 1893. On 6 June 1887 Mahon invited Unwin to speak, apprehensive that it was 'rather risky if it gets known to our boss that I am stirring up miners'. Unwin spoke again on 12 July and found inspiration:

> I tried to show them that far off as such a life may be they might still be happier for knowing about it and working for it . . . I couldn't say quite what I wanted, but I think they got an inkling. I felt very earnest, the tears nearly came into my eyes, they cheered a bit when I'd done. Oh Ettie, I felt as if I knew a bit of what it was to be inspired if the right words would only have come to me![17]

Unwin invited John Furniss, communist veteran of St George's Farm and the Christian Commune at Moorhay, to the Chesterfield Sunday Discussion Group; he himself lectured on Hinton. Carpenter contributed to the programme and was patron of the Sheffield Socialist Society, for which Unwin lectured on many occasions between 1886 and 1890. In

June 1889 he lectured as far afield as Leicester and that August organized a picnic for the Midland Counties Socialist Federation at Ambergate, a railway junction midway between Chesterfield and Derby.

Carpenter's commune still beckoned. Morris visited Millthorpe in 1886 and 1889 and was duly impressed, confiding to Carpenter that:

> I have spent . . . a vast amount of time designing furniture and wallpapers, carpets and curtains; but after all I am inclined to think that this sort of thing is mostly rubbish and I would prefer for my part to live with the plainest whitewashed walls and wooden chairs and tables. (Carpenter, 1916, p. 217)

Carpenter's asceticism also influenced Barry Parker's articles, 'Our Homes', which first appeared in the *Building News* in 1895. In one of Unwin's last *Commonweal* articles, 'Sutton Hall', he contemplated commandeering the country seat of the Arkwright family, to found his own commune:

> Small wonder that . . . we should fall to talking about 'the days that are going to be' when this hall and others like it will be the centre of a happy communal life. Plenty of room . . . for quite a small colony to live, each one having his own den upstairs where he could go to write or sulk, or spend a quiet evening with his lady-love or boon companion; and downstairs would be common dining halls, smoking rooms – if indeed life still needed the weed to make it perfect. And we chatted on, each one adding a bit to our picture; how some would till the land . . . and tend to cattle, while others perhaps would start some industry, working in the outbuildings . . . and taking care not to spoil our view with a hideous building or blight our trees with smoke. Others again would work in the mines bringing up the coal of which there is a good supply . . . we all felt, I think, more than ever determined that what might be shall be. (Unwin, 1889a)

Although the imagery and language of Morris is close, Unwin was more frank about the coexistence of art and industry. He also recalled the collegiate system with which he was familiar, which was also reflected in his designs for 'Cooperative houses' in the late 1890s.

In 1890 the Socialist League began to disintegrate. Paradoxically *Commonweal* carried 'News From Nowhere' (Morris, 1891) throughout much of the year, Morris' poetic swan-song and retreat into mediaevalism. In January 1891 Unwin still held that 'the ideal of socialism is to some of us a religion, and it does . . . not only tell us what is right but helps us to do it'; but he candidly admitted that 'it is because of that want of life and enthusiasm that the thing seems to drag so.'[18] By August of that year he confided to Ethel Parker:

> at one time I was sort of given up to socialism, it was my religion and I feel the loss of it as such. But I think it quite possible for some other side of the work besides agitation to take some place . . . I think that Barry [Parker] is feeling very much like we do that we need some central aim for our lives apart from just getting on and doing good among hands.[19]

Fulfilment was to come from his marriage to Ethel Parker in 1893; from his increasing involvement in housing work for the Staveley Company; and, from 1896, in partnership with Parker. Unwin's daughter, Peggy, regarded this period as a personal quest for a vocation:

> The reaching out through socialism, temperance, religion, living with labourers was trying to put satisfaction into a life that through work didn't interest him much. He was so very different when he felt he was doing something useful *through his work*.[20]

In 1891 Unwin first read *Fabian Essays*, which he pronounced as 'good from the Parliamentarian point of view'. Sidney Webb (1859–1947), Beatrice Webb (1858–1943) and George Bernard Shaw (1856–1950) had founded the Fabian Society in 1885; and despite Morris' scathing dismissal of democratic tactics there had been a steadily growing confidence that good government and allied professional skills could achieve a significant advance for socialism. Both Parker and Unwin were subscribers to Keir Hardie's Parliamentary fund in 1893, but Unwin himself did not join the Fabian Society until the turn of the century.

Partnership

In 1891 Unwin obtained from Robert Parker a grudging consent to his engagement to 'Ettie' and the same year a further partnership was proposed.

> Barry seemed to think that we might join some day and set up as architects, he doing the artistic part and me the practical.[21]

Unwin's close friendship with Parker began in 1881. He undoubtedly influenced a shy, sensitive boy with an artistic inclination towards a creatively satifying and socially useful career. From Parker, Unwin gained an aesthetic sense which overlaid a personal taste that had been pared down to the plainest essentials under Carpenter's tutelage. After school in Ashover, Derbyshire, Barry Parker entered T. C. Simmonds' 'Atelier of Art' [sic] at Derby, then enrolled for a few terms at the South Kensington School of Art. Decorative design, based on Owen Jones' massive *Grammar of Ornament* (1856) figured prominently in the course. From 1889 to 1892 Parker served articles under G. Faulkner Armitage (1849–1937),[22] a competent, if conventional architect of the 'Cheshire Revival' style, a richly eclectic northern Arts and Crafts variant (Allwood, 1987). Commissions included interior design and craft work. Armitage had also designed 'An Artizan's Room', displayed at the Manchester Jubilee Exhibition in 1887, where it was seen by Parker and Unwin. After acting as Armitage's clerk of works in Herefordshire, Parker began practice by designing three houses for his father in The Park, Buxton. The largest, 'Moorlands', completed in 1894, was the Parker home.

Figure 3 Ethel Unwin, photographed in New York, 1911. She provided quiet, sympathetic support to all Unwin's activities and participated in most of his conference engagements

Raymond Unwin married Ethel Parker (*see* Figure 3) in 1893 at a civil ceremony at Chapel-en-le-Frith, near Buxton. Barry Parker and his younger brother, Stanley, and Bruce and Katherine Glasier were the sole witnesses. The Unwins moved into lodgings in Chesterfield. Shortly afterwards, Barry Parker moved in to collaborate over the design of St Andrew's, Barrow Hill, built by the Staveley Company. Unwin designed the utilitarian exterior and Parker the interior fittings – pews, lectern, font, pulpit, chancel and altar rails and gaslights (*see* Figure 4) many of which effectively exploited ironwork techniques learned at Armitage's smithy. Parker also designed a mosaic reredos made by his brother-in-law.

It is paradoxical that Parker and Unwin should have first collaborated on a church design after the latter's decade of doubt, during which socialism became his religion. The Staveley Company had equipped Unwin with practical skills; the partnership of Barry Parker and Raymond Unwin was formed in 1896 on the basis of mutual respect.

Figure 4 St Andrews Church, Barrow Hill, 1894–5, interior perspective by Barry Parker (FGC Mus.). The first collaboration, with Unwin responsible for the design of the building, Parker for the fittings

'No partnership deed was drawn up – none was ever needed' (Parker, 1940b). The broad basis of 'the artistic' and 'the practical' lasted until 1914 and surely represented one of the most creative of all divisions of labour. St Andrew's became the prototype for secular successors – the community halls at the centre of their planned housing schemes.

Home and hearth

In 1911 Unwin declared 'the basis for all good city planning is the home of the citizen' (*Proceedings*, 1911, p. 97). This summed up the Parker and Unwin approach, in which they worked outwards from the individual home and hearth to the grouping of housing, the design of outdoor space and ultimately the Garden City and Garden Suburb. Unwin's concern for detail and quality in the design of working-class housing accomplished what Sir Frederic Osborn called 'the democratisation of architecture'. Aesthetic satisfaction was indispensable: Parker had headed his *Building News* articles 'Our Homes' with a favourite Emerson quotation exhorting the architect to 'build a plain cottage with such symmetry as to make all the fine palaces look cheap and vulgar' (Parker, 1895). Beauty would be 'increased to a maximum by the only true method of making all the necessary and useful things beautiful'. Morris had urged 'designers to be humble and begin once more with the style of well constructed, fairly proportioned, brick homes that look snug and comfortable'.[23]

Unwin eschewed the 'false convention of respectability' which demanded a parlour in addition to the living-kitchen in the 'two up two down' terraced house:

> Knowing that the family will practically live in the kitchen, he (the Architect) would think out the space needed to give room for doing work, taking meals and resting . . . In the living room he would plan . . . warm seats around the fire in winter . . . and seats for the summer near the windows, a good dresser for work . . . a table for meals, and a few shelves for books . . . Remembering that . . . labourers would have dirty and arduous work he would contrive to give a bath; and if nothing better could be done might put it into the scullery. In this way he would have obtained a cottage as nearly as possible fitted to the lives of the people. (Unwin, 1901a, pp. 64–5)

He claimed his period living with the Crees in Chesterfield had been a more valuable insight than theorizing. He strove to achieve Parker's precepts for:

> rooms where we have space to carry on the business of life freely and with pleasure . . . plain, simple and ungarnished . . . but honest . . . Then, if necessary, let the walls go untouched in all the rich variety of colour and tone, of light and shade of the naked brickwork. Let the floor go uncarpeted, and the wood unpainted, so that we may have time to think, and the money with which to educate our children to think also. (Parker, 1895, p. 108)

Unwin's son, Edward, was born in 1894 and his daughter Margaret (Peggy) in 1899. In 1896, upon joining Parker at Buxton, the family moved to 'The Lodge by the Beeches', Bank Hall, Chapel-en-le-Frith, a charming Arts and Crafts building designed in 1874 by W. Eden Nesfield (1835–88), an associate of Richard Norman Shaw (1831–1912). Freed from the convention of the Staveley Company, he wore homespun tweed suits and soft shirts. Peggy recalled 'we were clothed of course in Ruskin flannel – and it was years before I knew why it was Ruskin – plain living and high thinking were certainly the rule'. In 1898 the Glasiers moved to Chapel-en-le-Frith. They often joined the family circle around the fire, the symbolic centre of the home:

> the inglenook secured from draughts by high backed oak benches, which became bookshelves and cupboards on the outer side, specially designed to fit the simple brick lined hearth with its gleaming copper hood. There was no meaningless mantelshelf or useless ornament . . . everything in the room might have grown there. (Glasier, K. B., 1940)

Katherine Glasier also noted the Unwins':

> sincere belief in their fellow workers' right, not only to work and wage, but to interest and even joy in the doing of that work and assuredly to beauty in their surroundings.

Unwin hoped that Bruce Glasier might eventually join the partnership. Parker seems to have preferred employment of articled pupils to a

Figure 5 'The Artizan's Living-Room', sketch by Barry Parker, before 1895, as published in *The Art of Building a Home* (1901). Parker's interest in the reform of the design of working-class housing was undoubtedly stimulated by Unwin

politician *manqué*. Release from Staveley had enabled Unwin to resume politicizing, the Independent Labour Party and the Labour Church. The latter was strong in the north and its combination of religious fervour and aspiring political progress mirrored Unwin's personal traits. However, he now attempted to direct the ethical arguments to the substantive question of housing, to reflect 'as far as possible a truthful expression of the life that is to be lived there, instead of a mere echo of conventions'.

Concerning the coming revolution in domestic architecture

Between 1895 and 1901, Parker and Unwin gained their initial experience of house design and construction, which assisted the refinement of their design theory. The period culminated in their joint book, *The Art of Building a Home*. Publication of illustrated articles on the design of 'the smaller middle class house' was a phenomenon of the Arts and Crafts movement. Parker and Unwin were influenced by C. F. A. Voysey and M. H. Baillie Scott. British domestic architecture was highly regarded internationally; the Prussian Government sent the architect Hermann Muthesius (1861–1927) to prepare a detailed report, published in Berlin as *Das Englische Haus* (Muthesius, 1904).

Parker's sketch 'An Artizan's Living Room' (*see* Figure 5) which appeared in 'Our Homes', was their earliest working-class housing design,[24] possibly influenced by Armitage's Manchester Jubilee exhibit.

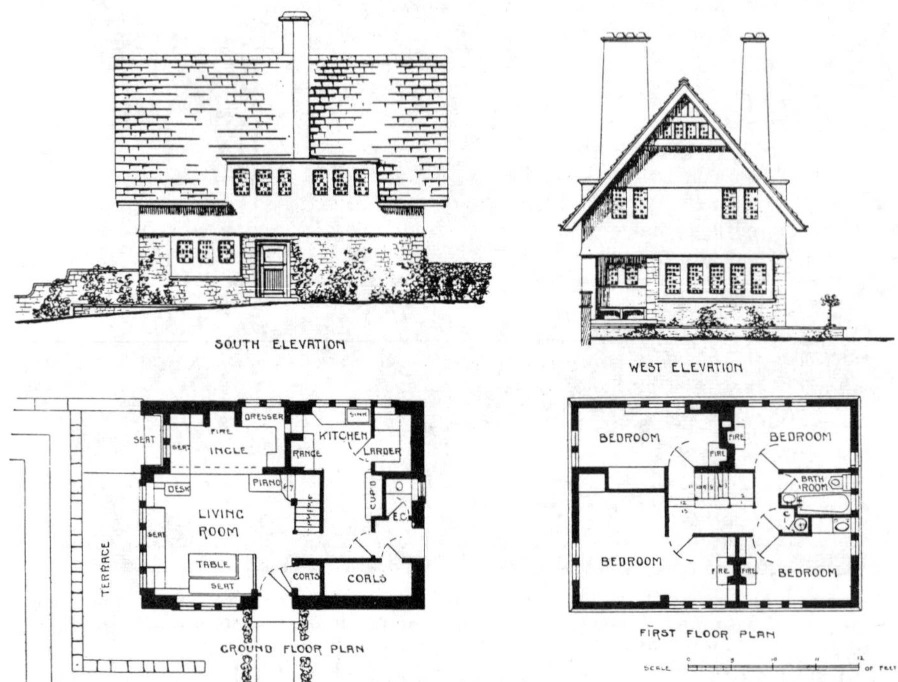

Figure 6 Unwin's design for a site near 'The Lodge by the Beeches', Chapel-en-le-Frith *c.* 1897, as published in *The Architect's Magazine* (1901). This project provided the means of working out a rational plan based on the functional requirements; it became the model for the dominant gabled ends of later housing groups

It also related to a plan for an unbuilt cluster of three cottages. In the Artizan's room the fireplace, flanked by rush-seated settles, formed an inglenook, breaking out of the conventional rectilinear box. The staircase was boldly exposed, anticipating twentieth-century open-planning, subsequently disliked by tenants at New Earswick and Letchworth. Despite Parker's fussy penmanship the underlying principles led towards the *machine à habiter*. Elsewhere Unwin's engineering and costing skills counterbalanced his partner's stylistic eclecticism. The late 1890s witnessed growing confidence in spatial design and refinement of form, reflecting consistent principles from the individual element to the total domestic environment, best exemplified at 'Chetwynd', Clayton, near Stoke-on-Trent (1899–1903) (Hawkes, 1986; Parker, 1901). Such accomplishments, however, lacked the social purpose sought by Unwin and his housing skills largely emerged through theoretcial models.

In about 1897 Unwin designed a house for himself, for a Chapel-en-le-Frith site, four square, vernacular, with a stone ground floor, rendered first floor and steep gabled stone-slated roof (*see* Figure 6). Internal planning concentrated family activities into a large living room with a focal inglenook and an open staircase. The ground floor was divided into overlapping activity zones, leaving a central space for family gatherings.

The parallel with Unwin's subsequent approach to site planning and grouping of houses is striking and the communal element was later externalized to foster neighbourly cooperation. It was emphasized that:

> each requirement has been considered and provided for . . . the shape and arrangement has been given . . . which seemed to suit those requirements . . . whatever the size of the house we think it should grow both as a utilitarian plan and an artistic creation out of the real needs of the occupants . . . the art of designing small houses and cottages consists . . . in working out such a convenient and comely setting . . . as shall enable [their] life to expand . . . actually stimulated by a congenial surrounding. (Parker and Unwin, 1901, pp. 132–3)

This prototype was developed as one element in the grouped housing designs for New Earswick and Letchworth, a tangible reflection of the communal cells identified by Unwin's early studies. Other prototypes also appeared in *The Art of Building a Home*. A quadrangle of 'Cooperative Houses for a Yorkshire Town' (*see* Figure 7), designed for an unidentified Bradford site in 1898–9, recalled Oxford Colleges and the Utopian vision of 'Sutton Hall'. Each dwelling included a large through living room and three to five bedrooms. The collegiate atmosphere was reinforced by cloistered colonnades leading to common rooms, tucked into internal angles where most bye-laws would have outlawed dwellings. Unwin pooled the space gained from the omission of parlours and exploited areas unsuited to development, turning problems to opportunities: an enduring characteristic of his work. Communal laundries and kitchens were designed to eliminate the waste of:

> thirty or forty housewives preparing thirty or forty little scrap dinners, heating a like number of ovens, boiling thrice the pans and cleaning them up again. (Unwin, 1901c, p. 105)

Another prototype involved a rural site and was more directly relevant to the design of New Earswick (to be considered in Chapter Three).

Theory had outstripped practice and by 1901 Parker and Unwin had built only three working-class cottages. A semi-detached pair in Cunnery Road, Church Stretton, Shropshire (1900–1) (*see* Figure 8), with roughcast walls, a hipped roof and a central gable, were seemingly insignificant in themselves and appeared derivative and Voyseyesque in character. Yet they served as prototypes for the first cottages at New Earswick. Lack of practical experience was outweighed by commitment. Unwin's earliest writing on housing carried an authoritative tone. This assisted his emergence from provincial obscurity in 1901–2, and his attraction of the major commissions for Letchworth and Hampstead in subsequent years. It was by any standards a remarkable achievement. The six months from the autumn of 1901 saw the publication of *The Art of Building a Home* and *Cottage Plans and Common Sense*, his appearance at the Garden City Association Bournville Conference and

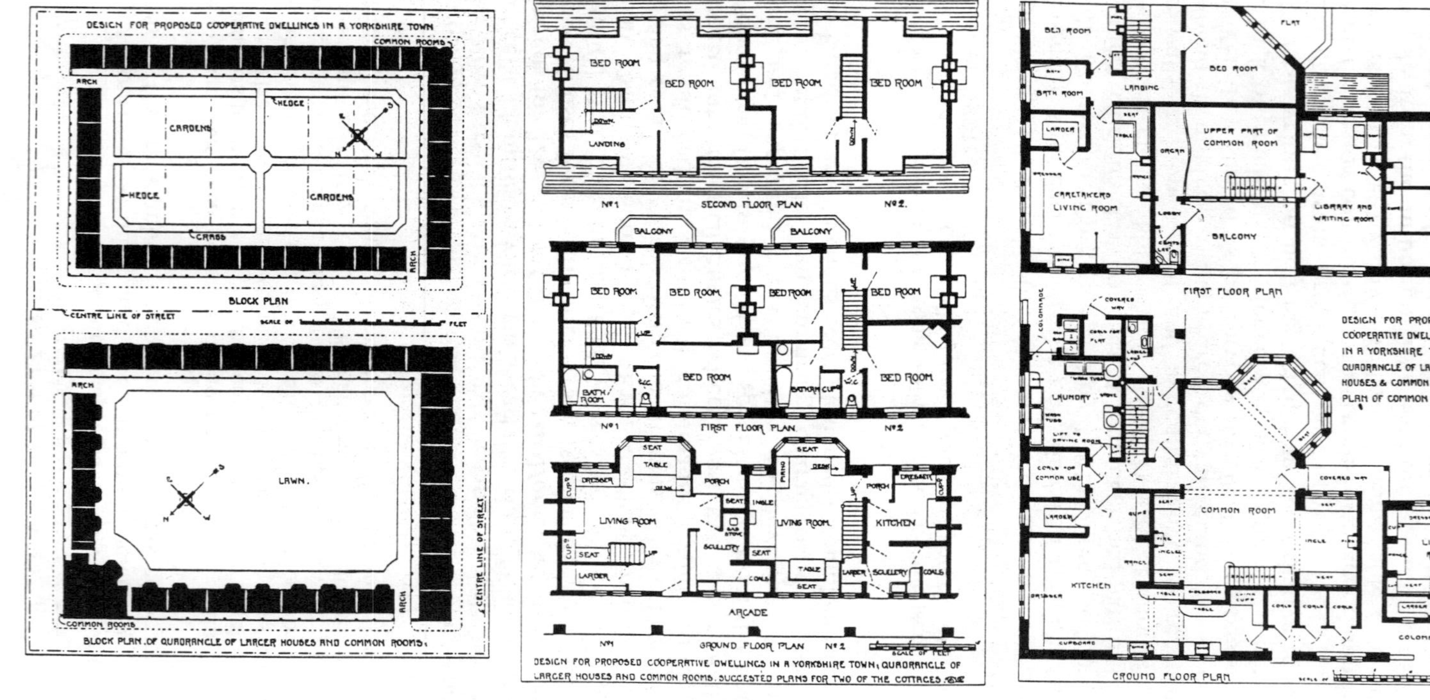

Figure 7 Quadrangles of Cooperative Housing, *c.* 1898 as illustrated in *The Art of Building a Home* (1901). This concept looked back to the collegiate model and forward to the rationalized block layout of *Nothing Gained by Overcrowding* (1912)

Figure 8 a) Cottages in Cunnery Road, Church Stretton, 1900–1. The built prototypes for New Earswick with a plan adapted for *Cottage Plans and Common Sense* (1902);
b) Nos. 1–2 and 3–6 Western Terrace, New Earswick, 1902–3. The generic likeness with Church Stretton and Starbeck cottages is readily evident

several key lectures. On 18 September 1901, just before the publication of *The Art of Building a Home*, the *Daily Mail* reported an interview with Unwin under the eyecatching byline 'Concerning the Coming Revolution in Domestic Architecture':

> 'There is no reason', he declared, 'why an artisan earning, say, thirty shillings a week should not possess a home as artistic in a modest degree, as that of his more wealthy neighbour'.

Illustrations showed 'An Artizan's Living Room', the Chapel-en-le-Frith design and an abortive project for a lakeland country house, embellished with price tags of £200, £500 and £10,000. This smacked of soliciting for work and Baillie Scott commented acidly on this in *The Builder's Journal*. *The Art of Building a Home* was well-received but with some critical comment on Parker's multifarious drawings of ingle-nooks. The proposals for communty design were little remarked upon. Unwin lectured to the Workmen's National Housing Council on 4 November and to the Fabian Society on 22 November 1901. The latter lecture, 'Light and Air and the Housing Question', appeared the following March as *Cottage Plans and Common Sense*, a landmark in the literature of housing design (Unwin, 1902).

Cottage Plans and Common Sense, 1902

The tract contained both a rational approach to housing design and pointers to layout techniques soon to be used at New Earswick and Letchworth. Unwin balanced individual and communal aspects, proposed standard plans, while recognizing their limitation, and, helped by the example of the LCC Architect's Housing Division, assisted the ascendancy of the professional housing designer.

He took first principles, 'shelter, comfort, privacy', and drew out general criteria and specific standards. Housing had to be freed from the bye-law strait-jacket. Sunlight was a key agent, to be:

> insisted upon as an absolute essential, second only to air space . . . every house should turn its face to the sun whence come light, sweetness and health. (Unwin, 1902, p. 3)

This would sweep away 'back yards, back alleys and abominations . . . too long screened by that wretched prefix back.' His quadrangle scheme had been rationalized (*see* Figure 9) and a maximum density of 20–30 dwellings per acre [8–12 per hectare] was suggested – the looser Garden City maxim of 'twelve houses to the acre' was still in the future. However, Unwin's analysis of the relationship between street length, frontage width and density looked forward to *Nothing Gained by Overcrowding*, 1912:

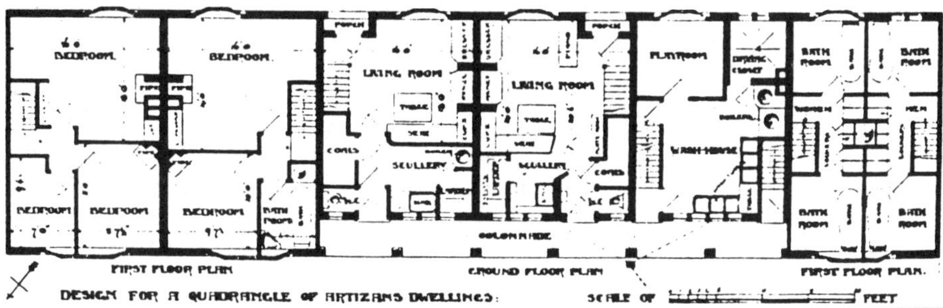

Figure 9 *Cottage Plans and Common Sense*, 1902. The quadrangle layout remained a favourite of Unwin's but was implemented comparatively rarely. The house plans are related to the early New Earswick types and have been rationalized from the earlier scheme for cooperative housing quadrangles

> the narrow house with its straggling projections required greater depth: and the deeper the houses the greater is the expanse of the side streets which has to be divided amongst them . . . if the quadrangle layout is adopted there need be no waste in the side streets, because the houses face all ways, and this would about balance the extra cost per house due to the wider frontage, while the saving of detached outbuildings and backyard walls would mean a considerable economy. (Unwin, 1902, p. 6)

Unwin's standard three bedroom house with 18ft. 9in. frontage had a net floor area of 930 sq.ft. (*see* Figure 9). The living room, including the stairs, was about 195 sq.ft., with, occasionally, a parlour of 126 sq.ft. The principal bedroom was 147 sq.ft., with two of 100 sq.ft. and a very small bathroom. These standards were close to those codified at New Earswick, Letchworth and Hampstead. Much of the furniture was built in and he advised:

> in planning the room the furniture should always be arranged and drawn in to make sure that the provision has been made for work, rest and play. (Unwin, 1902, p. 6)

This type plan was virtually identical with Nos. 3–6, Western Terrace, New Earswick. In emphasizing that 'the available room . . . be most liberally given where it will be most thoroughly and continuously used' (Unwin, 1902, p. 11), Unwin stated that rooms should serve multiple functions and bedrooms should include study areas. This 'activity' based approach to house planning supplemented area standards and looked forward even to the Parker Morris *Report* of 1961. Aesthetics were inseparable from functional considerations providing the marginal element 'which makes the difference between a mere shelter and a home'. Housing quality was thus equally as important as technical matters. This did not preclude standardization:

> when a quantity [of fittings] is required . . . no extra cost is entailed by having them well designed and of good proportions . . . That nothing can be spent on the ornamentation of artizans' cottages is no excuse whatever for their being ugly . . . a plain and simple building well designed is very far from being ugly. (Unwin, 1902, p. 12)

Cottage Plans and Common Sense marked an important advance in the literature of housing design. It set out a consistent and rational approach, balancing individual and communal aspects tempered by pragmatism. It recognized the importance of standards as well as their limitation and paved the way for the ascendancy of the professional designer in mass-housing. The long 'prentice period had ended.

3

New Earswick – Prototype for Community Design

> Villages like ours, in which an effort is being made to realise more wholesome living conditions . . . are watched with great interest by social workers throughout the country . . . we want at Earswick to do something towards the housing problem, and the value of our experiment will very much depend upon whether we are able to make it pay. If we . . . can pay something like three per cent . . . it is probable that we shall have many imitators.[25]

Joseph Rowntree (1836–1925) was speaking at the opening of the Folk Hall at New Earswick in October 1907, his gift to the model village which he had created to house his employees. The entire development had been designed by Barry Parker and Raymond Unwin. Rowntree followed the examples of Bournville and Port Sunlight. New Earswick's significance lay in its role as a prototype for Letchworth and Hampstead, with its layout and design elements also reflected in many developments of the period.

Joseph Rowntree, one of the most prominent Quaker businessmen, followed the precedent of the Cadburys' example by moving his cocoa works from the centre of York in 1898 to a site two miles north. Rowntree was concerned with the twin problems of poverty and housing. In 1898–9, his second son, Benjamin Seebohm Rowntree (1871–1954), undertook a systematic social survey of York, revealing the appalling housing conditions and economic deprivation of 25 per cent of the working class population. Published in 1901, *Poverty, a Study of Town Life* (Rowntree, 1901) made a great impact and also acted as a catalyst for action by Joseph Rowntree, who sought to place his accumulated wealth in trust for social and religious purposes. He examined the articles of the Bournville Village Trust and consulted both Cadbury's lawyer and Henry Vivian (1868–1930), Chairman of the Co-Partnership Tenants housing society. In December 1904 he formed the Joseph Rowntree Village Trust (JRVT), which took over the development of New Earswick (Waddilove, 1954). Bold objectives were specified:

> The improvement of the working classes . . . in and around the city of York and elsewhere . . . by the provision of improved dwellings with open spaces

> and where possible, gardens . . . and the organisation of village communities with such facilities for the enjoyment of full and healthy lives as the Trustees shall consider desirable.[26]

The Trustees, drawn largely from the Rowntree family, first met on 21 December 1904, and ratified 'a contract with Mr. Raymond Unwin, Architect, to act as consultant for the estate at a remuneration of 10s 6d per hour and out-of-pocket expenses'. Unwin had in fact been involved with the layout and design of the village for two years and this had presented him with the opportunity to develop early concepts of low-density housing into a prototype for community design.

Village antecedents

The village was a potent symbol for the Utopian commentators and a practical proposition in limited form. Estate owners continued to develop their own villages, often with the collaboration of eminent architects. Picking up the picturesque tradition, as exemplified at Nash's Blaise Hamlet in 1812, manufacturers adopted a village character for their own model communities (Tarn, 1973; Darley, 1975), notably successful at Port Sunlight and Bournville. Parker and Unwin were certainly aware of such developments and Unwin appears to have responded to a tentative commission from Isabella Ford of Adel Grange, near Leeds, a social activist and fellow disciple of Edward Carpenter. He recreated the visual harmony of the feudal village, which he described in 'Cooperation in building' (1899), reprinted in *The Art of Building a Home* (*see* Figure 10).

> The village was the expression of a small corporate life in which all the different units were personally in touch with each other, conscious of and frankly accepting their relations . . . It is this crystallisation of the elements in a village in accordance with a definitely organised life of mutual relations . . . which gives the appearance of being an organic whole, the home of the community, to what would otherwise be a mere conglomeration of buildings . . . The smallest cottage has its share of the village street on to which the Manor House also fronts . . . The sense of unity is further increased by general harmony . . . due to the prevalent use of certain materials, which are usually those found in the district. In the modern building estate all these elements of beauty are entirely wanting. The land is cut up into little plots all about the same size . . . such separation as exists only makes it possible for every house to block the view of some other . . . We cannot of course put back the hands of time, nor can we recreate the spirit which built the old churches that crown so many villages. The relationships of feudalism have gone, and democracy has yet to evolve some definite relationships of its own . . . we could, if we really desired it, even now so arrange a new building site . . . that it should have some little of the charm of the old village. (Unwin, 1901c, pp. 92–3)

This simile of crystallization, one of the most recalled images in

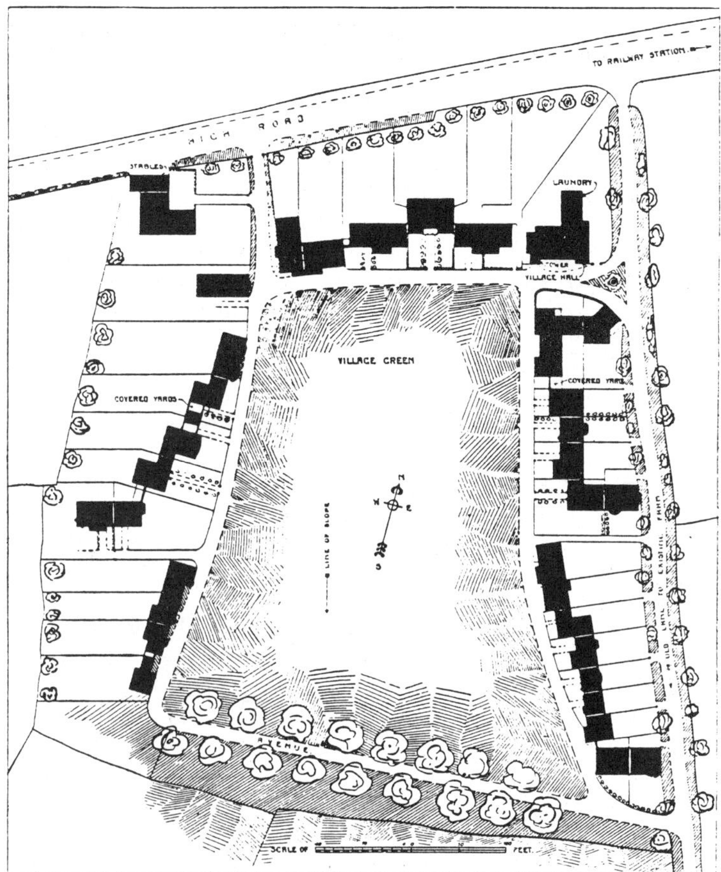

Figure 10 Plan of village green, *c.* 1899, as published in *The Art of Building a Home* (1902). This informal, open-ended grouping became an element of identity within larger schemes and was most completely realized at Westholm, Letchworth, in 1906

Unwin's writing over the next forty years, encapsulated the natural order of the elements of society, requiring perception to reveal and foster the underlying structure within an apparently amorphous mass. Villages remained perceptible as nuclei within the great industrial conurbations. Unwin chose the concept as the basis for planned neighbourhoods. In his prototype, with its crescent of housing around an open-ended green, Unwin gave prominence to a community hall, recalling the Barrow Hill Church. He looked forward to:

> the creation of streets with at least some unity and dignity of effect, and settlements that, if they may not have the charm of the old English village, shall at any rate look at home in their country surroundings. (Unwin, 1901c, p. 108)

In 1903 a further theoretical scheme, *Cottages Near a Town* (Parker

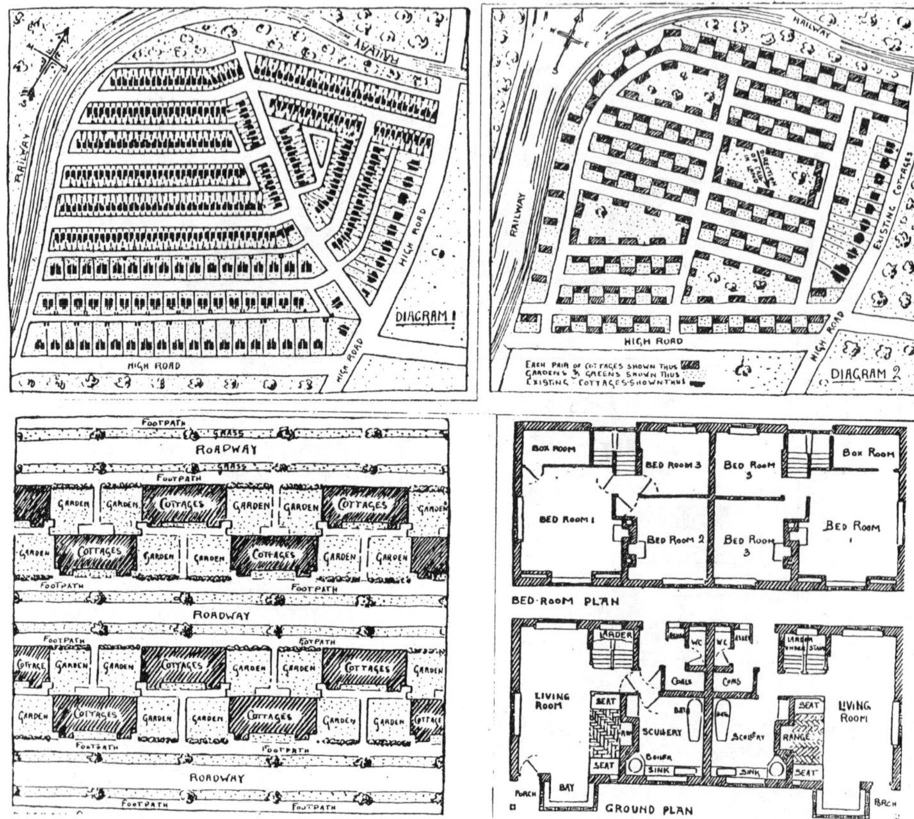

Figure 11 Cottages Near a Town (1903), designed the previous year for a site at Starbeck, Harrogate. The broken 'chequerboard' layout represented extreme reaction against the bye-law street. Although imperfectly resolved *Fabian News* felt the proposals to be more suited to Garden City development than the quadrangles of Unwin's earlier tract

and Unwin, 1903), overlapped the beginning of New Earswick, the first of the major substantive projects upon which Unwin's reputation as a planner, and, in collaboration with Parker, as a housing designer, rests. *Cottages Near a Town* was shown at the Northern Artworks Guild Exhibition in Manchester (*see* Figure 11). This was testimony to the broadening of the Arts and Crafts movement. Parker and Unwin were members of the Manchester Guild Council, alongside the progressive northern architect Edgar Wood (1860–1935). The scheme was designed for a 30-acre site at Starbeck, near Harrogate, West Yorkshire.[27] Two prototype cottages were built, larger versions of the pair built at Church Stretton. The layout rejected the relentless grid of bye-law development by siting the cottages in chequerboard formation, alternately brought forward to or pushed back from the street frontage. Diagrams contrasted a conventional layout of 424 terrace houses, alongside the chequerboard layout of 320 houses at 10.5 to the acre [4.2 to the

Figure 12 Cottages at Starbeck, 1903 (FGC Mus.): a) The gable dominated exterior represented a major step towards Garden City housing designs; b) The interior with its sturdy fittings evoked the traditional ideal of the farmhouse kitchen and was derived from Parker's early sketch of 'The Artizan's Living Room'

hectare]. Backyards were eliminated by bringing the coal-place, lavatory and ash-pit under the main roof. The relationship between the houses and the street grid was imperfectly resolved, probably as the outcome of inflexible bye-laws, giving an extravagant ratio of street length to houses served: a fault Unwin eliminated in working towards *Nothing Gained by Overcrowding*.

The wide-frontage houses had 912 sq.ft. area and the internal planning followed the principles of activity zoning, particularly the large living-room with its fitted furniture (*see* Figure 12a). The exterior design was complex, with the main roof punctuated by a large central gable; several small dormers possibly indicated Parker's close involvement (*see* Figure 12b), and added significantly to their cost: a factor which recurred at Letchworth and possibly prevented further development at Starbeck.

Nevertheless, the basic designs of 1901–3 and their variants were extensively developed and became virtually a kit of parts. While the early quadrangles had turned inwards to suggest collegiate self-sufficiency, *Cottages Near a Town* focused on the streets and the articulation of space enclosed by buildings around them, pushing housing design towards town-planning, first tentatively, then progressively realized at New Earswick, Letchworth and Hampstead Garden Suburb.

The layout of New Earswick and the first phase of development

Late in 1901 Joseph Rowntree purchased a flat, featureless 150-acre tract of land a mile north of his works. The site was bisected by the Haxby Road, running north to south, and bounded on the east by the sluggish, meandering River Foss. Alfred Walker, one of Cadbury's engineers, advised of likely difficulties with the alluvial subsoil, Raymond Unwin, whom Seebohm Rowntree (1871–1954) had met at the Garden City Association Bournville Conference, was engaged to prepare a layout plan. With Parker he designed the first phase of cottages.

A survey showing the existing farmstead, field boundaries, trees and hedgerows formed the basis for Unwin's first layout.[28] The Haxby Road was the generator for an irregular street-grid, with east–west roads taken from it at 600–700 foot intervals and north–south connectors distorted in the east by the course of the Foss. Unwin indicated blocks of four and six cottages in the south-eastern quarter. The development of Station Road – the southernmost of the east–west roads – and the southern portion of Poplar Grove followed this early plan closely. In one area the chequerboard pattern of *Cottages Near a Town* (1903) made a tentative appearance, together with loose quadrangles, while larger plots indicated houses 'for doctors, schoolmasters and ministers'. Public open spaces included a 5.4 acre [2.15 hectare] village green and recreation ground, on the site later developed for the primary school, flanked by an 'art and industry' institute. Elsewhere Unwin proposed a

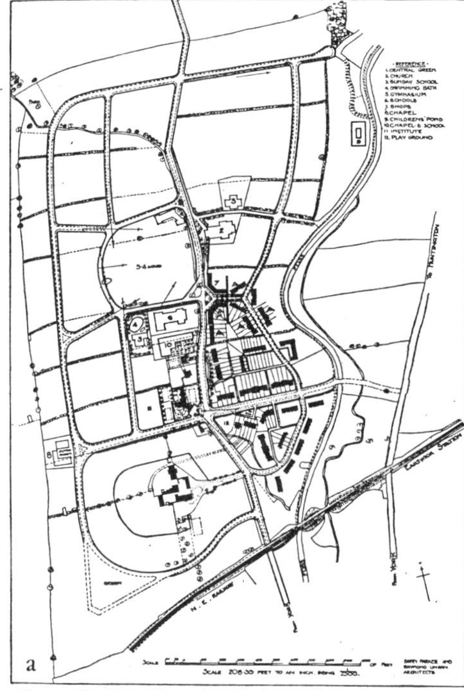

Illus. 171.—Plan of Earswick, near York, being built by The Joseph Rowntree Village Trust.

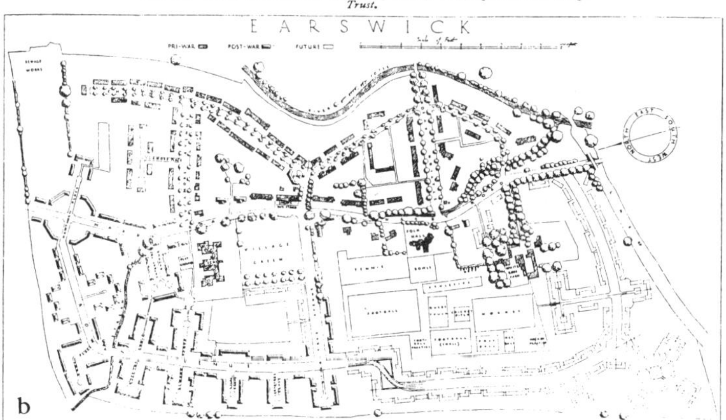

Figure 13 New Earswick layouts: a) Unwin's early layout, published in *Town Planning in Practice* (1909) includes the early proposals for community buildings; b) The contrast between pre and postwar development is readily evident on Parker's 1930 plan in which the cul-de-sac became a dominant motif

riverside park, boating lake, open-air swimming pool, allotments and local play areas. Strung out along Haxby Road were a temperance inn, three churches/chapels, a central church/institute, a gymnasium, a school and shopping parades. Provision of these was reduced. Much of the plan was diagrammatic and Unwin had not yet learned to design spaces between buildings or street pictures (*see* Figure 13).

This naive character was reflected in the first phase of cottage building.[29] Unwin was already concerned to match road standards to anticipated use. Haxby Road was a public highway and Station Road was constructed to prevailing bye-law width; but subsidiary roads such as Poplar Grove were treated informally, with a vestigial back alley to serve the rear of Western Terrace. Nos. 1 and 2 and 3–6 Western Terrace,[30] designed late in 1902, were closely related to the earlier prototypes discussed above. Nos. 1 and 2 Western Terrace took the hip roof and projecting gable of the Church Stretton design and added the bold, square bays of the Starbeck type. Nos. 3–6 Western Terrace, 16-ft. frontage cottages, with a central tunnel back-access, had plans that closely followed those from *Cottage Plans and Common Sense*, but their twin-gabled exterior coupled two pairs of the Church Stretton design. Nos. 7–13 Western Terrace, completed in 1905, were more fragmented, with projections for the parlour houses, as in the later Letchworth designs. The scene was set for the complex variations on basic types: a recurrent theme in Parker and Unwin housing.

The eastern-side houses in Poplar Grove (*see* Figure 14), backing on to the river, had the porch, coal-place and closet brought to the front. At New Earswick Joseph Rowntree encouraged tenant participation. On 30 October 1903 a residents' group met Seebohm Rowntree, Barry Parker and Raymond Unwin: preparation for the subsequent Village Council (Waddilove, 1954, pp. 78–81).[31] Residents criticized the 'back to front' arrangement in Poplar Grove and the open-plan with stairs rising directly out of the living-room. A partition wall was introduced, creating a corridor-like hallway in later repeats of the basic plan.

Building a community, 1905–15

In May 1905 Unwin was asked to prepare plans for a community hall. He advised the Trustees to relocate the site to the corner plot opposite the junction of Haxby Road and Station Avenue.[32] He exploited its visual potential with a diagonal siting, giving an oblique closure to views along both roads. He emphasized his intention by superimposed view-lines on the site plan, a technique he developed in 1905–6 through his enthusiasm for the analytical townscape technique of Camillo Sitte. The exterior of the Folk Hall realized the potential of its siting with roughcast walls and a dominant, steeply pitched pantiled roof. The interior had boldly engineered dark stained roof trusses starkly exposed above plain whitewashed brick walls, with a brick-lined inglenook to create a more intimate focal point. The name 'Folk Hall' evoked Geddes; the Rowntrees completed the trinity of interaction between 'Work' (the democratically run factory), 'Place' (the Model Village) and 'Folk' (Residents, Village Council and 'Folk Hall').

In February 1907, Seebohm Rowntree and Unwin prepared a construction programme:

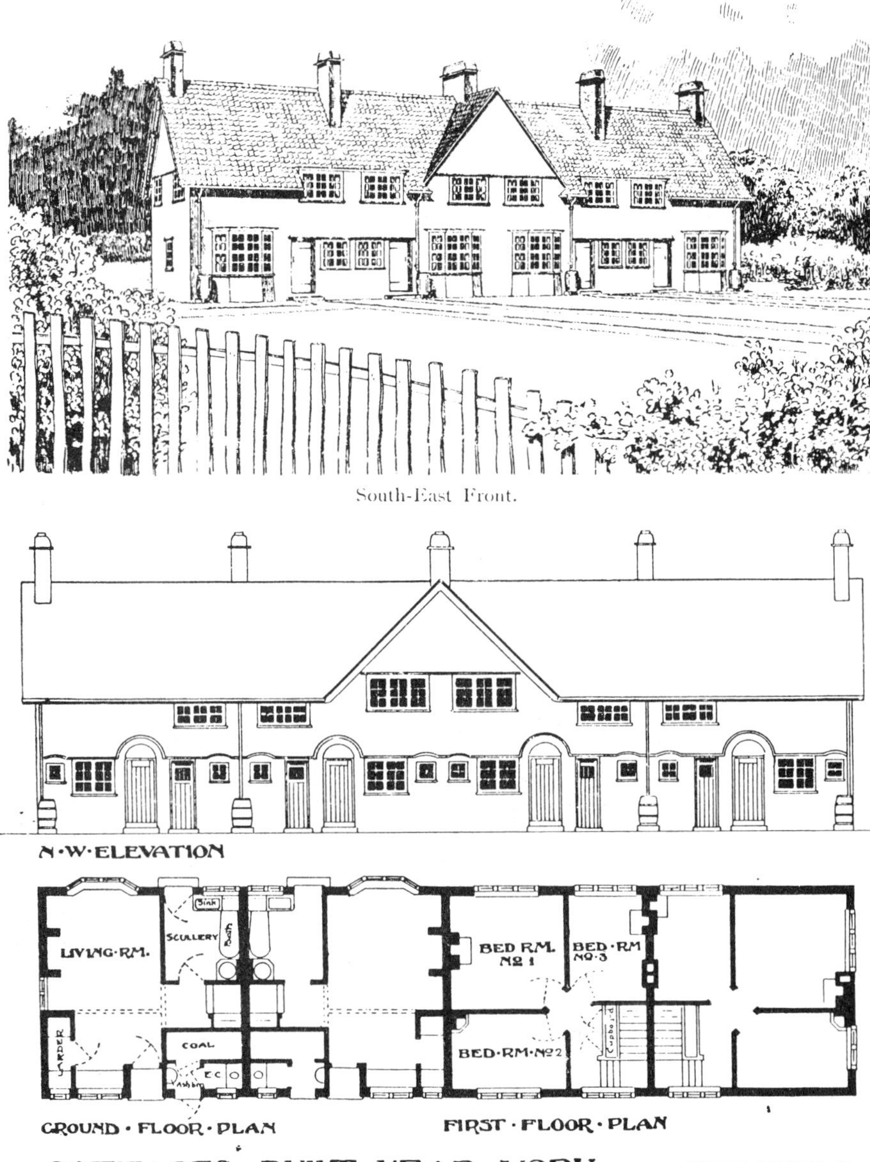

Figure 14 House type in Poplar Grove, New Earswick, 1904. The plain N.W. elevation shows the unwelcome prominence of the closet doors; tenants also criticized the stairs opening out of the living-room

a) Houses fourteen to the acre [5.6 to the hectare] to be let at 4s 0d per week – doubtful whether we can build these;
b) A small house with no hot water, and with bath optional to be let at 4s 6d per week – also fourteen to the acre;
c) A house like our present labourer's house – non-parlour to let at 5s 3d;
d) A parlour house to let at £16 0s 0d p.a.;
e) Larger parlour houses like blocks 46–49 to be let at £18 0s 0d p.a.[33]

Doubts about cheaper houses proved to be well-founded. Economic rent overpriced the smaller cottages and the relatively remote location entailed the concession of '33 minutes walking time to our Earswick estate' for Rowntree employees. By December 1907 there were few applications for cottages and more than one thousand vacant houses in York. Joseph Rowntree pondered whether the Trust would develop on the outskirts of a larger industrial town, or assist the Co-Partnership Tenants.

However, at the beginning of 1908, Unwin achieved his most economical designs. Ivy Place, a quadrangle bisected by Chestnut Grove, north of Station Avenue, was formed from plain terraces, with projecting ends, linked by archways at the corners. The designs were rationalized to eliminate bays and roof dormers. The modest floor area of 612 sq.ft. provided a living-room (with cooking range), back scullery (with bath) and three bedrooms for a net building cost, including garden layout, of £184 12s 9d. The gross cost, including overheads and fees, rose to £245 14s 9d. This required an 'economic' rent of 4s 6d, 5s 6d for the larger end units. Rates and water rates added another 11d per week, compelling some tenants to manage without a fixed bath. The Trustees reluctantly imposed a limit of 100 dwellings, reassessed annually. Late in 1908 the contracting department was in danger of closure, only saved by a programme of sixteen houses agreed the following January. Despite these setbacks the publicity was extensive and Seebohm Rowntree suggested that a few cottages might be let at reduced rents for being open to inspection. Visitors in 1909 included the German Garden City Association.

The years 1910–18 saw consistent development along Chestnut Grove, Sycamore Avenue and Sycamore Place, the first cul-de-sac in the layout. A new clerk of works, W. J. Swain challenged Unwin's extravagant design 'fads', particularly high-pitched roofs, gables and dormers. He claimed a saving of £119 for a block of four flat-roofed houses.[34] Unwin disagreed but with the assistance of Arthur Penty (1875–1937), a York architect recruited to his office, he prepared designs for Nos. 155–160 Chestnut Grove, with projecting gabled ends framing a concrete, flat-roofed centre. Designs by Swain for concrete bungalows, Nos. 1 and 2, and 21 and 22 Sycamore Place, were built in 1913. They were tidied up by John Stone of Unwin's Hampstead office. They did not prove watertight and were subsequently demolished.

By 1915 New Earswick had grown to 250 houses. Chestnut Grove and Sycamore Avenue repeated cottage types from Western Terrace. Focal sites received more individual treatment, as in the paired blocks either side of the bend in Chestnut Grove. A parade of shops with a distinctive concrete loggia facing Haxby Road was completed in 1912. The Primary School (1912) was an internationally recognized success. Rowntree authorized Unwin to make thorough studies of school design in Britain and on the continent, to which were added impressions of open-air schools seen in Chicago in May 1911. The single-storey building with low classroom wings had large folding windows and sun blinds to allow open-air teaching virtually all the year round. Penty was responsible for the low-key Georgian detailing. Space standards were 50 per cent higher than prevailing Board of Education requirements, and the hall, no longer hemmed in as with urban Board schools, was available for community use (Unwin, 1913c).

Parker's interwar consultancy

Following the November 1918 Armistice, Joseph Rowntree, by then in his mid-eighties, requested his son to:

> consult Raymond Unwin and ascertain whether . . . the Trustees . . . [should] erect . . . a maximum of 50 houses [incorporating] all the most up to date improvements that the Tudor Walters Committee . . . recommended so that they represent the 'last word' in cottage building.[35]

It was minuted that 'it is just possible that Mr. Unwin might regard the erection of these houses as an experiment of national importance and we might make use of his services'. Reluctantly Unwin declined and in February 1919 Barry Parker was appointed consultant on his return from working in Brazil.

Parker's revised layout for the village was based on *Nothing Gained by Overcrowding*, as amended by Unwin for the Ministry of Health, with the addition of a short cul-de-sac to the overall housing block. Parker's layout for the area west of Haxby Road prepared in 1920 achieved considerable saving in road length. The spine road, Rowan Avenue, was moved inwards to serve culs-de-sac, each of which had its own octagonal green. This was modified to give a tighter grouping (*see* Figure 13b), elevated to a minor art form, each road subtly varied and lined by the Rowan, Cherry, Lime, Crabapple and Almond trees from which they took their names. There was a progressive saving in road and service costs per house from £56 13s 0d pre-war to £45 15s 11d in 1923.

Parker examined every aspect of cottage planning, balancing conflicting preference for ground-floor or first-floor bathrooms against increased drainage costs or the request for larger bedrooms. He pointed out faults in the 1919 *Housing Manual* type plans. He conducted a detailed investigation into materials and techniques during the latter part of 1919 with the assistance of Harry Burr, the estate surveyor of Letchworth. It was concluded that traditional methods remained the most economical. Parker concentrated on standardization in bungalows 'built as Ford cars are built in which every part might be produced in large numbers'. These, in Rowan Avenue, were laid out on the 'chequer-board' pattern. The construction programme fluctuated. Rising construction costs and the unfavourable financial position of the Trust under the 1919 Housing Act forced cuts from eighty-two houses in 1920 to forty in 1921 and 1922. By 1924, when costs had fallen significantly, the initiative had decisively passed to local authorities. A modified programme was approved under the 1924 Housing Act and Parker proceeded a cul-de-sac at a time, with interwar construction finally halted in 1932 (Parker 1923, 1937).

Co-partnership housing 1901–14

New Earswick was matched in scale by many garden suburbs and villages. The Co-Partnership Tenants Housing Council, founded in 1906 under the leadership of the Liberal MP Henry Vivian, was the most significant organization registered under the Industrial and Provident Societies Act 1893. Constituent societies were registered as limited liability companies. Each tenant was required to invest, with a minimum share of £5 or £10. Surplus profits were distributed to tenant shareholders as credit for further shares and dividends were limited to 5 per cent. Vivian claimed that this encouraged:

> the driving force and stimulus to economy and the educational value which always arises from a sense of individual ownership, combined with safeguards to prevent this ownership expressing itself in an anti-social direction. (Vivian, 1906, p. 27)

Ealing Tenants Limited, the pioneer co-partnership organization, was registered in April 1901 to develop a site at Brentham on the northern outskirts of Ealing, a rapidly expanding town west of London. By September the first houses, Vivian Terrace, Nos. 71–87 Woodfield Road, were almost complete. The first phase of fifty houses completed by 1905 differed little from standard bye-law types (Johnson, B., 1977).

Vivian probably met Unwin in January 1905 when Garden City Tenants became involved in Letchworth. Work by the Co-Partners' consultant architect G. L. Sutcliffe (1864–1915) was often almost indistinguishable from that of Parker and Unwin. Vivian claimed that it was sound business sense to provide gardens, open spaces and landscaping as a setting for well-designed housing. His socialist beliefs notwithstanding, Unwin accepted that the co-partnership principle was in accord with his concept of village cells as the basis for planning:

> Instead of thinking and planning for a random assortment of individuals there is now a *whole* to be thought of . . . the principle of sharing . . . expresses itself in the harmony and beauty of the whole . . . I look to the principle of Co-Partnership to give us . . . a civic life which will once more infuse harmony and beauty into the homes, and into suburbs and villages.[36]

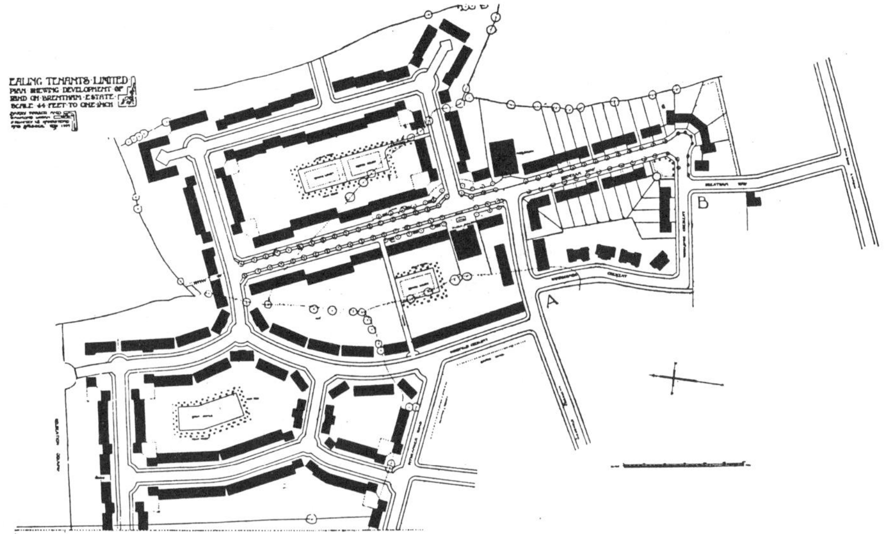

Figure 15 Plan of Brentham, 1907–8. This version was included in *Town Planning in Practice* (1909), and although later modified, the concept of large blocks with central communal spaces anticipated the layout shown in *Nothing Gained by Overcrowding* (1912)

In January 1907 Ealing Tenants purchased additional land at Brentham and Unwin's revised layout was followed until 1911. The large street block east of Brentham Way (*see* Figure 15), with its internal tennis courts, was surely a prototype for *Nothing Gained by Overcrowding* in 1912. Little of the detailed design was by Unwin. Most pre-1911 housing was by F. Cavendish Pearson and after that date by Sutcliffe. The junction of Brunner Road, Nevilles Road and Fowlers Walk took the form of a 'Y', illustrated in 1909 in Unwin's *Town Planning in Practice*. In 1911 further expansion required a modification of Unwin's layout but Sutcliffe was so well-versed in the design principles that the transition between the two is barely perceptible. Sutcliffe's best work at Brentham matches that of 'official' Parker and Unwin. The Brentham Club and Institute in Meadvale Road (1911) was an imposing composition with a tall Germanic tower forming a focal point in views along Denison Road, and diagonally along Holyoake Walk, closely following the precedent of the Club House on Willifield Green in Hampstead Garden Suburb.

Unwin planned several Co-Partnership developments (Abercrombie, 1910; Culpin, 1913, 1914). In September 1907 he prepared a layout for Anchor Tenants at Humberstone, near Leicester. In July 1910 Liverpool Tenants began the development of 25 acres of a 180-acre tract at Wavetree Nook, west of Queen's Drive, the city's ring boulevard. Unwin provided the layout and Sutcliffe designed the housing. In 1912 Coventry Garden Suburb Ltd. began development on co-partnership lines on a 10-acre [4 hectare] site off Radford Road, north-west of the city centre, only partly implemented. Penty designed the first housing groups, facing southwards over the open recreation ground in St Joseph's Road in a manner strongly reminiscent of Hampstead Garden Suburb, viewed from the Heath Extension. That same year. Glasgow Garden Suburb Tenants obtained an option on 200 acres [80 hectares] at Garscube on the city's northern outskirts. Unwin's layout plan exploited the steep contours and created an imposing formal centre on the brow of the hill that dominated the suburb. Only sixty houses were completed before 1914. In Wales, Cardiff Workers' Garden Village Society aimed at developing both middle and working-class housing on a 110-acre [44 hectare] site at Rhwbina. Unwin's ambitious layout contained a balance of formal and informal elements. A. H. Mottram (1886–1953), a former Hampstead assistant of Unwin's, was responsible for the architectural design and J. O. West, the former manager of Hampstead Tenants, supervised its construction by a direct labour force. In 1913 Unwin advised on the planning of a suburb at Town Hill, Swansea, producing a brilliant layout with ingenious zigzag access roads to overcome the steep gradients, reproduced in the Tudor Walters *Report* of 1918.

Although settlements fell short of the radical model of the self-contained garden city, by 1913 11,248 houses had been completed in such schemes. It is tempting to speculate whether the increasing volume of housing society development might have delayed the subsequent emphasis on state-aided municipal housing, had not the First World War intervened. However, the pioneer LCC cottage estates at Totterdown Fields (1901–13), Norbury, Croydon (1905–9), White Hart Lane, Tottenham (1904–14) and Old Oak, Hammersmith (1909–18) designed under the guidance of W. E. Riley (1852–1937), incorporated many of the best design features of the garden suburbs (Beattie, pp. 85-120). These, New Earswick and the Co-Partnership developments, spread widely the model of low-density housing development, heralding the unassuming character of much interwar housing.

4

The First Garden City – Vision and Reality

> I think Mr. Ebenezer Howard is greatly to be congratulated upon the fact that within five short years his visionary hopes for tomorrow have become the almost fulfilled realisation of today . . . The fortunate community living on this estate will rejoice . . . that the unearned increment . . . from the rents . . . will not go to enrich any individual landowner, but will be spent . . . to refine the lives . . . and exalt the minds of all who reside on the estate.[37]

So saying, Earl Grey opened the Garden City Estate at Letchworth on 9 October 1903. The Garden City became an important stimulus to state initiatives in housing and town-planning. Ebenezer Howard (1850–1928), describing his prototype in *Tomorrow: A Peaceful Path to Real Reform* (Howard, 1898),[38] sensibly left many details open to interpretation in the context of the selected site. There was little detail of the built form of the Garden City. Howard's diagrams, which indicated a Central Park flanked by public buildings, the Crystal Palace, radial boulevards and a circumferential Grand Avenue, transposed Buckingham's model town, Victoria (1849), from square to circular geometry. The 5,000 housing plots, 20 ft. by 100 ft., were comparable with bye-law development, but the 'Ward and Centre' diagram showed the Grand Avenue lined by crescents, comparable with Regents Park or Bath (*see* Figure 18a). Howard's own sketches showed terraces grouped into quadrangles for the majority of the housing. Howard envisaged implementation through a limited dividend development company – 5 per cent philanthrophy writ large. His inherent distrust of state intervention was evident in an early draft chapter, 'The Master Key',[39] in which he had summarily dismissed Parliamentary action. He had reservations about the capacity of the development company to build the Garden City itself.

Raymond Unwin translated Howard's mechanistic diagrams into an enduring framework for the First Garden City at Letchworth, forging his own approach to town-planning in the process. Howard's concept fitted the nineteenth century Utopian tradition, very different from the twentieth century pattern of development that emerged at Letchworth. In September 1901 Howard and Unwin had formed a bond of mutual respect at the Garden City Association's Bournville Conference. Unwin's paper 'On the Building of Houses in the Garden City' (Unwin, 1901d), both extended his own ideas on community design and acted as a brief for the Letchworth layout. He emphasized that the Garden City would be 'arranged in natural conformity with the land . . . with sites for our civic, religious and recreative buildings . . . dominating the city', a striking anticipation of the Town Square at Letchworth. Yet detailed differences would emerge: 'the quiet quadrangle' of housing was ousted by more fragmented short groups, as at New Earswick, and these became dominant both at Letchworth and Hampstead Garden Suburb. Unwin disclaimed 'the weak compound of town and country composed of wandering suburban roads lined with semi-detached villas' – yet reliance on the private small contractor brought them to Letchworth in significant numbers. Nevertheless the Bournville paper served as a marker for Unwin's continuing involvement with the movement.

The search for a site

Thomas Adams (1871–1940), Secretary of the GCA, had organized the Bournville Conference and followed through with further publicity (Simpson, 1985, pp. 11–13). In January 1902 he challenged John Burns (1858–1943), then a London MP and LCC Councillor, who had asserted that Garden Cities would not solve London's housing problems. Adams was critical of LCC cottage estates, emphasizing that decentralization and 'the laying out of such towns on a predetermined plan' were ancillary to the movement's cardinal principle of securing 'the unearned increment on the land'.[40] In July 1902 events moved forward with the flotation of a 'Garden City Pioneer Company' with £20,000 working capital. Its articles required the acquisition of a site upon which:

> to lay out, construct, manage and carry on any such garden city . . . to be carefully planned under the best expert advice, so that as the town grows, its factories and workshops, the houses of the people, the parks and open spaces, schools, churches and other public buildings, may be placed in the most convenient position. (Howard, 1902, pp. 174 and 180)

Furthermore, the surrounding agricultural belt would be 'placed under such restrictive covenants as may secure . . . the enjoyment for all time of the combined advantages of town and country life'. Town-planning had virtually arrived.

Adams, as Company Secretary, and Howard masterminded the search for a suitable site.[41] Criteria, drafted by a sub-committee, specified a freehold estate of 4,000–6,000 acres [1,600–2,400 hectares], with water supply and drainage, a railway and access to London or a major industrial centre. Lists of landowners were drawn up by county and agents were contacted. Confidential investigation inhibited premature speculation. By October 1902 the 6,000-acre [2,400 hectare] Chartley Castle estate, 8 miles north-west of Stafford, emerged as a strong contender.

Howard began to investigate industrial potential. By mid-November, however, the search widened to the Crouch Valley in Essex, Wytham Abbey near Oxford, Ribbesford near Bewdley, Worcestershire and 'Letchford Manor Nr. Hitchin' (*sic*). After receiving a critical report on Chartley, Unwin viewed the site with Adams on 11 January 1903 and was enthusiastic. His mining experience helped his assessment of potential building stone and brick earth, drainage and water supply:

> the higher portions running up from Chartley Hall . . . would make splendid residential districts. The grounds . . . including the castle mound . . . would make a charming public park at very small cost.

Adams concurred and recommended negotiation for an option to purchase.

The Board disagreed. Unwin visited two possible alternatives – Kirklington near Newark, Nottinghamshire, and Grendon, north-west of Atherstone, Warwickshire. Drainage problems eliminated the former but Grendon had excellent communications, particularly the main London and North Western Railway line from Euston. However, this, a canal and the River Tame appeared to rule out 'anything like a well-planned town being built . . . except at great cost'. In April 1903 Howard obtained an option to purchase Chartley for £285,000. Meanwhile, Herbert Warren, the Pioneer Company's solicitor, had recently purchased a practice at Baldock, Hertfordshire, 34 miles north of London on the Great North Road. The delayed appraisal of 'Letchford Manor' was soon under way: Warren and his clerk, James Brown, negotiated fifteen further options to increase the total area from 1,014 acres [405 hectares] to 3,818 acres [1,527 hectares]. The cost was £155,587, an average of £40 15s per acre. Early in July 1903 the Pioneer Company withdrew from Chartley.

The preparation of the plan

Unwin had been rather left out of things: on 16 July Parker wrote to Adams requesting further details. Adams replied that the partners would be consulted later. The Pioneer Company convened an Engineering Committee to obtain a layout.[42] H. D. Pearsall and H. B. Harris commissioned a report from H. Howard Humphreys, a London engineer and surveyor.[43] His report dealt with water supply, sewage disposal, road and rail transport, the position of the town centre, sites for factories and building materials.

The Hitchin–Cambridge branch of the Great Northern Railway ran south-west to north-east across the estate over the undulating outliers of the Chiltern Scarp. Humphreys advocated the construction of a station overlooking Norton Common and the shallow valley of the Pix Brook, along which he envisaged the main north–south road might run, possibly connected to the Great North Road beyond Willian village in the south of the estate. Unwin incorporated the line of this suggested road into his plan as 'Norton Way North – Norton Way South – Willian Way' but the connection to the Great North Road was never realized in this form. Between the Pix and the railway, a rounded plateau provided an ideal town-centre site, with 'numerous small plantations and other natural features which have the effect of preventing anything like monotony'. Factory sites, Humphreys felt, would best be placed to the leeward of the town, but improved technology would eliminate the tall smoking chimneys and dark satanic mills. The proximity of London and the growth of motor traffic would assist the development of manufacturing and engineering. Howard reported 'that Mr. Raymond Unwin had twice visited [the] estate for the purpose of reporting as [to] development'. Unwin submitted a rough plan and report in September 1903. The Engineering Committee minuted that 'the name of Raymond Unwin was mentioned in connection with the preparation of a plan . . . but no definite step was taken'. It began to look as if the prize might elude his grasp.

First Garden City Limited was registered on 1 September 1903. Its authorized capital was £300,000. However, investment was slow with only £181,026 secured by 1914. £93,934 had been mortgaged on the freehold, which inevitably inhibited development by the Company (Purdom, 1913). The architectural section of the Garden City Association, chaired by H. Clapham Lander (1869–1951), was invited to suggest consultants. Richard Norman Shaw (1831–1912), W. R. Lethaby (1857–1931) and Halsey Ricardo (1854–1928) were nominated. Shaw, the foremost architect of his generation, had in the 1870s evolved the richly eclectic 'Queen Anne' style, popularized at Bedford Park Garden Suburb in 1875. He declined the approach on the grounds of age. Lethaby, who had trained in Shaw's office, and Ricardo, were leading figures in the Arts and Crafts movement.

The Engineering Committee prevaricated pending completion of a contour survey by Humphreys. On 12 October 1903, the Company Board resolved that Lever and Howard should hold discussions with Unwin, while Herbert Warren sounded out [Sir] Aston Webb (1849–1930), RIBA President and one of the leading architects of Edwardian pomp and circumstance. His Victoria Memorial and the remodelling of The Mall as a processional route to Buckingham Palace intriguingly suggest that his involvement might have transformed the subsequent course of British town-planning.

On 20 October Howard, Lever and Pearsall held interviews. Lethaby was told that the Board required the best plan with the least trouble and was requested to participate with Ricardo in a limited competition. Next, at Howard's request, Parker was asked about Unwin's experience as an *engineer*. Asked how soon a plan could be prepared, Parker replied that he would need a week to ten days for site investigation and could submit the plan within five weeks. It was resolved:

> that the Secretary be instructed to write to Prof. Lethaby [*sic*] and Mr H. Ricardo and Messrs Raymond Unwin and Barry Parker [*sic*] . . . to . . . ask them independently to prepare a plan and submit the same to the Board, the fee for which would not exceed 100 guineas.[44]

The competition was under way without any indication of the assessment process. A third plan was prepared by Geoffry Lucas, a Hitchin architect and Sidney Cranfield, but no record of its commission has been found. Adams conducted Lethaby and Ricardo around the estate early in November. The Board had urged Howard to 'give special attention to . . . the first designing of the town'.

Unwin's plan was prepared in his Buxton office and on the Letchworth estate. The practice employed about six assistants and a secretary. Coordination of the domestic projects and the building of New Earswick required skilled management. Unwin was the more effective organizer, but neither he nor Parker were harsh taskmasters. They encouraged individuality; variable design standards were balanced by freshness and vigour. Among the Buxton staff, Robert Bennett (1878–1956), Wilson Bidwell (1877–1944), Cecil Hignett (1879–1960) and Albert Thompson (1878–1940) became successful architects in their own right. A more obscure assistant, Bowland Moffat (1880–1925), witnessed Unwin's 'quickness in grasping new ideas' as 'the Garden City scheme speedily took shape'. It was:

> a unique experience . . . quite out of the general range of architectural knowledge . . . and valuable in helping one to regard architecture not as apertaining merely to isolated buildings but as controlling whole towns and masses in one scheme.[45]

Unwin set off for Letchworth with Robert Bennett. They lodged at Letchworth corner on the Hitchin–Baldock Road, tramping over the estate, spending their evenings sketching out overlays on Humphreys' survey. Unwin confirmed the plateau west of the Pix valley as 'an exceptionally fine position for laying out a town centre . . . where groups of public buildings . . . would adequately dominate the whole area'. Significantly it was a natural feature which clinched matters:

> The three old oak trees which stood out solitary in the central town area were very helpful in fixing exactly the main axis line . . . I often remember, with a feeling of gratitude to them, the day when . . . they suggested to me the exact position, and Mr. Bennett and I were able to begin to lay the plan down on paper. (Unwin, 1913a, p. 228)

Completion of the final drawings at Buxton in December required the requisition of the Parkers' dining table at 'Moorlands'.

After Ricardo and Unwin had explained their plans to the Engineering Committee on 7 January 1904, the Board left the matter open pending a site meeting. On 28 January, the Engineering Committee compared the layouts with site plans prepared by the Great Northern Railway and cautiously recommended acceptance of the Parker and Unwin plan. The Board instructed Adams:

> to write to Mr Unwin for lithograph copies of his plan . . . and request . . . that he modify his plan in accordance with the railway company's plan . . . and also to inform him that his plan has been accepted, but only provisionally.

On 11 February 1904 it was finally resolved:

> That the plan be issued as the Company's plan.[46]

The plan[47] was publicly unveiled at a fashionable soirée in London's Grafton Galleries, where copies were distributed to Company shareholders.

The alternative layouts

Each of the three competition entries[48] paid deference to Howard's original diagrams. The Lucas and Cranfield plan was the least satisfactory, imposing a grid layout arbitrarily over the undulating terrain, with twin factory-belts running through the centre on both sides of the railway; Norton Common was shown as an elaborate Victorian park, with a grand boulevard running southwards to a vast town-centre piazza. The Lethaby and Ricardo plan was also poorly related to topography (*see* Figure 16). The industrial area was sited on the north-west, with sidings and a goods-yard on the town edge. The first impression of the town from the open terrain north of Wilbury Camp would have been industrial and difficult to screen with planting. To the leeward, the working-class housing and Norton Common would have received atmospheric industrial pollution. Lethaby and Ricardo favoured a compact grid layout, with the superimposition of major diagonals. They stressed that 'the city should not have the appearance of an overgrown village'. A mile-long axis led from the station to the town centre but this impressive concept would have been seriously weakened by its undulating line. The centre itself had triple axial roads converging on a square on the Pixmore slopes, the present location of the Hillshott School:

> a well-defined centre around which would be placed the town hall and other public buildings . . . rising in the middle of the central *place* would be a *campanile* to mark the heart of the city.

Unwin had noted Lethaby's remarks about the preservation of narrow seaward vistas in historic Constantinople and this was reflected around the main town square in both their plans. Lethaby and Ricardo reduced the entrances to their *place* to slits, heightening the sense of spatial release. Their housing adopted quadrangles with inner allotments as at

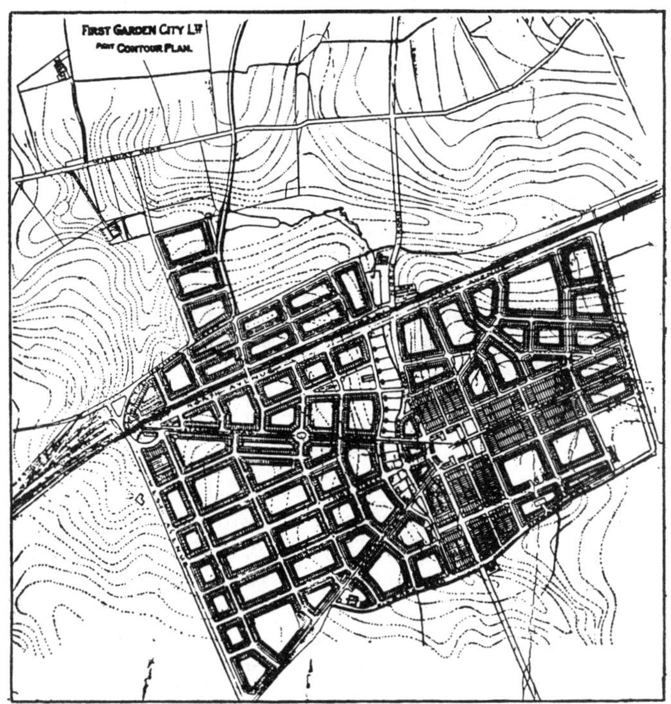

Figure 16 The Letchworth layout plan by Ricardo and Lethaby, 1903. Adams, and later Purdom, expressed a preference for its compact formality

Port Sunlight. As late as November 1909 Adams wrote to Ricardo that:

> the more concentrated development shown on your plan would not only secure a better architectural effect but would make the scheme more successful from a financial point of view.

Unwin's plan also appeared to be an exercise in formal geometery, but his carefully regulated major and minor axes effortlessly fitted the contour base (*see* Figure 17). The railway, the Wilbury–Norton road, the old Icknield Way, and the Hitchin–Baldock road were incorporated as east–west routes. Existing lanes - Letchworth Lane, Spring Road and Dunham's Lane provided fragmentary north–south communication. Unwin initially followed Humphreys' line for the main north–south route, eating into the eastern fringe of Norton Common, north of the railway. By April 1904, the road curved along the Common. It was ultimately run further east, creating a strip of building-land backing on to the Common. South of the railway, Unwin preserved the wooded Pix valley - now appropriately named Howard Park. The main axis, Broadway, ran at an angle from the Hitchin Road through the area reserved

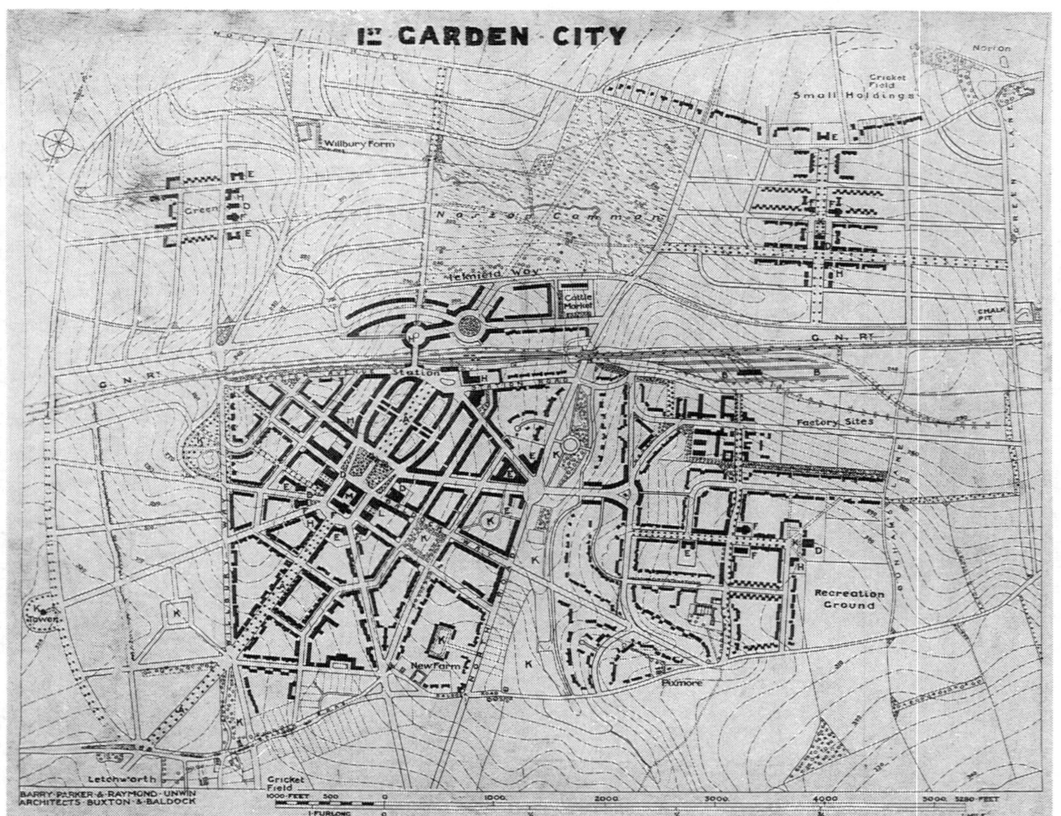

Figure 17 The 'original' Parker and Unwin layout for Letchworth, 1903. This layout, redrawn with minor modifications, was published in April 1904 as 'The Company's Plan'

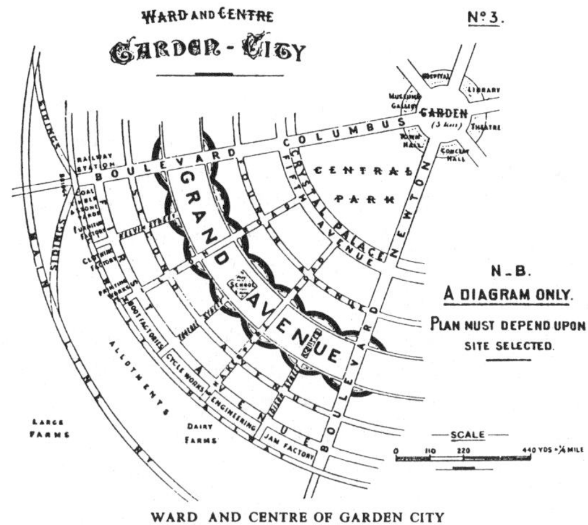

a

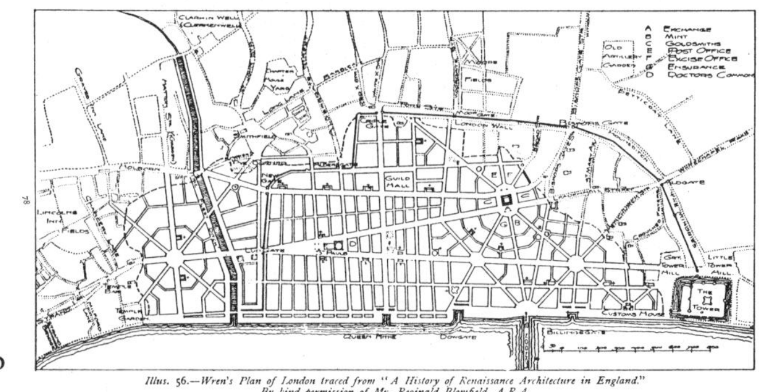

b

Figure 18 Influences on Unwin's plan: a) Howard's 'Ward and Centre' diagrams, from *Garden Cities of Tomorrow* (1902); b) Wren's City of London plan (1666) from *Town Planning in Practice* (1909): the area around the Exchange was the model for the treatment of the Central Town Square

for the Town Square (now J. F. Kennedy Gardens) to intersect the railway at the station site. The final length was paralleled by two sweeping curved roads, recalling the line of Unwin's favourite Oxford High Street. From Town Square radiated a web of minor axes, providing vistas from within and 'glimpses of that group of public buildings which would one day adorn that square, to those approaching the town' (Unwin, 1913a, p. 228). Minor roads connected the radials. The layout of the central area strikingly resembled the area surrounding the Exchange on Wren's City of London plan (1666) (*see* Figure 18b).

Outlying areas were informally treated. Beyond the Pix Valley at the east, two minor axes, Hillshott and Pixmore Way, were projected to guard against 'aimless wiggling', Unwin's *bête-noire* in site-planning. The upper slopes of Pixmore, developed for working-class housing, informally grouped as at New Earswick, had a defined neighbourhood centre, modified in detail later, but the guiding principles remained. The factory area, zoned as a broad belt either side of the railway, was concealed from the town centre by a bluff for which Unwin designed the Garden City Tenants' Birds Hill–Ridge Road housing scheme. North of Icknield Way lay the Norton Glebe where Unwin used field boundaries and hedgerows as the basis for an extensive housing layout. Between the preliminary plan and its implementation Unwin eliminated all north–south roads and two of the east–west roads in accordance with his principle of reducing road length relative to housing to a minimum.

In February 1904 he reworked the area between the Common and the railway, introducing a broad crescent and two interconnected circuses to bring the Broadway axis across the railway. These proposals were largely swept aside by the 1905 Cheap Cottage Exhibition. Adams considered that the axial line over the Common would make a convenient roadway. Unwin demurred, stating:

> we do not need more than a wide handsome walk . . . Having turned out the north and south road from one side of it, I should be very sorry to cut it in two with another road which . . . is less justified by the requirements of traffic . . . A broad grass glade . . . with perhaps a narrow paved way . . . would carry forward the axial line of the town, and provide . . . a short cut for pedestrians, the extra distance for vehicle traffic . . . would be very slight.[49]

The area north-west of the town centre contained another embryonic neighbourhood radically altered by Parker in the 1930s. The wide range of individual elements were largely integrated by Unwin's strong geometrical framework and tempered by a regard for natural features. Influenced by German practice, he developed the principles of land use and density zoning with definitions of town-centre, commercial and industrial areas and varied residential areas. Beyond the 'town area' agricultural land uses would predominate and development would be resisted.

Implementation and compromise

As consultants to First Garden City Ltd., Parker and Unwin were responsible for design control. The first houses constructed by local builders were of indifferent design, provoking Unwin to write to Howard stressing the importance of setting high standards. In July 1904 Adams advertised for an independent consultant at £200 a year. Unwin presented an impassioned justification of his position.

> People are expecting that the Garden City will be a more interesting and beautiful place than an ordinary new building suburb [*sic*], and its practical success will depend largely on this expectation being realised. The general effect . . . may yet be made or marred by the way in which the plan is carried out in detail. Two lines shown 50 or 60 feet apart on a plan . . . do not

constitute a design for a street, nor is it possible on such scale [Ordnance Survey 25″ (1:2500) base] to design the spaces where several streets meet and cross . . . The general effect will depend not only on the details of the roads, but on the planning of the buildings, and their arrangement on the plots, and the treatment of corner sites; . . . it seems to me very important to make suggestions to builders . . . The considering and passing of plans is another matter . . . it requires some experience to know what are the essential points to insist on . . . from the point of view of general effect.[50]

Unwin saw his work involving design briefs for each street and the articulation of space at junctions. Individual plans would be vetted with negotiation over detail where appropriate.

Despite his plea, the directors began to compile a shortlist. Unwin and Harry Burr, the Company's surveyor, prepared reports on their roles. The ambiguous nature of the resolution of August 4 suggests internal conflict:

That the Company employ an outside architect but that it would be distinctly experimental for one year, and that Messers Parker and Unwin be appointed at a salary of £200 and out-of-pocket expenses.

In the event the appointment was long-term. Unwin dealt with matters relating to the layout until the dissolution of his partnership with Parker in May 1914. Parker undertook the detailed design control. From 1914 until his retirement in 1943 Parker remained consultant architect to First Garden City Limited.

Control was variable and expedience often appeared to triumph. C. B. Purdom (1883–1965), one of the key figures in the Garden City and New Towns movements, then a junior accountant, witnessed conflicting opinions over design:

In the early days the consulting architects . . . set out to exert some control over the design of houses and to enforce the aesthetic interpretation of the building regulations but that attempt soon weakened . . . and for some years it practically disappeared . . . if the client were sufficiently determined he could put up much what he liked, as the buildings in the town bear witness. (Purdom, 1913, p. 69)

Unwin pressed for building regulations. The local Hitchin Rural District Council was permissive and while experimental construction was unlikely to be vetoed there was no guarantee of sound construction. Unwin's linking of aesthetic and constructional factors was evident from his first draft dated June 1904:

General Suggestions and Instructions Regarding Buildings other than Factories on the Garden City Estate
The Directors of First Garden City Limited are convinced that the high standard of beauty, which they desire to attain . . . can only result from simple, straightforward building, and . . . good and harmonious materials. They desire as far as possible to discourage useless ornamentation, and

to secure that buildings shall be suitably designed for their purpose and position.[51]

Unwin included building-area standards, building lines and grouping, aspect and prospect, boundary treatment and materials – many of the points stressed in *Cottage Plans and Common Sense*.

Control of materials, elaborated in the published 'Building Regulations' of 1905, was largely successful in practice. Welsh slate, reminiscent of bye-law terraces, was vetoed in favour of tiles. Unwin considered that the local yellow-grey gault bricks from Arlesey were drab and depressing and insisted on their being pebble dashed or colour-washed. Red facing bricks were readily permitted and widely used in the town centre. The 'Building Regulations' also included differential density zoning, related to the value of the dwellings, ranging from four to the acre [1.6 to the hectare] for houses costing more than £500, to twelve to the acre [4.8 to the hectare] for those costing less than £200. The smallest cottages had to include at least one living-room of not less than 144 sq.ft.

Townscape composition

Unwin found it difficult to coordinate development into the coherent groupings he had described as essential to the visual success of Letchworth. Adjustments to the layout in 1905 indicate his growing interest in spatial design (*see* Figure 19). The layout, particularly the town centre, remained a paper design. It had been prepared shortly before Unwin had studied Camillo Sitte's *Der Stadtebau nach seinen kunstlerichen Grundsatzen* [*City Planning according to Artistic Principles*] (1889) in Martin's corrupt French edition, *L'Art de Batir des Villes*. A Sittesque strengthening of the townscape potential of Letchworth began to emerge. The reworked junction of Leys Avenue, Gernon Road, Norton Way South and Hillshott pushed apart the first two roads, which led westwards and upwards into the town centre, creating a functionally more satisfactory site between them, subsequently developed for the Free Church. The staggered road junction was advocated by Sitte and broke the Gernon Road–Hillshott axis. The substitution of a rising shallow 'S' curve in place of the original straight line of Leys Avenue was visually effective, enabling the creation of sequential street pictures from its shopping parades.[52] Nearby Station Road was already laid out straight and Unwin introduced articulation of the building line, such as the shallow splays of Silver Birch Cottages (1905–7), for visual interest.

Judicious use of such techniques enabled Unwin to compose effective townscapes from individually undistinguished buildings, a point he emphasized later in *Town Planning in Practice* (Unwin, 1909, p. 208). The best example in Letchworth town centre is the visual sequence from Bridge Road to Leys Avenue, through Station Place (the town centre termination of the Broadway axis). The bridging point over the railway

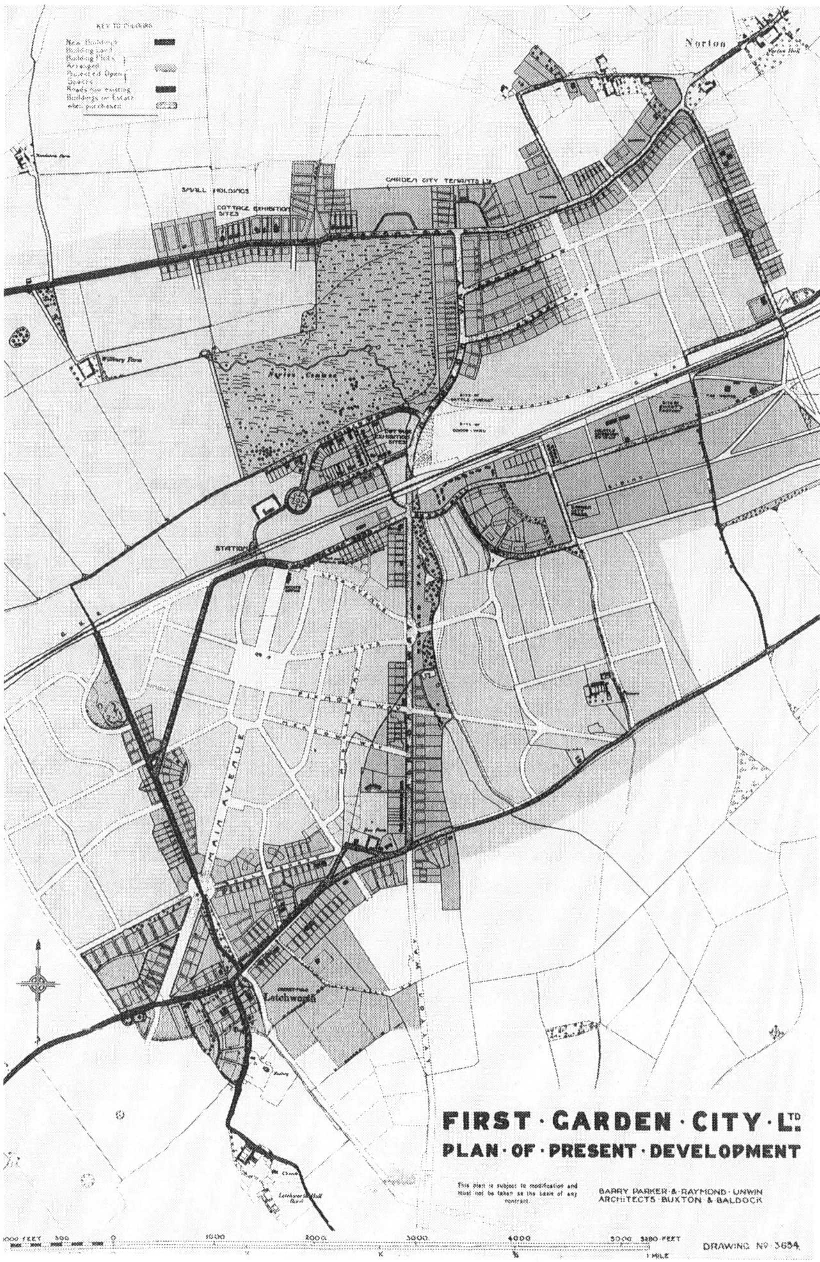

Figure 19 The Letchworth Plan, 1906 (LGC Corp.). The limited development and 'paper layout' of the town centre were a result of under-capitalization but enabled Unwin to introduce Sittesque modifications to the line of Leys Avenue, and diversion of Norton Way North behind building plots flanking Norton Common. Compare 17

Figure 20 Letchworth Town Centre, Broadway and Station Place. The 'stepped townscape' running across Station Place from The Colonnade to Broadway was the most impressive example of composing a varied townscape through articulation of the building line

was fixed early on although it was not constructed until 1930. In 1909, Charles Paget Wade (1883–1956), one of Unwin's Hampstead assistants, drew a fanciful mediaeval design for *Town Planning in Practice* (*see* Figure 46a). Below the playful fortified gateways lay the form of the triple-arched bridge, eventually built under Parker's guidance; beyond it lay a complex townscape based upon Unwin's articulated building lines (Unwin, 1909, Illustration 118). These evolved between 1905 and 1907. In the latter year he prepared a block plan indicating an angled recess centred on the axial line of the proposed bridge, partly filled in 1908 by a Neo-Georgian-style bank designed by Hugh Seebohm.[53] Unwin pulled forward the building line of Eastcheap–Station Place, partially closing off the westward vista from Leys Avenue in the process, with an effective 'stepped' townscape progression around 'The Colonnade', a dominant commercial building that also terminated the Station Road vista. The sequence to Broadway was enriched with the dominant Neo-Georgian-style First Garden City Estate Offices (Parker and Unwin, 1913–14), and the infilling by the stylistically similar National Provincial Bank (1926) (*see* Figure 20).

Elsewhere Unwin formed staggered road junctions, for example where Souberie Avenue crossed Meadow Way, although he did not attain the quadripartite enclosure of Sitte's favourite 'turbine plaza'. Multiple junctions created greater problems. The intersection of Broadway, Spring Road, Sollershott East and Sollershott West was complicated by a

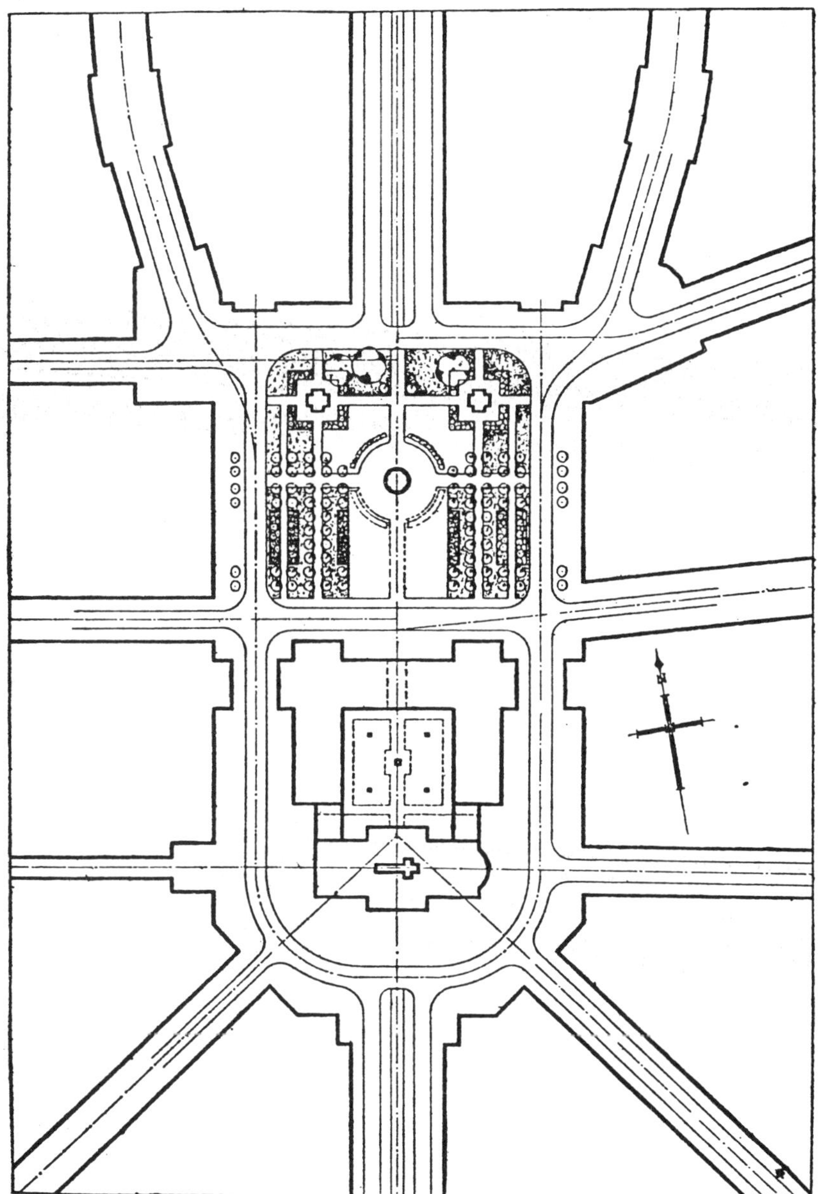

Plan of the Town Square, Garden City.

Figure 21 Letchworth Town Square layout 1912, published in Purdom's *The Garden City* (1913). The 'definitive' reduced square was adopted in 1912 and the outline of the major complex of buildings planted with Lombardy poplars requirement to include a tramway. Unwin's first layout was dated December 1904, designed with a triple carriageway for Broadway, with a tramway in one of the tree-planted margins. A revised scheme of July 1908 evolved in discussion with Walter Gaunt (1874–1951), Adams' successor as estate manager. The central roundabout, based on Henard's *carrefour à giration*, was one of the first in Britain, aptly named 'Sollershott Circus'.[54] The tramways were pushed to one side of the single carriageway of the length of Broadway from Hitchin Road; by the time the remaining length to Town Square was constructed in the 1920s the need for such a facility had passed.

The Town Square with its civic and religious buildings was intended as the visual climax of Letchworth. Unwin's original block plan was defective by Sitte's standards with a spatially loose arrangement. Unwin resisted the temptation to redesign the centre with the folksy groupings of his first plan for Hampstead Garden Suburb, prepared in February 1905. The provision for public buildings was overgenerous and many plots around the Town Square at Letchworth remained undeveloped for many years. Influenced by Lutyens' design for Central Square, Hampstead Garden Suburb, Unwin reworked its Letchworth counterpart in a formal layout. By 1907 he had linked church and civic buildings as a central group and in turn linked them to the perimeter buildings around the square with colonnades. The 4-acre [1.6 hectares] square to the north of the civic buildings was formally planted, with the three original oak trees in a place of honour on the axial sweep towards Station Place. East and west were oddly angled subsidiary *places* off which Eastcheap and Westcheap opened. This plan for Town Square was reproduced alongside Lutyens' proposals for Central Square, Hampstead Garden Suburb in *Town Planning in Practice* (Unwin, 1909, Illustrations 165, 166).

In 1910 visitors from the RIBA Town Planning Conference criticized the centre of Letchworth for its lack of civic design. Shortly afterwards, as the development became financially viable, Aneurin Williams, Chairman of FGC Ltd., announced that 'considerable attention has been given to the laying out of Town Square'. In May 1913, Gaunt unveiled a new plan (*see* Figure 21) (Gaunt, 1913). The Square had been reduced to 3 acres [1.2 hectares] comparable with Grosvenor or Belgrave Squares in London and would hold gatherings of 6,000–8,000 citizens. Formal planting began and the outline of the central group of buildings was planted-out in Lombardy Poplars. Alas, they remain: the buildings themselves progressed no further than a perspective by T. C. Watson Hart, their design 'freely adapted' from 'the works of Wren and other masters'. The civic buildings were enlivened by cupolas and the church had a Baroque spire rising on the Broadway axis. The linking colonnades were grafted rather unconvincingly on to the fronts of the simpler surrounding buildings (*see* Figure 21). Gaunt warned against lavish spending that might cause 'the toiler reproachfully [to] look at the civic centre outlay as something but for which his cottage might have been more economically built and rented'. Unwin had warned thus about 'civic art' a decade

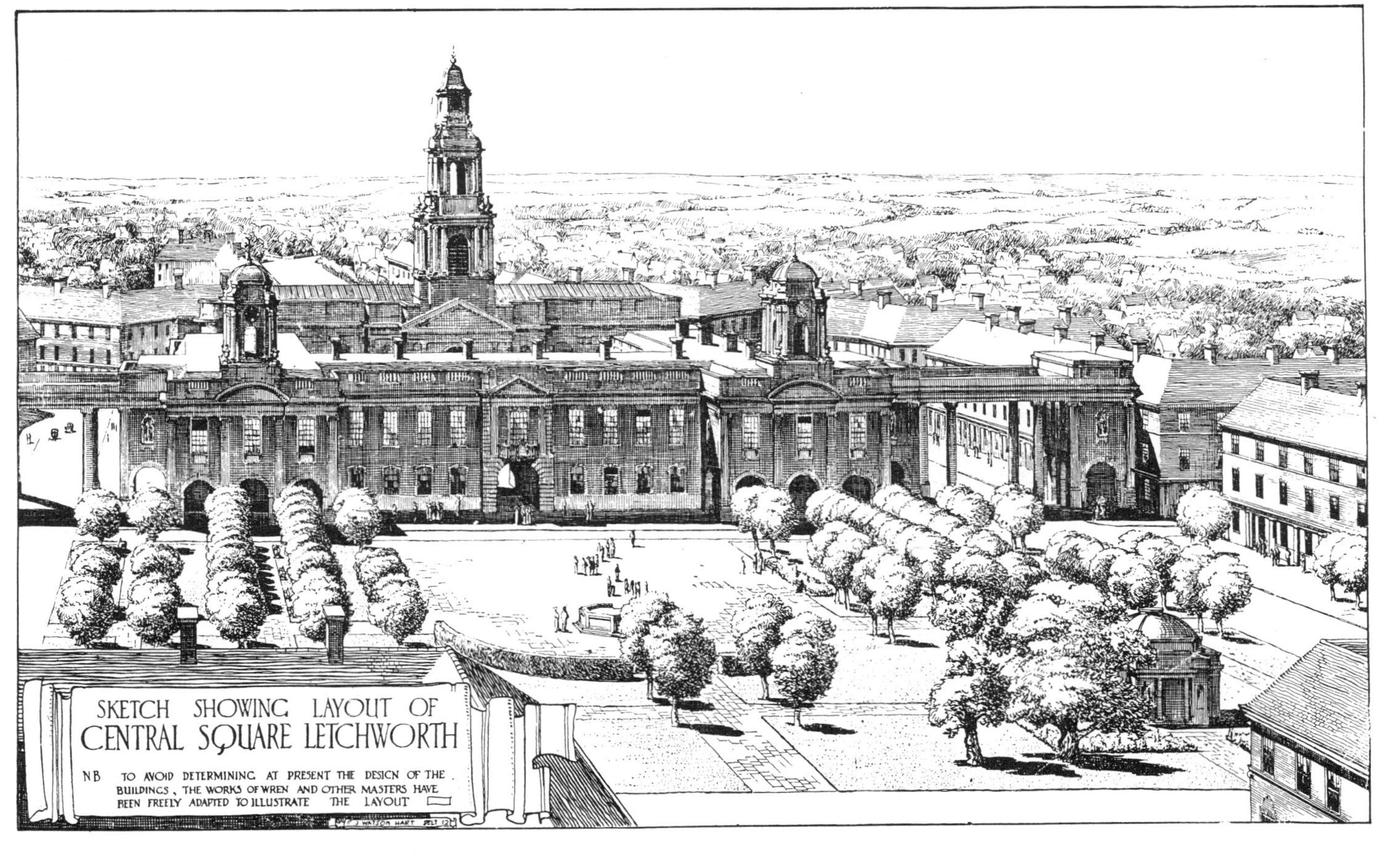

Figure 22 Letchworth Town Square 1912, perspective by F. J. Watson Hart (FGC Mus.). Modelled on 'the works of Wren and other masters', the buildings were never planned in detail and the First World War effectively precluded the realization of this grandiose concept

Figure 23 *Laneside/Crabby Corner*, Letchworth Lane, 1904. The former (left) was Unwin's home until his departure for Hampstead in 1906; the latter (right) was Parker's home 1906–35

earlier, but the caution of FGC Ltd. placed Letchworth at a disdvantage to Bournville and, particularly, Port Sunlight where groups of quasi-civic buildings added lustre to the overall visual quality.

The formal concept for the Town Square brought a design policy for Georgian-style buildings along the urban section of Broadway. This required Georgian-style buildings and reflected Unwin's moves towards a formal approach to civic design. The edict was not regarded as an unmixed blessing in Letchworth itself. Parker appears to have prepared an alternative Town Square layout. To Purdom the choice of an 'approved style' was anathema, notwithstanding his strictures over the lack of overall design control. He claimed that 'of all styles the Georgian is most out of keeping with the peculiar character of the town' (Purdom, 1913, p. 70). History has revealed the truths and limitations of these strictures. The Town Square was fitfully developed. The Museum (Parker and Unwin, 1914–20), the Grammar School (Parker, 1931) and the Council Offices (Bennett and Bidwell, 1935) all conformed but showed little individual sparkle, while later buildings appeared to be related only by visual inappropriateness for their setting.

Garden City domestic architecture

In 1904 Raymond Unwin leased a large plot of land in Letchworth Lane, a few yards south of the cottage where he had prepared the first sketch

Figure 24 Unwin's living-room, *Laneside*, 1904 (FGC Mus.). The setting for family and community life in the pioneer period of Garden City development

layout plan. Jointly with the Howard Pearsalls he built a pair of semi-detached houses, 'Laneside' and 'Crabby Corner' (both now extended as 'Arunside') (*see* Figure 23). Unwin's design rejected symmetry and expressed the differing requirements in a harmonious and subtly organized exterior. The building had roughcast walls and a dominant tiled roof, punctuated by dormers and capped by tall chimneys. It was, in essence, an enlarged version of the grouped cottages of New Earswick. The open-plan interior was based on his unbuilt design for his family home at Chapel-en-le-Frith. Unwin moved into 'Laneside'. The large living-room, with its copper-hooded fireplace, built-in window seats and cupboards, was sparsely furnished, with rush matting, trestle tables, a large settle, and slender rush-seated Clissett chairs (*see* Figure 24). The room became the setting for community life in the infant Garden City:

> No one entered more completely . . . into the pioneer life . . . innumerable societies were started . . . The Sunday evening services held in the Unwins' house were such as could be joined in by those of any, or no creed. (Parker, 1940b)

Yet Unwin stayed there for less than two years, moving to 'Wyldes', Hampstead, to oversee the planning of the garden suburb in the summer

Figure 25 The Parker and Unwin offices, Norton Way South, 1907. The adoption of the vernacular thatched-hall house once represented the ultimate in pastoral ideology. A mirror-image extension to accommodate Unwin's suite was never built but the building was tactfully extended by Parker in 1937 as his home

of 1906. That July, Barry Parker, newly married, moved into 'Crabby Corner', which remained his home until 1935. It was extended in 1914 with a Germanic three-storey sleeping tower. The domestic character also permeated the designs prepared in 1906–7 for the firm's Letchworth offices (now First Garden City Heritage Museum) in the parkway setting of Norton Way South. Parker chose the thatched mediaeval open-hall house as his model (*see* Figure 25), with the hall serving as the main drawing office (*see* Figure 26), and the raised solar as his private studio. There was room to accommodate a mirror-image extension for Unwin's office suite but this was never needed.

The domestic lifestyle of the Letchworth pioneers seems to have attained an idyllic Utopian quality (Brunt, 1942; Purdom, 1951; Miller, 1989). The 'simple lifers' included the freethinking middle-class teetotallers sporting smocks and sandals, and their hatless, gloveless, and, to conventional society, shameless womenfolk. Such esoteric pursuits as Vegetarianism, Theosophy and Esperanto flourished. Cartoons satirized the parsimony of the Parish Council – the local authority for Letchworth until 1919 – the Great Northern Railway and the philistinism of the estate manager, Walter Gaunt, whose well-publicized efforts to attract industry were often resented by the middle-class idealists. Howard, Unwin and others were caricatured (*see* Figure 27). Garden City Pantomimes, staged in the Parker- and Unwin-designed Mrs Howard Memorial Hall, satirized Letchworth life and 'the Spirit of

Figure 26 The drawing office, Parker and Unwin Letchworth offices, *c.* 1909 (FGC Mus.). Among the assistants present, Samuel Pointon-Taylor ultimately succeeded Unwin as chief Housing Architect at the Ministry of Health, while Cecil Hignett set up a successful independent practice

the Place'; a benevolent *djinn* took architects to task for their 'arty-crafty, ever so draughty' creations.

If the town centre of Letchworth was a partial success, the residential areas were another matter. Parker and Unwin designed individual and grouped houses, of the Arts and Crafts character. The aesthetic control process worked best in residential areas, curbing the visual excesses of conventional speculative development. Tree-lined roads such as Norton Way South attained a pleasing visual unity. Letchworth was notable for the quality of pre-1914 houses (Miller, 1989, pp. 59–87);[55] in addition to those by Parker and Unwin there were examples by Baillie Scott,

Two German ladies, who visited Letchworth last week, said on leaving: –" We are awfully disappointed in one thing: we were assured before coming that the people at Garden City were only half clothed, and that they all went bare-headed and wore sandals, and we have not seen one person of that sort! "

It really is too bad of folks
To come expecting something eerie,
We are just ordinary souls,
The right-side up, not " tapsalteerie."

Our architect is harmless quite,
Un' winsome, too, at present,
Our di-Rector ap-*Pears all* smiles,
Our Agent, *Gaunt*—but pleasant.

Figure 27 'What some people think of us', cartoon by Louis Weirter, 1909. A gentle local satire of the eccentricities of Garden City life, featuring Walter Gaunt (left), Unwin (lower centre), dressed in smock and sandals, and Howard Pearsall (right)

Curtis Green (1875–1960), C. Harrison Townsend (1851–1928), H. Clapham Lander, Courtenay Crickmer (1879–1971), Randall Wells (1877–1942), Robert Bennett, Wilson Bidwell and Cecil Hignett – the last three being 'graduates' of Parker and Unwin.

Publicity concentrated more on eccentricity rather than on the lasting legacy of housing design and layout. According to Purdom, the 1905 Cheap Cottages Exhibition 'gave the town the character of a village of tiny weekend cottages, not very well built . . . and gained the place a bad reputation before it deserved it' (Purdom, 1913, p. 501). This event was masterminded by Adams following publicity by J. St Loe Strachey, editor of *The Country Gentleman*, which voiced the problems of building agricultural workers' cottages at an economically viable cost. The exhibition site lay between the railway and Norton Common (*Book of Cheap Cottages Exhibition*, 1905; Miller, 1978, 1980). A cost limit of £150 per dwelling was set. Most entries were detached, giving little chance of attaining the coordinated design sought by Unwin. He was cautioned by the Board that 'architects must not be interfered with as regards details or matters of taste'. Among the most notable entries were two prefabricated reinforced concrete cottages: 158 Wilbury Road, designed by John Brodie, the Liverpool City engineer, and 'The Round House', 140 Wilbury Road, designed by Hesketh Stokes for Cubitts, the London builders, which had a sixteen-sided plan. The Exhibition, the first of its kind, attracted 60,000 visitors. Unwin's interest in building technology was kindled, leading to his involvement, in 1920, with the Ministry of Health demonstration site at Acton and the *Daily Mail* Ideal Home Model Village of 1921, at Welwyn Garden City.

More significant were the housing estates that consolidated earlier achievement at Bournville, Port Sunlight and New Earswick. Parker and Unwin initially developed their design themes in the Garden City Tenants' estates (Miller, 1979b, 1989). The Letchworth branch of the Co-Partners undertook development in 1905–10. The first, Eastholm Green, surrounded the village green from *The Art of Building a Home* with a loose grouping of detached and semi-detached houses, one pair of which, probably designed by Unwin himself, won a prize in the Cheap Cottage Exhibition. Westholm Green (1906–7) commanded views of Norton Common and was flanked by groups of cottages, with multiple gables and dormers breaking the steeply pitched roofs (*see* Figure 28), comparable with designs for Station Road, New Earswick. Parlour cottages gave emphasis to group centres and ends. Westholm Green and its successor, Birds Hill (1906–7), created a design kit, capable of varied assembly to fit specific site conditions. In addition to a village green, Birds Hill included a cul-de-sac to enable development in depth, a central 'backland' playground and a planted buffer zone demarcating the housing from the adjoining factory area (*see* Figure 29a).

Birds Hill was locally controversial for weekly rents of 4s 6d [22½p] for a two-bedroomed non-parlour cottage to 8s 6d [42½p] for three- and four-bedroomed parlour types, which were claimed as a result of extravagant construction, pricing the housing beyond the means of

Figure 28 Westholm Green, 1906, built by Garden City Tenants Ltd. This layout at last enabled Unwin to realize his village green model, designed in 1899. Compare 10

labourers. Unwin defended his designs with costings and attempted to turn the tables by declaring that a 9d [4p] a week average wage rise would solve the problem. He reiterated:

> if Garden City stands for anything it surely stands for this: a decent home and garden for every family . . . This is the irreducible minimum. Let that go and we fail utterly. And if we succeed utterly, what then? A beautiful home in a beautiful garden and a beautiful city for all. (Unwin, 1906a, p. 111)

However, he designed simpler, cheaper cottages and looked again at standardization. None of the Co-Partners' subsequent developments was quite so exuberant as Birds Hill.

The largest of the Garden City Tenants' estates was Pixmore (1906–10), a 16.35 acre [5.35 hectare] neighbourhood block south of Ridge Road, developed with 164 houses, at twelve per acre net, excluding roads, the Institute and recreation grounds (*see* Figure 29b). Unwin progressively eliminated through roads. Pix Road zigzagged through the centre to serve 71 houses, but its width was only 18 ft. between fences, with no room for footpaths. Today the estate centre is choked with parked cars, unthinkable at the time of construction. Housing groups were simpler than at Birds Hill, but corner groupings were given careful thought and the splayed terraces framing the junction of Pix Road and Broughton Hill were illustrated in *Town Planning in Practice* (Unwin, 1909. Illustrations 267, 268).

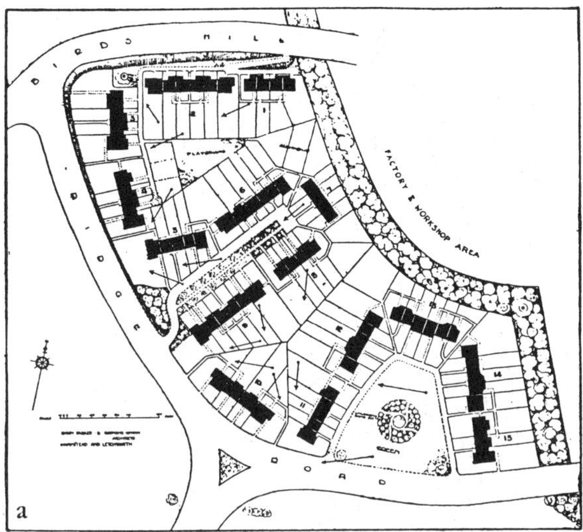

Garden City Tenants. Bird's Hill Estate, Letchworth. Irregular lay-out to suit site, with plantation defining the area.

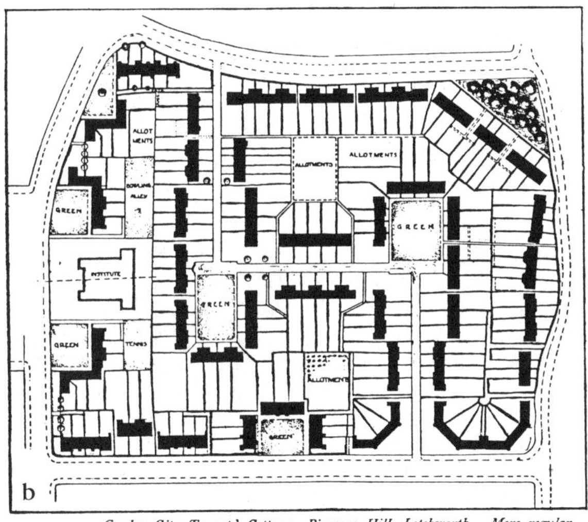

Garden City Tenants' Cottages, Pixmore Hill, Letchworth. More regular lay-out, with carriage drive developing central area.

Figure 29 Garden City Tenants' housing schemes: a) Birds Hill, 1906; b) Pixmore, 1907–9. Plans illustrated in *Town Planning in Practice* (1909), which indicate Unwin's growing confidence in techniques of site layout and increase in scale towards the self-contained neighbourhood unit

By 1907 Letchworth was developing a significant industrial base. The early estates had partly met the initial housing demand but low-cost labourers' housing remained a pressing need. Few industrialists provided company housing. FGC Ltd took a more direct role from 1907, through its subsidiary Letchworth Cottages and Buildings Ltd.; by 1911 this had constructed nearly 200 cottages, many costing under £150. The groups

Figure 30 Rushby Mead housing scheme, 1911: a) Setback cottage group designed by Bennett and Bidwell; b) Rushby Walk cul-de-sac, with groups by Parker and Unwin (left and centre) and Crickmer (right) and retention of original hedgerow

in Common View designed by Parker reduced brickwork to a minimum and brought down the roof, with bedroom windows under catslide dormers.

In August 1911 the Howard Cottage Society was formed (Miller, 1979b). Ebenezer Howard was one of its directors. In 1912, Frederic Osborn (1885–1978) was recruited as secretary. The first project set high standards. Development along Rushby Mead, facing Howard Park, began in 1911, with a layout by Unwin in which he reworked his early admiration of village groupings in terms of the more analytical approach of Sitte. The gentle curve of the road followed the bed of the Pix Brook, which had been culverted through Howard Park. Existing trees and hedges were preserved and the building line articulated to form a picturesque sequence. Three firms of architects designed successive housing groups, but their work blends unobtrusively, complemented by cream roughcast walls, rich red tiled roofs and green painted woodwork.

Southwards from Birds Hill, the first two blocks, set behind long gardens, the right angled returns and frontage block, were designed by Bennett and Bidwell. Rushby Walk, an early cul-de-sac included two groups by Parker and Unwin and two by Courtenay Crickmer (*see* Figure 30). South of Hillshott Unwin created an enclosed ***place*** with the road taken diagonally between blocks set at right angles to each other, a convincing fusion of Sittesque design principles with the open form of Garden City development. Its visual successor, Jackmans Place, developed by Letchworth Urban District Council in 1919–21, was designed by Bennett and Bidwell and was based upon the layout principles set out by Unwin in *Town Planning in Practice* and the Tudor Walters *Report*.

Before then, local authority construction had been sporadic. Hitchin Rural District Council built four cottages on Icknield Way in 1912 and wartime conditions promoted more extensive construction in 1915–16.

Unwin's achievement at Letchworth

Raymond Unwin officially resigned as consultant architect to FGC Ltd. in May 1914, upon dissolution of the partnership with Parker. Purdom's claim that 'Unwin, fighting a losing battle, fled during 1906 to Hampstead Garden Suburb . . . and Letchworth hardly saw him again' (Purdom, 1951, p. 53) is melodramatic overstatement. Unwin drew strength from turning problems to opportunities. He continued to modify, refine and adapt the plan until 1914. Well into the 1920s, whenever the Unwins returned for social gatherings, the brothers-in-law would withdraw to confer informally about development of the Garden City.

Purdom viewed Letchworth as the supreme test of Unwin's creative and administrative abilities.

> No one architect, however able, could control a town or lay down laws for its growth. And when the condition of architecture in this country is considered . . . and generally the incompetence of those who practise it, it must be obvious that Mr. Raymond Unwin, venturesome as he is, was undertaking a task too great for any man. (Purdom, 1913, p. 39)

Figure 31 Aerial view of Letchworth, 1937 (Letchworth GC Corp.). At this period the sinews of the plan still stood out in sharp relief, revealing the sporadic infilling of the town centre

The limitations of aesthetic control were apparent where the Company felt it was more important whether development took place than what it looked like. Nevertheless, the Letchworth system moved beyond landlord covenants towards modern development control. Applications that seriously violated density or building standards were rejected. Designs by local architects, versed in Garden City principles, were approved. The majority of the applications from builders or designers with no great visual sensitivity were generally given the benefit of the doubt, without seriously compromising cardinal principles.

Like Howard, Unwin had visualized a complete town, which his plan aimed at creating in the rolling North Hertfordshire landscape:

> although the centre and the main framework of roads dominate the planning, the greater part of a town consists of the dwellings of its citizens, and Letchworth came into being mainly to express the new ideas [associated with] Mr. Howard and the Garden City Association. That every house should have its garden and should be placed that all its rooms should be flooded with light and sunshine, unblocked by other houses or by its own projections, were the main ideals. It was necessary to break away from the customary type of street with its endless rows of houses . . . hideous in appearance . . . and squalid . . . The break was successfully made . . . not without its mistakes . . . it is true . . . The great thing is that a new and vastly improved standard was set up and applied to the whole of a town in place of the deplorable one which had well-nigh become universal. (Unwin, 1913a, p. 229)

In 1909 Frederick Law Olmsted Jr., son of the great American landscape architect, visited Letchworth. He felt the road network was almost too reminiscent of the ubiquitous American gridiron but 'the number of ill-considered designs seemed to be no more than is reasonably to be expected as the price of a healthy state of active experimenting'.

He concluded:

> Age is what Letchworth seems mainly to need; age, the growth of vegetation, and the quality which comes from painstaking care in the commonplace work of maintenance, repair and adaption to use on the part of those who live in it. (Olmsted, 1909, p. 199)

The intervening eight decades have brought this maturity, as Letchworth has mellowed to Arcadia, aided by Unwin's original respect for natural features and subsequent planting and landscaping. From the air, the sinews of the plan still stand out (*see* Figure 31), clothed in greenery that conceals many of the design errors that once seemed so important, and evoking Howard's objective of a synthesis of town and country.

5

Hampstead, the Unique Garden Suburb

> When the deeds for the land were signed I was reminded by the Vice Provost of Eton that it was Henry VIII – Henricus Octavius – a man and a king who signed the deeds at the sale of those lands; and the person who signed the deeds at the purchase . . . was Henrietta Octavia, a woman and not a queen, but for many years a 'general servant' in Whitechapel – buying them with the money of democracy for the homes of democracy. (*Cottages with Gardens for Londoners*, *c.*1907, p. 18)

On Thursday 2 May 1907, Henrietta Barnett thus inaugurated Hampstead Garden Suburb by turning the sod for the first pair of Co-Partners cottages, Nos. 140–2 Hampstead Way. Raymond Unwin handed the spade to her and Henry Vivian, Chairman of the Co-Partners, commended his organization's combination of commercial viability with cooperative ownership. Alfred Lyttelton, Chairman of the Hampstead Garden Suburb Trust Ltd. stressed the benefits of an estate planned:

> not in the manner of the speculative builders, but in opening out and not breaking the vista of views in which Hampstead was so rich. There were many communities . . . in which the squire and the parson and those who clustered round . . . parsonage or manor lived together harmoniously with no sign of tyranny or patronage on one side, or of a servility or loss of independence on the other. (*Cottages with Gardens for Londoners*, *c.*1907, p. 14)

These comments sprang from Unwin's paper, 'Cooperation in building' (Unwin, 1901c), also of seminal significance as a catalyst for Henrietta Barnett's concept of a garden suburb for all classes.

Henrietta's dream

Henrietta Barnett (1851–1936) was a contemporary of Ebenezer Howard (Barnett, 1918; Grafton Green, 1977; Slack, 1982). Drawn into the circle of Octavia Hill (1838–1912), a pioneer of housing reform and also of the common land registration movement, she met and soon married Samuel

Augustus Barnett (1844–1913), who felt a vocation for work amongst the poor. From 1873 to 1906 he was Vicar of St Jude's, Whitechapel, amid some of the worst East End slums. In 1884 he founded Toynbee Hall, the first of the University settlements, which sought to bring Oxford graduates into contact with slum dwellers. Stern moral rectitude coloured the Barnetts' approach to social problems. Degredation was a reflection of sin and alms an unjustifiable palliative. Self-discipline and self-reliance were the keys to salvation. However, experience taught them that overcrowded housing undermined their efforts at spiritual guidance directed towards moral and spiritual matters.

In 1880 they acquired a weekend house on the northern fringe of Hampstead Heath which was soon nicknamed 'St Jude's Holdall'. *En route* to Russia in 1896, Henrietta Barnett learned of proposals to extend the London Underground Railway northwards to Hampstead. 'It required no imagination to see the rows of ugly villas such as disfigure Willesden . . . therefore there was nothing else to do but enlarge the Heath' (Barnett, 1918, 2, p. 312). Having identified a major goal she refused to be diverted by technical, financial or procedural obstacles and sought the recruitment of influential followers whose role was to lubricate the wheels of progress. By November 1902, Parliamentary sanction had been granted and finance raised to build the Hampstead 'tube' to Golders Green. The Wyldes Estate, owned by Eton College, became ripe for development. In June 1903, assisted by Robert Hunter, a founder of the National Trust, Henrietta Barnett mobilized the Heath Extension Council, to purchase 80 acres [32 hectares] to form a permanent open space and obtained an option to purchase for £48,000. She broadened the campaign to acquire the remaining 243 acres [97 hectares] for development of a 'Garden Suburb for the Working Classes' and announced in the *Hampstead and Highgate Express* on 28 November 1903:

> The conditions of building are those which ensure the establishment of not [*sic*] a 'garden city' but a 'garden suburb' in which every house, however humble, will be productive as well as pleasurable. The plan, however, will necessitate the provision of some shops, and some houses of a larger size and more extensive gardens.

The identification of a 'garden suburb' probably reflects the wide publicity accorded to the opening of the Garden City estate at Letchworth a few weeks before. The Garden City Association took a great interest in her proposal and one of her early supporters, Howard Pearsall, became a director of First Garden City Ltd. Henrietta Barnett organized her 'veritable showman's happy family' (Barnett, 1928, pp. 6–7); two Earls (Lords Grey and Crewe), two lawyers (Sir John Gorst and Sir Robert Hunter), two Free Churchmen (Herbert Marnham and Walter Hazell), a Bishop (Dr Winnington Ingram) and a woman (herself), the 'syndicate of eight' described in her letter to the press. The syndicate became a 'Steering Trust' in May 1904 and worked in parallel with the Heath Extension Council. She had possibly considered enlisting local authority support. The press had linked the LCC cottage estate at Tottenham with the Garden City. However, the LCC was uncooperative and even refused to pay the stamp duty on the transfer of the Heath Extension.

The choice of Raymond Unwin as planner rekindled his youthful acquaintance with the Barnetts. Henrietta Barnett later claimed that it arose almost on impulse:

> In September 1904 I was called away suddenly from Whitechapel by the serious illness of one who was very dear to me, and stuffing a few more dull documents into the bursting bag, I tore off for the train. Amid the anxieties attending the illness I read on and on, not noticing who wrote what, until putting down I said 'That's the man for my beautiful green golden scheme' [*sic*]. (Barnett, 1928, p. 7)

She could scarcely have remained ignorant of the publicity about the formal launch of Unwin's layout for Letchworth earlier that year. In November 1904 she attended the York conference of the National Union of Women Workers, at which Unwin spoke on 'The Improvement of Towns' (Unwin, 1904), which also presented a convenient opportunity to visit New Earswick. Following his youthful consultation of Samuel Barnett, Unwin had resolved his vocational dilemma; through the efforts of the Rowntrees, Howard and now the Barnetts, the vision outlined in *The Art of Building a Home* was assuming material form. Henrietta Barnett had an equally clear concept: late in 1904 she had a drawing prepared for her old nurse, to whose sickbed she had rushed, showing the Heath Extension, flanked by houses, with a distant church spire, a remarkably close anticipation of the form the Suburb would take.

The evolution of Unwin's layout

In December 1904 Unwin was given permission by Eton College to survey the proposed Heath Extension, assisted by a contour plan prepared by Howard Humphreys who had undertaken a similar task at Letchworth. Henrietta Barnett redoubled her efforts to enlist support for her bid to spread 'the contagion of refinement' to working-class life and housing. Philosophically and physically, Hampstead Garden Suburb compromised purist Garden-City ideals by endorsing the outward spread of the metropolis. The constitutional and financial basis was, however, virtually identical. Following Morris, Unwin had attacked suburban development, in *The Art of Building a Home*:

> When a modern town begins to sprawl . . . what desecration of scenery follows . . . modern suburbs specially offend in coming between [the historic centre and the rural surroundings]; so that however the city may be fitted to beautify the landscape, we cannot see it from the fields, nor can we catch a refreshing glimpse of the cool green hillside from amongst our busy streets. (Unwin, 1901b, p. 84)

Characteristically, he turned problems to opportunities through the physical framework for the realization of Henrietta Barnett's social objectives. Preservation of the Heath Extension brought about a 'refreshing glimpse of the cool green hillside' to many. Hampstead Garden Suburb was surely one of the most creative of all compromises.

In February 1905, Henrietta Barnett brought her proposals to a liberal readership through *Contemporary Review* (Barnett, 1905); Patrick Geddes and Charles Booth were among those who commended the scheme. She virtually presented a development brief, reflected in Unwin's preliminary layout, published on 22 February. Several of her ideas were expressed in Unwinian language. Reference to cottages with tenth-acre plots and the formula for subsidizing road costs from the more affluent properties carried the hallmark of his 'robbing Peter to pay Paul'. The 'essential condition that the dwellings of all classes be made attractive . . . as are the cottages and Manor houses of the English village' virtually sprang from *The Art of Building a Home*.

As the nucleus, the Heath Extension gave the Trust a monopoly of amenity through frontage development judiciously exercised to serve social ends: a foretaste of 'positive discrimination':

> Under strict building covenants some of the most attractive portions of this land will be leased (not sold) to the rich in 1, 2, 3 acre plots . . ., it is hoped that these . . . will produce a large ground rent. Beyond it is proposed that smaller plots should be set apart for people of humbler means . . . always providing that the fundamental principle is complied with that the part should not spoil the whole, nor that individual rights be assumed to carry the power of working communal or individual wrongs . . . Every acre which fetches a large price will release other acres [for] . . . cottages for the industrial classes. (Barnett, 1905, p. 232)

With land at £150 per acre and allowance for road costs, she envisaged development of 80 acres with small cottages. The suburb would benefit from 'being planned, not in piecemeal . . . but as a whole':

> The houses will not be put in uniform lines, nor in close relationship, built regardless of each other, or without consideration for picturesque appearance. Each one will be surrounded with its own garden, and every road will be planted with trees, and not be less than forty feet wide. Great care will be taken that these houses should not spoil each others' outlook. (Barnett, 1905, p. 235)

Broader community needs would be met with 'houses of prayer', lecture rooms and clubs, shops, baths and wash-houses, bakeries and cooperative stores – in abundance comparable with Unwin's provision in the preliminary plans for Letchworth and New Earswick. The sick, the elderly, the handicapped, the single and orphan children would be accommodated in housing quadrangles. The stigma of charity would be avoided and the security of the site would provide potential for profitable development, but without sacrificing amenity.

Unwin's February 1905 layout[56] took as its prime determinants the 80-acre tongue of the Heath Extension, the central hillock commanding views westward to Harrow, where Henrietta Barnett herself had determined to site the Churches and the Institute, and approaches from North End Road, Hoop Lane and Finchley Road. The subsequent evolution of the plan provides clear evidence of Unwin's understanding of Camillo Sitte and of the influence of Lutyens, but it also marked Unwin's own distinctive contribution to site-planning. As already noted, he had studied the corrupt French Sitte translation, *L'Art de Batir des Villes*.

The character of the first Hampstead plan contrasted both with the suburb as built and with Letchworth. Unwin rejected the formal central framework of Letchworth in favour of amorphous tree-lined roads, flanked by fragmented groups of cottages, with a loose-knit villagey centre. The picturesque, almost artless, informality of New Earswick reasserted itself. His zeal in fulfilling Henrietta Barnett's requirements was rewarded by her approving handwritten comments upon her copy of the plan (*see* Figure 32).[57] The early quadrangles from *Cottage Plans and Common Sense* and chequerboard street rows from *Cottages Near a Town* reappeared. School sites were reserved in the '70 acres [28 hectares] allotted to the homes of the industrial classes at 10 to the acre'. Areas east and north of the Heath Extension were reserved for 'the homes of the rich', but Unwin criss-crossed the plots with view lines indicating distant prospects from less favourably placed areas. It all suggested 'a place for everyone' with, as a proper corollary, 'everyone in their place' but it failed to demonstrate the underlying sense of ordered design, so conspicuous in the Letchworth plan. The central citadel of religion and knowledge was a casual concept, with the church tower forming the sole focal point among open-sided quadrangles of cooperative housing and parades of shops. Although the vista from the centre to the Heath Extension was suggested, its visual potential was not fully realized. The overall effect was restless and aimless, as in self-conscious German extension plans later criticized by Unwin in *Town Planning in Practice*.

The two-year gap between the preliminary plan and commencement of development gave ample time for revision and refinement of the layout. In March 1906, Hampstead Way was realigned to avoid the demolition of the outbuildings of 'Wyldes', the seventeenth-century farmhouse that shortly afterwards became Unwin's home and offices. The 'artisans' quarter', developed under the aegis of the Co-Partners, had not attained a definitive layout at the time of the May 1907 inauguration. The Heathgate – Central Square – Erskine Hill area, the northern cottage sector and the sliver of land south of the Heath extension remained fluid. As late as 1908–9 neither the Central Square nor the northern cottage sector between Addison Way, Willified Way and Hampstead Way had been finalized. Not until April 1911 did a relatively definitive plan emerge for the 243-acre [98-hectare] 'Old Suburb' (*see* Figure 33), just as the Trust and the Co-Partners were negotiating for the

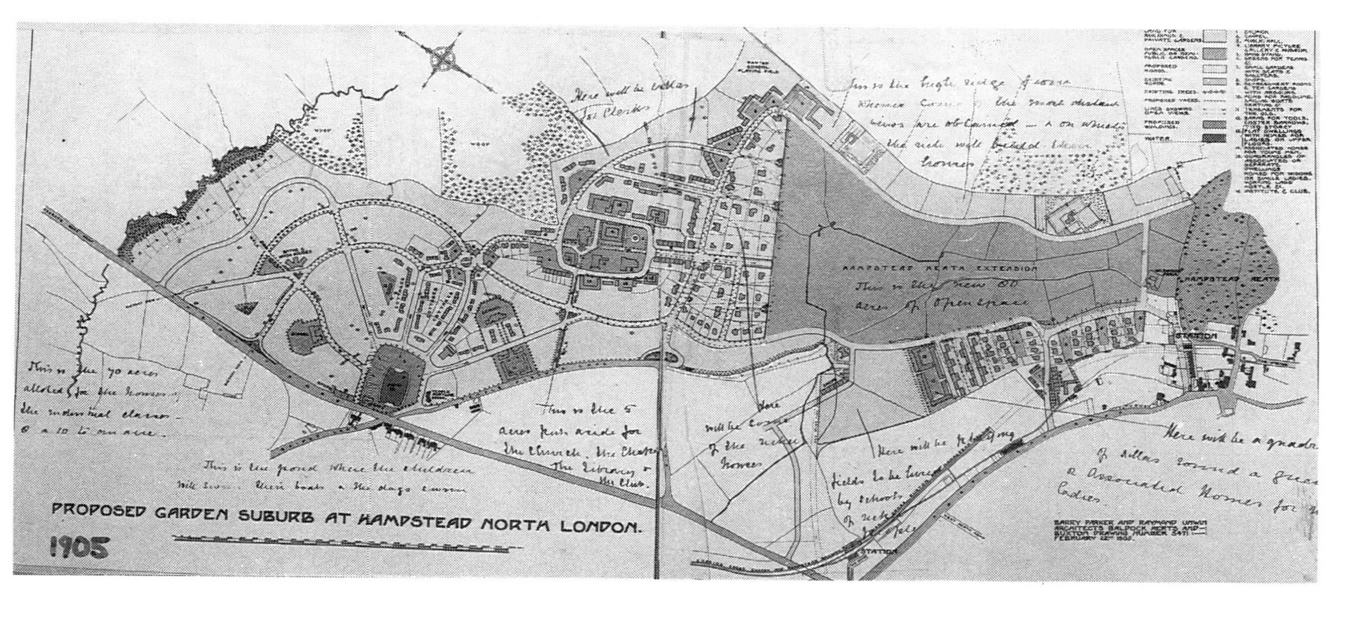

Figure 32 Unwin's 1905 plan for Hampstead Garden Suburb (HGS Archives). This copy, printed to aid fundraising, includes Henrietta Barnett's handwritten comments

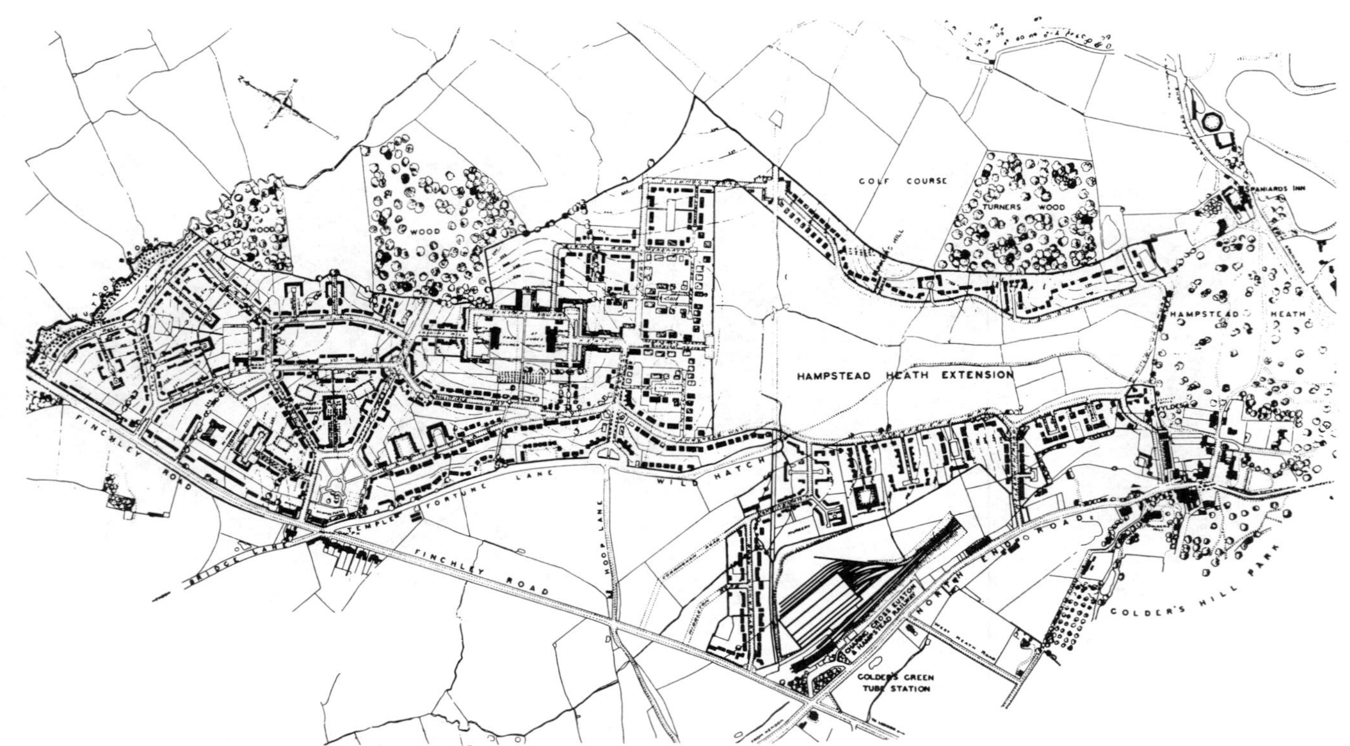

Figure 33 The 'definitive plan' of the 'Old Suburb', 1910–11. While the final layout of the 'Artizans' Quarter' and the distinctive pattern of culs-de-sac S.W. of the Heath Extension are shown, Central Square and its approaches were still somewhat diagrammatic

addition of the 412-acre [165-hectare] 'New Suburb' to the north and east. Implementation of the layout required immunity from the restrictive bye-laws of the Hendon Urban District. On 21 February 1906, Henry Vivian introduced a private bill in Parliament; it received the Royal Assent that August as the Hampstead Garden Suburb Act 1906, the first British town-planning legislation. It empowered the Hampstead Garden Suburb Trust to make its own bye-laws, subject to the approval of the Home Secretary. It decreed that the Garden Suburb was to be 'created for persons of all classes, with gardens and open spaces and other special amenities and facilities for persons of the working-class and others'. It fixed an average net density of eight houses per acre: an important anticipation of nationally adopted standards. Implications for highway design were highly significant: footpaths became optional and grass margins might be substituted. Any road under 500 ft. length was defined as an 'accommodation road' and might be as narrow as 20 feet between front property boundaries and still include planting. Other roads were to be 40 ft. wide with grass margins or planting. The Act enabled the use of culs-de-sac and closes that would have infringed the local bye-laws. Unwin exploited the design potential:

> such drives [the accommodation roads] have been extensively used in developing the Estate, and many different groupings of the houses have been rendered possible by their use . . . these very small roads are very much like the drive of a gentleman's house . . . the full twenty feet being set apart for the roadway, but the remaining part [left from a drive of twelve to sixteen feet] left as a grass margin. (Unwin, 1911e, p. 85)

Unwin had advocated the substitution of lightly paved 'carriage drives' for bye-law streets in *The Art of Building a Home*. This feature, anticipating the modern concept of a road hierarchy, impressed the Danish architect-planner Steen Eiler Rasmussen (1898–1990):

> the road net is differentiated . . . it is like a tree with branches, an organic pattern channelling traffic down to the smallest leaves of the plant. (Rasmussen, 1957, p. 286)

The Trust also prepared its Building Regulations, which followed those for Letchworth in including public health and construction requirements, internal planning standards and design advice. Unwin emphasized that:

> The company's architects do not ask for elaborate elevations, but attach importance to the proportions of buildings and their parts, also their suitability to a particular site, and to other buildings in the vicinity.[58]

Unwin reminded architects that all elevations were to be regarded as open to view; that they should ensure a sunny aspect for each house, with care taken not to block the outlook from neighbouring properties. He implemented these policies through his consultancy role of approving plans for each plot.

Lutyens and the Central Square

On 28 May 1906, the 'Steering Trust' approved both Unwin's appointment and that of an additional eminent consultant:

> Mr. Raymond Unwin of Baldock, Architect, being present having offered for a fee of £1500 to 1) Prepare in consultation with Mr. E. L. Lutyens of 29 Bloomsbury Square, W. C., Architect (whose fee is to be paid by the [Trust] Company) complete plans for the laying out of the estate as a Garden Suburb, such plans showing all proposed roads and open spaces.[59]

Unwin prepared a detailed road, plot and drainage layout, to the satisfaction of G. E. Strachan, a civil engineer also retained at Letchworth. The involvement of Lutyens was largely confined to the Central Square and its approaches.

Edwin Landseer Lutyens (1869–1944) was already recognized as a supremely accomplished designer of country houses, who was now developing a taste for the grand manner (Weaver, 1913; Hussey, 1950a, 1950b). Alfred Lyttelton (1857–1913), the new chairman of the 'Steering Trust', had commissioned a country retreat, 'Grey Walls' (1900–1) on the links at Gullane, east of Edinburgh. He possibly persuaded his colleagues that Unwin's preliminary plan was too informal and lacked an adequate central focus. As at Letchworth, Richard Norman Shaw had also been approached and had again declined involvement. Lutyens' influence was increasingly reflected in designs from Unwin's Hampstead office.[60]

It would be misleading to credit Lutyens with the tightening-up of the overall layout. Certainly the arbitrary curves were eliminated but the general framework remained; composed housing groups succeeded the artless scatter of the preliminary plan. This also reflected Unwin's own correction of aesthetic shortcomings and contact with Lutyens served to reinforce a growing appreciation of formal design. Unwin smoothed Lutyens' relations with Henrietta Barnett, cryptically described to Herbert Baker (1862–1946) as:

> A nice woman but proud of being a philistine – has no idea much beyond a window box full of geraniums, calceolarias and lobelias, over which you can see a goose on a green. (Hussey, 1950b, p. 187)

Lutyens' influence was most immediately felt in the finalization of Central, North and South Squares, Erskine Hill and Heathgate, the latter giving an axial vista to the Heath Extension. Unwin's preliminary plan had already shown this with a focal church tower (*see* Figure 34a). He prepared a revised layout in the winter of 1906–7, introducing radical alterations to the central area.[61] A Sittesque-enclosed *place* terminated the Temple Fortune Hill axis, articulating the awkward change of direction into Erskine Hill, which had been straightened to lead upwards into the north of Central Square, complementing the Heathgate approach (*see* Figure 34b). The picturesque building groupings had been eliminated

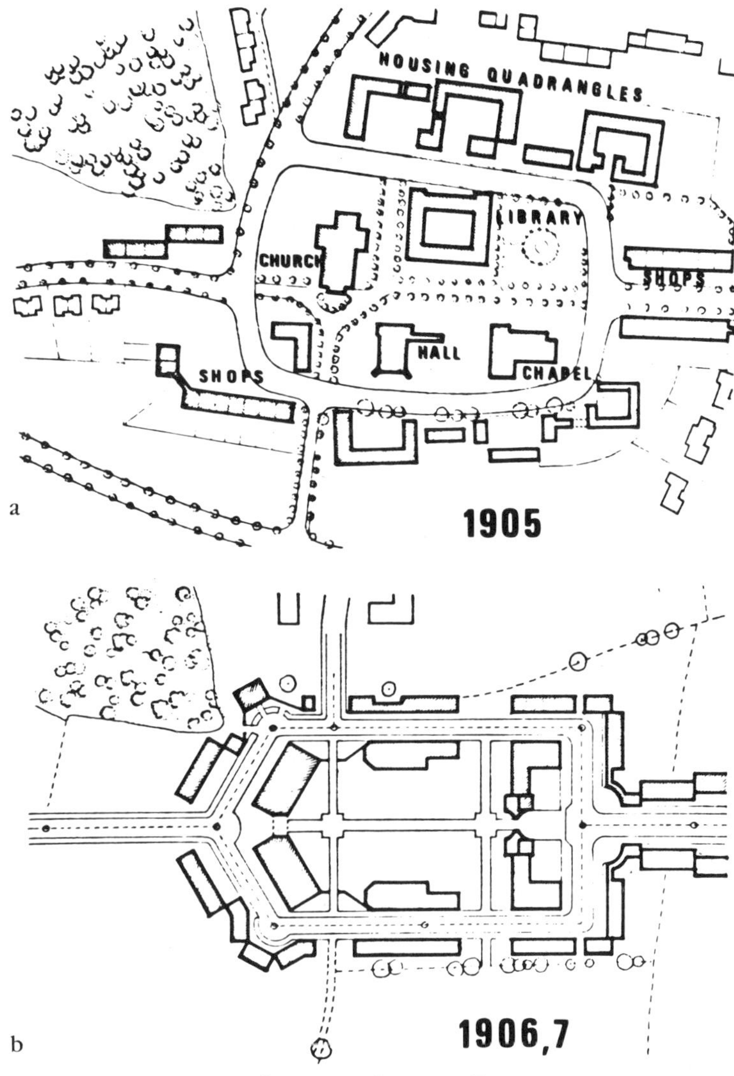

Figure 34 The evolution of Central Square: a) Unwin's 1905 layout; b) Transitional scheme 1906–7. Unwin's formal grouping of picturesque buildings were ousted in favour of an axial arrangement reflecting the influence of Lutyens

and a large central double quadrangle substituted, with a perimeter road between the outer and inner building masses. The Heathgate axis was emphasized by twin buildings, with corner towers, between which a narrow pathway led into the inner quadrangle. In the absence of detailed drawings, the attribution of this layout must be based on circumstantial evidence.

The most likely author appears to be Lutyens. The block layout may be compared with his designs for Rossall Beach (1901) a residential suburb north of Blackpool. This involved a central complex with a domed church, flanked by twin 'L'-form colonnaded blocks, resembling the Hampstead layout. In addition, the twin towers of the Hampstead layout may have been influenced by Lutyens' 'Wrenaissance' design for the London County Hall Competition, which took up most of 1907. The precedent of Greenwich Hospital, by Inigo Jones, John Webb and Christopher Wren, possessed a seminal significance for both Lutyens and Herbert Baker; it is not surprising that its layout should have been tried for Central Square. Among Lutyens' sketches there also exists a Palladian design with a lofty *campanile* modelled upon San Giorgio Maggiore, Venice.

These concepts may have proved too grandiose for Henrietta Barnett. The Board approved a layout by Lutyens on 5 March 1907 but it was not until 1908 that the familiar 'trinity' of St Jude's Church, the Free Church and the Institute emerged. The layout was based upon a 'linked plaza' sequence described by Sitte, in which each major axis was closed off by one or other of the buildings. Unwin acknowledged Lutyens' achievement of:

> a more formal arrangement . . . in order to secure two most desirable points, namely a sufficient sense of enclosure in the built up portions of the square and a sufficient degree of openness to preserve . . . open views . . . towards the west . . . (Unwin, 1911e, p. 8)

To achieve the latter the roadway along the west was eliminated, creating pedestrian links with the surrounding residential areas. Finalization of details brought some differences. Unwin proposed 'to attach the Vicarage, halls and Sunday schools to the church and chapel to complete to some extent the enclosure on three sides of this larger *place* [Central Square]', an arangement, illustrated in *Town Planning in Practice*, which would have robbed the buildings of the geometrical clarity and bold massing that were Lutyens' hallmarks.[62] He rose magnificently to the design challenge of a unified ensemble on a prominent site, to be curbed by Henrietta Barnett in April and May 1909 (Percy and Ridley, pp. 148, 168, 182, 213–14).

> I want a certain height of building in a certain place for general effect. Mrs B. dead against this certain height on the grounds of other houses being overshadowed. They would naturally like not to disappoint Mrs. B., the pioneer of the movement and the mother of Hampstead . . . Unwin warns me it will make things difficult. Alfred Lyttelton in agreement and enthusiastic. (Hussey, 1950b, p. 191)

The cornice line of the churches was lowered to line with the surrounding houses in North and South Squares, and clerestories were deleted (*see* Figure 35).[63] The massive roofs are undeniably impressive, recalling the great mediaeval barns. The churches framed the Institute, only partially completed to Lutyens' final design, with a deep central

Illus. 167.—Hampstead Garden Suburb. Sketch showing the arrangement of buildings on the Central Place. Mr. Edwin L. Lutyens, Architect.

Figure 35 Sketch for Central Square, 1909 from *Town Planning in Practice*. This shows St Jude's with a clerestorey and an 'attached hall', and complete frontage development by the Institute

courtyard creating a tight spatial enclosure in contrast to the openness of Central Square opposite. Detailing of the complex abounded in Lutyens' characteristic quirks, allied to a rich palette of materials, including red and grey bricks, Portland stone dressings and deep red handmade tiles.

The linked houses of Erskine Hill – North Square – South Square – Heathgate were integral to Lutyens' concept. Their high cost and dissension in the Board (Percy and Ridley, 1985, p. 182) resulted in only a small portion being implemented to Lutyens' detailed design. The houses on the west of North Square and Erskine Hill exhibit a panache, lacking in the more conventional Neo-Georgian design of the remainder of North Square by G. L. Sutcliffe.[64] The much later South Square by A. S. G. Butler was a pale adumbration of Lutyens' manner.

Life and work at 'Wyldes'

In 1906 Unwin moved into 'Wyldes'. He revelled in its links with the artists John Constable and John Linnell and the writers William Blake and Charles Dickens. His own household welcomed 'all kinds and conditions' of society. The black boarded barn was converted into an office suite, with extra living accommodation above; Unwin added a new wing in 1910. The modest rooms with their rush matting, oriental rugs, elegant rush-seated Clissett chairs and crammed bookcases suggested a master's lodging.[65] Unwin became the master of a modern guild,[66] with his protégé, Albert Thompson, as office manager. At peak periods, up to forty assistants were employed, with consultancies for scattered Co-Partnership developments and local authority town-planning, in addition to Hampstead.

Assistants were allowed to make their individual contribution, giving a freshness and variety to housing that might so easily have become stereotyped. Samuel Pointon Taylor (1884–1958) had, under Parker's tutelage, designed individual houses before concentrating upon grouped housing. In 1919 he joined the Ministry of Health, ultimately succeeeding Unwin as chief housing architect. Frank Bromhead (1881–1972) had worked for Alexander Harvey at Bournville. He designed parts of Birds Hill, Letchworth, and Asmuns Place at Hampstead. The Bohemian eccentricities of Charles Paget Wade (1883–1956), a dilettante affectionately known as 'The Brigand', who sported knee breeches, a parrot and mediaeval weaponry, were adjuncts to brilliant draughtsmanship in the style of Kate Greenaway and Randolph Caldecott. Wade added touches of whimsy to the 'Great Wall', which divided the Suburb from the Heath Extension (*see* Figure 46b), and to the Rotherwick Road 'gateway'. He drew many of the finest illustrations for *Town Planning in Practice*. He retired to the Cotswolds after the First World War to create his private Utopia at Snowshill Manor. Appropriately the office included a guild socialist, Arthur John Penty (1875–1937), a York architect. He designed some of the most distinctive buildings in the Suburb, notably the Temple Fortune shops and flats.

Visitors were impressed by Unwin's synthesis of life and work, hearth and home. His first floor sitting room included a study corner where he would retire from family activities to work late into the night. His bold pencil sketches were worked up by interaction with his assistants, with attention to detail a vital ingredient in the Suburb environment. Ernst May (1886–1970), the German architect-planner whose Frankfurt housing in the 1920s integrated Garden-City principles with the burgeoning modern movement, worked at 'Wyldes' in 1910. He recalled Unwin relaxing on a reclining couch, while May himself worked on his own translation of *Town Planning in Practice*, and Etty Unwin read aloud (May, 1903, pp. 427–8). H. E. von Berlepsch Valendas (1849–1921), the German Garden City enthusiast, characterized Unwin as 'a worthy successor to Ruskin and Morris' (Berlepsch Valendas, 1912, p. 135). Later, the Danish architect, Steen Eiler Rasmussen, commented similarly. The sole dissenter was Penty, perhaps resentful as an assistant after greater autonomy in York. He left the practice in March 1914 with bitter memories:

> Lutyens who was Consulting Architect to the Suburb would not pass his [Unwin's] designs . . . but when I began to design for him everything went through with little alteration . . . I was able to do some very good work for him. But after 4 years or so he began to think he had designed the job himself. He began to dictate to me in a way he did not at first and my position was becoming impossible. But I was afraid to leave because as prices had in 1912–3 gone up by 25%, domestic work was being stopped . . . So I hung on until it came about that he had no work for me to do.[67]

The cordial relations between Unwin and many of his assistants perhaps puts the matter into context.

Co-Partnership housing

The Hampstead Garden Suburb Trust Limited, successor to the 'Steering Trust', convened its first meeting on 12 March 1907 under the Chairmanship of Alfred Lyttelton, with Sir Robert Hunter, one of the founders of the National Trust, Frank Debenham, Robert Marnham, Henry Vivian and Henrietta Barnett. On 1 May 1907 the Wyldes estate was finally conveyed to the Trust for £107,500, an average of £442 8s per acre.

Vivian had announced in March 1906 that the Co-Partners would participate significantly in development. If the 70 acre 'artisans' quarter' was less striking than Central Square, it nevertheless arguably exerted a more immediate influence over the course of British town-planning. The soft curved roads of the preliminary plan were ousted by more purposefully straight lines, which imparted a striking geometrical clarity that was profoundly to influence housing layout and design. Natural features again provided a starting point:

> Immediately north of Central Square . . . the plan shapes itself somewhat in the form of a basin, the lowest point being adjacent to the junction of Finchley Road and Temple Fortune Lane . . . an open space should form the terminal feature along roads radiating from this point . . . a pond is arranged at the centre point to which all roads converge. (Unwin, 1911e, p. 8) (*see* Figure 36a)

By March 1907 a detailed layout had been prepared for the Co-Partners' offshoot, Hampstead Tenants. The central green was shown flanked by cottage groups, an arrangement regrettably revived in the 1920s when Queen's Court was built, eliminating the green and reflecting pool. The layout was an advance on estates at Letchworth. Asmuns Place, was a brilliantly handled cul-de-sac (*see* Figure 36b), terminating in a broad 'T', enabling varied groupings around a bowling green and playgrounds. The road was treated as a 'carriage drive', with broad greensward margins and a kerbless road (*see* Figure 37). Footpaths led to backland allotments and tennis courts. Cottages, designed by Frank Bromhead and Charles Wade, ranged from two-bedroom types, with living-room and scullery, to compact three- and four-bedroom parlour types. Baths were housed in sculleries, staircases led out of living-rooms. Through rooms, common at New Earswick and Letchworth, had largely disappeared. The first cottages in the Suburb, Nos. 140–2 Hampstead Way, near Asmuns Place, had roughcast walls as at Letchworth (*Cottages with Gardens for Londoners*, c.1907). The major part of Asmuns Place was built in dark brown London stock bricks, with red dressings; tile creased 'tunnel back' archways and tilehung gables added variety.

The design principles were developed in Hampstead Way, Asmuns Hill, Temple Fortune Hill and Willifield Way (*see* Figure 38) (Taylor, 1971). Setbacks and projections ensured a varied street picture, often symmetrical about the street axis. 'Y' road junctions lent themslves to effective groupings, as at Willifield Way and Temple Fortune Hill, with

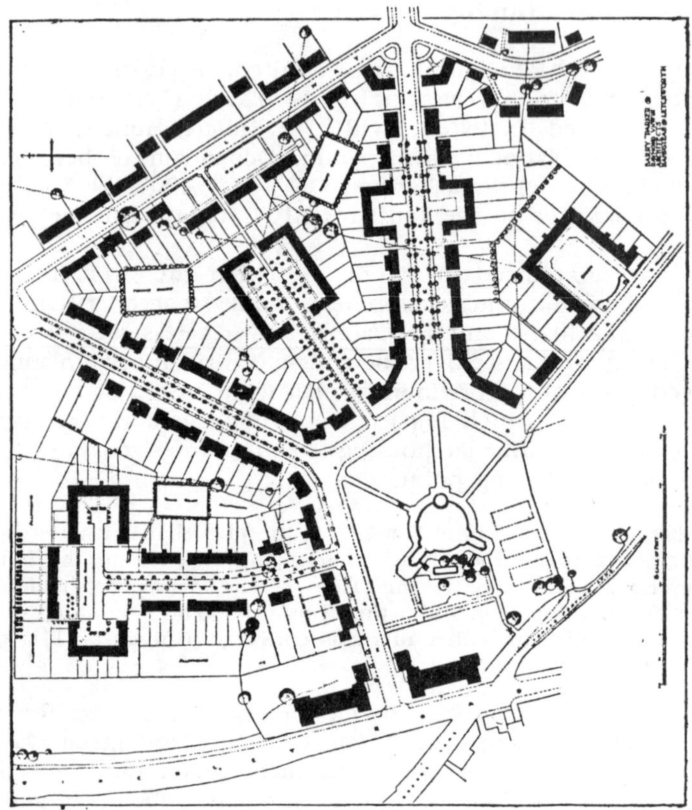

a

Illus. 235.—Part of Hampstead Garden Suburb developed by the Hampstead Tenants, Limited, and laid out for cottages.

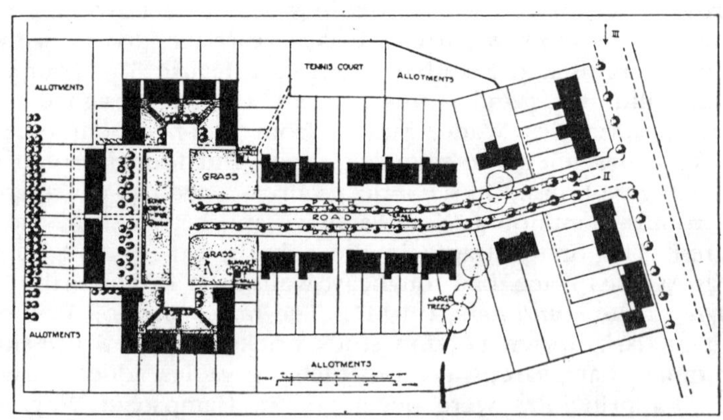

b

Illus. 280.—Arrangement for developing greater depth of land planned for groups of cottages, very similar to Asmuns Place, built by The Hampstead Tenants, Ltd.

Figure 36 The 'Artizans' Quarter', Hampstead Garden Suburb, 1909: a) General layout; b) Asmuns Place. In the overall layout, Unwin's techniques for grouping of housing are at their most comprehensive. Asmuns Place represents a more intimate design

Figure 37 Asmuns Place, 1907–8 (HGS Archives). Asmuns Place was a classic cul-de-sac layout, with a lightly paved road and sensitive landscaping

a hexagonal space, designed in 1909 by Courtenay Crickmer – 'Crickmer Circus'. This arrangement was repeated by Parker and Unwin on Addison Way. The Tenants' Club House, located between the 'artisans' quarter' and the middle-class housing, sought to encourage social fellowship. Charles Wade's design featured a tall Germanic tower to provide a focal point to views along Willifield Way (*see* Figure 39). Its destruction by a wartime landmine deprived the Suburb of a characteristic visual accent.

Wade was also involved with 'The Orchard'. Located in the backland between Asmuns Hill and Temple Fortune Hill, Unwin at last realized a complete housing quadrangle, built in 1909 to provide 57 flats for beneficiaries of the 1908 Old Age Pensions Act. Pathways passed beneath low sprung brick arches into the inner quadrangle. Detailing was subtle: timber balconies set against the brick gables and dormers produced an intimate, non-institutional atmosphere. Regrettably the building was badly neglected and was demolished in 1972. Other specialized housing schemes included Waterlow Court, a brilliant Baillie Scott design built in 1909 by the Improved Industrial Dwellings Company for single business ladies. Homesfield, a cul-de-sac off Erskine Hill designed by Parker and Unwin in 1911, was influenced by Lutyens. It provided accommodation for groups variously described by Henrietta Barnett as 'waifs and strays', 'retired domestics' and '16 old dears, weary and worn'.

In November 1907 the Co-Partners began to negotiate for larger plots.

Figure 38 Asmuns Hill from Hampstead Way, 1912 (Unwin Collection, Manchester University). The pair of cottages to the left of the junction marked the inauguration of the Suburb in 1907. The central landscaped garden, with its proposed reflecting pool, was regrettably built over in 1928 for Queens Court

Second Hampstead Tenants, registered in April 1909, commissioned the finest Parker and Unwin designs including the large houses in Hampstead Way facing the Heath extension (1910), Reynolds Close (1910–11), Corringham Road and Corringway (1911–12), Rotherwick Road (1911) and Addison Way (1911–12). Reynolds Close, a classic Parker and Unwin cul-de-sac, had a 20 ft. roadway with a spacious 'T' head, serving 25 generously sized linked houses and forming a compact ensemble (*see* Figure 40). The architectural treatment was restrained – dark brown brick, oak framed leaded light casement windows and timber loggias and balconies. The focal building, Penn House, was symmetrical, recalling country Queen-Anne style. Handling of the space between the buildings to suggest a corporate identity was characteristic of Unwin's work, represented here by the inclusion of tennis courts at the head of the cul-de-sac. Heath Close nearby was subtly varied and a restrained foil to the mediaevalism of the gateway to Waterlow Court. The junction of Corringham Road and Hampstead Way formed a gateway to the Heath Extension, which Unwin emphasized with a bold angled corner block with a fretted first floor balcony commanding views towards the unspoilt heathland. Corringham Road passed through a spacious quadrangle framed by four formal pavilions with classical motifs and

Figure 39 The Clubhouse, Willifield Green, 1912 (Unwin Collection, Manchester University). A visual and social centre, intended to promote mixing between the social strata of the Suburb. The building with its tall Germanic tower was destroyed by a land mine during the Second World War

brick and stone chequerboard treatment, reflecting the influence of Lutyens. Close by, Corringway terminated in a mews, with ground floor garages beneath chauffeurs' flats. *The Builder* was rather put out by this:

> What have they done to deserve such a punishment? Surely there might be arranged a small inferno for motors only, leaving the families to inhabit, like others, the paradise of the Garden Suburb. (*The Hampstead Garden Suburb and its Architecture*, 1912, p. 255)

The same observer praised Parker and Unwin's Addison Way flats, framing the junction with Hogarth Hill, as confirmation 'that an architectural effect can be obtained even where the tenants pay only 5s 9d [29p] per week'. This masterly composition, a hollow hexagon built across a falling site, held the roof eaves constant so that the two-storey houses on Hogarth Hill became a three storey block with ground floor flats and balcony-access maisonettes north of Addison Way. The spatial enclosure was emphasized by projecting pairs of Germanic hip-roofed towers from the block ends (*see* Figure 41). Further along Addison Way were two-storey cottage blocks with a central triple-arch motif: a Penty design of 1911–12 repeated in Sycamore Avenue, New Earswick.

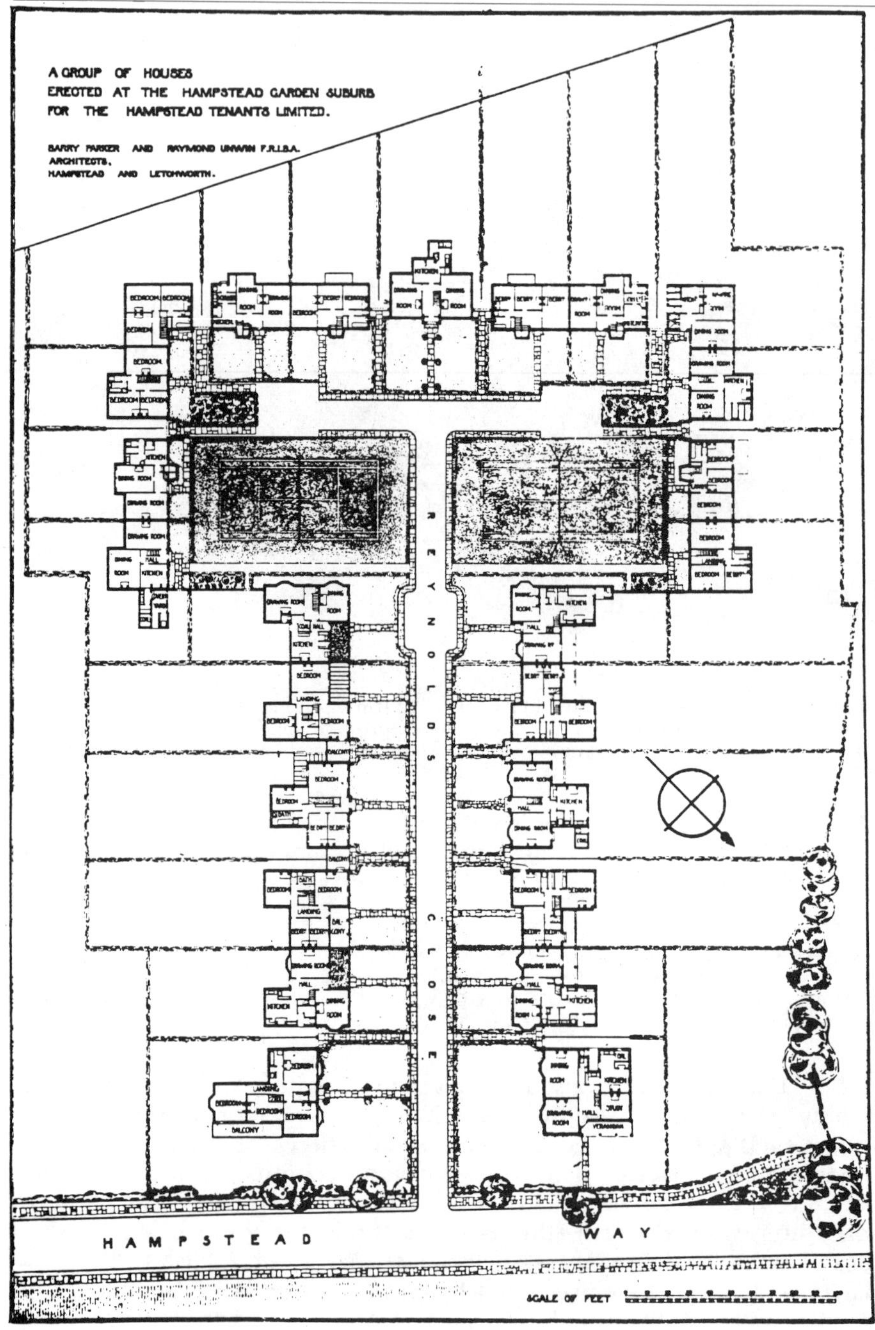

Figure 40 Reynolds Close, 1910–11. Spaciously grouped, linked middle-class houses in a form that pointed forward to the Radburn layout of 1929

Figure 41 Addison Way, junction with Hogarth Hill, 1911–12 (Unwin Collection, Manchester University). One of the finest of Unwin's groupings set around a 'Y' junction, framed and emphasized by pairs of towers

The coordination of design

Much of the development was based on individual plots. Unwin was conscious of design inconsistencies at Letchworth when he wrote:

> The Town Planner may lay out on the best lines the main thoroughfares and *places* . . . may follow with the best designs for arranging the plots, the building lines . . . but the aim is almost sure to be frustrated by the work of those that follow. The designs may be good, but for the want of any co-ordination the result will be little more that an inharmonious jumble. It is hoped that the general introduction of town planning . . . will encourage the individual building . . . as a unit in a larger picture. (Unwin, 1911e, p. 84)

To encourage good design, The Garden Suburb Development Company was founded in July 1907 (*Town Planning and Modern Domestic Architecture*, 1909, pp. 33–4). Their roster, a 'who's who' of domestic architecture, included Michael Bunney (1873–1926), Courtenay Crickmer (1879–1971), E. Guy Dawber (1861–1938), W. Curtis Green (1875–1960), Geoffry Lucas (1872–1947), Edwin Lutyens, Barry Parker and Raymond Unwin, M. H. Baillie Scott (1865–1945), C. Harrison

Figure 42 The Temple Fortune gateway, Finchley Road, 1910. This impressive 'gateway', with its Germanic hip-roofed tower, is shown in a preliminary design illustrated in *Town Planning in Practice* (1909)

Townsend (1851–1928), Herbert Welch (1884–1953) and Edgar Wood (1860–1935).

The company's own development included visually prominent sites. The concept of the 'Great Wall' dividing the Suburb and Heath Extension originated in Unwin's early writing.

> In the old towns we admire . . . we notice that the country comes up clean and fresh right to the point where the town proper begins . . . In the oldest cities we sometimes find a wall, with the country coming right up to the gates which adds to the effect. (Unwin, 1901b, p. 84)

This boundary treatment was already shown on the 1905 plan, but Unwin's enthusiasm for German mediaeval fortified hill towns finalized a concept that helped unify the view from the Heath Extension while retaining the views outwards. The pavilions and gazebos were fancifully detailed by Charles Wade. Unfortunately only half the proposed length was completed. The central terraced section, 'Sunshine Corner', formed the gateway to Heathgate and framed the axial view of the spire of St Jude's. The residential area north of the wall was laid out with culs-de-sac and closes, quiet, traffic-free backwaters that subsequently influenced Radburn. Linnell Close (1909–11) was flanked by generous Queen Anne houses, largely designed by Michael Bunney.

In 1909 the Development Company commissioned Edgar Wood to design the Wellgarth Road 'gateway' leading from the Heath Extension towards North End Road, a crescent of tall brick houses, with tall stone-mullioned windows and parapeted concrete flat roofs, oddly suggestive of Lutyens' Castle Drogo. Although this bold concept was abandoned,

Unwin was surely broadminded enough to have accepted the radical design of his old Northern Artworker colleague. The most successful 'gateway' was at Temple Fortune on the Finchley Road (1909), two massive blocks of shops, with flats above – Temple Fortune House and Arcade House (*see* Figure 42). These defined the entrance into the Suburb from the straggling ribbon development. Penty prepared the detailed design, a boldly assertive and eclectic composition. The projecting block ends with their Sussex half hip roofs and delicate ironwork balconies were successful townscape features, decisive visual accents when viewed obliquely. The side elevation of Temple Fortune House, split into two slightly staggered blocks, had a soaring brick tower, capped by a hipped roof modelled on the *Markusthurm* at Rothenburg (*see* Figure 44). The picturesque massing did not impair functional efficiency. The ground-floor shops formed an imposing podium for the flats. The buildings were designed to be viewed from all sides, especially Arcade House whose rear elevation was intended to face the focal green of the 'artisans' quarter'. The service area was ramped and sunk, with a bridge linking the rear balcony and the gardens. The Temple Fortune group was completed in 1911 by the imposing Temple Fortune Court flats, a Penty design, with details influenced by Lutyens.[68]

Hampstead Garden Suburb was notable for its consistently high standard of architecture and firm design-control policy exercised through the Trust. The Suburb influenced the adoption of statutory planning significantly but replication proved elusive, especially through the 1909 Housing and Town Planning Act.

The 'New Suburb'

In 1911 the Co-Partners began negotiation with the Ecclesiatical Commissioners for a further 300 acres [120 hectares] and the Trust sought to add 112 acres [45 hectares] to the Suburb. Unwin was anxious to plan the 'New Suburb' in harmony with the existing one. In May 1911 he embarked for Boston *en route* to Philadelphia for the Third National City Planning Conference. On the voyage, he worked each day and:

> as the *Bohemian* neared the lightship nearly all details had been completed providing cottages, chapels and market places on a 400-acre tract.[69]

Unwin's hectic initial three-week visit to the United States left lasting impressions and he encountered a reciprocal appreciation of his work at Hampstead, 'the most poetical side of city planning'. Elated, he wrote to Henrietta Barnett that 'the zeal of the Americans for "city planning" . . . and especially for the Garden Suburb side of it has converted our journey into something like a triumphal procession' (Barnett, 1918, II, p. 322). He sped home on the *Lusitania* to present his plans to the Trust.

Figure 43 Unwin's plan for the 'New' Suburb, 1911–12. This layout, only part of which was implemented, gave evidence of his growing predilection for formal layout frameworks

The layout provided a formal framework for land east of the 'Old Suburb' (*see* Figure 43) (Unwin, 1912a, pp. 6–10). Northway and Southway were projected from the centre line of the Free Church and St Jude's to the junction with Bigwood Road and thrust boldly eastwards as divergent axes. Middleway, aligned on the centre of the Institute, was interposed as the central prong of a trident. To complement the dominant hill-top location of the Institute, Unwin envisaged an enclosing quadrangle of domestic-style buildings, with a central tree-lined path leading upwards from Bigwood Road. Addison Way was extended as a long, straight road, with the Market Place as a new shopping centre. Further 'gateways' from The Bishops Avenue and East Finchley led towards a central boulevard and square, 'The Forum'. North of Addison Way [Falloden Way] the rising ground towards Finchley was more informally treated; the Co-Partners tightened up the layout in 1913–15 with Eastholm, Midholm and Westholm. Implementation of the new plan was halted by the outbreak of the First World War, but its formal potential was indicated in the London Society *Development Plan for Greater London* (1919).

In 1913 Unwin was commissioned by Finchley Urban District Council to prepare a town-planning scheme, under the 1909 Act, for the undeveloped north-east margin of the 'New Suburb' (Unwin, 1913b, pp. 141–2). It was hindered by Parliamentary sanction for construction of the circumferential North Junction Railway. This would have cut across the unspoilt valley of the Mutton Brook and carved into the hillside north of Addison Way. In the 1920s the expedient upgrading of Addision Way as Falloden Way, a link from the Great North Road to the Barnet bypass, severed the north of the Suburb. Much of the detail of the 1912 plan was modified by the Co-Partners in the 1920s, and the 'New Suburb' lacks the distinctive character of the 'Old Suburb'. Little of the Finchley UDC scheme survived.

The influence of 'The suburb salubrious'

Hampstead Garden Suburb elevated the art of site design, effectively combining formal and informal elements. Its eclectic visual expression ranged from the English vernacular, through Queen Anne and Georgian, to the Grand Manner, with a dash of German romanticism, characterized by Berlepsch Valendas as:

> an agreeable simplicity of architectural expression . . . Mass and silhouette play the essential part, not a crowding of decorative motifs . . . the happy union of art and calculation, as it is so typical of the English people. (Berlepsch Valendas, 1912, p. 164)

The Suburb has been acclaimed as the supreme achievement of the English domestic revival integrated with the emergent art of town-planning. Authorities such as Clarence Stein (1882–1975) (Stein, 1949, p. 203), Steen Eiler Rasmussen (1898–1989), (Rasmussen, 1967, p. 392), Sir Nikolaus Pevsner (1902–84), (Pevsner, 1951, p. 59), and Nicholas Taylor (Taylor, 1973, p. 72), have added lustre to its reputation, with consensus over its status as 'the most nearly perfect example of that unique English invention and speciality, the Garden Suburb'. Adulation may provoke radical reaction as with Charles Edward Jeannerat [Le Corbusier] (1887–1965). While an assistant of Peter Behrens (1868–1940), the German pioneer of modern architecture, he painstakingly traced illustrations of Hampstead. During the First World War he designed a small garden suburb in northern France, St Nicholas d'Aliermont,[70] with a cul-de-sac of wide-fronted semi-detached houses, alternately setback and pulled forward, emulating Parker and Unwin's *Cottages Near a Town*. From the early 1920s, however, Le Corbusier spearheaded the revolt against what he regarded as romantic sentimentality and embraced the modern movement.

Emphasis on design obscured Henrietta Barnett's social purpose. Hampstead Garden Suburb was a dangerous model, as single-minded Garden City protagonists realized. The emergent housing and town-planning movements were lured towards the easier suburban option. Influence on legislators was clear-cut: witness Henry Vivian personally leading visiting groups of fellow MPs, or John Burns, who caught its character as 'the suburb salubrious'.[71] The ambitious expansion plans of 1911–12 may have been a measure of success, but the emergence of the local authority's responsibility for working-class housing, the sharp rise in postwar construction costs and the upward spiralling of property values combined to undermine the original social objectives.

Henrietta Barnett presided over development until her death in 1936, ever reminding Trustees of their social obligations. Shortly before her death she had obtained an option on one of the Co-Partners sites for working-class flats. Her colleagues prevaricated and later, when they proposed its development as her memorial, they found it had been sold.

Although Unwin severed his official connection with the planning of the Suburb in December 1914, his presence remained. Visiting architects and town planners were given a guided tour and a 'socratic' discussion on planning philosophy. Unwin's successor, J. C. S. Soutar, appointed in April 1915, retained the consultancy until 1951. Relations with the Co-Partners became increasingly strained following Vivian's resignation from the Trust in 1919; reorganization removed their dividend limitation.[72] By 1936 it was regrettably concluded that Hampstead Garden Suburb then reflected the impossibility of meeting the original social objectives, but did not invalidate their intent.

The development of Hampstead Garden Suburb posed far fewer problems than did Letchworth as a self-contained town. The land would have been built upon in any case. Good, bad and indifferent garden suburbs spread in the interwar years, easy alternatives to planned decentralization to self-contained Garden Cities. Large council estates on garden suburb lines resulted from the 1919 Housing Act, such as the LCC's Watling, St Helier and Becontree estates, Birmingham's Kingstanding, Liverpool's Speke and Manchester's Wythenshawe, many of them approved by Unwin during his civil-service career. Planned regional decentralization required bold intervention. Simultaneously Hampstead Garden Suburb represented both a prototype for interwar suburbia and remained a unique achievement that could not be repeated. Its quality remained as tantalizing as the distant prospect of its central 'trinity' of Churches and Institute set against the backcloth of the Heath Extension, viewed from the traffic-choked north London roads, bordered with the pale imitators of the 1920s and 1930s.

6

The Theory of Housing and Town-Planning, 1901–14

Unwin's position in the forefront of planning rested not only on his practical achievements but also on his contribution to the evolution of planning theory. His best known publications, *Town Planning in Practice* (Unwin, 1909) and *Nothing Gained by Overcrowding* (Unwin, 1912b) were internationally acclaimed and widely influential. His approach was omnivorous, rarely confined to a single topic but rather stressing the interrelationship between different scales of community and civic design. The close relationship between the theoretical approach of *Cottage Plans and Common Sense* (Unwin, 1902) and *Cottages Near a Town* (Parker and Unwin, 1903) and New Earswick, Starbeck and Letchworth was of crucial significance in developing Unwin's skill as a housing architect. Themes from earlier work were continually developed and refined. Material in both *The Art of Building a Home* (Parker and Unwin, 1901) and *Town Planning in Practice* was of earlier provenance than the publication date.

A number of recurrent themes emerged reflecting Unwin's key interests in physical planning. His early identification of a broad, overall framework to give a sense of form to urban development was described with conviction at the Garden City Association Conference in 1901 (Unwin, 1901d). Planning became a process applicable to any level of settlement size or to any problem involving the equitable distribution of population or resources. Unwin was influenced by Geddes' synoptic vision of the city region, allied to a socialist faith in planning as a fairer agent of distribution than the market. Pragmatically Unwin distinguished a series of operative levels, from the individual to society as a whole. His earliest work concentrated on the individual home related to the community unit, the focus of his housing design and site-layout techniques. This was characterized as the 'detailed level' in the division described in *Town Planning in Practice*. Above this lay a broader level, the context into which detailed site-design meshed, concerned with factors such as the major highway network and primary land uses. Unwin soon identified a strategic viewpoint, developing work by Howard and Geddes. This will be discussed in greater detail in Chapter Eleven.

The *character of towns* as an historic and aesthetic concern stemmed from Ruskin and Morris but was also related to Unwin's discovery, in 1904, .of the work of Camillo Sitte, which added a more analytical dimension (Sitte, 1965; Collins, 1965). It also focused upon the *individuality* of towns, in contrast to Unwin's perceived philistine monotony of the Victorian industrial city. Unwin took the topic, debated in Germany, of *irregular versus formal* planning. *Town Planning in Practice* represented an interim assessment, although it is often cited as definitive evidence that formal planning was anathema to Unwin. His view that there were distinct merits in a broad formal approach to town design was already present during 1904–9 but was significantly strengthened before 1914.

The relationship between highways and buildings was an important theme in *Town Planning in Practice*, whether at civic-centre scale, allied to the tightly enclosed Sittesque *place*, or access roads, culs-de-sac and their associated housing groupings. Experience at Letchworth and Hampstead enabled Unwin to contrast his open layouts with the hard-paved bye-law alleys and streets. The fact that the latter were significantly more expensive, serving the derided terraced houses, later formed the basis of his proposition 'Nothing Gained by Overcrowding' (to be discussed in Chapter Seven).

Town planning in practice

Unwin's major book (Unwin, 1909)[73] appeared as the first national town-planning legislation was approved. He candidly admitted its hasty assembly from material garnered over the previous decade, embellished by his best assistants at 'Wyldes'. The subtitle 'An introduction to the Art of designing Cities and Suburbs' related to the extended realm of *The Art of Building a Home*. The original title *The Art of Town Planning* was also a close transliteration of Martin's title for the French translation of Sitte.[74] In 1932 Thomas Adams evaluated the book's influence:

> It helped to raise the conception of town-planning above the level of political discussion which centred round the problems of protecting property against alleged interference with private rights. It visualised town-planning as the art of town architecture. (Adams, 1932, pp. 54–5)

Much of its strength lay in its detachment from the limited horizons of the 1909 Act and its relationship to the emerging internationalism of planning. Unwin acknowledged the assistance of Parker, Geddes, Lutyens and Horsfall, and also the German pioneer, Joseph Stübben (1845–1936) and the American, Charles Mulford Robinson (1868–1917). The international bibliography contained references to Stübben, Berlepsch Valendas, Theodor Goecke and Paul Schultze-Naumburg (Unwin, 1909, pp. 405–11).

The architectural emphasis was assisted by illustrations from Charles Wade, evoking fairytale mediaeval townscapes, populated by poke-bonneted, besmocked figures out of Kate Greenaway's books for children. This imagery labelled Unwin as a mediaevalist, whereas he strove to maintain a balanced view of the aesthetic divide. Unwin's enthusiasm for Sitte permeated the book. Its content was loosely structured with a philosophical introduction, followed by practical advice on planning the town as a whole and the detailed design of sites.

The necessity of planning

In introducing 'Civic Art' in *Town Planning in Practice*, Unwin extended the argument rehearsed in *The Art of Building a Home*: that beauty was indispensable at all levels. He contrasted nineteenth century technical advances with their aesthetic poverty, following Morris who had provided the initial stimulus for Unwin's involvement with environmental design. The necessity of beauty in the home had been emphasized a decade earlier; this realm was now to be extended to the town as a whole. A favourite Morris quotation was reiterated:

> Beauty, which is what is meant by art . . . is . . . no mere accident of human life . . . but a positive necessity . . . if we are to live as Nature meant us to – that is unless we are content to be less than men. (Unwin, 1909, p. 9)

It was to be innate and organic, not imposed or applied, and integral with functional considerations, as Lethaby had urged, through the 'well doing of what needs doing'. Unwin contrasted a corrugated-iron market building with the wasteful extravagance of ornamental railings for the town park. His approach would reverse the priorities:

> First, let our markets be well built and our cottage areas well laid out; then there will soon grow up such a full civic life, such a joy and pride in the city as will seek expression in adornment. (Unwin, 1909, p. 10)

Planning's objective was to increase the opportunities to realize a fuller life. Unwin remained convinced of the potency of environmental determinism. The Aristotelian maxim that 'a city is a place where men live a common life for a noble end' had been used as the basis for a 1904 lecture and took its place in the philosophical introduction to *Town Planning in Practice* (Unwin, 1904, 1905, 1909, p. 11).

The hovering omnipresence of Morris had influenced Unwin's formulation of planning. The early designs for grouped housing focused as much on the notion of community and interdependence as on individual requirements. Unwin drew from Morris a hatred of the suburb as the embodiment of middle-class pretence, interposed between the historic centre of town or village and its unspoilt rural setting. Oxford, where Unwin grew up, was a prime concern. He may possibly have heard Morris' lecture, 'Art under plutocracy', given under Ruskin's chairmanship, at University College in November 1883:

> 'Need I speak to you,' Morris declared, 'of the wretched suburbs that sprawl around our fairest and most ancient cities? Must I speak to you of the degradation that has so speedily befallen this city [Oxford] . . . which, with its surroundings, would, if we had a grain of commonsense, have been treated like a most special jewel, whose beauty was to be preserved at any cost. (Morris, 1883, p. 170)

This imagery was reflected in Unwin's 'Building and Natural Beauty' and 'Co-operation in Building', published in 1901 in *The Art of Building a Home*, but written earlier (Unwin, 1900–1; 1901c). He berated the sprawl, squalor and false gentility that interposed themselves between town and country: 'miles of jerry cottages built in rows, or acres of ill assorted villas, each set in a scrap of so-called landscape garden' (Unwin, 1901c, p. 94).

He nevertheless recognized that decentralization was inevitable and looked to planning for redemption:

> the state or municipal landlord might relieve the overcrowding in towns by developing hamlets and villages in the outlying districts wherever they had, or could get, suitable land. (Unwin, 1901c, p. 103)

It was possibly this statement that alerted Howard to Unwin. Letchworth and Hampstead provided testimony to Unwin's abilities, both to plan a large settlement *de novo* and to redeem the suburb, which was, after all, the prime subject for the 1909 legislation.

Survey–analysis–plan

An historical survey of planned towns and a discourse on formal and informal beauty preceded the concise fourth chapter of *Town Planning in Practice* that discussed the city survey. Unwin acknowledged the influence of Geddes. Parker had visited the Outlook Tower in Edinburgh in the 1890s but Unwin did not meet Geddes until 1905.[75] Unwin also referred to Seebohm Rowntree's survey of York, T. R. Marr's of Manchester and Charles Booth's account of the East End of London as indispensable for indicating the social and sociological context, particularly when graphically presented. He recommended preparation of maps of public buildings and buildings and places of historic value, interest or beauty. Traffic and transportation surveys, following the example of the Royal Commission on London Traffic, would enable preparation of estimates of capacity and proposals for improvements. Finally the regional context would be drawn with geological, geomorphological and climatic surveys. Unwin emphasized 'the designer's first duty . . . to study his town, his site, the people, and their requirements'. Like Geddes he felt that 'the city which seeks to design its future requirements must first know itself thoroughly and understand its own needs' (Unwin, 1909, p. 146).

Only through a thorough survey and analysis could a successful plan be prepared, balancing functional efficiency with aesthetic individuality drawn from the surroundings. Implementation presented a further opportunity for cooperation and Unwin wondered whether parts of the survey might be undertaken by citizens' groups. The formulation of the plan was another matter and demanded the consummate artist. Once the planner had mastered the elements of his city, his technical and organizational powers would be focused on the interrelated problems, together constituting the 'kindly hand of necessity, guiding him into the right path' (Unwin, 1909, p. 149). He visualized the planner tramping across the site, as he had at Letchworth and Hampstead, seeking natural features to suggest the lines of major roads, residential and commercial areas and industrial estates. A major priority would be a central group symbolizing the spiritual, temporal and intellectual aspects of good government. From these the 'designing genius' might 'seize upon the ductile mass of requirements' and forge the plan 'anchoring . . . to the few absolutely fixed points, brushing aside minor obstacles . . . modifying or bowing to major ones . . . to mould the whole into some beautiful or orderly design' (Unwin, 1909, p. 149).

The conciseness of this chapter, an interlude in the aesthetic argument that dominated the book, perhaps obscured the fact that it contained the essence of planning, the classic process of survey–analysis–plan and the concept of a broad, overall framework through which to guide and control development.

The broad framework

Unwin's concept stemmed from his 1901 Bournville Conference paper, which described a process capable of generalization for more universal application than the Garden City. Unwin perceived a plan:

> arranged in conformity with the land . . . sites for our civil, religious and recreative public buildings . . . have been determined, dominating the city. Wide avenues or roads must be planned to lead off from . . . all directions, so that glimpses of open country shall be obtained . . ., and vistas leading up to the finest buildings shall greet the visitor from every direction . . . In the arrangement of [residential areas] . . . a complete acceptance of natural conditions must be combined with some definite design. (Unwin, 1901d, pp. 69-70)

Beyond that, 'a community inspired with some ideal of what their city should be' would achieve 'something more worthy to be expressed in its architecture than the mere self-centred independence and churlish disregard of others which have stamped their character on our modern towns' (Unwin, 1901d, p. 72).

Initially, however, regulation would be needed to prevent 'the hopeless jumble of blue slates and red tile, of brick, stone and plaster' so characteristic of the conventional suburb. An advisory committee, representative of 'practical skill and artistic taste' (a combination strikingly resembling the division of labour between Unwin and Parker), would possess 'an absolute veto on monstrosities' (Unwin, 1901d, p. 74). Unwin had followed the process in his substantive work – a broad development plan, detailed design briefs and aesthetic control exercised by a committee – which looked beyond the regulation of development through bye-laws or covenants, and forward to the planning process introduced through the 1909 Act and subsequent legislation.

The overall concept was refined by subsidiary factors. The overall balance was to be secured by 'giving due expression of the right proportional importance of each need' (Unwin, 1904, p. 4), a reflection of his personal philosophy 'that everything matters but nothing overmuch'. Plans would grow organically from site considerations but yet reflect a definite sense of design. These points were self-evident truths – 'nothing is needed but that someone should think of them and suggest them at the right time' (Unwin, 1904, p. 5).

Key aspects of the broad framework providing for the planning of settlements as a whole were elaborated in Chapters Five, Six and Seven of *Town Planning in Practice*. This ranged around the aesthetic divide 'formal versus irregular', to be discussed in detail below. Unwin was perhaps conscious that he had understated the necessity of an overall coherent approach, for in the 'Introduction' to the second edition of the book he underscored 'the importance of following out in town planning the proper order as well as the proper principles of design' (Unwin, 1911c, p. xvi):

> First, the main centre must be determined upon, and the secondary centres selected in proper relation and proportion with it. Then the main framework of roads must be arranged again in proper relation and proportion to the main and subsidiary centres. The main lines of communication, from centre point to centre point, from the main centre to the surrounding suburb, from residential areas to centres of commerce or employment, should all have been provided by this main framework of roads. This will divide up the area of the town into a series of spaces. In each . . . less important roads should be designed strictly in relation to the main roads . . . Each of these areas left within the framework . . . may thus be treated with an individuality of its own to suit the purpose for which it is required, whether for large residences, small residences, business premises or factories . . . All the important elements of relation and proportion may thus be satisfied without in any way destroying the symmetry and beauty of the whole design. (Unwin, 1911c, pp. xvi–xvii)

Unwin reiterated the principles in 1911, at the Third National Conference on City Planning, held in Philadelphia:

> First, there is the life of the community, for which an outward form of expression is required. This is the root and basis of the whole work. The study of the social condition of the community cannot be too thorough . . . second, the site upon which this community is to dwell . . . Finally there is the detailed design. (*Proceedings*, 1911, p. 101)

Influenced by the RIBA Town Planning Conference 1910, Unwin concluded that planning represented essentially an architectural problem, with the urban designer thinking:

> much more in building . . . masses and groups than merely in straight lines . . . the principles are simply [those] of architecture applied on an extended field, and equally apply whether it is a central town or residential suburb. (*Proceedings*, 1911, p. 102)

Unwin's 1911 visit to the United States enabled him to broaden the framework of planning to include the regional-strategic level; at Chicago he witnessed the civic consciousness fostered by Daniel Burnham's great plan of 1909. The proposal for neighbourhood playgrounds and community centres within half a mile of each home brought potential for social reconstruction, with:

> the amorphous mass of humanity . . . beginning to take on a definite relation to the centre . . . as particles in a chemical solution group themselves into beautiful crystalline form about some central point of attraction. (Unwin, 1912c, p. 45)

This simile of crystallization looked back to Unwin's early studies of rural communities; planning represented a means to regain the sense of identity lost through nineteenth-century urbanization. At the overall level he relished the experience of being driven round the Chicago park system, pronouncing that 'this green girdle is indeed a wonderful creation'. The role of open space in controlling and articulating suburban development underlay his subsequent work for the Greater London regional Planning Committee.

In a 1911 Cadbury Lecture in Civic Design,[76] given at the University of Birmingham, Unwin ranged across the full scope of his subject (Unwin, 1912d). The need for overall control had assumed primacy, indicating his growing interest in management. He advocated 'the same guiding oversight and direction in developing the opportunities, the same correlation of all the different parts, which are so essential for a great modern industrial concern'. Town planning was, he claimed, 'simply the medium through which this organising movement finds its practical expression' (Unwin, 1912d, p. 11). The process was 'essentially a synthetic art' consisting 'of assembling and marshalling many parts, co-ordinating many activities for their mutual benefit and combining the individual forms of expression so as to produce a healthy, convenient and beautiful city' (Unwin, 1912d, pp. 11–12). Success demanded 'cordial co-operation of many experts . . . the architect, the surveyor, the engineer, the valuer, the economist, the sociologist and even the antiquarian'. The town-planner, although still likely to be an architect, must also be capable of acquiring generalist knowledge of all fields in order 'to assign the contribution of each its proper place in the whole'. Aesthetics were integral:

> Beauty is, indeed, intimately associated with use, fitness for purpose and function . . . [these] dictate certain lines of development, but usually they are not exact lines, rather they are limits of deviation . . . It is the duty of the town planner, in so far as he is an artist, to learn those limits well, seldom to transgress them, and then only to attain results overwhelmingly worthwhile. (Unwin, 1912d, p. 15)

Having urged the creative imagination to soar, Unwin reminded his audience of the 'greatest good fortune [that] it has happened in England that town-planning has actually developed from an attempt to improve the homes and lives of individual members of the community'. *Garden Cities and Town Planning* considered Unwin's lecture 'as expressive of the ideal as well as the practical, and the sociological as well as the economic' (Unwin, 1912d, p. 11). We can already sense the synoptic scope of his Columbia University lectures of the 1930s, and it was regrettable that this clear statement of objectives did not appear in the revised edition of *Town Planning in Practice*.

The Example of Germany

In *Town Planning in Practice* Unwin cited *The Example of Germany* (Horsfall, 1904), as one of the seminal influences on the introduction of town-planning in England, in the transition from public health and housing reform to the formulation of a mechanism to regulate the use and development of land. Horsfall had described legally binding plans for urban extension, with the allocation of parks, primary land-use zoning and differentation of building height and density, allied to the coordinated construction of transport infrastructure. Implementation demanded competent, efficient local authorities. Horsfall had observed the 'Lex Adickes' of Frankfurt, a local statute that long remained the envy of Unwin and the British planning pioneers (Horsfall, 1904, pp. 78–80; Bullock, 1977, pp. 203–23). Land required for rational urban-extension planning might be appropriated, highway reservations deducted and the remainder redistributed to owners as workable building plots. In Köln, the 1901 Building Regulations had introduced district zoning, with a band of 'open development' [*sic*] running around the lines of the old fortifications, with articulated lower-density suburbs beyond.

Unwin quickly assimilated Horsfall's work and in the late 1890s may have been directly aware of it. The first reference to it appeared in November 1904 in 'The Improvement of Towns', a lecture given in York (Unwin, 1904, 1905). He spoke of German local authorities who were:

> not only empowered but . . . instructed to prepare building plans in advance, of all growing districts, to arrange the streets in the most convenient, beautiful and economical way, to define the height of buildings, fix the building lines and areas, and even to determine the class of building,

> forbidding, for example, blocks of dwellings except where large open spaces are adjacent, and excluding all offensive factories or trades from residential districts. (Unwin, 1904, p. 3)

Copious German examples were included in *Town Planning in Practice*, and were discussed both for their aesthetic character and for the principle of orderly urban extension.

The influence of Sitte

It is in the extensive discussion of the aesthetics of town-planning that the original concept and title of Unwin's book, *The Art of Town Planning* is most strongly felt. The *aesthetic* example of Germany, primarily viewed through the work of Camillo Sitte (1843–1903) assumed dominance and was an aspect of *Town Planning in Practice* that most concerned reviewers.

Unwin's discussion and analysis of townscape character was initially drawn from Morris. In the late 1890s, with a growing family and a small income, Unwin had few opportunities to travel for pleasure, unlike Barry Parker who made extensive 'sketching tours' between 1894 and 1901, visiting France, Northern Europe and Italy. Unwin studied his partner's water colours and photographs with enthusiasm and only in the mid-1900s was able to visit Germany. Etty Unwin long remembered her husband's 'tears of joy' on entering Rothenburg, a Bavarian hill town, as if in fulfilment of a pilgrimage (*see* Figure 44).[77]

The influence of Sitte was similarly indirect. *Der Städtebau nach seinen Künstlerichen Grundsätzen* was originally published in 1889, but Camille Martin's French translation, *L'Art de Bâtir des Villes*, appeared in 1902. Unwin had studied French at night school and in 1904 analysed the translation, unaware of its distortion. Later he corrected the impression given by Martin of contrived informality, which, as has been shown, influenced the preliminary plan for Hampstead Garden Suburb early in 1905.

Sitte's thorough analysis of historic European cities had led him to conclude that their visual richness stemmed from an organic relationship with their topography that provided crucial lines of deviation from imposed geometry. Sitte believed that these effects had been consciously designed; many German town planners broke away from the bold grid-and-web plans of late-nineteenth century town-extension plans. 'Formal versus irregular' planning was keenly debated. Sitte, often held up as the champion of informality, was less dogmatic, recognizing the importance of the individuality or *genius loci* of a town above arbitrary aesthetic prescriptions, based on prevailing fashion.

The approach was bound to appeal to Unwin, who related Sitte's analytical techniques to English townscapes. He stressed the 'great urgency that some knowledge of the art of town building [an almost literal translation of Martin's title] shall be communicated both to the

Figure 44 Rodergasse und Markusthurm, Rothenburg (FGC Mus.). The informal picturesque townscapes within and the clear delineation of the fortifications without the Baverian hill towns, served as potent models for Unwin's approach to civic design and overall city planning

public . . . and to those professionally engaged so that they may carry out civic improvements in the way which will produce the greatest convenience and beauty',[78] an objective he fulfilled in *Town Planning in Practice* (Unwin, 1909). Its first six chapters have been assessed as 'pure Sitte-artistry' (Collins, 1965, p. 138). It would, however, be over-simplification to regard Sitte as the *fons et origo* of Unwin's work; like Sitte, he remained receptive to contrasting ideas, and a rational enthusiast for the Sittesque approach.

For example, in his 1906 Cambridge lecture, 'The improvement and laying out of towns', Unwin warned against too informal layouts, citing the firm, concave line of Oxford High Street (always one of his favourite examples) against the 'aimlessly wiggling line' found in some over-self-conscious German examples.[79] Sitte had warned that 'sundry curves, twisted streets' and attempts to recreate 'accidents of history . . . *ex novo* in the plan' should be avoided (Sitte, 1965, p. 111). Only through analysis of historic townscapes and by application of the principles to modern conditions could urban design evolve. In 1906–10 Unwin made contact with many leading German planners including Joseph Stübben (1845–1936), Theodor Goecke (1850–1919), A. E. Brinckmann (1881–1958) and Werner Hegemann (1882–1936). The exchange was two-way and in 1906 Unwin stated 'that in planning and arranging of residences our continental bretheren may be willing to learn from us' (Unwin, 1906b, p. 418).

The character of towns

In *Town Planning in Practice* Unwin introduced the subject through a historical survey, attempting a distinction between those 'definitely designed' and 'those which have grown gradually without any pre-arranged plan', and between the fortified walled, contained town and the unfortified or open town, the 'regular planned' and the 'definitely designed but irregular' town (Unwin, 1909, Chapter II). Greek and Roman, Renaissance and Baroque plans jostled alongside mediaeval cities. Charles Wade's illustrations of the latter, both real and imagined, were generously spaced throughout the book, evoking the townscape of an imaginary Golden Age (*see* Figure 45). It is these that still impress; they also undoubtedly drew attention from Unwin's textual advocacy that a formal or ordered approach might be more appropriate to contemporary planning. He included British and American plans – Oxford, the Wren Plan for London, Bloomsbury, Bournemouth, Washington and Philadelphia – to illustrate the divide between formal and irregular towns. He drew on the periodical *Der Städtebau* for contemporary German plans, including Köln, with suggestions by Sitte for adjustments to relate more sympathetically to existing features and property boundaries. Flensburg (Henrici), Zchernitz (Gurlitt) and Stuttgart (Fischer), the latter reflecting 'irregularity for its own sake', were also included. He concluded by advising the architect to base his own decision on 'the relative importance of carrying out some symmetrical design, and, on the other hand, of maintaining existing characteristics of the site with which he is dealing' (Unwin, 1909, p. 114).

This advice was amplified in the third chapter of *Town Planning in*

Illus. 183.—*Sketch of an irregular* Y *junction showing how the curve in the direction of the road closes the view.*

Figure 45 Pictorial treatment of irregular road junction by Charles Wade, from *Town Planning in Practice* (1909). The inclusion of a diminutive layout plan was a Sittesque presentation technique

Practice, 'Of formal and informal beauty'. As early as 1901 Unwin had warned against 'meandering in a false imitation of so-called natural lines' and advocated 'that beauty in orderly design for the creation of which alone power has been given to us' (Unwin, 1901d, p. 69). It was vital to seek broad effects rather than finicky detail. A degree of underlying order was essential to allow the plan – and more importantly the ultimate settlement – to be comprehensible, but he stopped short of a forced symmetry, 'only appreciable on a paper plan or from the car of a balloon' (Unwin, 1909, p. 137). Both at Letchworth and Hampstead Unwin secured the best of both worlds, for each is readily appreciated at ground level or from aerial photographs. And at Hampstead the buildings underscored the aesthetic debate significantly, with the set pieces of Lutyens' Churches and Institute rising above the picturesque roofscapes of the surrounding residential areas. Although Unwin strove to present a balanced view, in 1909 he continued to feel that informal groupings were a more natural and organic expression of the concept of community.

Reviewers of *Town Planning in Practice* concentrated on aesthetics and reflected the rise of Neo-Georgian architecture and Beaux Arts Classicism at the expense of the Arts and Crafts movement. Wade's imagery seemed to emphasize that Unwin stood entirely for spatial enclosure and incontrovertibly against the vista. The *Architectural Review* accused him of 'dallying' and declared that 'Palladianism is the only course which can bring about that unanimity which is essential to success', citing the 'City Beautiful' formality of contemporary American plans.[80] In reviewing the book in the RIBA *Journal*, H. V. Lanchester (1863–1953), himself a civic designer, juxtaposed a selection of Unwin's illustrations with Burnham's great Chicago Plan, to indicate 'the distance we have to go if we are to arrive at a uniform standard in the matter of civic design'.[81] In December 1909, Unwin addressed the Society of Architects on town-planning, effectively illustrating the aesthetic divide by the informality of Rothenburg ('The Peasants' City') and the formal radiating plan of Karlsruhe ('The Ducal City'). He made a virtue of 'dalliance' in the search for the *via media*, pointing out:

> the elements of a new synthesis . . . The problem before us really is how to weld together into one harmonious whole the undulating surface and irregular lines of our country and the definite lines and ordered arrangement characteristic of good design. (Unwin, 1910c, p. 92)

The period 1910–12 strengthened Unwin's appreciation of formal design. In Berlin in May 1910 he admired the bold axial line of *Unter den Linden* and the strategy for the preservation of open space (Unwin, 1910d). The RIBA International Town Planning Exhibition revealed the aesthetic diversity of planning and the progress of the American 'City Beautiful' movement (RIBA 1910a, 1910b; 1911). His visit to the United States in May–June 1911 further strengthened his appreciation of the formal approach and:

> the increasing knowledge of town-planning work would lead me to emphasise even more the importance of formality and order in design . . . from the scale and breadth of treatment in the great town-planning schemes of America . . . the natural and proper part that formality and symmetry play in architectural grouping, and by the careful study of Classic and Renaissance planning . . . the importance of maintaining simple, orderly, broad lines of design . . . we find lacking in many German plans [with] . . . undue concentration on a somewhat forced picturesqueness. (Unwin, 1911c, pp. xvii-xviii)

At a subsequent debate on the 'formal versus irregular' issue at the Architectural Association in October 1911, Stanley Ramsey (1882–1968), who with Charles Reilly (1874–1948), Stanley Adshead (1868–1946) and Patrick Abercrombie (1879–1957), was promoting the revival of the Neo-Georgian style through the Liverpool University Department of Civic Design, opened the discussion by confessing himself 'a formalist of the worst description', but concluded, correctly, that 'Mr Unwin was a greater formalist than his paper led them to believe' (Unwin, 1911f, p. 272).

Despite Unwin's changing views, *Town Planning in Practice* remained unrevised. The fifth Chapter, 'Of Boundaries and Approaches', laid great stress on the demarcation of town and country. In *The Art of Building a Home* (1901) Unwin had emphasized the importance of a clean break and the visual potential for boundary features, gateways and

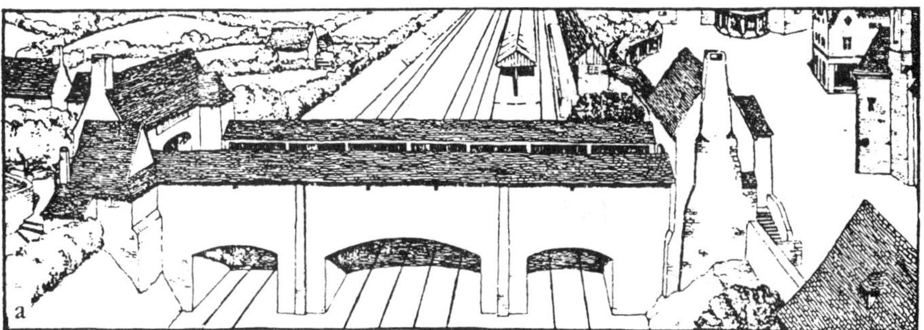

Illus. 118.—*Suggested Railway Bridge for Letchworth, Garden City.*

Illus. 110.—*Hampstead Garden Suburb Boundary Wall.*
Being built by The Garden Suburb Development Company (Hampstead), Limited.

Figure 46 Boundaries and approaches from *Town Planning in Practice* (1909): a) Railway bridge and Station Place, Letchworth. The whimsy of the fortified railway bridge remained unrealized, but Unwin's techniques for townscape composition can be glimpsed at top right of the sketch; b) The 'great wall', Hampstead Garden Suburb. This became one of its most successful features, clearly defining the boundary of the Heath Extension with the housing area beyond

walls, as he had subsequently designed for Hampstead Garden Suburb (*see* Figure 46) (Unwin, 1901b, p. 84).

Unwin elaborated this in *Town Planning in Practice*, addressing himself to the articulation of urban form by open space. It was vital to 'secure some orderly line up to which the country and town may each extend and stop definitely, so avoiding the irregular margin of rubbish-heaps and derelict buildings which spoil the approach to almost all our towns today' (Unwin, 1909, p. 163). The gateways to historic Rothenburg, and the continental 'green girdles' formed by demolition of ancient fortifications, were extensively illustrated.

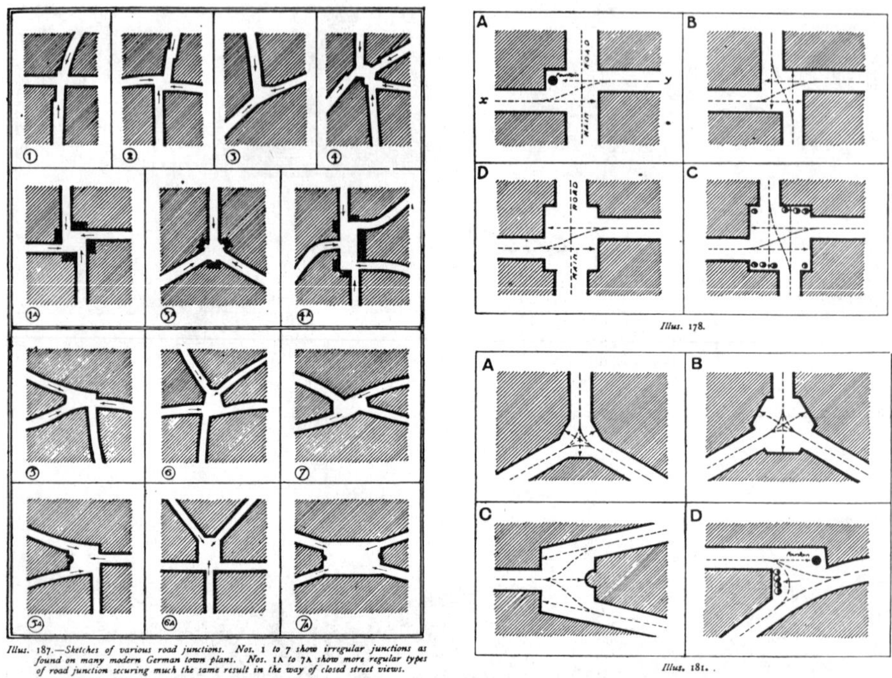

Figure 47 Treatment of road junctions to form places from *Town Planning in Practice* (1909). These include the 'turbine plaza' in which each arm of the junction is closed off visually

In Chapter Six, 'Of Centres and Enclosed Spaces', Unwin concentrated on spatial enclosure, following Sitte. Diagrams illustrated 'built up churches' as an integral part of the urban fabric, rather than isolated in grand, open squares,[82] irregular *places*,[83] with the famous 'turbine plaza'[84] in which the axis of each approach into a town square was terminated by a building, and grouped *places* to set off major public buildings (*see* Figure 47). The emphasis upon the term *place* posed some problems of definition and translation but it was evident that Unwin had grasped the essence of Sitte's approach:

> A place . . . should be an enclosed space . . . resulting from a fairly continuous frame of buildings, the breaks in which are small in relative extent and not too obvious. If we examine a series of ancient *places* . . . the entrances into them are usually so arranged that they break the frame of the buildings very little if at all. (Unwin, 1909, p. 197)

Size would be related to the scale of surrounding buildings – deep and narrow in front of Gothic cathedrals, broad and shallow in front of classical set-pieces. Unwin illustrated the Greek *agora*, the *Piazza San Marco* in Venice, the *Place de la Concorde* in Paris, and, of course, many mediaeval 'organic' examples. The spatial analysis of the German town of Buttstedt emphasized the spatial counterpoint of the mediaeval

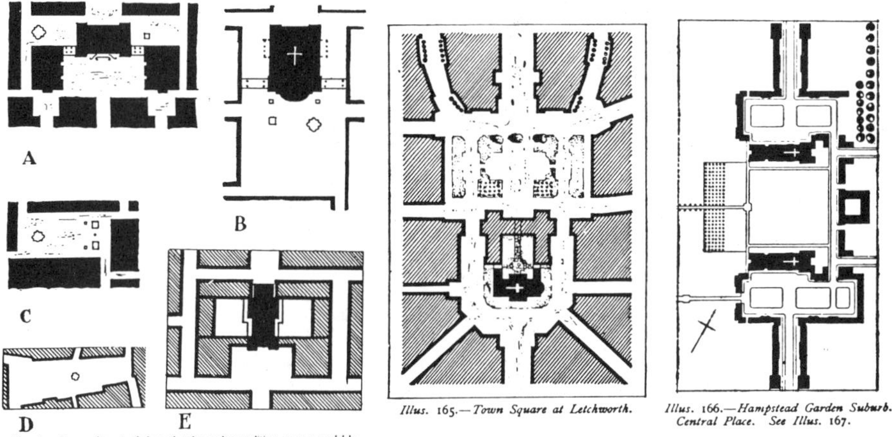

Figure 48 Grouped places from *Town Planning in Practice*, incuding Town Square, Letchworth and Central Square, Hampstead Garden Suburb. The redemption of the Letchworth Town Square with colonnades, as recommended by Sitte, is evident as is the early proposal for 'attached' vicarages and halls at Hampstead Central Square to achieve a tighter spatial grouping

city.[85] For modern examples Unwin reproduced the Town Square at Letchworth and the Central Square at Hampstead Garden Suburb, albeit that the former had been designed before his study of Sitte. The latter was shown with the attached halls and vicarages, which Lutyens subsequently modified (*see* Figure 48).

Highways and urban design

Highway design and its relationship to civic design was emphasized in the seventh Chapter of *Town Planning in Practice*. The concept of a hierarchy of highway standards had stemmed from Unwin's advocacy of lightly paved 'carriage drives', flanked by landscaped margins, to serve housing groups in place of the uniform bye-law grid of streets and alleys. In 1904 he posed the rhetorical question: 'Why should it not be allowed to reduce the actual roadway and footway to a width reasonably proportional to the traffic on condition that the remaining space be planted with trees and shrubs and laid down as grass margins?' (Unwin, 1904, p. 7), a precept followed at Hampstead Garden Suburb (*see* Figures 49a and b), aided by the local Act of Parliament. Overall he examined briefly grid and web plans, remarking on the visual monotony of the formal grid and the difficulty of treating the oblique triangular junction sites in the latter. Consideration of the space around road junctions led to further examination of Sitte's work. Unwin was not prepared to accept offset junctions without question, a point over

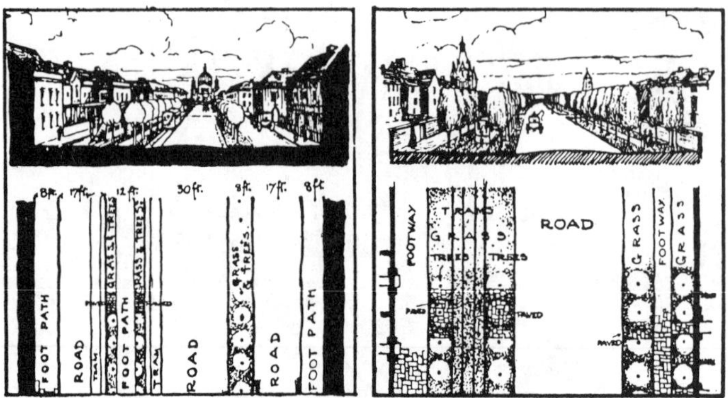

Illus. 176.—*Designs for Broadway, Garden City, Letchworth.*

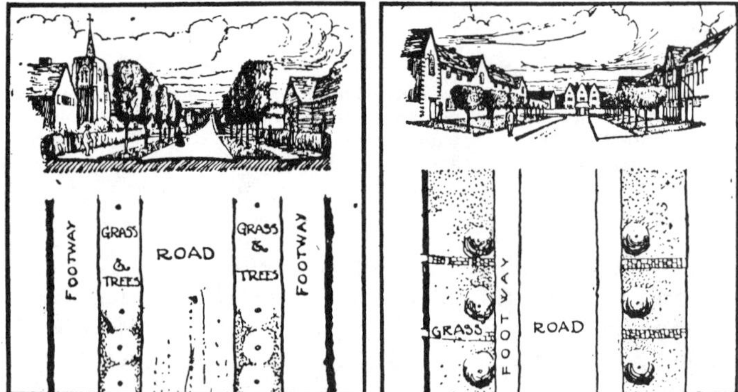

Illus. 228.—*Examples of lighter building roads and drives as used at Earswick, Letchworth, and Hampstead.*

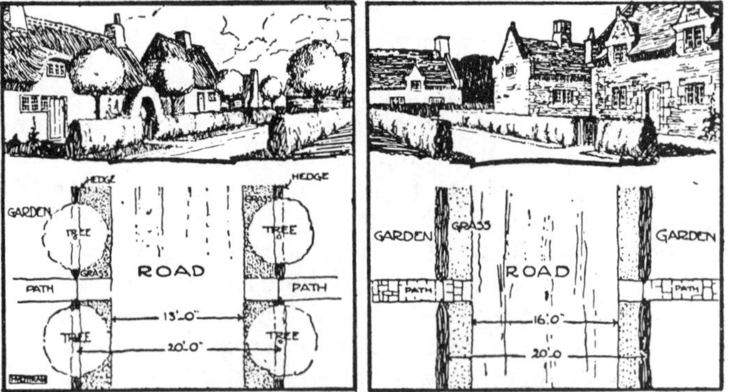

Illus. 228*a*.—*Examples of lighter building roads and drives as used at Earswick, Letchworth, and Hampstead.*

Figure 49 Road sections from *Town Planning in Practice* (1909). Standards adopted for Earswick, Letchworth and Hampstead were illustrated, indicating the variety of treatment and planting and the differentiation of width to reflect anticipated traffic levels, and a desire to integrate aesthetic and functional elements in an anticipation of the hierarchical approach to highway design which Stübben had criticized Sitte. Unwin agreed that major road junctions required the main line to be carried through; for multiple junctions he advocated the gyratory roundabout, Eugene Henard's *carrefour à giration* already deployed at 'Sollershott Circus', Letchworth (Unwin, 1909, pp. 237–9). Large volumes of traffic demanded multiple track roads, a German innovation (*see* Figure 49c).

On the aesthetic question, Unwin discussed the German debate on 'crooked versus straight streets' [*krumme oder gerade Strassen*], which affected the character of planned urban extensions in a fundamental manner. Sitte had been relatively undogmatic and Unwin appears to have been unaware that Martin had fabricated a chapter on the issue in his translation, when he wrote in *Town Planning in Practice* that Sitte had done scant justice to the:

> directness; convenience and economy; the symmetry and simplicity of the street picture . . . in spite of the general absence of straight streets in mediaeval towns . . . they have both use and beauty of their own, and that they may with advantage be freely used by the town planner. (Unwin, 1909, pp. 249–50, 259–60)

Unwin the engineer recognized that functional efficiency was not to be compromised by aesthetic theory. Rather, he reiterated that the functionally efficient solution would possess its own inherent beauty. Curves should take the form of bold concave or shallow 'S' lines, following Unwin's ideal of High Street, Oxford. The planting of streets should be bold, with avenues to bring visual unity where the buildings might be uncoordinated. For suburban areas he advocated smaller tree species – almond, plum, crab apple, hawthorn, rowan, beech – which had given Letchworth its verdant character.

Unwin developed his interest in the interface between planning and highway design over the next few years. In a November 1913 lecture, 'Roads and Streets', he defined the road hierarchy with greater clarity:

> Proper organic planning of road systems with a main frame of arterial highways, with secondary roads linking them up . . . and mere building streets not used for through traffic, will enable roads of many varying widths to be safely used . . . If the main and secondary roads are properly planned, the through traffic will always follow them; and provided due space is secured between the buildings for light and air it is economical that the road width which is not wanted on minor roads should be added to the main thoroughfares where it is urgently required. (Unwin, 1914b, p. 16)

This anticipated both the Radburn traffic-free superblock and Sir Alker Tripp's highway-precinct theory by many years.

Site design

Chapters Eight to Twelve of *Town Planning in Practice*, contained a manual on residential layout. Unwin emphasized the necessity of fitting within an overall guiding framework:

> in site planning the first consideration will be the arrangement of the buildings and the development of the site to the best advantage, whereas in town planning the first consideration must be the general convenience of the town and the arrangement of main roads . . . where town-planning is undertaken by municipalities it will certainly be well to leave a good deal of freedom in the matter of site-planning . . . to the owners or societies who may be developing the land. (Unwin, 1909, p. 289)

The twin levels corresponded to the local authority preparing the guiding framework under the 1909 Act and the developer filling in the detail. The visual effects illustrated throughout *Town Planning in Practice* were most appropriate to site design. They required detailed control, preferably backed up by landowner covenants as at Letchworth and Hampstead Garden Suburb. Unwin conceded that often the planner 'must lay out his streets and *places* often with a very imperfect knowledge of what will be the character of the buildings surrounding them' (Unwin, 1909, p. 208).

Site design and housing layout had originally brought Unwin to prominence. By 1906 his contribution at the Seventh International Congress of Architects, 'The Planning of Residential Districts and Streets', concentrated on site design (Unwin, 1906b). His techniques had advanced through practical work and study of Sitte. Articulation of building lines, setbacks, angled groupings and open greens represented his transposition of Sittesque techniques to the low-density Garden City and were useful in avoiding monotony where house types were repeated.

Characteristically this also served a social objective. 'Most successful of all is when the buildings . . . can be grouped together . . ., so that the unit . . . ceases to be the individual house or cottage, and becomes the group' (Unwin, 1906b, p. 425). Economy was also achieved. Unwin had been criticized over the cost of Garden City housing and he reiterated principles for standardization in his paper 'Cottage Building in the Garden City'.

> If cottages are to be built cheaply they must be built in groups; thorough organisation of the building operations must be secured; a sufficient number must be built . . . to effect the great economies which arise from . . . repetition . . . it is very important to standardise the various parts . . . Too much care cannot be taken in designing doors and windows . . . Where groups of cottages must be kept absolutely simple, good results will depend largely on the arrangement of them. Here, as in so many other cases, our forefathers have shown us the right way. (Unwin, 1906a, p. 109)

The grouping and arrangement of cottages was extensively dealt with in *Town Planning in Practice*. There was little advice on internal planning, however. Chapter Eight, 'Of Site Planning and Residential Roads', further developed the theme of the harmonious relationship between highways and buildings. At the detailed level Unwin was more inclined to advocate informality, with layouts that would incorporate worthwhile site features, hedgerows or trees, while economizing on road lengths. He included diagrams of daylight and sunlight and advocated careful consideration of aspect to gain maximum amenity. Fine-tuning followed basic layouts in which massing of building in relation to natural features was worked alongside the road pattern.

The spacing of roads was crucial. Unwin discussed the relationship of plot frontage to density and road length per plot, an analytical technique which led to *Nothing Gained by Overcrowding* in 1912. He concluded that a plot depth of 150 ft. [46 m] would allow flexibility of building line but avoid back-to-back overlooking. An average frontage of 24 ft. [7.3 m], and roads 300 ft. [91.4 m] apart, gave a net density of 12 houses to the acre [4.8 to the hectare], a standard evolved from the Letchworth Building Regulations where a coverage of one sixth plot area gave a house of 1152 sq.ft. [15 sq.m.], on a one twelfth acre plot (Unwin, 1909, pp. 321–7). Although Unwin retained comparative densities of up to 20 houses to the acre [8 to the hectare], all elements of the density argument in *Town Planning in Practice* now appeared to converge upon '12 to the acre', ratified as *the* urban density standard in the Tudor Walters *Report* of 1918. Support literally sprang from grass-roots level:

> Twelve houses to the net acre of building land, excluding all roads, has been proved to be about the right number to give gardens of a sufficient size to be of commercial value to the tenants – large enough that is to be worth cultivating seriously for the sake of the profits, and not too large to be worked by an ordinary labourer and his family. This figure . . . has now been fairly well tested . . . at Bournville, at Earswick, at . . . Letchworth, at Hampstead and at many other places. (Unwin, 1909, p. 320)

The ninth Chapter of *Town Planning in Practice*, 'Of Plots and the Placing of Buildings', functioned as a detailed manual of layout design (Unwin, 1909, pp. 319–74). The 70 acre 'artisans' quarter' at Hampstead Garden Suburb and its component elements demonstrated the almost infinite variety of street picture and spatial groupings that might be generated. Road junctions were of especial significance, with closing features such as screen walls and small pavilions (*see* Figure 50). Triple junctions, which combined better visibility for approaching traffic, with the potential for enclosing space, were exemplified by 'Crickmer Circus' at the junction of Willifield Way and Temple Fortune Hill and by the Baillie Scott-designed grouping at the Hampstead Way junction on Meadway. The monotony of the corridor–street might be mitigated through gentle angled splays of the building line as in Station Road, Letchworth. More informal layouts were represented by Birds Hill and Pixmore.

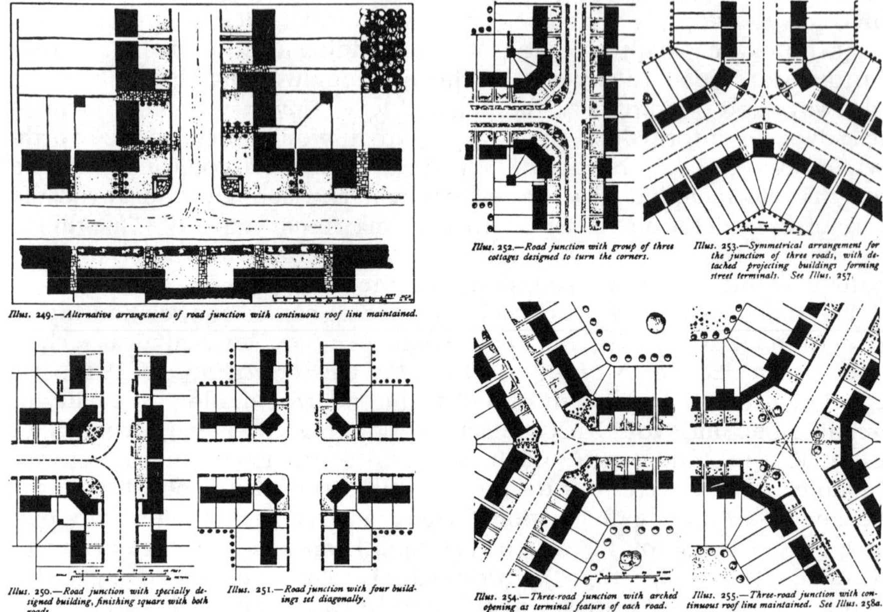

Figure 50 Housing groupings around road junctions from *Town Planning in Practice*, 1909. Publication of Unwin's major book confirmed a shift in emphasis to exterior space and the composition of street pictures, influenced by Camillo Sitte

Varied groupings suggested outdoor rooms, with formal greens as at Linnell Close and Lucas Square, Hampstead, bringing the early quadrangles into the life of the street without sacrificing their corporate identity. The cul-de-sac was exemplified by Asmuns Place and variants. Unwin was convinced that more widespread use would follow the recognition that:

> The character of modern traffic, particularly . . . motor traffic, has rendered frontage to the main road anything but desirable for residence; the dust, the noise, the smell are all objectionable features. (Unwin, 1909, p. 317)

The cul-de-sac was the logical culmination of Unwin's hierarchy of roads. It was more economical to construct and had great potential for landscaping. A series of culs-de-sac would present the opportunity for independent pedestrian routes in several parts of Hampstead Garden Suburb, leading to the updating of Garden City layout principles to the motor age at Radburn, New Jersey in 1928–9.

Town Planning in Practice extended its concerns far beyond the 1909 Act. The distinction between the ideal and the practical was not always clear but it emphasized the importance of creativity beyond quantifiable standards for satisfactory community design. As Thomas Adams, himself a surveyor, observed, Unwin's strength, perhaps paradoxically, lay in his detachment from procedural problems. The influence of the book was primarily seen in housing layouts. It was supplemented three years later by *Nothing Gained by Overcrowding*, which played a vital role in advancing the ***principles*** of Garden-City housing and town-planning rather than the ***fine detail*** with which *Town Planning in Practice* was so intimately concerned.

7
Nothing Gained by Overcrowding

'Nothing Gained by Overcrowding' was perhaps one of the few revolutionary catchphrases coined by planning. It is arguable that its judicious application accomplished an environmental change in the interwar period, which even the most optimistic proponents of the cause would initially have considered to be in the realms of wishful speculation. It was used as propaganda by the Garden Cities and Town Planning Association, who published it in 1912, and by others, including the National Housing Reform Council, for whom Unwin presented one of his preliminary versions. As will be shown, his argument was somewhat devious, but, allied to the provision of the 1909 Housing and Town Planning Act that density limitation did not bring an automatic right to compensation, the way was prepared for codification of the new standards as national policy. In addition, *Nothing Gained by Overcrowding* contained an important statement on the necessity for regional-strategic planning, which in turn formed the basis for Unwin's interwar work on population and resource distribution and for his role as Technical Adviser to the Greater London Regional Planning Committee.

Precursors

By 1900–1 Unwin had developed an analytical approach both to highway design and housing layout. He had drawn attention to the anomaly of the costly bye-law streets and alleys contrasted to the lightly paved carriage drives serving country houses. At the same time he had sought optimal layouts, such as the quadrangles of *The Art of Building a Home*[86] and *Cottage Plans and Common Sense*, where communal gardens and open spaces were substituted for back alleys, coal houses and privies of bye-law development. The open-centred quadrangle block appeared on the Brentham plan of 1907, virtually identical to that shown in *Nothing Gained by Overcrowding* five years later.

In *Town Planning in Practice* Unwin examined the economic and functional factors of roadbuilding. Initial cost would be met by the developer, and subsequent maintenance by the local authority, who had attempted to minimize their future outgoings by insisting upon uniform hard-paved roads and alleys, irrespective of the number of houses served or probable amounts of traffic. Such roads were likely either to be inadequate for major radial routes, or grossly extravagant for housing alone. Unwin concluded:

> this excessive cost [£5–£8 per lineal yard for a roadway, with twin pavements 40–50 feet [12.2–15.2 m] total width] tends to limit the frontage of houses. Where an attempt is being made to build cottages under £200 in cost, the charge of £3 per yard for the half share of the road becomes a serious matter, and the houses must suffer, both in size and frontage. (Unwin, 1909, p. 302)

If planning controlled density, a point would be reached where the cost of the additional road length necessary to serve more houses outweighed the increased return from the greater number. Unwin compared twin blocks, each 600 ft. [183 m] by 400 ft. [122 m], developed with perimeter housing. A constant 150 ft. [46 m] plot depth was used, leaving a tract of land 300 ft. [91 m] by 100 ft. [30 m] in the centre. If a 45 ft. [13.7 m] bye-law road was run through the centre, Unwin argued that the perimeter frontage lost, together with increased road costs made development within the block uneconomic:

> We shall . . . lose 0.45 acres which, at £300 per acre . . . £135. We should have to make 400 feet of new road . . . 30s per foot, or £600, making a total £735 . . . unless we can increase the value of the land by more than £735 we shall gain nothing whatever . . . and might just as well have left the open space in the centre to be used as a recreation ground or allotment ground. (Unwin, 1909, pp. 327–8)

If lighter roads were permissible, as at Hampstead Garden Suburb, it would be possible to develop in depth economically. Unwin's formula, however, relied on the substantially higher costs of the bye-law street. He was not alone in attempting to break away from the bye-law strait-jacket. In December 1910 an article in *The Surveyor and Municipal Engineer* illustrated a rationalized form of terraced development, virtually eliminating the derided back projections, with a block layout having a central communal open space (Slater, 1910). Unwin continued to refine the basic proposition. In February 1911, at Liverpool, he described the effect of density limitation on housing design to a National Housing and Town Planning Council conference (Town Planning Conference at Liverpool, 1911, pp. 265–7). He presented diagrams showing alternative schemes ranging from twenty houses to the acre to a minimum of ten. The difference in ground rent per plot, was £2 16s 9d [£2.84], or less than 5d [2.25p] per week, whereas the plot areas were 172 sq. yds. [17 sq.m.] against 423 sq. yds. [42 sq.m.]. The greater amenity value of the larger lower-density plots became the lynch pin in Unwin's argument. He also reiterated the savings from lighter road construction, citing a thirteen-acre estate at Acton, where a saving of £2,000 had been offset against a proportionately higher plot area per house. In May 1911 the paper was published (Unwin, 1911d) as Unwin presented the theme at the Philadelphia Conference on City Planning (*Proceedings*, 1911, pp. 105–6). Later that year a new 'Introduction' to *Town Planning in Practice* included another variant on the same material (Unwin, 1911c, pp. ix–xiii). He had considered six alternatives with 20-acre [8-hectare] sites developed from 9.6 to 25 houses per acre [3.85–10 to the hectare]. All used a 23-ft. frontage house. In the 'definitive' form *Nothing Gained by Overcrowding* showed a house frontage of 16–18 ft. [4.9–5.5 m], with an alternative 20 ft. 6in. The other densities, 12, 14 and 20 houses per acre, were suppressed to heighten the extremes.

Nothing Gained by Overcrowding – the exemplar of site design

In January 1912 Unwin delivered a Manchester University Warburton Lecture, 'The Town Extension Plan' (Unwin, 1912c). He urged the widespread use of the 1909 legislation to control and articulate suburban development. *Nothing Gained by Overcrowding* was presented in virtually its final form, with a strategic dimension absent from its precursors. The University published the lecture and the Garden Cities and Town Planning Association the tract (Unwin, 1912b).

Hypothetical 10-acre [4-hectare] sites were shown diagrammatically alongside each other to demonstrate (*see* Figure 51):

> That the greater the number of houses crowded upon land, the less economical is the use being made of it, the higher the rate must the occupier pay for every available yard of the plot, and the smaller will be the total return to the owners of the land in increment value due to building operations. (Unwin, 1912c, p. 52)

These sweeping claims were supported by tables:

Table 7.1 *Nothing Gained by Overcrowding*. Comparative plot sizes, densities and costs

	SCHEME I with land at £500 per acre	SCHEME II with land at £500 per acre	SCHEME III with land at £250 per acre
Number of houses	340	152	152
Average plot size	83.5 sq.yds.	261.5 sq.yds.	261.5 sq.yds.
Cost of roads	£9,747 0s 0d	£4,480 10s 0d	£4,480 10s 0d
Cost of land	£5,000 0s 0d	£5,000 0s 0d	£5,000 0s 0d
Total cost of land and roads per house	£43 7s 6d	£62 7s 5d	£45 18s 6d
Equivalent ground rent per week	8d	11¾d	8½d
Price of plot per sq.yd.	10s 4½d	4s 9¼d	3s 6d

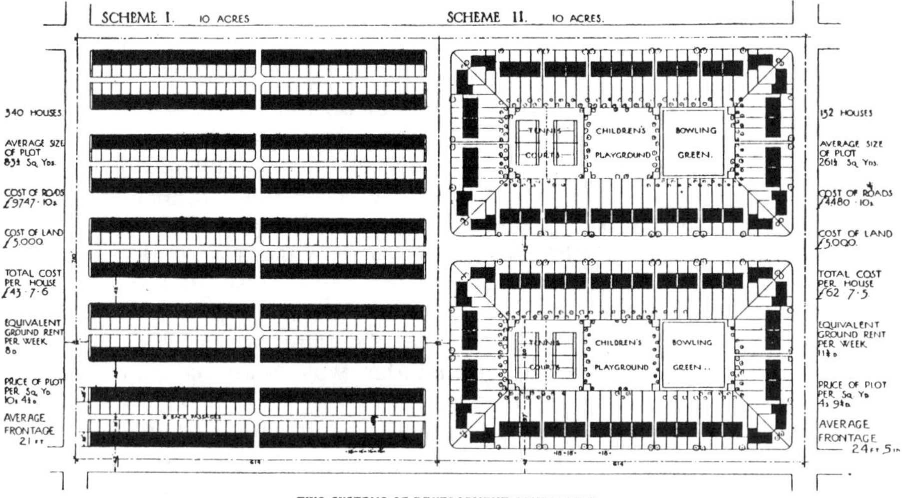

Figure 51 *Nothing Gained by Overcrowding*, 1912 the two systems of development contrasted. In spite of Unwin's flawed logic, the promise of reduced road and service costs, and the benefits of increased garden size, the concept exerted a powerful influence on the First World War reconstruction debate on housing

Unwin assumed the same unit cost of land, ignoring the fact that Scheme II would require 22.36 acres [9 hectares] for the same number of houses, with an acquisition cost of £11,184 4s 2d, rather than the £5,000 shown. Total road costs were £10,021 1s 4d rather than the £4,480 shown. This was evident from the 'total cost of land and roads per house' but the global figures were omitted. Furthermore the total road cost per dwelling, not shown, was, at £29 9s 8d [£29.48], actually higher for open development than the £28 6s 8d [£28.33] of the conventional layout, notwithstanding Unwin's contention that bye-laws required extravagant highway provision. The latter required only 13.20 ft. [4 m] per dwelling compared to 17.42 ft. [5.31 m] for open development. In reality Unwin's analysis went no further than the virtually self-evident fact that the higher the density, the greater the proportion of any given site to be covered by roads and buildings, drastically reducing the garden area. It was also necessary to include inefficient linking roads in the bye-law scheme, so that the decrease in density from 34 to 15 dwelling units per acre was matched by a more than threefold increase in plot area from 83½ sq. yds.[8 sq.m.] to 261½ sq. yds. [26 sq.m.]

Unwin capitalized on the propaganda value through his concept of 'plot value'. He calculated ground rent by dividing plot areas by road and land costs. Thus the 83½ sq. yd. plot would rent at 8d per week; the 261½ sq. yd. plot at 11¾d. Unwin joyfully seized on this and declared to his Manchester audience:

> Now I ask you, if there are two shops and one of them offered 83 marbles for 8d and the other offered 261 marbles for 11¾d would not the youngest

> player know which was the best offer? (Unwin, 1912c, p. 54; Unwin, 1912b, p. 7)

He tactfully omitted to describe the effect on the lad who had only 8d to spend! But therein lay the nub of the matter. No amount of special pleading could disguise the fact that, failing subsidy, the additional land and road costs must inevitably be recovered through higher rents.

There were other questionable assumptions. *Nothing Gained by Overcrowding* carried the subtitle *How the Garden City type of Development may benefit both Owner and Occupier.* The benefit to the occupier-tenant was seen as the better value of the increased plot area, and the inclusion of the communal open space. This land was in part deducted from individual plots and the remainder was 'marginal development land' shown on the early block diagram in *Town Planning in Practice*, combined to provide two tennis courts, a children's playground and a bowling green. Construction and maintenance costs would surely have been added to rents; after all Unwin referred to such land yielding 'at any rate some revenue' in *Town Planning in Practice*. He had tellingly emphasized that bye-law streets, constructed willy-nilly at the developer's or tenants' wishes, represented the most expensive form of open space. As road costs per house were actually higher, and overall road costs substantially higher, in Unwin's open-development model, any benefit to the tenant was more apparent than real. House construction costs were totally ignored but they would certainly have been higher. That a tenant might, even if able to afford the higher rents, have preferred a cheaper house with a smaller garden at a lower rent was, if considered at all, probably rejected as heretical.

The landowner would have received a greater reward from the increased land take and the developer would have made a substantially greater capital outlay, before exacting his tribute from the tenant. Unwin had assumed that ground rent would not rise proportionately with plot size, crediting the developer with a rare degree of altruism. He had assumed that density limitation would be imposed through planning and perhaps felt that public authorities should implement the new standards. Yet they would have been charged with the recovery of all costs from 'economic rent' prior to the 1919 Housing Act. Planning had a crucial role in assisting the transformation, as subsequently did the more positive housing role of the public sector. It might have been expected that unit land costs for the larger site might diminish due to the larger take; Unwin postulated that voluntary landowner agreements might also reduce them through quicker turnover to satisfy the increased demand. To illustrate this he fixed the total increment to that of the bye-law scheme and spread it over the greater area required for open development, thus significantly lowering both the unit cost and the total return. First Garden City Ltd. at Letchworth were disposing of development land at prices that reflected densities from their zoning plan, but they had originally acquired the estate at agricultural value: circumstances unlikely to be replicated in the suburban extensions developed under the 1909 Act. Nevertheless, town-planning would help to reduce the price of suburban land by eroding the high expectation of bye-law densities. Unwin calculated the effect of this by presenting Scheme II with land cost halved to £250 per acre, giving a weekly ground rent per week of 8½d [4p], a mere halfpenny more expensive than Scheme I, the bye-law development. His political convictions underlay his contention that:

> It is the obvious duty of the community to provide for the right system of development, and not be turned aside because of the hardships that may fall upon a few individuals who have laid their plans on the assumption that they would continue to be allowed to do something which has proved to be detrimental to the community . . . It is possible that no change can be introduced, however beneficial, that will not cause individual hardships. (Unwin, 1912b, p. 17)

Such hardships should, he had always asserted, be borne by those most able to sustain them.

The block layouts represented a landmark in the evolution of site planning. Unwin had urged the incorporation of communal amenities since the 1890s. Their backland location retained the maximum frontage for building with accessibility from all houses by a safe pedestrian route. It only required the superimposition of the cul-de-sac, extensively used at Hampstead Garden Suburb, to create the Radburn superblock, the American innovation of the 1920's updating the Garden City to the motor age. As early as 1914 Unwin experimented with double and even quadruple blocks, in a preliminary layout for the Marino estate on the outskirts of Dublin (Miller, 1985, p. 178).

Nothing Gained by Overcrowding consolidated Unwin's writing and reputation. Whatever the detailed shortcomings, the tenor of his argument carried conviction and popular appeal; 'Nothing Gained by Overcrowding' became a convenient rallying cry, particularly when allied to the substantive achievements of New Earswick, Letchworth and Hampstead (*see* Figure 52). It is worth looking ahead to see how the proposition fared in post-1919. The Garden Cities and Town Planning Association reissued the tract in 1918, and in December 1919, Unwin reworked his basic thesis for the Ministry of Health periodical *Housing* (Unwin, 1919a). He reported that land costs had fallen from the 1914 average of £300 per acre (substantially below the £500 assumed for *Nothing Gained*) to £212 in 1919. The cost of roads and sewers had risen over the same period from £5 8s 0d [£5 40] per linear yd. for a 36 ft. highway (Unwin had assumed £7 5s 0d [£7 25] for a 42 ft. highway) to £11 6s 0d [£11 30]. Based on these two factors alone, open development was only a little more costly and was moreover prescribed by statute. Illustration of alternatives with up to 34 dwellings per acre was largely academic. Land, road and sewer costs for the five alternatives differed little from the Ministry-approved layout, with the latter at £67 13s 4d [£67 67] per plot against £63 per plot with the highest-density scheme. Net costs per square yard per plot ranged from 33s 11d

The Garden City Method of Development.

FRONT GARDENS TO HOUSES UNDER TOWN PLANNING.

The By-Law Method of Development.

ORDINARY SUBURBAN VILLAS, SHOWING AMOUNT OF SPACE FOR FRONT GARDEN.

21

Figure 52 *Nothing Gained by Overcrowding*, 1912: Hampstead Garden Suburb and the Bye-law Suburb. The use of photographs, in addition to Unwin's analytical diagrams, gave the publication great propaganda value and stressed the Arcadian quality that Hampstead had gained within five years of inauguration

[£1 70] for the 340 sq. yd. plots of the Ministry approved layout to 17s 6d [87½p] for the 73.6 sq. yd. plots of the highest-density scheme. Using the ground-rent calculations from *Nothing Gained*, the difference was much smaller at 1s ¾d for open development and 11¾d for the highest-density scheme.

The increased plot widths now required a cul-de-sac to provide additional development frontage, visibly reducing the efficiency of the layout, as Unwin himself had prophesied, where it cut through to the backland. A major inconsistency lay in his statement that:

> frontage is quite as important as . . . number of houses per acre. The relatively high cost of road-making at the present time increases the importance of the economy of road frontage. (Unwin, 1919a, p. 162)

Why did he not attempt to rationalize narrower frontage houses, using earlier designs, rather than increase frontages more than 10 ft. over those shown in *Nothing Gained*? Would that have been an unacceptable compromise with low-density standards a *fait accompli*? The vital issues of the abnormally high building costs and shortage of labour and materials were omitted. Alongside these, land and road costs were almost incidental. Perhaps the article was intended to reassure local authorities of this.

The Garden Cities and Town Planning Association republished *Nothing Gained by Overcrowding* in 1933. Six years later Frederic Osborn (1885–1978) corresponded with Unwin about the necessity of preparing a strong analytical case for low-density cottage development to counteract the growing appeal of high-density high-rise flats to architects and intellectuals. In 1946, at the dawn of the new-towns programme, Osborn wrote to Barry Parker urging him to revise the document.[87] Parker candidly replied that although *Nothing Gained by Overcrowding* had been widely influential, it had been hindered by the calculations. With the postwar distortion of costs and the effect of planning on land values, any figures were likely to be 'fictitious, fanciful, undeterminable, unpredictable and enigmatical'.[88] Analysis suggests that this had perhaps always been the case. If so, it was a formidable achievement to build, metaphorically speaking, the post-1919 housing programme on such an insecure foundation.

The strategic implications of *Nothing Gained by Overcrowding*

The spread of low-density suburbs brought the necessity to consider overall urban form at a strategic level. Yet Howard had applied Garden City principles to the replanning of London. As early as 1906, Unwin hinted at the articulation of surburban expansion following an overall strategy:

> We may see to it that each new town extension is defined and has limits set . . ., each planned as a whole and finished with some comely edge. Should the town need to extend still further, a belt of meadow, park or wooded grove can be reserved and the defined area maintained.[89]

Here is the concept of the green belt or green girdle, studded with satellites drawn from the ring boulevards of continental cities, and Howard's reference to the extension of Adelaide, South Australia, beyond a defined park belt. At the 1910 RIBA Town Planning Conference, Unwin suggested two major alternatives:

> In considering the general form . . . that town development should take two extremes may be mentioned. Either the town may extend in solid continuous rings, like the rising of flood water in a shallow basin, or it may increase by the growth of numerous detached townlets spreading from some centre, such as an existing village or a railway station on the outskirts of the town . . . The essential idea that after a certain size the development of a city should be by the formation of supplementary centres on the outskirts, and . . . the importance of securing that the indefinite expansion of these and the central town should be checked, and that the defining belts of park, woodland or open country should be reserved, seems to me of the utmost importance. (Unwin, 1911b, pp. 248, 250)

Unwin's visit to Chicago in 1911 was another catalyst in developing this overview. The Manchester University Warburton Lecture of January 1912 and *Nothing Gained by Overcrowding* both presented the strategic dimension:

> I venture to suggest that the ideal form of town will consist of a central nucleus, surrounded by suburbs each grouped around some subsidiary centre representing the common life of the district . . . around which should be located municipal or administrative buildings, its places of worship, its educational, recreational, and social institutions . . . Between each of these suburbs there might well be reserved some belt of open space, parkland, woodland, agricultural or meadowland, which would at once define one suburb from another, and keep the whole of the inhabitants in intimate touch with ample open space. (Unwin, 1912c, pp. 47–8)

The implications of his many references to 'crystallization' were reflected in this concept: a combination of Howard's Social City cluster with the planned expansion of German cities.

The application of Garden-City principles to suburban growth was illustrated by a handsome aerial perspective, drawn by A. H. Mottram (1886–1953), one of Unwin's leading assistants (*see* Figure 53). It showed a formally planned central city with a radial road network converging on a semicircular crescent, open to a river front. To the right lay a railway line serving an extensive industrial estate and dockyard. The city had absorbed several old villages. Green reservations along valley bottoms articulated the pattern of settlement in a polynuclear form. The drawing incorporated motifs from the plan of

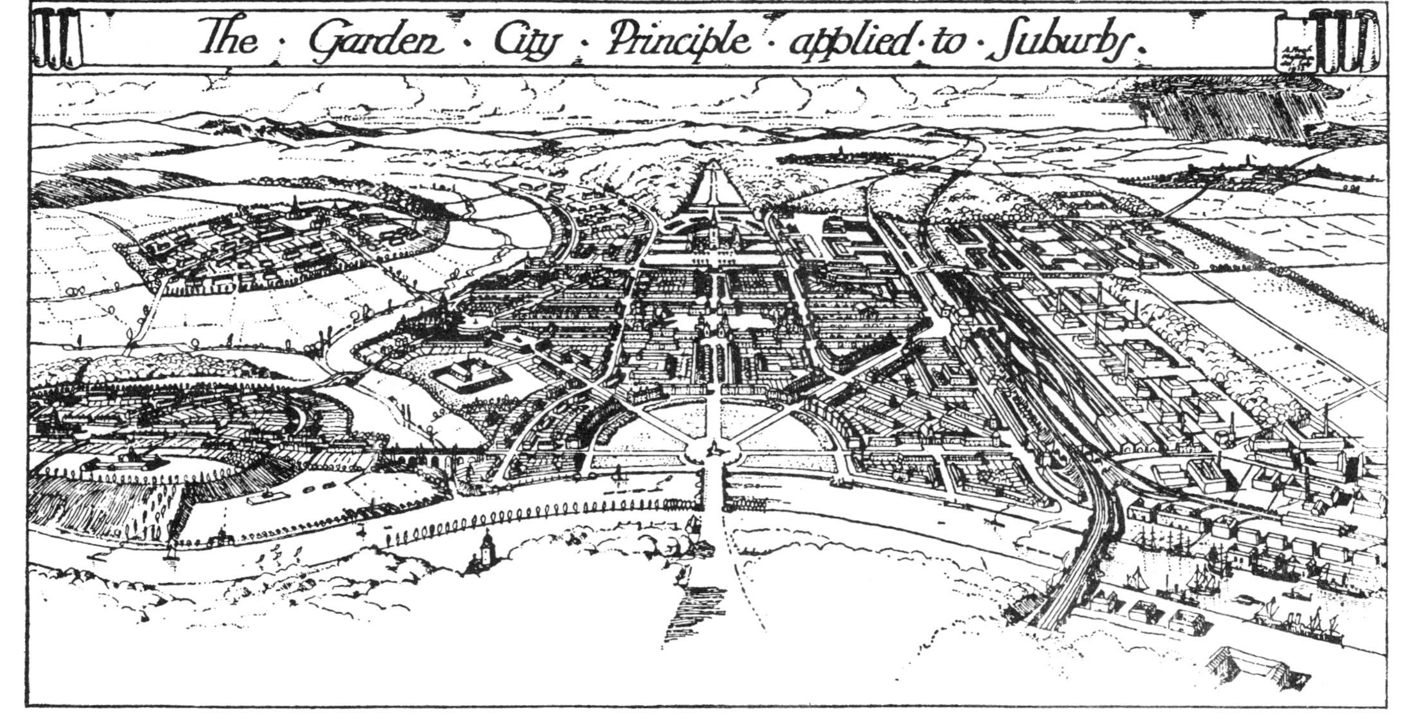

Figure 53 *Nothing Gained by Overcrowding*, 1912: the Hampstead Garden City principle applied to suburbs. The urban cluster articulated by belts of open space was an elaboration of Howard's 'Social City' (1898), and was the model Unwin ultimately expanded for his strategic approach to Greater London

Hampstead Garden Suburb – the semicircular crescent and converging radials was clearly derived from the 'Artisans' Quarter', while the major axis leading to a distant church recalled Central Square. The layout strikingly anticipated Adshead and Ramsey's plan for Dormanstown, near Middlesbrough, Teesside (1918).

The diagram, a springboard to Unwin's views on regional strategic and ultimately national planning, appeared with the Warburton lecture and in *Nothing Gained by Overcrowding*. In the 1920s it illustrated Unwin's paper *The Overgrown City*, (Unwin, 1922) prepared for the Russell Sage Foundation of New York and appeared as a model displayed by the Ministry of Health at the British Empire Exhibition at Wembley, London, in 1924.[90]

Initially Unwin appears to have accepted without comment the increases in population and area predicted in the calculations that accompanied the Warburton lecture and *Nothing Gained*. The lecture took the 17,000 average annual population increase for Greater Manchester and contrasted the 100 acres [40 hectares] required to house it at 34 dwelling units per acre, with the 227 acres [91 hectares] required for open development at 15 d.u. per acre. Land acquisition costs were £50,000 and £113,500 respectively, adding values of £45,000 and £102,150 over agricultural use. Unwin argued that the additional £57,150 created by 'the Town Planning Act may prove to be the handsomest gift this country has made to its landowners for a long time!'. Density limitation would tend to reduce the inflated levels attained for bye-law development and he suggested that the total increment would be spread over the greater area required for the low-density development. Working the Manchester figures back to the land price, Unwin reached a figure of £248 10s 0d per acre, which, Unwin claimed, reduced the plot unit ground rent from 11¾d to 8½d:

> I have tried it with dearer and cheaper land, with more costly roads and less costly ones . . . the general results come to exactly the same thing. In other words our overcrowding system of development is so absolutely uneconomical, it wastes so much of our land in roads, that actually it would be possible, giving the landlord the same total increment from every house that is built . . . to provide the plot of 261 sq. yards for 8½d. per week in place of a plot of 83 sq. yards which costs 8d. per week. (Unwin, 1912c, p. 58)

Part of the land would be park belts up to 300 yds. wide to separate town and suburb. Increments generated by building value would be shifted further out. Unwin did not discuss compensation for the removal of building value. He was optimistic that planning would remove acute local congestion and provide 'better distribution and more economical use of land'.

The cornerstone of his argument was the geometrical theorem that the area of a circle increases proportionately to the square of its radius. Unwin claimed that the rate of outward expansion would diminish due to the greater area available as the radius increased. Expansion of Manchester

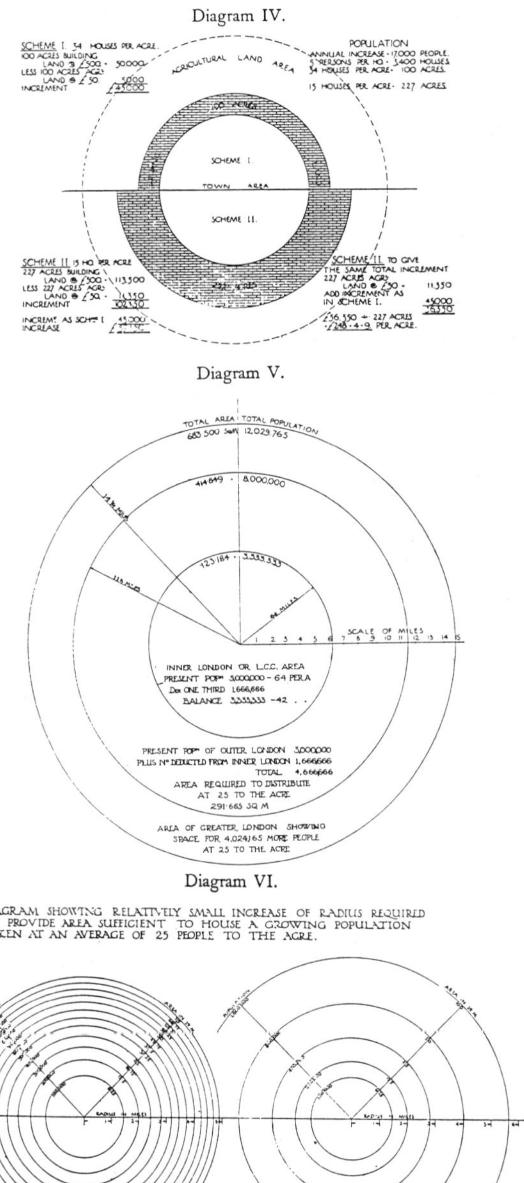

Figure 54 *Nothing Gained by Overcrowding*, 1912, the strategic implications. The interwar spread of Greater London was clearly implicit, but interwar attempts at overall control of the amorphous mass proved to be of little avail

at the restricted density, over ten years would increase the radius of its area from 2¼ to 2¾ miles [3.6–4.4 km.]. The additional half mile would house a population of 170,000, assuming that only half the area available would be built upon, with green wedges and girdles to articulate the new development into a 'federal' cluster (Unwin, 1912c, p. 60).

In *Nothing Gained by Overcrowding*, Unwin turned to Greater London, and graphically presented his prediction of its future enlargement (*see* Figure 54). The LCC area was, in 1912, equivalent to a circle of 6¼ miles [10 km.] radius, housing a population of 5 million at an average of 64 persons per acre [26 to the hectare]. Unwin proposed a one third reduction overall to allow inner-London housing improvement, and outward movement into the Metropolitan Police Area, represented by a circle of 14¾ miles [23.6 km.] radius. Its existing population, beyond LCC limits, was 3 million and with immigration would increase to 4.6 million. Unwin set the gross density of new development at 25 persons, 5 dwellings per acre [10 persons, 2 dwellings per hectare], the Hampstead Garden Suburb figure. This redistribution would be to increase the radius of the developed area from 6¼ to 11½ miles [10–18 km.], housing a total population of 8 million. The undeveloped outer band of 3¼ miles [5.2 km.] to the boundary of the Metropolitan Police Area would accommodate an additional 4 million, developed under the same conditions. The increase in peripheral development would make travel patterns more complex, but Unwin ignored the potential generation of circumferential in addition to radial movement (Unwin, 1912b, pp. 13–16, diagrams V, VI).

Unwin's prophecy of low-density suburban growth of outer London was self-fulfilling in the interwar years. The implementation of a structured hierarchy of planned neighbourhoods and articulation of the sprawl by open space was haphazard at best. At face value, Unwin's tract appeared to legitimize the suburb through application of Garden-City standards, which annoyed younger protagonists of the movement, notably F. J. Osborn (1885–1978) and C. B. Purdom (1883–1965). 'I never liked Unwin's examples', Osborn wrote to Barry Parker many years later. 'They made people think we wanted to expand London to one continuous urban tract'.[91] Unwin himself became acutely conscious of the dangers of the apparent open-ended commitment when he advised the Greater London Regional Planning Committee in the late 1920's.

8

Foundations for a Public Career

The conference circuit 1906–14

Between 1901 and 1914 Raymond Unwin attained a high profile in housing and town-planning; his appearance at Bournville in 1901 had initially marked him as an articulate and persuasive advocate and within five years he had achieved international recognition.

By mid-decade the Garden City had been accepted as an important contribution to European housing reform. At the Seventh International Congress of Architects, hosted by the RIBA in London in 1906, Unwin's work was placed alongside that of such established continental masters of urban design as Joseph Stübben (1845–1936), Charles Buls (1837–1913) and Eugene Henard (born 1849). Unwin became involved with the RIBA Town Planning Committee, where his presence must have augured well for securing a central role for the architect in town-planning.

In 1910 there were major conferences in Germany and England. Unwin was a delegate at Berlin and Düsseldorf in May–June 1910. The events were organized with teutonic thoroughness. Werner Hegemann (1882–1936), one of the leading figures in civic design, assembled a comprehensive exhibition, much of which Unwin borrowed for display in London. The German capital and the Grosses Berlin Competition presented him with the challenge of the metropolitan scale and the context for bold, formal planning, not previously emphasized in his work or writing (Unwin, 1910d).

Unwin was a prime organizer of the RIBA International Town Planning Conference, particularly the exhibition held at the Royal Academy (RIBA 1910a, 1910b; 1911). The event was presented with a full panoply of ceremony under the Patronage of His Majesty King George V and the Presidency of Leonard Stokes of the RIBA. The 64 Vice Presidents included Lords Temporal and Spiritual, the Maharaja of Baroda, Kitchener of Khartoum, Thomas Hardy and Ebenezer Howard. More than 1,300 delegates attended, packing the City Guildhall for the inaugural session, receiving and discussing 43 papers, with visits to Bournville, Port Sunlight, Letchworth and Hampstead Garden Suburb. Neither before nor since had town-planning enjoyed such prestige.

The Exhibition was comprehensive (RIBA, 1910b).[92] German material filled six galleries and part of a seventh, with the Central Hall dominated by a model of Hellerau Garden Suburb, Dresden. Grosses Berlin, the Vienna Ringstrasse and Karlsplatz, together with many urban extension plans, showed the range of German planning. The American exhibits included Burnham's Chicago Plan of 1909, which stole the show. English Garden Cities and Suburbs made a muted impact but appealed to continental delegates. The emergent British school of civic design was represented by Mawson's proposals for Southport and Dunfermline and Prestwich's transformation of Port Sunlight. Richard Norman Shaw's grandiose proposals for the Quadrant, Regent Street, and Piccadilly Circus, indicated his equality to the task of reconstructing Nash's fine ensemble as an Edwardian Baroque set-piece more appropriate to a modern Imperial capital. In the small Black and White Room, Patrick Geddes, 'that most unsettling person', hovered in the midst of the raw material of the Edinburgh Civic Survey, ready to ensnare unsuspecting visitors.

John Burns (1858–1943), President of the Local Government Board (LGB), which administered the narrowly defined procedure of the 1909 Act, gave a rousing opening address 'which lifted the subject into the realm of the poetical, while it was properly and severely practical at times'. Much of the content dealt with London, yet he also emphasized, as befitted his Labour origins, the popular basis for planning in a style very close to Unwin's:

> We have to think of the great mass of mankind . . . and the responsibility rests with us to see that the labourer is provided with infinitely better housing and street accommodation . . . The great town planning movement must not end in a few cities getting all the talent, most of the money, and the best of the improvements . . . For reasons industrial, social, commercial and Imperial, town planning must go hand in hand with better housing, wider roads, higher wages and increased sobriety . . . Plan the town, but spread the people. Make wider roads but do not narrow tenements behind. Dignify the city by all means, but not at the expense of the health of the home and family life of the average workman and citizen. (RIBA, 1911, p. 66)

It was a *tour de force* embracing the housing and social emphasis, which Unwin had stressed over the years, with an appeal to architects and civic designers. Stanley Adshead concluded that 'it is clear that the future of town-planning rests very largely with this man' (Adshead, 1910, p. 183), an evaluation not confirmed by Burns' subsequent action. The event was 'essentially an architects' conference'; most delegates probably felt that 'the Act should have specified that an architect should be in charge'.[93] Even the *Architectural Review* commented upon the scant treatment of the local authority and the landowner, essential parties to statutory planning.[94]

Unwin was unanimously elected a Fellow of the RIBA. His public career developed rapidly. In May 1911 he was one of the British delegates to the Third National Conference on City Planning held in Philadelphia. On his return, Sir Oliver Lodge offered him the Cadbury Lectureship in Civic Design at Birmingham University. He travelled to Canada in 1913, to Toronto, Montreal and Winnipeg, and advised on the planning of Halifax, Nova Scotia (*Canada and Town Planning*, 1914, pp. 88–89). He missed the 'First International Congress of Town Planning and the Organisation of City Life' at Ghent, but as RIBA delegate, had submitted a paper on urban-extension planning to be considered in his absence.[95] In May 1914 he addressed the Imperial Health Conference on garden cities. That fateful August he was one of the organizers of a London University International Planning summer school.[96] John Nolen (1869–1937), one of the leading American planners and A. E. Brinckmann (1881–1958), one of the younger followers of Sitte, were prevented from attending due to the impending international crisis. The event broke up as war was declared on 4 August.

The Town Planning Institute

The 1910 RIBA Conference served as a challenge to other professional bodies. The RIBA Town Planning Committee's circular ('Suggestions to promoters of town planning schemes', 1910), a document in all probability drafted by Unwin, recognized that 'the preparation of all the data upon which the design must be based hardly falls within the province of the architect, and it would seem that this formulation of the city's requirements . . . is the proper sphere of the surveyor (aided, of course, by the engineer, the valuer, the economist, the sociologist and the antiquarian)'.

In the Easter of 1909, Thomas Adams, returning from a National Housing Reform Council visit to Germany, discussed with Unwin and others the concept of an interdisciplinary institute for all professions engaged in planning (Cherry, 1974, p. 57). In January 1913, *Town Planning Review* reported meetings of a group of architects, engineers and surveyors. That July a 'provisional committee' was appointed – five architects: Adshead, Lanchester, Lucas, Soutar and Unwin and three surveyors: Adams, Davidge and Pepler. John Burns presided over the Inaugural Dinner of the Town Planning Institute in January 1914. The following May, Adams was elected President, with Unwin and J. W. Cockrill as Vice-Presidents, Pepler as Treasurer and Geddes as Librarian (Cherry, 1974, pp. 59–60). At one of the earliest meetings Unwin presented 'Town Planning in Relation to Land Values' (Unwin, 1914c).

As senior Vice-President, Unwin played an important role, particularly after Adams' departure for Canada in the autumn of 1914. He succeeded as President in 1915. Unwin considered meetings 'a useful interlude, taking us for a time out of the all-pervading atmosphere of war' (Unwin, 1915b). He was saddened by the decision to expel honorary German members, including Brinckmann, Eberstadt and Stübben, but heartened to learn that Hegemann had started a new career in the USA.

Festinate Lente: the Ruislip–Northwood UDC Scheme

John Burns had introduced the Town Planning Bill in the 1908 Parliamentary Session but it failed because of lack of time. Reintroduced, it received assent on 3 December 1909, a modest beginning for statutory town-planning to secure 'the home healthy, the house beautiful, the town pleasant, the city dignified and the suburb salubrious'. Developed land was excluded. Land with imminent development potential was the focus of the procedure, following German extension practice. The foundation of Garden Cities was neither hindered nor furthered (Minett, 1974). Emphasis upon suburban development brought accusation from Purdom that the 'good wine' of the Garden-City concept had been weakened with 'the water of town planning'. Others, Unwin included, could reflect that Garden-City housing standards had been given legal imprimatur remarkably quickly.

The weakness of the Act lay in permissive operation and cumbersome procedure. Local authorities required Local Government Board sanction to prepare schemes. They undertook widespread consultation, weighted on the side of objection and delay, published details in the *London Gazette* and laid them before Parliament for forty days. Approval took several years. Of the 172 schemes prepared under the Act, a mere thirteen were fully approved. This opened up a gap between Whitehall and the local authorities, emphasizing procedural etiquette above plan content or implementation, despite LGB inspectors of the calibre of Adams and later of Pepler and Unwin.

The content of the schemes was often bland. Primary land-use zoning, density limitation, the provision of open space and the reservation of main-road lines were the most usual features. By contrast Unwin's *Town Planning in Practice* showed an elusive and idealistic vision. As a consultant, Unwin became involved with the Ruislip–Northwood Urban District Council (UDC) Scheme, one of the first prepared under the 1909 Act (Miller, 1984, pp. 14–15), and later with the Finchley UDC Scheme. In addition, schemes were prepared for Quinton–Harborne–Edgbaston and East Birmingham through the initiative of J. S. Nettlefold (1866–1930), a Birmingham City Councillor and one of planning's most enthusiastic early advocates (Cherry, 1975).

The Ruislip–Northwood scheme aimed at providing a broad, articulated framework for the development of 6,585 acres [2,634 hectares] in Middlesex, 14 miles from central London: in many respects a prototype for the interwar suburb, when most development occurred in Ruislip–Northwood. As at Hampstead Garden Suburb, railway improvements, particularly the electrification of the Metropolitan and District line, acted as catalyst. The 1,276 acre [510 hectare] Ruislip Manor estate was owned by King's College, Cambridge, and the

Ruislip–Northwood UDC were alerted to the dangers of uncontrolled building in a largely rural area, which might impose unreasonable costs for roads and sewers. In fact preparation of the Ruislip Manor Estate layout proceeded in harmony with the UDC scheme. This resulted from close cooperation between William Thompson (died 1914), one of the most active supporters of planning, who became Chairman of the Ruislip Manor Company in April 1910, Edmund Abbott, Clerk to Ruislip–Northwood UDC, Frank Elgood, Chairman of the Ruislip–Northwood UDC Town Planning Committee, himself an architect, and Unwin, retained as a consultant by King's College. The solicitors to King's College had also acted for its sister foundation, Eton College, over the conveyance of the Wyldes estate to the Hampstead Garden Suburb Trust.[97]

The Ruislip Manor Estate, in the centre of the area, was a narrow swathe, four miles by half a mile, undulating and wooded in the north, with a large reservoir in the centre and development land towards the south. In July 1910 a layout competition was held with Sir Aston Webb and Unwin as assessors. In August the UDC passed a preliminary planning resolution and deposited at the LGB a map indicating the whole unbuilt area (Aldridge, 1915, pp. 532–3). On 12 August a site inspection was attended by Adams for the LGB, Elgood and Abbott of the UDC, and Unwin and Thompson for Ruislip Manor. The first owners' conference took place on 30 November. The King's College solicitor, J. S. Birkett, drew parallels with Hampstead Garden Suburb where private legislation had saved £10,000 in roadmaking costs, an advantage that planning would bring to Ruislip–Northwood. Thompson undertook that the competition-winning plans would be made available to the local authority.

In January 1911 the competition results were announced. The winners were A. and J. C. S. Soutar (the latter would succeed Unwin as consultant to the Hampstead Garden Suburb Trust in 1914). A design division between 'formal' and 'irregular' was strongly marked. *The Builder* noted:

> it is clear that direct and comprehensible lines of layout have been regarded as of the utmost importance . . . The first premiated plan . . . is typical of a number of others which are based on a main axial road . . . and also employ diagonal roads in order to give the most direct access possible to outlying portions.[98]

The major axis was cunningly terminated to avoid bridging the reservoir, leaving much of the Copse Wood to the north in its natural state, while opening up the southern portion for building, at ten houses to the acre, with 837 acres [335 hectares] residential development, 225 acres [90 hectares] open space and 184 acres [74 hectares] occupied by roads (*see* Figure 55b).

The Council's formal resolution seeking authority to prepare the scheme followed shortly afterwards. The LGB Local Inquiry was taken by Adams on 16 February 1911; authority to proceed was confirmed a month later (Aldridge, 1915, pp. 532–3). Completion of the draft scheme in July 1912 was preceded by the construction of houses in Manor Way. Had they not conformed with the scheme, the Act would have enabled their demolition without compensation. A further conference took place in November 1912. Adams took the second Local Inquiry on 17 and 18 April and 12 May 1913,[99] but the LGB draft order of intent to approve the scheme was delayed until 2 June 1914. It was laid before Parliament on 30 June, and belatedly received formal approval on 7 September 1914, by which time the outbreak of war had postponed development.

The Ruislip–Northwood scheme developed into a complex affair. The LGB was not entirely to blame for the delays. Unwin analysed virtually every clause in the draft schedule to the scheme, suggesting copious amendments, supported by Abbott and Elgood.[100] Everyone aimed at matching the high standards of Hampstead Garden Suburb. For example, the November 1912 conference saw a long discussion between Unwin, Soutar and Elgood over the importance of the design treatment of corners and building up to the back of the pavement line to frame the street picture. King's College tabled many objections concerned with responsibility for road construction and maintenance at the second Local Inquiry in April–May 1913. Adams noted that Unwin had given evidence on behalf of the RIBA over the controversial issue of aesthetic control. Adams considered that it would 'not be desirable to confer power on a local authority to veto design'. Unwin pressed the matter and obtained a private meeting with Burns, who personally approved the inclusion of the measure, subject to a right of appeal to the LGB.[101] A departmental memorandum considered that the weight of documents bore 'witness to the immense amount of time and labour which the preparation of a town-planning scheme gives up to this stage . . . it is desirable to . . . discourage elaboration'.[102]

The Approved Scheme consisted of an Official Map showing the road framework and land-use zoning proposals (*see* Figures 55a), and an 88 clause Schedule that incorporated detailed layout and construction standards (Aldridge, 1915, pp. 529–612). Roads ranged from major arteries, with a 60 ft. [18.25 m.] reservation, 26 ft. [8 m.] carriageway and planted margins, through a variety of culs-de-sac with a minimum 20 ft. [6 m.] reservation and 14 ft. [4.25 m.] carriageway, to a 7 ft. [2.1 m.] carriageway restricted to serving a residential quadrangle. Building lines were articulated and built-up corners permissible. Residential densities ranged from 4 dwellings per acre around the secluded Northwood woods to a maximum of 12 south of the Metropolitan Railway. Eleven shopping centres, 29½ acres [11.8 hectares] of 'compulsory' and 185 acres [74 hectares] of 'optional' commercial land were allocated, with a 243-acre [97 hectare] factory zone adjoining Northwood Junction. One hundred acres [40 hectares] were reserved as private open space, with agreement on 150 acres [60 hectares] of public open space.

Constructional standards and minimum room sizes followed the Hampstead Garden Suburb Building Regulations. Clause 56 to the Schedule contained the controversial powers of aesthetic control, generally comparable with those exercised by the estate owners at Letchworth and Hampstead. Building designs considered to be 'injurious to the amenity of the neighbourhood' could be rejected, or amendments specified, which implied that the Council would take professional design advice on a regular basis (Aldridge, 1915, pp. 590–1). In cases of dispute the RIBA President could be called upon to appoint an arbitrator. Abbott and Elgood, albeit hesitant over its practicability, were confident that 'the clause is a step in the right direction'.[103]

The Ruislip–Northwood scheme was much more complex than its Birmingham counterparts. Nettlefold commented that:

> [although] the smaller place [Ruislip–Northwood] has dealt much more thoroughly and effectively with the various problems . . . the general provisions . . . seem . . . a little too elaborate. They go into more detail than is advisable. Town planners should aim for simplicity of regulations and elasticity of detail. (Nettlefold, 1914, pp. 124, 128)

The Quinton–Harborne–Edgbaston scheme had gained a year over its rival but even with a broad-brush approach it was a lengthy undertaking. Nettlefold considered that 'the greatest obstruction of all to genuine and effective town-planning' (Nettlefold, 1914, p. 180) was the LGB under Burns. The department's reactionary 'poor law' image lingered long.

Housing investigation and legislation, 1912–14

Just before the First World War, private-sector housing construction declined sharply because of increased building costs. It became a live issue with the Liberals and Conservatives. Rural matters, ownership and development of land were also investigated. A Departmental Committee of enquiry into Buildings for Smallholdings was appointed in February 1912 by the President of the Board of Agriculture, Walter Runciman. The brief was to report on housing and farm buildings with a more general investigation of rural labourers' cottages. Convenience of planning, economy of construction and 'the possibility of reduction of cost by the use of new materials and methods of construction' were to be examined in detail. In the summer of 1912, Unwin travelled to Sweden to visit smallholding colonies.

The *Report*, published in March 1913, (*Buildings for Smallholdings*, 1913) attempted to set 'the minimum space to accommodate decently an average family': a theme long familiar from Unwin's writing, but this was his first opportunity of advocacy in a government report. The

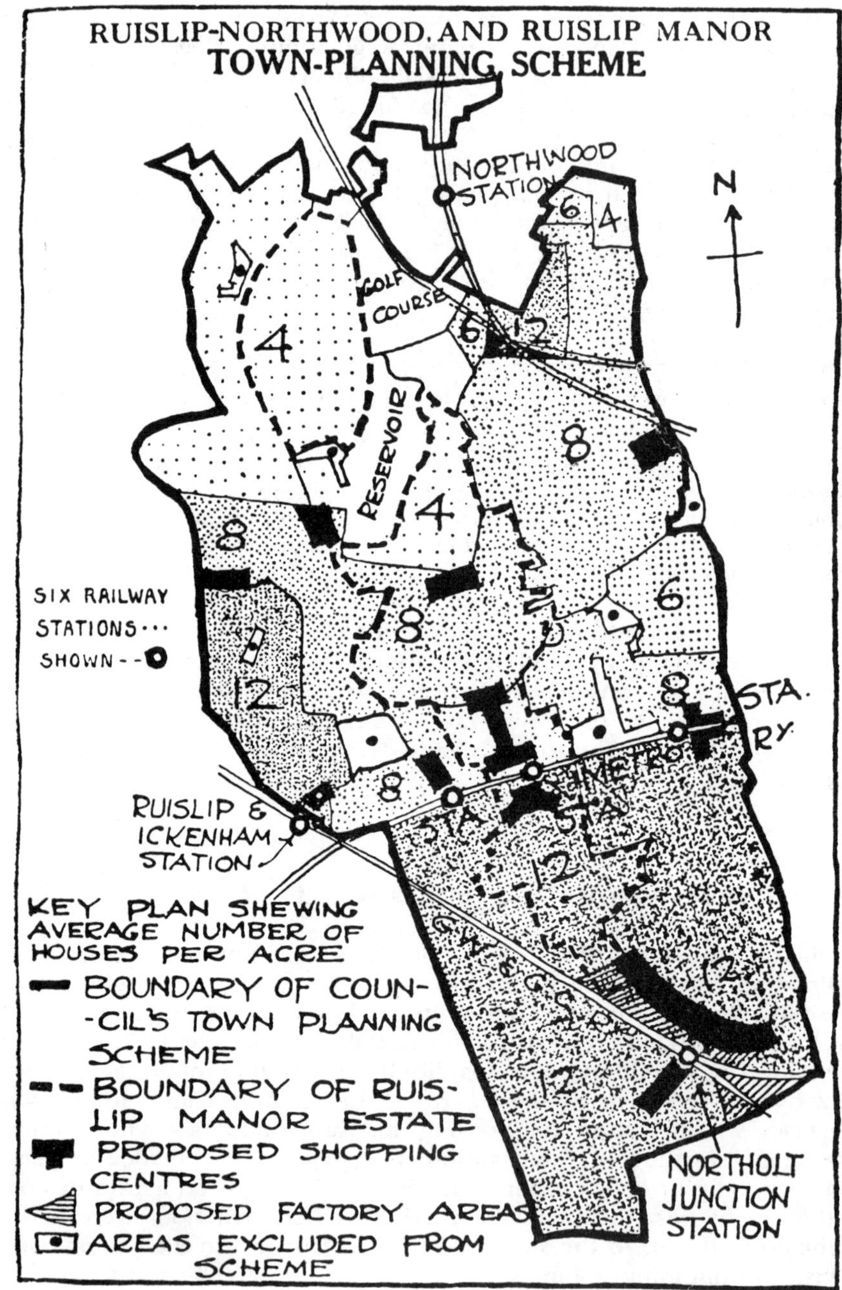

Figure 55 Ruislip-Northwood town-planning scheme, 1910–14: a) Overall zoning proposals showing differential residential densities

THE RUISLIP MANOR TOWN PLAN.

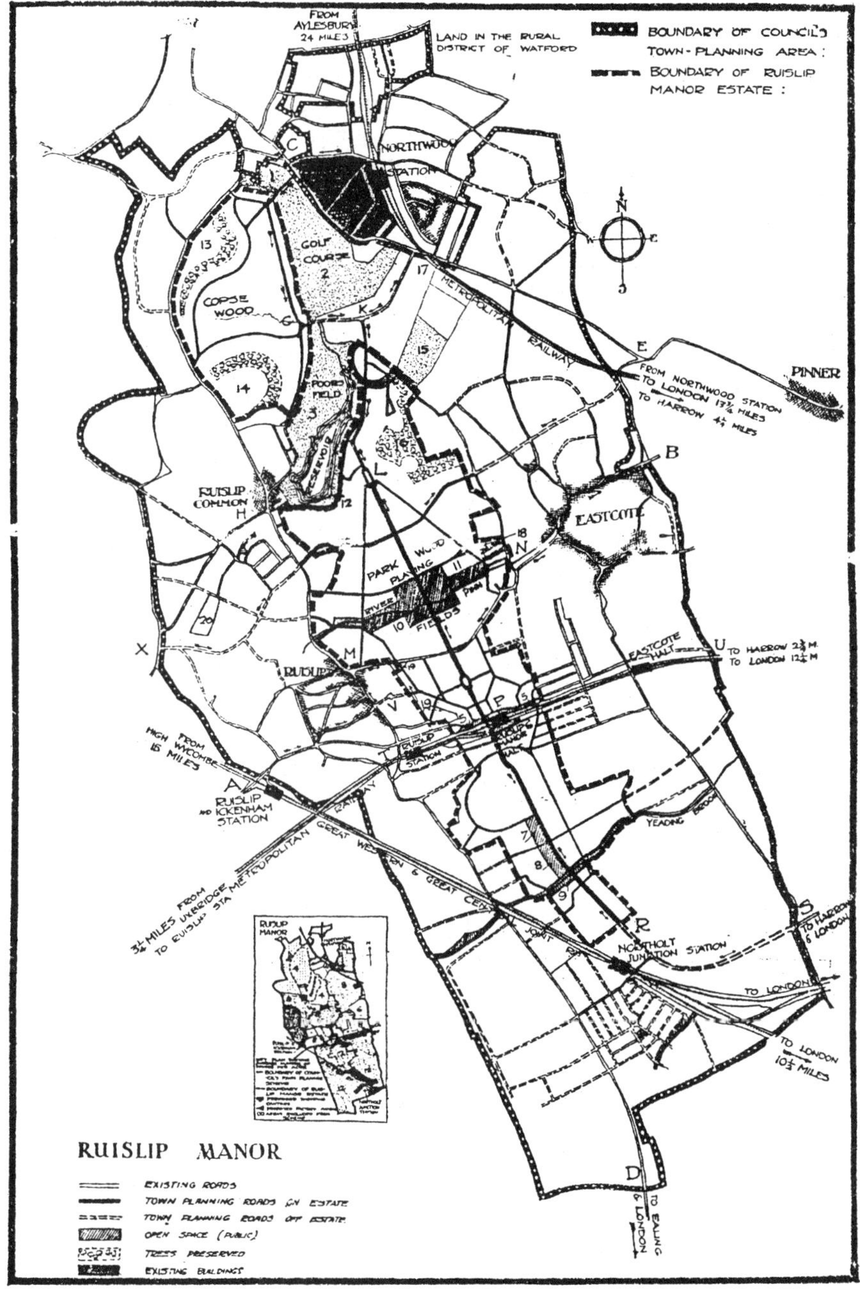

b) Ruislip Manor plan, a modified version of Soutar's competition-winning layout, 1911, set within the UDC planning framework

Smallholdings Committee housing standards were clearly derived from the Letchworth and Hampstead building regulations (*Buildings for Smallholdings*, para. 151). In addition to a room-by-room design brief, building materials were also examined, including a section on the use of concrete at New Earswick and Hampstead. The *Report* was the transition from the 1905 Cheap Cottages Exhibition at Letchworth to the Ministry of Housing demonstration site at Acton in 1920 and Unwin's further emphasis on the investigation of building materials through the Building Research Station. Thirty model plans included several Parker-and-Unwin types.[104] Most interesting were specially designed 'minimum plans' for compact semi-detached cottages, with simple, rational elevations in which the picturesque dormers and gables were replaced by low-pitched, hipped, slated roofs, a form prominently featured in the 1918 Tudor Walters *Report*.[105] With sash windows, the 'people's Georgian' cottage of interwar council-housing estates evolved (*see* Figure 56). The designer is unknown. The image conflicts with Unwin's earlier philosophy of reflecting vernacular traditions. However, in parallel with his moves towards formal town-planning, his detailed investigation of construction and materials led to his appreciation of the potential for a more universal housing prototype. Whether or not the instigator of the prototype, Unwin was the link between the pre- and postwar reports and manuals.

In November 1913, Runciman appointed a further committee to advise on 'plans, models, specification and methods of construction of rural cottages'. The attractively presented *Report* (Advisory Committee on Rural Cottages, 1914) indicated collaboration between Unwin and his committee colleague Lawrence Weaver, editor of *Country Life*. It appeared two weeks after the outbreak of war in August 1914. Weaver had made available the regional winning designs from a *Country Life* cottage competition, to which were added Parker-and-Unwin types and those from the Smallholdings *Report*. The text reiterated the earlier conclusions and added a short section on grouping and layout, recognizably by Unwin. Working drawings of the 23 plan types and model specifications were available.

A more comprehensive investigation of rural life had been undertaken by Seebohm Rowntree, following a personal request by David Lloyd George, then Home Secretary. The *Report* (*The Land*, 1913, 1914), indicated mounting concern over housing, gross overcrowding, insanitary conditions and high rents. Private enterprise was unable to respond and Rowntree urged that local authorities be made responsible for meeting his estimated shortfall of 120,000 rural dwellings. There were also detailed committees of inquiry into Scottish and Irish housing – though not in England and Wales, which made quantification of needs difficult and contentious.

Both the ruling Liberals and opposition Conservatives contemplated housing legislation. In July 1914, Walter Runciman introduced a Bill to enable the provision of working-class housing in rural areas, and housing for government employees, the latter to cater for the strategically vital Rosyth Naval Base on the Firth of Forth in Scotland. Controversy over the allocation of £3 million for the rural housing forced the separation of the Rosyth clauses into the Housing No. 2 Act 1914, approved a week before the outbreak of war. The Admiralty's unwillingness to ease the housing shortage at Rosyth had brought strong criticism.[106] In July 1913, Unwin had been appointed to plan a 300-acre [122 hectare] garden village. His layout strung the principal access road around the shallow valley site, with culs-de-sac taken off it.[107] Implementation became inextricably tangled with a Dunfermline Burgh planning scheme. Eventually a government-funded public-utility housing society, later known as the Scottish National Housing Company, undertook construction. The remainder of the Bill was modified, with powers valid for only a year. The two 1914 Housing Acts were overtaken by circumstances but they represented a precedent for an interventionist strategy of housing provision, followed through both during and after the war.

'Mr. Unwin at the L.G.B.'

After the outbreak of war the housing and town-planning branch of the Local Government Board initially operated normally. The Ruislip–Northwood scheme moved slowly to final approval and the Board continued to advise local authorities. Following Adams' departure for Canada in October 1914, George Lionel Pepler (1882–1959), later to be one of the most persuasive influences in the spread of statutory planning, was recruited for the Arterial Road conferences and planning in Greater London. In December 1914, at the age of fifty-one, Raymond Unwin was appointed as the Board's Chief Town Planning Inspector. Herbert Samuel, who had succeeded Burns, later claimed credit for recognizing that 'Raymond Unwin was the best man for the job' (Unwin, 1937d, p. 588). *Garden Cities and Town Planning* jubilantly proclaimed:

> It is difficult to express the debt which both the garden city movement and town planning owe to Mr. Unwin. It is largely due to his influence and example that town-planning in this country is proceeding on sane lines and has been saved from either mediaeval rectilinearity or grandiose flamboyance. The worship of the letter to the killing of the spirit which has characterised the German school, has been supplanted by the sweet reasonableness of the British school, and it is certain that this country must now take the lead in town-planning. (Mr. Unwin of the Local Government Board, 1914, pp. 208–9)

Chauvinistic hyperbole aside, was Unwin's 'sweet reasonableness' enough to advance the cause and quality of town-planning? Hitherto he had provided a practical examplar: henceforth he would work as a relatively anonymous civil servant. He would monitor local-authority initiative and evaluate proposals and progress, an administrative role

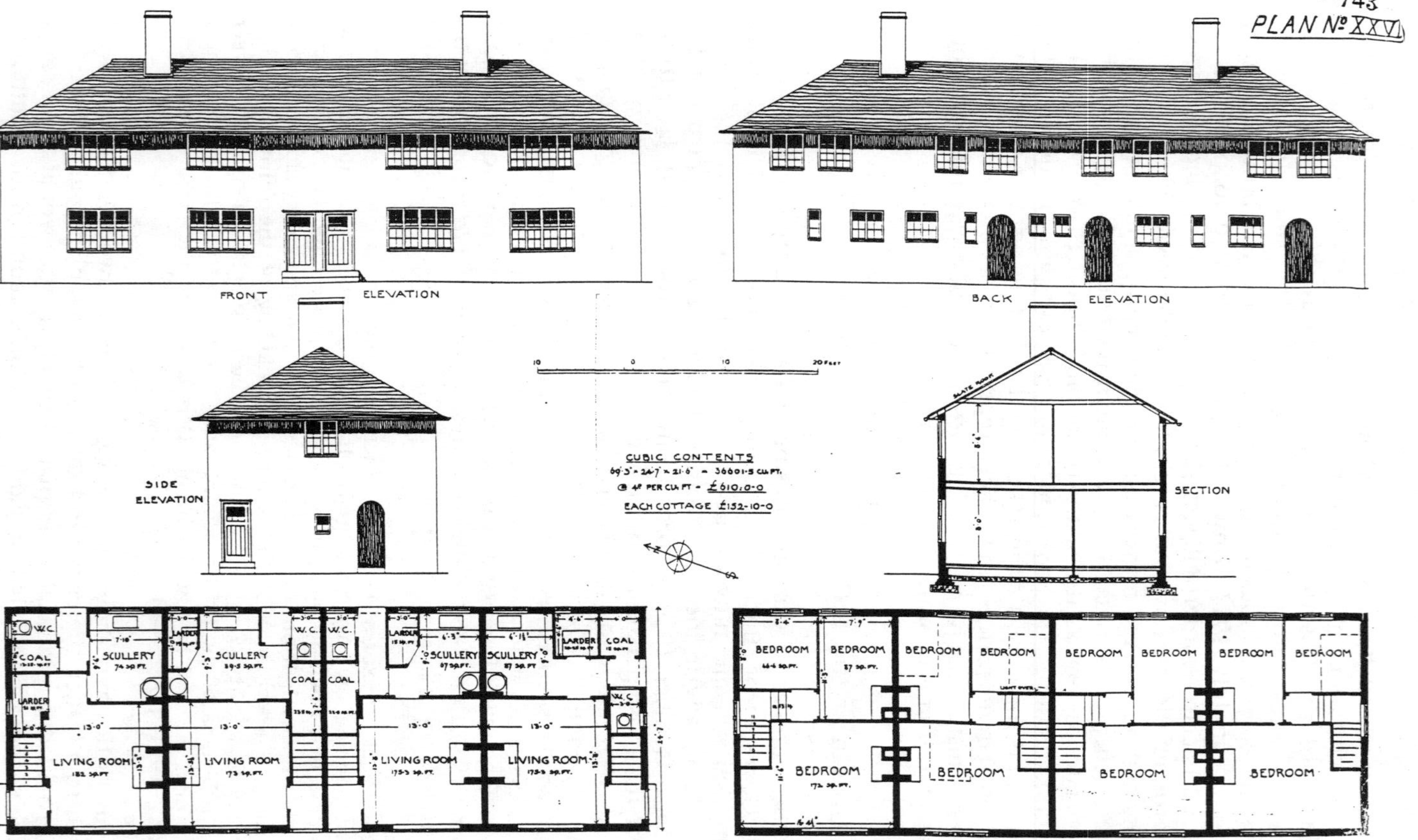

Figure 56 The rational house from the *Smallholdings Buildings Report*, 1913. This plain design, with its unbroken hipped roof, was used at Gretna and became a standard feature of many interwar council estates

that he fulfilled with characteristic efficiency but which presented few opportunities for the creative spark. His daughter recalled that financial necessity played a part in his decision:

> he wasn't making all that much money before 1914 and when war came there was a complete shutdown of private practice. He could have gone back, but by then [in 1919] he had become intrigued with the problems of government and proved himself a very able administrator.[108]

Unwin served the planning inspectorate until the summer of 1915, busy with Local Inquiries for the Hale, Wrexham, Colne, Birmingham South, Stetchford and North Yardley (Birmingham), Mansfield and Nottingham schemes.[109] He recommended modifications including the incorporation of additional land, the preservation of open space and greater cooperation with neighbouring authorities. Stetchford and North Yardley was the most complex. Unwin's 116-page report included the assessment of leading evidence from Neville Chamberlain (1869–1940), then Chairman of the Birmingham City Town Planning Committee. 1915 was the peak year for preparation of schemes under the 1909 Act, with a total of 49 authorized, in preparation or adopted, covering a total of 77,202 acres [30,880 hectares]. The momentum fell away rapidly and work of immediate national importance had been found to deploy Unwin's energies and coordinating skills to the full.

Dublin and Sao Paulo

In spite of the war Unwin was involved in planning outside the English mainland during 1914–16. At the time of his visits, Ireland was still an integral part of the United Kingdom. The brief Brazilian consultancy was an indication of the extensive international currency of Garden City design standards. In 1912, Unwin had been considered as a possible consultant for the Imperial capital of India, New Delhi (Irving, 1981, p. 40). Lutyens was appointed and his work extended over eighteen years, representing a milestone in formal civic design. It is difficult to believe that Unwin would have sympathetically responded to the task.

Geddes drew Irish attention to *Nothing Gained by Overcrowding* in his evidence to the Dublin Housing Inquiry in 1913. In the spring of 1914, Unwin visited Dublin to lecture on 'How Town Planning may solve the Housing Problem', urging citizens to 'learn to take the comprehensive view', fostering civic pride simultaneously with shame for the slums. Geddes organized a Civic Exhibition from 17 July–15 August, a charade played out against Home Rule agitation and the worsening international crisis. Geddes had persuaded the Viceroy, Lord Aberdeen, to offer a £500 premium for a Dublin Town Plan competition. The Citizens' Housing League urged the City Corporation to invite

Geddes and Unwin to comment on their housing and slum-clearance proposals. On 25–6 August they met city officials and toured the inner areas' suburban fringes (Miller, 1985, pp. 263–7).

Their joint report was forwarded from 'Wyldes' on 26 September.[110] The 'inner city' material reflected concern for conservative surgery and rehabilitation of housing: Geddes' daughter, Norah, was working with the Women's National Health Association in Dublin. Unwin was concerned with the wider application of Garden City principles, as in *Nothing Gained by Overcrowding*, and urged the Dublin Corporation to:

> acquire land on the outskirts . . . and build . . . garden suburbs of adequate size to support their own social life, recreation and culture.

'The Garden City Principle applied to Suburbs' had been the manifestation of Unwin's regional–strategic view. It was the concept subsequently filled out in detail in Abercrombie's winning Dublin City Plan.

A site at Marino, on the north-western outskirts, appeared to be 'second to none in Dublin . . . on grounds of accessibility, economy and beauty alike'. Unwin, Geddes and F. C. Mears planned the 96-acre [38.4-hectare] site, with 1,100 houses, 11.5 to the acre [4.5 to the hectare]. Trees and natural features were preserved. The layout was palpably Unwin's, incorporating a differentiated road network with 'green paths' for a kind of proto-Radburn pedestrian circulation. A formal approach led from Fairview Road, opposite a large park to be laid out on land reclaimed from Dublin Bay. A long central axis led into the estate through a hexagonal circus, a feature found at Hampstead Garden Suburb that recurred at Jardim–America. The central feature was a long, narrow green, 800 by 150 ft., flanked by tree-lined avenues and paths. The housing blocks were laid as a distorted grid, derived from the diagrams in *Nothing Gained by Overcrowding*. Double and quadruple blocks were indicated, the latter with a central school site. The housing superblock had virtually arrived.[111]

Marino was developed but the plan was totally altered. The first official Corporation layout, prepared in 1919 by H. T. O'Rourke, the Dublin City Architect, retained the axial theme but took a more restricted site and was realigned to require demolition of Marino House, a masterpiece of Irish–Georgian architecture. The final, mid-1920s plan for an extended area had a grandiose geometrical layout, with a central circular recreation ground and branching culs-de-sac.

The Unwin–Geddes report reproduced housing standards from the Rural Labourers' Cottages Report. Unwin also recast the City Architect's scheme for Fairbrothers' Fields following the principles of *Nothing Gained*, incorporating Dublin land and road costs. The remainder of the report dealt with civic design and urban renewal, with suggestions later taken up by Abercrombie and the Kellys. The report was a mixture based on the authors' individual experience and a brief survey.

Much of it was critically received by the Corporation: the City Architect felt that 'a typical example of the English Garden Suburb' would prove 'thoroughly impractical within the congested area of a large city'. Nevertheless, the Royal Institute of the Architects of Ireland (RIAI) and the Civics Institute commended the proposals. The subsequent appointment of O'Rourke as City Architect assisted the acceptance of Garden-City standards.

In 1916, Unwin returned to Dublin (Miller, 1985, pp. 282–96). The destruction of Lower Sackville Street (O'Connell Street) during the Easter uprising had brought confusion over responsibility for rebuilding a principal commercial thoroughfare, dominated by the handsome Georgian Post Office where the insurgence began. The professional bodies were keen to ensure that the opportunity for civic enhancement was not lost. The RIAI pressed for legislation for land acquisition, civic improvement and strict design control, following the precedent of the German *Lex Adickes*. The Fire and Property Losses Association, the owners and lessees, wished to rebuild as quickly and cheaply as possible, with any embellishment funded from the public purse. The Dublin Corporation was caught in the middle, seemingly unwilling to take decisive action.

The Home Secretary, Herbert Samuel, promised legislation to bridge the gap between the opposing factions and provide some public finance for a visually satisfactory construction. On 2 August 1916, the Dublin (Emergency Provisions) Bill was introduced in the House of Commons. A heated debate by Irish MP's over the second reading caused suspension of the session. Speculation on the identity of 'the King's High Planner' was rife. It was confirmed that Unwin would negotiate with the Corporation and other parties to secure agreement on amendments to the legislation. The major points of contention were in Section 2 of the Bill, empowering the Dublin Corporation to control design through bye-laws and Section 4, with its compulsory-purchase provisions.[112]

In August 1916, Dublin Corporation invited the RIAI President, Caulfield Orpen, Kaye Parry of the Civics Institute, the City Architect and Professor Unwin (*sic*) to attempt to overcome the deadlock. The negotiations were probably conducted 'off the record'. However, Unwin's cousin, Christy Booth, resident in Dublin at the time, remembered arriving at the Royal Hibernian Hotel to meet him for luncheon. Orpen informed her that a stormy meeting was in progress, then returned at 4.00 p.m. observing, 'Just now they were at each other's throats, but now he has them eating out of his hands', a vivid evocation of Unwin's persuasive 'sweet reasonableness'.[113]

The City Architect was empowered to 'require reasonable alterations to be made in regard to the design [of buildings] and materials to be used' in the reconstruction of Lower Sackville Street. Uniform, imposed elevations were rejected but the harmony of a Georgian style advocated.[114] Announcement of agreement was made at a Civics Institute luncheon, held in Unwin's honour on 18 November when civic and professional leaders vied with each other to emphasize arrival at 'a point of agreement which they had never dreamt of, by the intervention of Mr. Unwin'.[115] Unwin also lectured on 'The Replanning of Dublin', warmly commending the Abercrombie–Kelly proposals and urging detailed study and discussion, for 'only by such means can the citizens obtain a complete grasp of the problems, and give their representatives a national [*sic*] mandate to go forward'.[116]

The compromise agreement was incorporated in the Dublin Reconstruction (Emergency Provisions) Act, 1916.[117] A development control system was created, which gave the City Architect a month to achieve 'reasonable alterations' to design, building line or materials. Arbitration could take into account the additional costs incurred by the City Architect's requirements, under approved public funding, towards the expense incurred through meeting the 'public interest' safeguarding of visual amenity. The Act was criticized as being too limited,[118] and the rebuilding it achieved was undistinguished. Although design intervention was recognized in mainland planning, the concept of providing 'amenity' funding for higher standards did not find favour.

In 1916, Unwin was commissioned to provide a layout for Jardim–America, a garden suburb to the west of the rapidly expanding Brazilian provincial capital, Sao Paulo. Its Director of Public Works, Dr Victor da Silva Freire, had visited Letchworth and Hampstead. The City Improvement and Freehold Land Company had acquired a 240-acre [96-hectare] site adjoining the grid layout of an earlier town extension. The requirement for 50 ft. [15 m.] streets ruled out the visual intimacy of Letchworth and Hampstead. Unwin added diagonals and a few curved streets to break the grid. He widened the central Avenida Brazil to form a boulevard, crossing diagonals in a central hexagonal circus recalling Sollershott and Crickmer Circuses at Letchworth and Hampstead. Subsidiary curved streets helped to minimize traffic short-cuts. Block centres included open spaces. The development included very low-density, largely detached houses on generous plots.[119] Unwin was unable to travel to Brazil, but, in January 1917, Barry Parker arrived for a two-year sojourn, during which period he developed the layout, designed many individual houses and gave advice on the planned extension of Sao Paulo and other Brazilian cities (Parker, 1919, pp. 143–51).

The Ministry of Munitions' housing initiative

It is ironic that a major housing initiative resulted from problems associated with munition production and supply during a war of attrition.[120] The enterprise was linked to the political ascendancy of David Lloyd George (1863–1945). Existing plants were located where a vast influx of workers would exacerbate overcrowding, or, for strategic reasons, were developed in remote areas, which lacked infrastructure.

The Well Hall Estate at Eltham, on the south-east fringe of Greater London, was the first to be built, to provide accommodation for the increased workforce at the Woolwich Arsenal (Culpin, 1917; Beaufoy, 1950). The 1,200 houses and flats were designed in ten days in January 1915 in the Office of Works under the direction of Frank Baines (1879–1933), who subsequently served on the Tudor Walters Committee. Designed in haste and quickly built, its image stressed permanence. The cottage groupings and the wilfully informal road layout evoked the composed street pictures and spatial enclosures illustrated by Charles Wade in *Town Planning in Practice*. Unwin's moves to endorse more formal and rational layouts of housing design had probably led him beyond picturesque over-indulgence, however accomplished. Pepler approved the plans on behalf of the LGB. The estate was an expensive undertaking, with costs of up to £1,000 per dwelling, three times 1914 prices. Subsequent housing schemes were much simpler.

In 1915, the Prime Minister, Herbert Asquith, appointed a Munitions of War Committee, expanded in the subsequent coalition government as an autonomous Ministry of Munitions under David Lloyd George, with Christopher Addison, Winston Churchill and E. S. Montague as group heads. The new Ministry oversaw all aspects of supply and production of raw materials for, and manufacture of, armaments, including the iron and steel, chemical and engineering sectors. Employment, welfare and housing relating to ordnance factories came under state control. Staff were brought in to man the juggernaut: in July 1915, Raymond Unwin was seconded as Chief Housing Architect to the Explosives Department.[121] Pepler remained at the LGB, but headed a team that undertook munitions work, and private consultants were extensively employed, among them Gordon Allen, W. Curtis Green and Adshead, Abercrombie and Ramsey.

Policy demanded the priority construction of large ordnance factories in remote areas and the expansion of existing plants. The private sector, debilitated by recruitment of its labour, could not respond and the Housing Act 1914 and Defence of the Realm Act 1915 were used as the basis for state action. Unrest in overcrowded Barrow-in-Furness and on Clydeside over expensively rented housing underlined the urgency of the situation. By 1919 the Ministry had secured temporary hostel accommodation for 10,800 workers and had built 2,800 temporary cottages and 10,800 permanent houses on 38 widely scattered sites, with canteens, social halls, shops and churches to serve the major schemes.

Unwin set to work with vigour. His daughter recalled him:

> as concerned as the next man about winning the war, and I think glad to feel he could help in that direction by doing what he knew and did well . . . He was . . . very concerned about what would happen after the war, at home and in international affairs. But he did not share mother's pacifist attitude. He did feel the war had to be won. Not that she wanted it to be lost, but she found it harder to see any good coming out of any war.[122]

Unwin established a close rapport with Addison, which was to continue through the latter's tenure of the Ministries of Munitions, Reconstruction, and Health. In January 1916, Seebohm Rowntree took control of the Welfare Section (Briggs, 1961, Chapter V). He and Unwin resumed an acquaintance formed at New Earswick, of significance in influencing postwar housing policy.

In June 1915 the Ministry decided to build a vast explosives plant in Dumfriesshire on the Solway Firth, divided into nitro-glycerine production at Dornock, a cordite plant at Mossband and magazine production at Longtown. Townships were to be built at Gretna and Eastriggs and temporary billets requisitioned at Carlisle (Addision, 1925, pp. 154–5). Layouts were prepared under Unwin's direction and he made frequent site visits. The Gretna site lay to the south-west of the old village on the Carlisle–Glasgow road and sloped gently to the Solway. South of the east–west Annan road, a grid layout served temporary hutments. Construction exhausted precious timber supplies; brick structures, some built as hostels but ultimately convertible into permanent homes, became the norm.[123] The major axis of the plan, Central Avenue, aligned on the tower of Gretna Green church, was projected southwards to command a distant view of Skiddaw, one of the major peaks in the Lake District. On a site visit Unwin checked the line and to the consternation of the surveyors, asked them to correct it. It was, they groused, the first day in three months that it had been possible to see that far![124]

Central Avenue, the main approach from the station, included shops, cinema and an institute (*see* Figure 57). The precise, economical Georgian style became a model for interwar suburban centres. Civic design was achieved through projection and recession of the building lines, producing a series of subsidiary spaces off the main axial vista. A more spacious *place* was envisaged at the junction of Annan Road and Central Avenue, with enclosure across the minor axis after the manner of the junction of Heathgate and Meadway at Hampstead Garden Suburb. North of Annan Road there was permanent housing. Central Avenue split to form an impressive boulevard with a central grassed reservation; it was ultimately intended to be projected northwards to the site of a new station on the Carlisle to Dumfries railway. The northern-sector layout balanced formal and informal elements. Linked housing groups and greens opened off the curving Victory Avenue, which led from Annan Road to a more formally composed *place* in front of the Roman Catholic church.

Courtenay Crickmer from Letchworth was resident site architect, leading a team which included Geoffry Lucas, Evelyn Simmons and F. C. Bowers. Early buildings incorporated the roughcast walls and picturesque dormers of Letchworth, but later groups pioneered the simplified 'people's Georgian', with brick walls, sash windows and low-pitched, hipped, slated roofs (*see* Figure 58). Linking walls and outbuildings created a pleasant ensemble, made more familiar through the 1919 *Housing Manual*. The Gretna school, with its large, airy

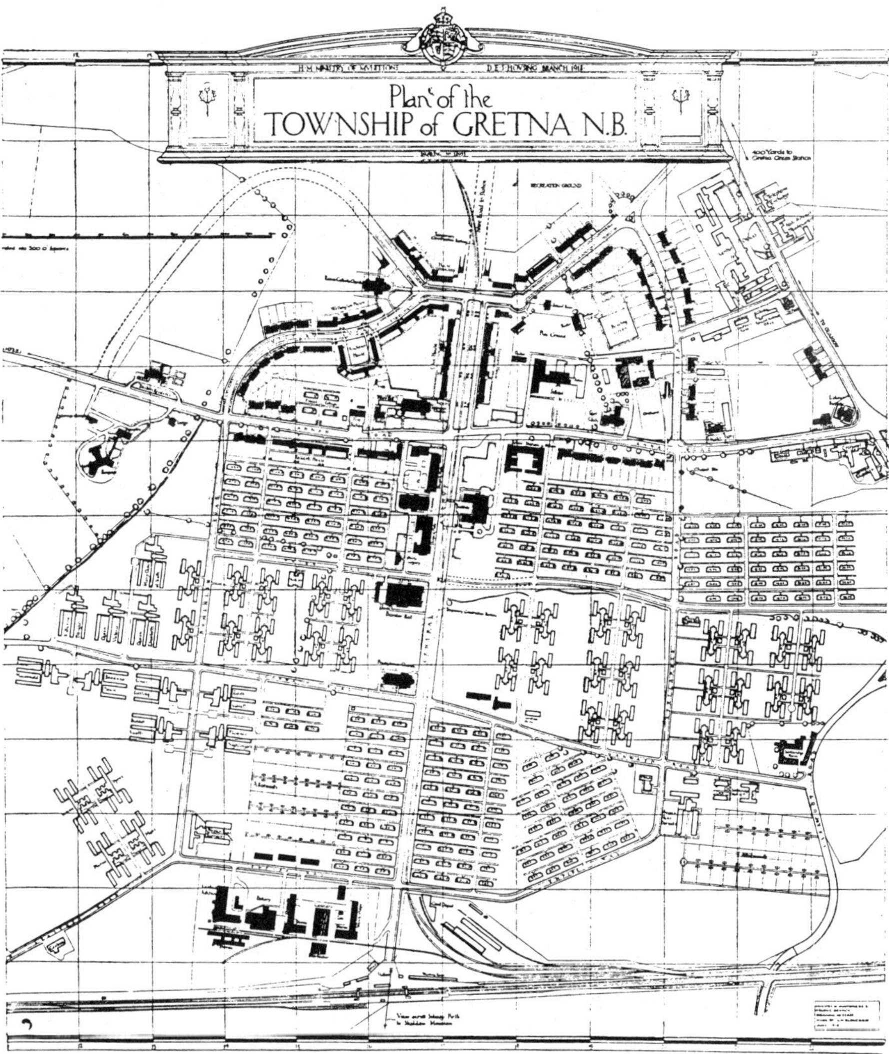

Figure 57 The Gretna layout, 1915–16. The major unifying element was the central axis, around which Unwin created a visually varied village centre with diverse community buildings

Figure 58 Gretna housing types, 1916–18 (Cruse collection): a) The staff residences designed by Courtenay Crickmer, reiterated the dominant stair tower from his Letchworth designs; b) The Girls' Houses, convertible to family dwellings, in which the tranisition to the 'peoples Georgian' of the *Housing Manual*, 1919, is readily apparent

classrooms and generous windows, was clearly modelled on Unwin's New Earswick design. The three churches were the most impressive individual buildings: notwithstanding his agnosticism Unwin had lobbied hard to obtain funds for permanent structures.[125]

Gretna comprised 427 timber huts, 47 timber hostels, 127 brick houses and 12 brick hostels. There was a vast canteen, serving 17,000 meals daily. Eastriggs lay 4½ miles westward and was slightly smaller, with a higher ratio of permanent buildings – 165 temporary cottages, 16 temporary hostels, 160 brick houses and 17 brick hostels.[126,127] The township occupied the site of an old farmstead and Unwin's layout preserved an existing tree-lined avenue. The overall character was more fragmented than Gretna and there were fewer communal buldings.

The Explosives Department also developed Mancot Royal, Queensferry, a site on Deeside 4 miles west of Chester. The layout represented Unwin's more rational approach, with a varied grid incorporating existing hedges and trees. The central offset road junction, with its small central green and fourfold focal points, represented the modified 'turbine plaza' developed from Sitte. Ewart Culpin felt that:

> in many respects this plan is the most satisfying [of the munitions communities]. It is simple and direct, the setbacks in the groups of cottages along the main roads are effective and there is an appropriate degree of dignity maintained in the general expression.[128]

At Mancot there were 191 brick cottages to only 6 convertible hostels. The simplified Georgian style was used throughout.

The wartime munitions communities attracted international acclaim. Due to censorship, it was not until late 1918 that the achievements could be appreciated on the home front. Unwin and Crickmer collaborated with Thomas Adams over the publication of Gretna in Canada. Adams commended:

> the policy of developing new model communities which will help to win the war by making labour more effective, and help to reconstruct Britain after the war as a result of broad vision and the exercise of prescience during the war. (Adams, 1918, p. 33)

The impact in the United States was direct. In 1917 Culpin had sent photographs of Well Hall, Gretna, Eastriggs and Mancot to the American Institute of Architects, who despatched Frederick Lee Ackerman, an observer of British housing and planning since the 1901 Bournville Conference. His articles stimulated the Federal government to appropriate funds for housing schemes to be constructed by the United States Housing Corporation and the Housing Division of the Emergency Fleet Corporation. Yorkship, New Jersey, Hilton, Virginia and Atlantic Heights, New Hampshire, begun in 1917–18, all bore traces of their transatlantic precedents. Unwin was well aware of their development and appears to have undertaken an unspecified 'mission' to the United States in the summer of 1918.[129]

9

Housing for Heroes

Planning for reconstruction

Unwin's general influence on post-1919 housing has long been recognized, but his role alongside the policy-makers has been difficult to establish, notwithstanding his prominence on the Tudor Walters Committee. In fact, his prescription of housing standards from the turn of the century onwards, already described, prepared the ground for involvement with Seebohm Rowntree on the work of the Housing Panel and was arguably decisive in gaining acceptance of the new standards for post-1919 housing – and, moreover, predated Tudor Walters.

The concept of a bold state initiative for postwar reconstruction assumed prominence from March 1916 (Johnson, 1968; Orbach, 1977; Swenarton, 1981). Herbert Asquith convened a committee to study the rebuilding of a peacetime economy, with housing and public works as key elements. On 20 April the National Housing and Town Planning Council urged the LGB to declare a commitment to excellence in housing standards.[130] The Reconstruction Committee began to formulate a housing policy in June 1916. As Johnson observed in his classic account of the Reconstruction movement:

> If there was one moment when official planning turned the corner from minimal to maximal goals, this was it. Henceforth no mere restoration, no efficient but conventional process of demobilization would pass for true fulfilment. The slogan 'Homes for Heroes' was still to be invented but after June 1916 housing and reconstruction were linked. (Johnson, 1968, p. 18)

The Committee identified interlinked topics: the numerical deficiency as the basis for a public programme; dwelling type and accommodation; density and estate layout; constructional standards; the development agency; and financial inducements. On 30 November, Vaughan Nash, Secretary to the Reconstruction Committee, outlined a confidential draft programme in 'The Housing Question'.[131] He estimated that a wartime housing deficit of 150,000 would reach 200,000 by the end of 1917 and 70,000 working-class houses would subsequently be required annually. Private enterprise would not meet this need. The LGB proposed a

Treasury grant to cover the increased cost assessed as resulting from wartime conditions. Under an agreement between the LGB and the Ministry of Munitions, such grants had fluctuated between 35 and 70 per cent. Assistance would only last while 'abnormal' conditions prevailed. Expenditure would be heavy. Based on wildly optimistic assumptions of a 20 per cent grant and a £500 dwelling cost, £12 million would be required to make good the deficit, with £4.2 million annually to sustain the programme in England and Wales.

A firm programme was formulated as planning for reconstruction gathered momentum from February 1917 under the Premiership of David Lloyd George. He sought 'persons with ideas' to grasp an opportunity unparalleled 'even by the French Revolution' (Webb, 1952, p. 82). Sectional panels of the Reconstruction Committee were convened for Education, Control of Industry, Wages and Employment, and Housing and Local Government. The Fourth Marquis of Salisbury (1861–1947), a past-President of the Garden Cities and Town Planning Association, took charge of Housing. His group included John Hills and Leslie Scott, both progressive Conservatives, the latter to win distinction through involvement with rural housing and land acquisition; Thomas Jones, deputy secretary of the War Cabinet; Seebohm Rowntree and Beatrice Webb. The group was hyperactive. Members lobbied for the adoption of their hobby-horses, creating difficulty for securing overall co-ordination. However, consistent progress was made. Although Beatrice Webb saw Rowntree as 'more a philanthropist than a capitalist . . . eager to spend his time and money in working up special subjects . . . [but] too modest and hesitating in opinion to lead' (Webb, 1952, pp. 86–7), his work largely shaped the group's conclusions, which had been discussed informally with Unwin beforehand. Unwin was able to draw on his Munitions experience to provide information on labour, materials and cost. Although not a member, he was party to and in many respects a shaper of the panel's policies.

The panel's first meeting on 19 April 1917 shaped its future course. Rowntree was requested to prepare a memorandum, tabled on 8 May,[132] which contained the elements of the report presented in October to Christopher Addison who had succeded as Minister of Reconstruction. The housing deficit in England and Wales at the end of 1917 was estimated as 175,000, with a subsequent annual requirement for 75,000. Ending the war in 1918 would bring an immediate need for 250,000 houses, plus 50,000 in rural areas: 300,000 overall, eventually accepted as the target. Rowntree stressed that:

> It is of supreme importance that the plans for the erection of the required houses should be ready by the time that the War ends: it follows therefore that any measures proposed should be readily agreed to by Parliament.

The logic was incontrovertible. Rowntree recommended the creation of a professionally skilled Housing Board, investigation of standard designs and materials requisition. He proposed state-aided construction, but local-authority ownership of the completed housing. The cost would be 50 per cent above prewar levels and the grant might reach £25 million. A 'dual valuation' was suggested, at the initial 'inflated' level and three years later for a 'normal' figure to be paid by the local authority. Salisbury warmly endorsed the proposals and sent a copy to Viscount Rhondda, President of the LGB. As Briggs recorded, Rowntree:

> saw far beyond the public health aspect of housing policy, the professional nineteenth century pre-supposition of housing reformers, to housing as a 'social service'. (Briggs, 1961, pp. 137–8)

Rhondda requested consideration of a new, enlarged Ministry – a 'Ministry of Health'.[133] Christopher Addison subsequently became its first incumbent.

Unwin assisted Rowntree, citing as precedents the Ministry of Munitions' negotiation of agreements with local authorities. He and Rowntree proposed Regional Commissioners, to liaise between local authorities and the Ministry and advise on land acquisition, town planning and transportation.[134] Rowntree combined 'the advantages of state direction and control, with those which come from a large measure of decentralisation' and thought that the Commissioners might organize construction. Unwin stressed local responsibility:

> I think it is very important to maintain small units of autonomy and cultivate a definite local community feeling . . . As compared with transit, water supply etc., the actual building of cottages, however, is a matter rather of filling in the details of a big scheme, and I am inclined to favour the development and encouragement of small units for handling this detail problem . . . There is no doubt that all these things interlock, the one with the other, and in essence, that all form part of the complete subject of town planning, which really should include the whole organisation and disposition of the services and other provision for aggregations of population.[135]

Unwin visualized a regional strategic approach, with local authorities guided towards fulfilment. The system did not work well and was abandoned in the retrenchment of 1921. Unwin's comments hinted of a later examination of population and resource distribution at national level, which culminated in the work of the Barlow Commission.

Unwin also proposed an 'Emergency Housing and Town Planning Department'. Under the Director would be a Chief Technical Officer, with responsibility for the preparation of model plans, passing local authority housing schemes and estimates and supervision of the Regional Commissioners who would ascertain the housing requirement, vet plans and estimates for confirmation by the central department and give town-planning advice. A Chief Administrative Officer would coordinate a central-supply department and legal matters, supervise construction and certify payments.[136] Much of this structure was created within the Ministry of Health in 1919, with Unwin taking the key role of Chief Housing Architect.

The Tudor Walters Committee

Rowntree and Unwin considered the systematic research of 'methods of construction, choice of materials, purchase and distribution, and economies in building construction'. With the size of the programme 'an economy of even a few pounds per cottage would result in a large total saving', with further benefits through standardization. It was imperative to recognize the challenge of:

> novel materials and methods of building . . . which need scientific investigation to prove their durability, to define the scale limits of their use . . . before they can be recommended . . . It was thought that the Industrial Research Committee would carry out investigation of points put to them by the proposed Committee.[137]

The Committee, to which Unwin referred, was to undertake a comprehensive study of housing under the guidance of the LGB. Its eight members would include an architect, a builder, an engineer and an industrial chemist. On 14 June 1917, Rowntree wrote to Sir Horace Munro at the LGB to urge its President, Viscount Rhondda, to appoint the Committee without delay, adding 'I think Unwin would make an excellent Chairman'.[138] On 26 July, Rhondda's successor, Hayes Fisher, appointed Sir John Tudor Walters (1868–1933), a Liberal MP, Chairman of the London Housing Board and a Director of the Hampstead Garden Suburb Trust, as Chairman of the Committee. Their brief was:

> to consider questions of building construction in connection with the provision of dwellings for the working-classes in England, Wales and Scotland, and [to] report upon the methods of securing economy and despatch in the provision of such dwellings. (Tudor Walters, 1918)

Membership included three architects: in addition to Unwin, Frank Baines of the War Office and Sir Aston Webb, distiguished past-President of the RIBA. Most of the Committee's papers appear to have been destroyed.[139] A few surviving papers include a draft by Unwin proposing a fourfold subdivision of the subject, indicative of his leading role in its work:

1) Materials and supply, which would work closely with the Ministry of Reconstruction;
2) Construction, which would consider innovative techniques and work closely with the Industrial Research Committee;
3) Organisation and Labour, which would deal with the reorganisation of the building industry during the transition to normality; and a
4) Plans committee, which would cover both house plans and layout, and ascertain whether standardised plans might be appropriate.[140]

It was a comprehensive brief, posing questions left unanswered; yet a remarkable amount was achieved in a comparatively short time, reflecting commitment from all involved. Unwin proposed the detailed investigation of eight standard dwelling types, all three-bedroomed, with parlour and non-parlour variants; he collaborated with Rowntree over calculating the quantities of materials required for the construction of 500,000 dwellings.

The Committee held 26 full meetings, 39 sub-committee meetings, examined 150 expert witnesses, and analysed copious written submissions (Tudors Walters, 1918, para.1). The *Report*, published in October 1918, contained the most comprehensive analysis of working-class housing, but the War Cabinet had still not settled the financial arrangements. Many of the witnesses had experience of Garden-City housing, including Adshead, Crickmer and Alwyn Lloyd. Lloyd had assisted Unwin at 'Wyldes' before involvement with Welsh co-partnership housing. Seebohm Rowntree doubtless gave testimony about New Earswick, while W. J. Swain would have referred to the experimental concrete cottages there. A. S. Barnes of the Department of Scientific and Industrial Research (DSIR) had already invited Unwin's collaboration over the development of experimental building science. The LCC Architect, W. E. Riley (1852–1937), had gained more experience of council housing than any other. Building contractors, manufacturers, trade-union officials, public health inspectors and housing-association managers made individual appearances.

The fifteen-month working period of the Tudor Walters Committee was marked by a growing rift between Hayes Fisher, whose department was responsible for housing, and Christopher Addison, Minister of Reconstruction from July 1917. Addison, progressive in outlook, regarded the Housing Panel as a valuable ally in advocating a radical new state-aided housing initiative. With Unwin influential over the Tudor Walters Committee, and maintaining fruitful contact with Rowntree, it was likely that the *Report* would contain a bold prescription. By contrast, Fisher personified the 'poor law' image of the LGB, with his cautious, non-committal attitude to housing. The LGB ignored the Housing Panel Memorandum drafted by Rowntree. The LGB had written to local authorities and, despite an incomplete response, Fisher claimed that a total of 100,000–150,000 houses would suffice. He disagreed fundamentally that 'the new schemes [should] be models for imitation by future builders', adding that density limitation would involve 'increased cost, not only in land purchase, but also . . . in streets, drains, water mains etc.'. Addison's riposte was clearly based on *Nothing Gained by Overcrowding*:

> The opinion of competent town-planning authorities does not agree . . . that the limitation of the number of houses to the acre involves increased cost in streets . . . The opportunity . . . of raising the standard both in design and layout of the houses must not be lost.[141]

Fisher's obduracy persisted through the winter of 1917–18. After a stormy meeting, Addison referred to the LGB thinking 'they can do a job sixty times greater than before on the existing staff of "three men and a boy''' (Addison, 1925, II, p. 216). The Tudor Walters *Report* was complete by the spring of 1918 but publication was delayed. The Board sponsored a Cottage Design Competition in association with the RIBA.[142] Most of the entries reflected the picturesque individuality of early Garden-City architecture, rather than the contemporary rationalized approach. Confusion was created after the announcement of the winning entries in April 1918 and the Board refused to clarify their status.

Unwin's position was difficult. Evidently *persona grata* with Fisher, to the extent of appointment to the Tudor Walters Committee, he had steered its work towards the Housing Panel's ambitious programmes, allied to Garden-City housing standards, albeit that they had been endorsed in the prewar rural housing reports. He had ignored the Board's limited responses, and archaic circulars. Yet his permanent post remained with the Board and his public career might have foundered had not Lloyd George supported the creation of the Ministry of Health.

In May 1918 the Commons requested the publication of the Housing Panel's memorandum, more than a year after Rowntree's first draft. It called for 300,000 houses *to be built during 1918* [author's italics] and concluded:

> Every endeavour should therefore be made to complete the preliminary work such as the choice and acquisition of sites, the layout of the land, the plans of the houses and the specification of materials. (Housing in England and Wales, 1918, para. 49)

Its belated appearance underlined the lack of preparation.

The Tudor Walters *Report*

The Tudor Walters *Report* was published in October 1918, a few weeks before the 11 November Armistice. It represented the most comprehensive statement on low-density housing. Not surprisingly, it affirmed the efficacy of Unwin's work from *Cottage Plans and Common Sense* onwards. It restated the housing need of 500,000. Unwin and Rowntree had worked on that basis. An annual programme of 100,000 new houses would be required once the deficit had been made good (Tudor Walters, 1918, Part I, para. 1). The Committee did not expect the private sector to meet working class needs until building costs had stabilized. Anticipated labour and materials shortages and high costs would require intervention of a powerful executive Central Housing Authority and Regional Commissioners. To alleviate overcrowding, towns were urged to acquire suburban land, provide infrastructure and proceed with simplified town-planning schemes, leasing sites to housing societies and manufacturers for development in accord with the overall guiding principles. The suburban focus of the 1909 Act, rather than Garden-City or Satellite development, was confirmed as the model for the majority of schemes. Sites were to be selected with convenient access to local employment and estates were to include social, educational, religious and recreational facilities. Natural features would be incorporated into layouts, attaining individuality and a marginal element of beauty:

> To be content merely with satisfying the utilitarian ends . . . would be false economy. The care and thought which are required to secure economical provision . . . may at the same time make of the necessary parts of the plan a coherent design, grouped round some central idea and preserving any existing views and features of interest and beauty, within the limits prescribed by convenience and due economy. By so planning the lines of the roads and disposing the spaces and the buildings as to develop the beauty of vista, arrangements and proportion, an attractiveness may be added to the dwellings at little or no extra cost, which we consider should not only not be omitted, but should be regarded as essential to true economy. (Tudor Walters, 1918, Part V, para. 57)

The authorship of such passages is as evident as if they had appeared under Unwin's name.

The Committee endorsed densities of 12 dwellings per acre [4.8 per hectare] for urban schemes, and 8 per acre [3.2 per hectare] for rural. Road widths would be proportional to anticipated traffic levels. Rising expectations over the sixty-year life of the housing would justify the inclusion of a parlour wherever possible. Three bedrooms were to be well-nigh universal. Type plans illustrated both parlour and non-parlour houses, some derived from Hampstead and Letchworth,[143] with a distinction between those where cooking took place in the living-room and those with the cooker in an improved scullery. Frontages ranged from 16ft. 4in. [5 m.] to 27ft. 9in. [8.5 m.]. The relationship of parts was the key to a successful plan (*see* Figure 59) (Tudor Walters, 1918, Part VI, paras. 98–140).

> The total space which can be provided in a cottage is so small that it is of paramount importance that the whole of it should be put to the best possible use, and that it should be allotted to the different rooms and parts according to the degree of importance which each may serve in the general life of the family. (Tudor Walters, 1918, para. 143)

'Desirable minimum sizes of rooms' were reproduced from the Rural Cottages Report and set 180 sq. ft. [18 sq.m.] living-rooms, 120 sq. ft. [12 sq.m.] for parlours, 80 sq. ft. [8 sq.m.] for sculleries and 150 [15], 100 [10] and 65 sq.ft. [6.5 sq.m.] for bedrooms in non-parlour house types. The text stressed that 'the effective size of a room cannot be judged solely by its floor area'. Total floor areas ranged from 766 sq.ft. [76 sq.m.] for the minimum three-bedroom, non-parlour house illustrated, to 1,150 sq. ft. [115 sq.m.] for the largest three-bedroom parlour type.

Economy of planning produced simplicity of form, with low-pitched hipped roofs, unbroken by dormers, as on the diagrams illustrating grouping principles. No elevational details were included. Flat-roofed

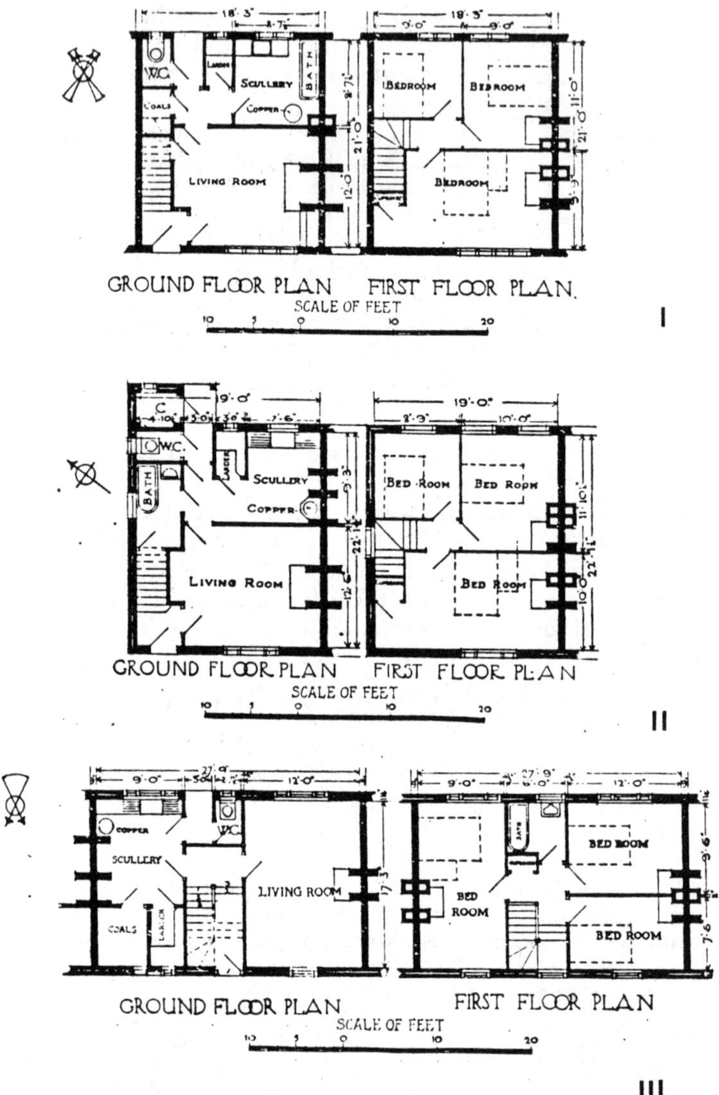

Figure 59 Tudor Walters type plans, 1918. Athough the plans and their variants were developed from a list prepared by Unwin in 1917, the report included many types used at Letchworth

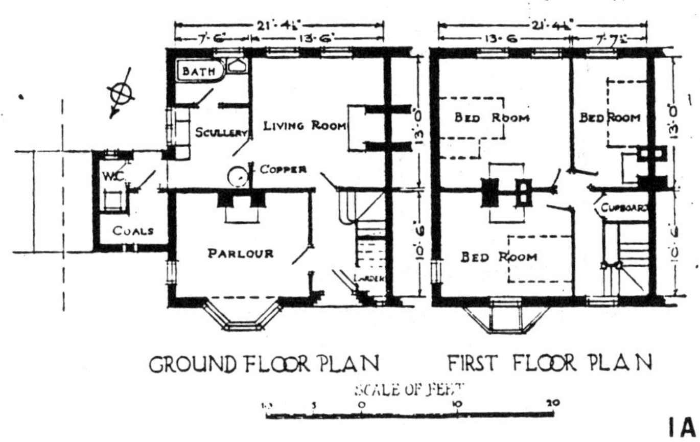
BATH
SCULLERY
LIVING ROOM
W.C.
COPPER
COALS
PARLOUR
LARDER
BED ROOM
BED ROOM
CUPBOARD
BED ROOM
GROUND FLOOR PLAN
FIRST FLOOR PLAN
SCALE OF FEET

IA

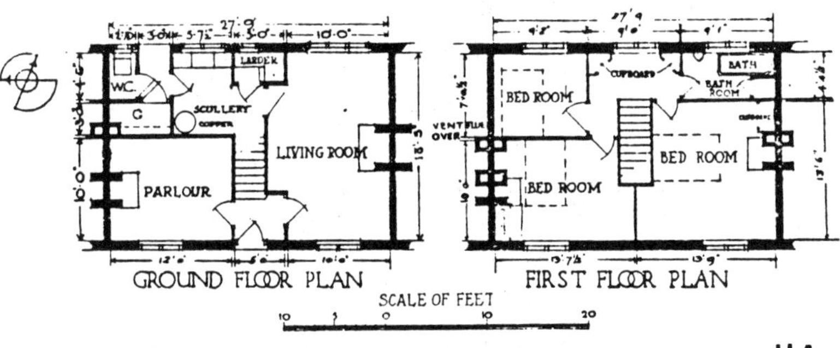
LARDER
W.C.
C
SCULLERY
COPPER
LIVING ROOM
PARLOUR
BED ROOM
CUPBOARD
BATH
BATH ROOM
VENT FLUE OVER
BED ROOM
BED ROOM
GROUND FLOOR PLAN
FIRST FLOOR PLAN
SCALE OF FEET

IIA

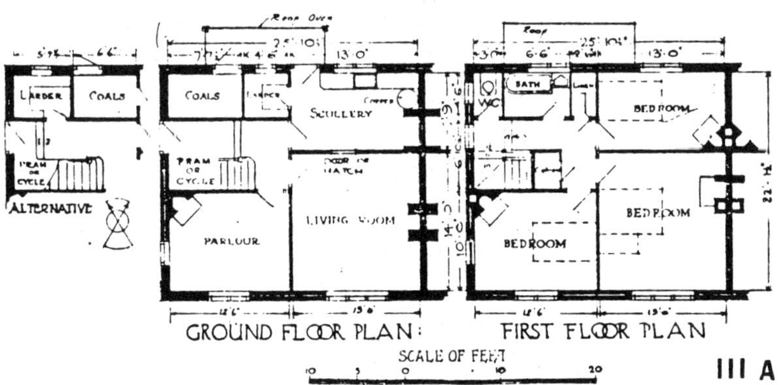
LARDER
COALS
PRAM OR CYCLE
ALTERNATIVE
COALS
SCULLERY
PRAM OR CYCLE
PARLOUR
LIVING ROOM
BATH
W.C.
BED ROOM
BEDROOM
BEDROOM
GROUND FLOOR PLAN
FIRST FLOOR PLAN
SCALE OF FEET

III A

cottages might be judiciously included on urban sites. Site-planning advice followed *Nothing Gained by Overcrowding* and showed simplified groupings around road junctions, village greens and even a complete Unwin layout, prepared for the Glasgow Housing Society though not identified.

The 'rational' approach involved research into every 'component . . . and process concerned with Housebuilding' to secure 'the greatest economy and efficiency'. To eliminate bricklaying (the most expensive walling construction) research into new materials appeared promising and timber substitutes were to be studied. Organization of the munitions factories and motor manufacture influenced advocacy of standardization of elements for assembly into different 'models'. Definition of performance criteria for foundations, walls, floors and roofs paved the way for the work of the Building Research Station. The Committee had examined priority materials allocation and labour. It appeared essential to reorganize the construction industry to eliminate restrictive practices and to introduce management techniques.[144] Finally, the role of the professional designer was underscored by the recommendation that every housing scheme should be architect-designed (Tudor Walters, 1918, para. 349).

The Committee united on a charter for the state provision of enlightened working-class housing. The basic principles of the Tudor Walters *Report* remained unchallenged until publication of the Dudley *Report* (*The Design of Dwellings*, 1944), also a wartime initiative. Only in 1961 did the Parker Morris *Report*, *Homes for Today and Tomorrow*, modify the design approach by substituting family activities for the numerical standards for room sizes. Even this had been anticipated by Unwin in *Cottage Plans and Common Sense* in 1902. The boldness of the Tudor Walters *Report* was widely commended, even by critics.

The Tudor Walters *Report* was followed by two further government reports. In November 1918 the *Report* of the Departmental Committee on Bye-laws, which had begun in 1914, at last appeared (Local Government Board, 1918). Unwin was a member, together with Henry Vivian, leader of the Co-Partnership Tenants. Restrictive bye-laws had long been regarded as an impediment to progressive housing design and layout. Many architects, including Lanchester, Soutar and Sutcliffe, were called. On 21 February 1917, the Ministry of Reconstruction appointed a Women's Sub-Committee on Housing (Ministry of Reconstruction, 1918). They criticized the Munitions housing at Gretna and the prizewinners in the LGB cottage competition. They were also adamant about the separation of cooking from living areas and about the provision of a separate bathroom, both ambivalently treated in the Tudor Walters *Report*.

The uncertain will to build

Political will for action remained uncertain in the late autumn of 1918. In November, Addison introduced the Ministry of Health Bill to create a super-Ministry to take charge of the housing programme. He was invited by Lloyd George to become its first Minister. Sir Aukland Geddes succeeded Hayes Fisher at the LGB: during Geddes' short tenure, Unwin was invited to return. The Armistice of 11 November brought housing to centre stage. Lloyd George called a snap General Election and his campaign pledge of 23 November of 'homes fit for heroes' came to symbolize reconstruction (Orbach, 1988, p. 64). A Ministry of Reconstruction proposal for materials requisition and building licences was defeated, but Geddes' formula for a 'penny rate' limit on the losses that local authorities would incur on their housing schemes was approved (Johnson, 1968, pp. 325–6). This open-ended offer, enacted in 1919, induced local-authority action, but, in the context of escalating building costs, fuelled by lack of control over materials or inessential building, it led to sudden retrenchment in July 1921.

Unwin and Rowntree both voiced their aspirations for the forthcoming housing initiative to which they had contributed so positively. Unwin gave 'Housing: the Architect's Contribution' at the RIBA on 11 December 1918. His quest for rationalization and efficiency had not clouded the personal basis for design (Unwin, 1919c, p. 50):

> If you are seeing the cottagers sitting round their winter evening fire, you cannot through forgetfulness so plan your house that the fireside is a passageway . . . it is not our function to prescribe the mode of life [to] suit the kind of houses we should like to build . . . it is our duty rather to understand the modes of life and the ideas which inspire the people.

The Tudor Walters types were:

> not intended to become stereotyped designs or to be slavishly copied, [rather] to set a minimum standard [to be] improved upon, adapted in each case to the position, the site and form of grouping adopted. (Unwin, 1919c, p. 51)

Tradition was a guide to inherent fitness for purpose in housing design, and, implicitly, for regaining social cohesion:

> In past times a continuous tradition of planning and design was handed down . . . developing with the ever-growing complexity of life . . . admirably adapted to national habits and local conditions. That tradition was rudely broken by the great industrial revolution which was responsible for a hasty urbanisation and the careless wholesale production of cheap hovels for factory hands. It is time for us to take up again that tradition. (Unwin, 1919c, p. 57)

The socialist evangelist re-emerged. William Dunn, H. V. Lanchester and S. B. Russell, all involved with wartime housing, rose to praise Unwin's contribution and commitment to postwar excellence. Russell declared 'for that [Tudor Walters] *Report* Mr Unwin can justly claim chief credit' (Unwin, 1919c, p. 60).

Rowntree spoke on 'Housing after the War' at the Royal Society of Arts. With Adshead's chairmanship and contributions from Henry Aldridge of the National Housing and Town Planning Council and Ewart Culpin of the Garden Cities and Town Planning Association, the event became a forum on housing policy. Rowntree drew upon Land Inquiry and Housing Panel experience and looked to the construction of 325,000 houses in 1919 as a valuable employment generator. His statement that returning soldiers 'will not be put off with vague promises' hinted at growing preoccupation with social unrest. He drew heavily on Unwin's precepts and emphasized:

> It is of supreme importance that full advantage be taken of this unique opportunity. In the past a private builder could put up any house no matter how ugly . . . and lay out his building estate as unwisely as he liked if only he complied with the minimum requirements of local bye-laws . . . But now we have a chance of actually transforming it [housing] in a single year. Let us make the most of this chance. (Rowntree, 1918, p. 71)

For once the staid social analyst was carried away by enthusiasm: he must have known of the impossibility of such a rapid transformation in the context of political uncertainty.

In January 1919 Addison moved to the LGB prior to its reconstitution within the Ministry of Health. He gloomily reported that:

> for all effective purposes we were starting from scratch . . . without Housing Commissioners and without plans prepared or land acquired; without the power to foster the production of materials, and with a financial scheme that contained no penalty upon extravagance. (Addison, 1925, II, p. 216)

In fact Geddes had begun to appoint Commissioners. The Central Directorate was headed by Sir James Carmichael with Unwin and S. B. Russell as joint Chief Architects. The twelve Regional Commissioners included Davidge and F. M. Elgood.

The Housing Act 1919 and the *Housing Manual*

A new Housing and Town Planning Bill was presented to the Commons in the spring of 1919 (Cherry, 1974, pp. 681–4). It incorporated the major recommendations of the Tudor Walters Committee and established the provision of working-class housing as a statutory duty of local authorities, aided by the state. Although envisaged as a temporary expedient, the principle of local-authority provision of housing for those unable to obtain it in the market place endured for sixty years.

Local authorities were required to prepare programmes based on their assessment of need, to be financed through long-term loans and state subsidies on the 'penny rate' formula. They were also empowered to acquire land for sale or lease and to aid public-utility housing societies. The Ministry might act in default and recover costs. Lloyd George commended the measure as a 'bulwark against Bolshevism' for which the anticipated cost of £20–£40 million appeared well justified (Johnson, 1968, pp. 345–7). Housing provision would redeem the pledge to returning soldiers, would represent an employment generator and would stimulate economic activity through maximum involvement of the private-sector building materials and construction industries.

Town-planning provisions were secondary to housing but simplified the 1909 Act procedure. Addison was wary of compulsion. Sir John Tudor Walters, paraphrasing Unwin, considered that housing and town-planning were inseparable.

> Do not let us . . . fill up all the little bits of spaces in the centre of our towns with badly planned houses. Let us go right out into the suburbs of our towns and cities; let us have belts of new housing schemes round our towns, planned and laid out on lines that are spacious and generous in their conception and execution. (Cherry, 1974, p. 682)

During the Committee stage, supporters of the National Housing and Town Planning Council achieved their objective of compulsory town-planning, with amendments requiring every borough or district council with a population greater than 20,000 on 1 January 1923 to prepare a scheme. The Act received Royal Assent in July 1919 and widespread commendation. The major exception was the Garden Cities and Town Planning Association, whose New Towns Group, led by C. B. Purdom and F. J. Osborn had hoped for state provision of Garden Cities and Satellite towns ('New Townsmen', 1918; Johnson, 1968, pp. 422–5). Ebenezer Howard had purchased the first 1,250 acres [508 hectares] of the site of Welwyn Garden City in May 1919 (Beevers, 1988, pp. 158–67). However, aside from the principle of self-containment, most significant elements of Garden City layout and housing design had been municipalized.

The legislation was accompanied by a design *Manual* (Local Government Board, 1919). It summarized Tudor Walters' recommendations and emphasized the need for 'good houses, adequate in size, equipment and amenity to afford satisfactory dwellings for a working-man's family'. Housing schemes would 'mark an advance on the building and development which has ordinarily been regarded as sufficient in the past, and . . . should serve as a model or standard for building by private enterprise in the future'. Commissioners would give preliminary advice on choice of site, size of programme, design and materials. Location was linked to urban expansion, population trends, accessibility to employment and education and to preparation of planning schemes. Densities were fixed at 12 houses to the acre for urban schemes, 8 to the acre for rural locations. *Nothing Gained by Overcrowding* was reiterated by a statement that 'the cost of the land bears a small proportion to the total cost of a scheme'. A technical appendix on 'The Lay-out of Schemes'

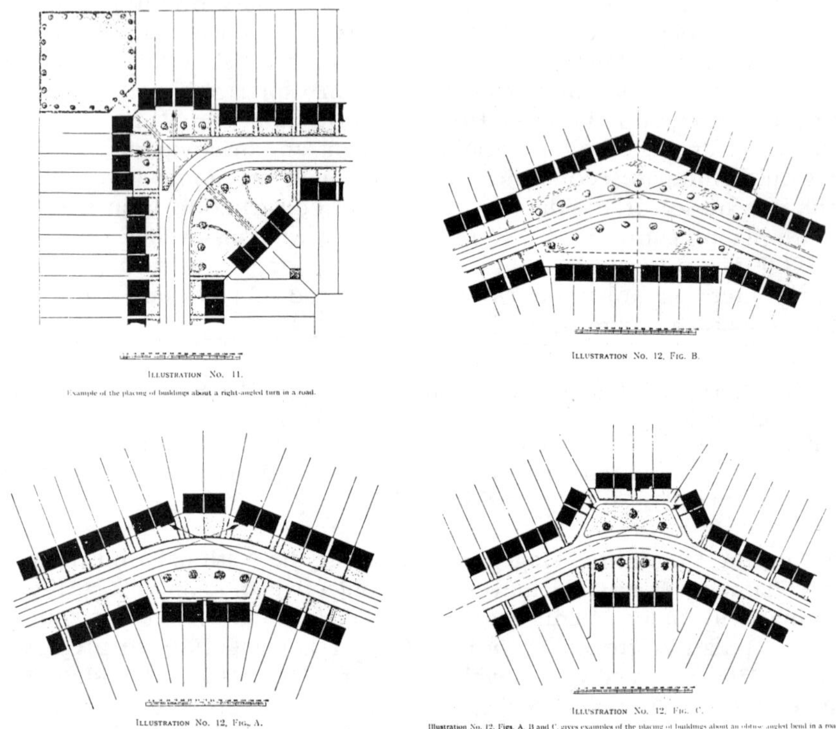

Figure 60 The *Housing Manual*, 1919: layout and grouping techniques. The diagrams were simplified versions of examples from *Town Planning in Practice*.

contained diagrams familiar from the Tudor Walters *Report* and some redrawn in simpler form from *Town Planning in Practice*, indicating Unwin's close involvement (*see* Figure 60).

The *Manual* included a set of 'typical plans'. It was stressed, possibly by Unwin, that:

> ***these plans have been prepared*** with due regard to the areas desirable for different rooms. They are only ***for general guidance and are not intended to hamper initiative or to prevent full expression being given to local customs and traditions, or the use of local building materials*** [italics in original]. (Local Government Board, 1919, paras. 34, 37)

The designs marked the eclipse (*see* Figure 61), in official circles, of the informal, Arts-and-Crafts-influenced early Garden City style, with which Unwin and his contemporaries had been so closely identified. The 'rational' house, which had made a tentative appearance in the Smallholdings *Report* in 1913 (*see* Figure 56), had been featured in the munitions communities and now appeared to reign supreme (Swenarton, 1981, pp. 144–8). The low-pitched hipped roof became a standard feature of interwar housing. In private sector construction it was often

Figure 61 The *Housing Manual*, 1919: a) Four-bedroom parlour house; b) Three-bedroom non-parlour house. Although parlour houses represented the ideal, rising costs soon eliminated all but the simplest of the type plans, and area standards were progressively reduced throughout the 1920s

embellished with mock gables to differentiate it from the public-sector corporate image. Rectangular outlines, with bays used only to increase undersize rooms, were the order of the day. The bay became a symbol of private-sector development. Although the *Manual* mentioned grouping, the illustrations were of semi-detached pairs. This became the dominant building form in many council estates, and virtually universal in private-sector development. The generous spacing made it difficult to achieve continuity and closure of the street picture. Emphasis was placed on linking with outbuildings, screen walls and arches which disappeared as subsidies were reduced. The effect of the *Manual* on the morphology of housing was both swift and profound.

Accommodation was closely prescribed. The standard dwelling would contain living-room, scullery, three bedrooms, bathroom and w.c., with 'a considerable proportion of houses having parlours and also a certain number . . . having more than three bedrooms'. These types were designated 'Class A' and 'Class B' respectively. The Tudor Walters advocacy that a parlour should be included if at all possible had thus been diluted: only four of the twelve plan-types included a parlour. The archaic nomenclature which referred to 'living-room' and 'scullery' ensured that the most common arrangement would be to include a range or cooker in the former. The private sector eliminated this, though the 'kitchen' was often smaller than the 80 sq. ft. [8 sq.m.] minimum public-sector scullery. The private sector equalized the living spaces, from the public sector 180 sq. ft. [18 sq.m.] living-room and 120 sq. ft. [12 sq.m.] parlour, to a 150 sq. ft. [15 sq.m.] 'dining room' and 'lounge'. With the private sector recovery from the mid-1920s, 'homes for heroes' became 'semis for bypasses'.

Great expectations

The appointment of Christopher Addison as the first Minister of Health on 25 June 1919 began the great experiment in housing in earnest. The campaign had received a regal send-off that April at Buckingham Palace where King George V addressed local authority representatives:

> It is not too much to say that an adequate solution of the housing question is the foundation of all social progress. Health and housing are indissolubly connected. If this country is to be the country which we desire . . . a great offensive must be undertaken against disease and crime, and the first point at which the attack must be delivered is the unhealthy, ugly, overcrowded house in the mean street, which we all of us know too well. (Aldridge, 1923, pp. 153–5)

The concept of a direct attack on the slums was a popular misconception of the 1919 programme, which was primarily intended to make good a numerical deficiency through new construction. Although the issue was examined by the Unhealthy Areas Committee in 1920–1 it was not until the 1930 Housing Act that legislation enabled widespread clearance.

Housing built under the 1919 Act was identified with Christopher Addison: it would perhaps have better justified the eponym 'Unwin' for his part in formulating and advocating the new approach. Initially he had hopes of optimal achievement. In July 1919, at the Architectural Association in London, he 'laid stress on the fact that town-planning was the basis of social reconstruction' (Unwin, 1919e, pp. 188–9). Expectation was high as local authorities started to prepare their programmes. The Ministry publicized innovation through its illustrated periodical, *Housing*. Unwin wrote on site layout. In December 1919, he reworked *Nothing Gained by Overcrowding*, revealing the reduction of land prices and the doubling of road costs. The extra cost of building at 12 houses to the acre against 21 had fallen from 19 per cent in 1914 to 4 per cent by 1919 (Unwin, 1919a, pp. 146–8; 162–3). Unwin edited an issue on 'Site Planning', emphasizing that housing should embrace town-planning (Unwin, 1920d, pp. 41–3). Schemes should provide open space and community buildings, with sites for larger houses to attain a degree of social mix. Unwin urged flexibility, pointing to the need for monitoring and the regular revision of plans. His Ministry group included Samuel Pointon Taylor (1884–1958) who had served his apprenticeship at Letchworth and Hampstead, and F. Longstreth Thompson (1890–1973), later to become a partner of Thomas Adams.

Unwin's article, 'The City Practical' (Unwin, 1920a, p. 267) developed the earlier 'Garden City Principle applied to Suburbs', again illustrated by the 1912 perspective showing articulated urban expansion. Unwin considered the concept equally applicable to fringe cottage sites and satellites with up to 100,000 population, possibly alluding to the LCC estate at Becontree, near Dagenham, Essex. Manchester and Birmingham were also building large fringe satellites. In 1924 Unwin's perspective was displayed as a model at the British Empire Exhibition (William Ellis, 1924, pp. 231–4, 275).

Enthusiasm failed to mitigate the chaos as costs soared. The three-bedroomed, non-parlour house, optimistically costed at £300 in wartime, reached £704 in October 1919 and peaked at £930 in August 1920 (Ministry of Health, 1920, I, p. 24). Material costs rose sharply as they were used for non-essential buildings. By September 1919, the Ministry had received applications to acquire 4,600 acres [1,872 hectares] of land, capable of accommodating 460,000 houses, but only 43,299 had reached tender stage (Johnson, 1968, p. 434). The Housing (Additional Powers) Act 1919 awarded a flat-rate subsidy of £150 per dwelling for private-sector construction of up to 100,000 houses, which ultimately accounted for 39,186 of the 213,821 houses completed under the 1919 Acts.

The Ministry pressed on with further work – standardization and new methods of construction and an examination of the 'unhealthy areas', organized by a Housing Advisory Council under the Chairmanship of Sir John Tudor Walters. Members included Neville Chamberlain, William Dunn (1859–1934), an architect with wartime housing experience, R. L. Reiss (1883–1959), a lawyer who had assisted Rowntree's land investigation and became an influential supporter of the Garden-City movement, and Henry Aldridge, the housing reformer. Council members served on specialist sub-committees.

Unwin was a member of the Standardisation and New Materials Committee and also of the RIBA Science Standing Committee, both of which collaborated with the Department of Scientific and Industrial Research (DSIR) (Atkinson, 1971, pp. 446–8). Late in 1919 a Building Research Board (BRB) was established under the Chairmanship of Lord Salisbury, with H. S. Weller, a civil engineer, as its first Director. Its first headquarters was a five-acre 'demonstration site' at East Acton (Acton Housing Scheme, 1920), which featured experimental pairs of houses, many involving concrete systems or components. The BRB disseminated its research through articles in *Housing* (Special Methods of Construction, 1919). By March 1920 24,000 houses were under consideration. 'Dorlonco', steel-framed houses with rendered panels, were used by Adshead and Ramsey at Dormanstown (Pepper and Swenarton, 1980, pp. 81–92), the Dorman Long company village near Middlesbrough. The 'Duo-Slab', with cast *in situ* frame and concrete infill panels, became popular while traditional materials were scarce. Rationalized traditional construction was exemplified by Barry Parker's bungalows at New Earswick, 'built as a Ford car is built' (Joseph Rowntree Memorial Trust, 1920, pp. 254–5). The independence of the BRB ensured its survival following the 1921 retrenchment.

The work of the Unhealthy Areas Committee suffered directly. A publication *Manual on Unfit Houses and Unhealthy Areas*, I, 1919 actually preceded its investigative work. The *Manual* illustrated the comprehensive redevelopment of dense urban sites. Unwin was an advocate of this approach, although not a member of the Unhealthy Areas Committee. Neville Chamberlain, with experience of slum clearance and reconditioning of housing in Birmingham, chaired the Committee which included Pepler and Reiss. The Committee's *Interim Report* of March 1920 (Ministry of Health, 1920) dealt with the problems of Greater London, and the *Final Report* of April 1921 reinforced the earlier findings with evidence from Birmingham, Liverpool, Leeds and South Wales. Both concluded that the solution to the slum problem required the extension of town-planning to built-up areas, enabling linkage between clearance and reconstruction and suburban or satellite decentralization. In an addendum to the *Interim Report*, Reiss proposed land nationalization to overcome the problems of acquisition, compensation and betterment. Although the Committee was cut short, its recommendations were taken up by Unwin for the Marley Committee in the 1930s and ultimately by the Barlow Commission which reported in 1940.

Crisis and retrenchment

While the Ministry set up a comprehensive advice-and-research structure, its performance was judged by the completion rate and cost of housing. Its *Annual Reports* for 1919–22 relayed the key issues, somewhat belatedly. Addison struggled to retain governmental commitment in the face of severe inflation. Sniping from Cabinet colleagues intensified as performance lagged and costs rose. The *First Report* reviewed the situation to March 1920, describing the structure of the new Ministry. 1,553 out of 1,865 housing authorities had submitted programmes involving 3,387 layouts, 2,704 of which had been approved, providing for 161,307 houses. 370 authorities had begun work on 52,031 houses but *none* had been completed (Ministry of Health, 1920, I, p. 14). It was galling to set this against calls for 300,000 completions during the first year of peace. The sharp rise in costs was virtually all borne by central government due to the 'penny rate' formula. Austen Chamberlain, Chancellor of the Exchequer, called for a limit to the programme (Johnson, 1968, p. 495). Addison suggested controls unacceptable to the Conservatives in Lloyd George's coalition and looked for more unorthodox solutions.

In mid-1920 the Ministry investigated the Building Guild, a

Manchester-based workers' cooperative backed by the Co-operative Wholesale Society Bank. The Guild agreed a 'cost plus' tender basis and was promised twenty contracts. According to their leader, S. G. Hobson, this was 'a glorious act of faith on the part of Addison and Unwin' (Hobson, 1938, pp. 227–8). After sixteen contracts were awarded the Bank withdrew backing. The Guild's appeal to the National Federation of Bulding Trade Operatives for assistance was rejected. Guild socialism, an appealing concept to the followers of Morris, failed to win support from its natural allies in the harsh postwar world. By December 1920 the outlook appeared bleak. Unwin wrote to his daughter Peggy, newly married and settled in the United States, of deep disillusionment and impending crisis:

> Those in power seem to have lost any glimmering of an idea . . . of a new order and are working steadily to recover the pre-war position . . . the only one they can understand. I think nearly all the projects . . . of the Ministry of Reconstruction have for the time being been dropped: Whitley Councils, Builders Parliaments and such like no longer figure in the government's thoughts. There is of course a good deal developing: many hopeful movements which before the war would have seemed great.
>
> We have managed to get about £1,000,000 of work into the hands of the Building Guilds before Addison ratted; he has now yielded to the Master Builders Federation and between them they will wreck the scheme if they can. The government may come a cropper this Winter through a combined unemployment and Irish crisis . . .The financial pundits I hear, think it will take about 3 months to tide over the slump and then things will begin to mend – if we hold together till then.[145]

The government held on, but Addison resigned in the spring and was demoted to the Minister without Portfolio. By March 1921 only 25,878 local-authority, 1,930 public-utility and 13,703 subsidised-private dwellings had been completed (Ministry of Health, 1921, p. 56). The annual rate of 70,000 was not revealed until 1922. Costs had peaked in August 1920, then fell slowly. In July 1921, Austen Chamberlain obtained a 176,000 house limit to the 1919 Act subsidies. Addison resigned the same month, following humiliation before the Commons (Johnson, 1968, pp. 497–8). His successor at the Ministry of Health, Sir Alfred Mond, had already disbanded the Regional Commissioners and withdrawn *Housing*; and disaffected staff, including Reiss, had resigned.

The Addison Act legacy

Under the 1919 Housing Acts, 167,883 local-authority houses, 4,745 public-utility-housing society houses and 39,186 private-sector houses were built. The best of these attained the individuality that Unwin had stressed as inseparable from good architecture. Ministry staff vetted plans in detail. Although this delayed construction, it set high standards. Unwin must have been heartened to see the newly created Letchworth

Urban District Council make full use of its housing powers. Their first two schemes encapsulated contrasted design approaches. Jackmans Place, by Bennett and Bidwell, stressed continuity from housing society schemes, notably Rushby Mead. The Crescent, designed by Courtenay Crickmer, who had worked as Unwin's site architect at Gretna, used the simplified hip-roofed house types found in the *Housing Manual*.

Unwin was impressed by the work of the London County Council under its newly appointed architect, George Topham Forrest (*c.*1870–1945). The largest scheme, Becontree, was virtually a self-contained satellite and the Watling, Bellingham and St Helier estates also attained an impressive scale (London Housing, 1928, 1931, 1937; Jackson, 1973, pp. 291–9). Barry Parker, as consultant to several local authorities, submitted his schemes to Unwin at the Ministry, almost reviving the old partnership. Parker's work maintained a distinctive character even with stringent cost limits. His subtle variations on cul-de-sac layouts, or bold octagonal groupings around road junctions, contributed to the individuality of schemes at Newark-on-Trent, Bridport, Wakefield, St Neots and, later, at Loughborough.[146] Unwin also admired schemes designed by Percy Houfton, a Derbyshire architect he had known in the 1890s, for the Chesterfield and Ashbourne Rural Districts. In his lectures, Unwin illustrated the Stanmore Estate at Winchester, designed by Curtis Green, and the more formal approach of Adshead and Ramsey at Newburn-on-Tyne.

Notwithstanding the emphasis on using architects, many schemes were prepared by district surveyors with little design competence. The Ministry's guidance was crucial, but it fluctuated during the period 1919–21. In May 1920 *Type Plans and Elevations* appeared (Ministry of Health, 1920), which presented designs 'which could be used without alteration': a motley collection. There was a momentary reversion to the steeply pitched roofs and gables, with designs for tile districts. Plans were long and shallow rather than square and compact and more suitable for sloping or hilly sites. An asymmetrical roof with subsidiary rooms pushed well into the loft also found favour. Full Bills of Quantities were available for the standard designs (Swenarton, 1981, pp. 159–60). At the end of 1920 *Housing* published a design for a block of four cottages derived from the early 'rational' types illustrated in the Smallholdings *Report*. Detailed guidance was eclipsed and many subsequent schemes became mere stereotypes.

The mid-1920s

As Addison Act subsidies ran out in 1922, the average cost of a three-bedroomed non-parlour dwelling slumped to £378. Shortly before, Sir Eric Geddes had claimed in Parliament that the cost would remain at £1,000.

The mid-1920s Housing Acts promoted greater numbers but represented ideals eroded by penny-pinching. Neville Chamberlain, as

Minister of Health, promoted the 1923 Housing Act, which introduced a flat-rate subsidy of £6 per house per annum for a maximum of twenty years (Aldridge, 1923, pp. 192–4). By October 1925, 122,719 houses had been completed under its provisions. The area of a three-bedroom non-parlour house was pared to 850 sq.ft. [85 sq.m.] but restored to 950 sq. ft. [95 sq.m.] after protest. Costs stablized at between £378 and £425 between 1922 and 1925. Ministry staff exerted less detailed influence. Yet Aldridge maintained that standards were safeguarded by:

> the quiet and unassuming, but watchful services of Mr. Raymond Unwin and Mr. Pepler . . . the local authorities who have had their layout plans criticised and returned with suggestions as to their amendment will be most ready to join in the recognition of a public service wisely rendered by a public servant. (Aldridge, 1923, p. 297)

Ramsay Macdonald's short-lived Labour administration passed the Housing (Financial Provision) Act in 1924, identified with John Wheatley, the Minister of Health. Housing problems had worsened since 1919, despite the construction of 284,000 houses including 48,000 from the private sector. It was hoped to raise the annual construction rate from 90,000 to 225,000 by 1934. Subsidies per house were increased to £9 per year for forty years, with a higher discretionary rate of £12 10s for rural housing. The Wheatley Act remained in force until 1933 and promoted the construction of over 400,000 houses.

Housing quality remained of prime concern to Unwin and he was cautiously critical in his RIBA lecture of November 1925, calling for a rekindling of the idealism of 1918:

> How much of it [housing] adorns, how much disfigures our land . . . When the first housing scheme [Addison Act] was launched . . . standards of health, accommodation and design were set, and a continuous effort was made to reach and maintain those standards . . . In 1923 [Chamberlain Act] the reverse arrangement was made, the central authority undertook a limited financial obligation only, and laid down but a few and general conditions . . . estimates of cost are generally approved [i.e. submitted for Ministry approval], but plans of layout and of houses are not submitted . . . except in the case of difficulty as to cost . . . Much that I see inspires me with hope . . . But I also see much which falls short of this standard and no little that inspires apprehension as to what may be happening in some places . . . reproducing many of the worst evils of the nineteenth century builder. A layout devoid of interest or merit, plans inconvenient and uncomfortable, aspect neglected, north living rooms and south larders; and . . . elevations consisting of incongruous features unhappily combined . . . That we should still be destroying the remaining beauty of our land by development such as described can only be regarded as spendthrift extravagance. (Unwin, 1925a, pp. 42–3)

Unwin's audience included Pepler, Adshead, Davidge, Ebenezer Howard, I. G. Gibbon from the Ministry of Housing and Colonel C. H. Bressey from the Ministry of Transport. Davidge drew attention to the anonymity of Unwin's bureaucratic role:

I think it is a national loss that he [Unwin] has to spend his time in the humdrum dreariness of the so-called Ministry of Health, when he might be enthusing the nation as a whole. Dr Unwin is a national possession. (Unwin, 1925a, p. 834)

Table 9.1 Reduction in area standards of local authority housing, 1919–27

	'A' type (non-parlour)	'B' type (parlour)
Dec. 1919	882 sq. ft. [88 sq.m.]	1007 sq. ft. [100 sq.m.]
Dec. 1923	801 sq. ft. [80 sq.m.]	948 sq. ft. [95 sq.m.]
Dec. 1927	786 sq. ft. [79 sq.m.]	904 sq. ft. [90 sq.m.]

In 1929 Unwin tabulated the declining area standards (Unwin, 1929a, p. 834).

Design, too, remained a prime concern. In 1926 the Housing (Rural Workers) Act promoted satisfactory accommodation in rural areas. The newly formed Council for the Preservation of Rural England was drawing attention to the erosion of rural amenity through ugly, sporadic development. The Ministry prepared a new *Manual* (Ministry of Health, 1927) which urged the importance of matching rural vernacular traditions. Unwin was involved with its preparation and its text recalls *The Art of Building a Home*. He became involved with CPRE meetings and conferences. In 1930 he was appointed to the CPRE–RIBA Joint Committee on the Control of Elevations. Asked by a young architect if he had considered the educational value of an exhibition of good and bad design, Unwin wryly replied: 'Yes, but I concluded that the public might prefer the bad examples and decided against it!'[147]

During his last years at the Ministry, Unwin worked under Neville Chamberlain who discharged his housing and planning responsibilities efficiently. Completions rose from 173,426 in 1924–5 to a record 238,914 in 1927–8, with the cost of a three-bedroomed non-parlour house falling to £368 in March 1928 (Ministry of Health, 1928). That November, Unwin 'passed the 65th milestone happily and with no recognisable jolt'.[148] He accepted the post of Technical Adviser to the Greater London Regional Planning Committee and viewed his farewell reception at the Ministry, held on 7 December 1928, as 'a splendid start to my new job'.[149] One hundred and fifty colleagues bade him farewell. Sir Arthur Robinson, the civil-service Head of the Ministry, presented him with a framed, illuminated address in Latin, signed and sealed by Chamberlain. Unwin's 'retirement' was to prove unusually fruitful; that evening he attended a TPI examination committee and worked late into the night on correspondence for the International Garden Cities and Town Planning Federation.

Wythenshawe

The Manchester satellite at Wythenshawe was one of the most ambitious interwar local-authority projects. Its scale and character anticipated the first generation of post-1945 new towns (Simon, 1935; Creese 1966; Day 1973; Deakin, 1989). Although its early development was shaped by Barry Parker's consultancy from 1927–41, Unwin was also involved. Manchester's housing programme sprang from the enthusiasm of Alderman W. D. Jackson, Chairman of the Public Health Committee and E. D. (later Lord) Simon, Chairman of the Housing Committee (whose wife, Sheena, also took a direct interest in housing and planning matters). In March 1920 Patrick Abercrombie reported that 'the Wythenshawe estate stands out as the one piece of unspoilt land suitable for building in the immediate vicinity of Manchester' and recommended the creation of a satellite, separated from the city by a green belt. That December the Corporation resolved to negotiate for purchase of the 2,568-acre [1,027-hectare] estate, but agreement was not reached until August 1926. Simon had already purchased Wythenshawe Hall and presented it to the city.

Ministry loan sanction was sought and in October 1926 Raymond Unwin and W. G. Weeks held a public local inquiry.[150] Unwin had already been involved in discussions about the city's housing programme. Chamberlain subsequently approved the purchase of the estate for £210,000. Although the land lay outside the city boundary, the large LCC estates, notably Becontree, created a precedent. It was recommended that additional land should be purchased to develop a self-contained satellite. By 1929 the landholding reached 3,547 acres [1,419 hectares], comparable with the original Letchworth Garden City estate.

In January 1927 the Corporation convened the Wythenshawe Estate Special Committee to manage and plan the development. The Town Clerk contacted Unwin, requesting advice on a consultant. The appointment of Barry Parker that August hinted of the old partnership. The Committee called upon Parker:

> to use all the resources known to town planning to develop it [Wythenshawe] on the best possible lines from the point of view of amenity . . . and financial advantage to the city.[151]

Parker's plan was regarded by Lewis Mumford, the eminent American sociologist-planner, as a bold updating of Howard's Garden City to suit the motor age.[152] The detail represented a logical development of the block system from *Nothing Gained by Overcrowding* to the scale of the Radburn neighbourhood superblock, incorporating the optimal hexagonal grids of the Canadian planner, Naulan Cauchon. Parker's first report to the Committee, presented in 1928, incorporated a full road hierarchy.[153] Most revolutionary were the parkways, developed in their mature form in his 1931 plan and a reflection of his enthusiasm for

American practice. The first section of the Princess Parkway was opened in 1933, running through a generously landscaped belt up to 400 ft. wide: striking confirmation that the most efficient functional arrangement gave the greatest scope for beauty. The parkways were intended to articulate neighbourhood blocks, linking the central Wythenshawe Park with the peripheral green belt.[154] Unwin's enthusiasm for parkways in his Greater London Regional Planning Committee *Reports* seems to have stemmed from Parker's pioneering work at Wythenshawe.[155]

Implementation was frustrated by hostility from the rural districts in whose areas the land lay, which necessitated private legislation to incorporate the estate within the city boundary. The depression and cutbacks in housing finance mitigated against achievement of the full potential. Parker was sixty at the time of his appointment but he continued to attend the monthly meetings of the Committee until his retirement in March 1941. During that period, relations with the Manchester City Architect became strained. Parker discussed problems with Unwin; in January 1932 his brother-in-law advised him to retire following the tabling of a motion to dispense with his services.[156] Assured of the continued support of the Simons, Parker soldiered on. It is tempting to speculate on what the partnership of Parker and Unwin might have achieved, given a healthier economic and political climate. Following Unwin's retirement, it would have been possible to have picked up the threads, but perhaps the two had moved too far apart by then. Notwithstanding the difficulties, however, Wythenshawe had outstripped the combined population of Letchworth and Welwyn Garden City by the mid-1930s, and represented perhaps the most striking example of the municipalization of the Garden City.

From the Presidential platform, 1931–3

The 1930 Housing Act turned the emphasis from local-authority construction of new housing towards slum clearance and redevelopment, tardily following up the recommendations of the Unhealthy Areas Committee almost a decade before. Housing constructed under the new Act was to be within the reach of the poorly paid. By 1930–1 local-authority housing construction had declined to 58,349 against 225,368 private-sector completions (Ministry of Health, 1931, p. 101). Unwin pressed for widespread use of the Act, although he was concerned at the downturn in local-authority construction at a time of rising unemployment. In 1931 he was elected President of the RIBA for a two-year term.[157] In his Presidential Address that November the zeal of the young evangelist reappeared:

> It is difficult to explain why slum or semi-slum conditions are still so widely tolerated today . . . so much that we do accomplish in the way of education and other social services is so obviously wasted because of bad housing

conditions . . . I confess that every visit paid to the East End of London rouses in me the latent revolutionist. The time is surely ripe to tackle our slum problem on an adequate scale, to plan and rebuild our East Ends . . . Brains and hands in excess of those required for the work are available; and their unemployed owners are receiving sums that could make a handsome contribution to the cost . . . I am convinced that the project is well within the powers and resources of our country . . . should other and more orthodox means fail we may yet be called upon to provide a leader who, taking a lesson from Ruskin and his Oxford road makers, will gather round him a volunteer band of unemployed architects and operatives, and will lead them in a new crusade to clear and rebuild the slums. (Unwin, 1931a, pp. 6–7)

In December 1931, Unwin analysed the Ministry of Labour *Gazette* to correlate the sharp rise in construction-sector unemployment with the downturn in housing. Influenced by the economic theories of John Maynard Keynes, he advocated a bold, nationally led housing programme, claiming that savings on the dole would bring a £75 discount from each employee against the cost of each house (Unwin, 1931c, p. 805). During 1932 the situation worsened and Unwin stepped-up his campaign. In his second Presidential Address that November, 'Housing: the present opportunity', he argued that unemployment had arisen:

purely from an incapacity to take advantage of the situation. What a splendid opportunity is afforded by the 250,000 available operatives . . . to overcome some of the enormous arrears . . . [by] building decent homes to live in and efficient factories to work in . . . We can legitimately rejoice that something over one and one half millions of families . . . have been provided with improved homes . . . When, however, full credit has been made for the progress and improvement so far made, we must admit that little more has been done than to provide improved accommodation for the increase of our people, leaving the old urban populations still living in the degraded and muddled conditions which were inherited from the nineteenth century. (Unwin, 1932c, pp. 7–8)

His solution lay in 'MORE PLANNING AND BETTER PLANNING' (his capitals) and a national strategy to conquer 'creeping economic paralysis'. The following month in 'Housing and Unemployment' (Unwin, 1932b), he reiterated his argument for a subsidy made up of dole money to promote construction. A favourable omen was the MOH report that local authorities could build houses for £350 all-in, to be rented at 8s 0d [40 p] per week. He remained deeply sceptical of the capability of the private sector:

to expect private enterprise to solve the housing problem . . . much less to solve the slum problem, is as unfair to private enterprise as it is to the slum dweller. (Unwin, 1932b, p. 11)

As he wrote, 1924 Housing Act subsidies were terminated and this helped to intensify his campaign. He convened a private meeting at the

RIBA on 13 January 1933 (Unwin, 1933c, pp. 173–4), to discuss the formation of an independent non-partisan Public Utility Housing Board. At the end of the month Sir Austen Chamberlain chaired a conference on the subject. The Board would operate from a position intermediate between a private developer and a public-authority works' department. Keynes had calculated existing multiplier benefits from Unwin's proposal to convert the dole to wages, claiming that:

> expenditure of £30 millions on housing would probably increase the national income by £60 millions . . . save the country £15 millions in unemployment relief, and increase income from taxes by £12 millions. (A National Policy for Public Housing, 1933, p. 278)

Keynes and Unwin described the proposals in *The New Statesman* (Unwin, 1933d, pp. 155–6). In a March broadcast Unwin characteristically sought a *via media* 'between two extremes of housebuilding'. Housing provision was now:

> as much a necessity as pure water, electricity or education, all of which have been made public services. That the housing of the poorer sections of the community should be made a definite public service is really the substance of the proposal. (Unwin, 1933f, pp. 433–5)

Government participation was necessary as a guarantee to secure low interest and ensure that cheaper finance brought lower rents. Some supporters, including the Simons, felt that Unwin was insufficiently bold and that the Board should undertake the entire housing responsibilities of the MOH. The Government rejected the scheme because it involved a public cost and subjected private enterprise to unfair competition. However, Unwin's proposals were more enthusiastically received in the United States, which he visited in November 1933. He remained fiercely opposed to cutting standards and acceptance of high-density, high-rise flats in slum clearance areas. The LCC began to build extensive flatted schemes from the late 1920s, when the large cottage estates were completed. Unwin viewed the trend with alarm (Unwin, 1934c).

Throughout the 1930s he continued to move in official housing circles. In 1936–7 he was a member of the Rural Housing Sub-Committee of the Central Housing Advisory Committee. They found sporadic action by rural councils, as legislation was not strong enough to ensure that needs were met, particularly those of agricultural labourers. There was also the need for more reconditioning. The main recommendations were embodied in the Housing (Financial Provisions) Act 1938. Housing management had long been Unwin's concern and he had frequently advocated the social methods pioneered by Octavia Hill in the late-nineteenth century. In 1938 he was a member of the Management of Municipal Estates Sub-Committee which recommended that local authorities should be concerned both with the care of the house and its tenants. It was also recommended that the Institute of Housing introduce social aspects into its syllabus. Public Utility Housing Societies had played a valuable role in constructing and managing housing since the 1840s. Unwin had worked closely with the Co-Partners at Letchworth, Hampstead, and on scattered sites. After 1919 such organizations were eclipsed by local authorities. In 1936 a new Housing Act empowered local authorities to encourage and collaborate with Housing Associations. Unwin joined the Sub-Committee of the Central Housing Advisory Committee appointed to consider this matter. The *Report*, published in 1939, advocated greater publicity for the potential benefits of housing societies and that local authorities should advance them working capital.

Technical research for housing

Unwin's interest in the rationalization and standardization of building elements was expressed as early as 1902 in *Cottage Plans and Common Sense*. His involvement with materials research for the Department of Scientific and Industrial Research in 1917 was a natural corollary to his work on the Tudor Walters Committee. This led to the quasi-autonomous Building Research Board, with its demonstration site at Acton, both strongly influenced by Unwin. In the early 1920s, research was divided between different institutions. The MOH looked into advanced prefabricated systems such as the 'Weir', 'Atholl' and 'Wild'. In January 1925, selected local authorities were offered a grant of £200 per house for the construction of semi-detached pairs. The previous October, Unwin became Ministry representative on the Building Research Board until his retirement in December 1928. He was influential in the Board's decision to acquire a permanent headquarters for the Building Research Station (BRS) at Garston, near Watford. He collaborated with Dr Stradling, the Director, to encourage housing-oriented research. Links were fostered with the RIBA through Unwin's long membership of the Instutute's Science Standing Committee, which he chaired from 1927 to 1929.

Unwin's interest was the 'efficiency of buildings from the standpoint of the user', and in formulating scientific standards to measure 'amenities' such as daylight and sunlight. At Garston a model house was constructed to measure heat losses through walls, flues and roofs and light transmission through different types of glass. In 1931 the BRS developed the heliodon for calculating and evaluating the amount of sunlight for any day of the year relative to model housing layouts. The BRS compiled a report on *The Orientation of Buildings* (Atkinson, 1971, pp. 447–8).

Unwin chaired the Building Research Board from 1933 to 1939 and was remembered as 'critical, but always kindly and constructively critical'. In 1934 the MOH established a technical committee to examine the construction of working-class flats. The BRS provided a schedule of materials and their performance relating to the major structural elements, together with detailed advice on thermal and acoustic transmission and fire resistance. In 1936 Unwin wrote in his introduction to the *Annual Report* of the BRB that the advance of scientific knowledge of building materials might enable performance rather than rule-of-thumb constructional methods to be used as the basis for regulating building standards. This led to the substitution of the Building Regulations for the old Model Bye-Laws in 1965. Technical information amassed by the BRS was published as a new constructional textbook, *Principles of Modern Building* (Fitzmaurice, 1938).

Unwin's involvement with the BRB was much less known alongside his widespread identification with housing and planning. Yet it was equally significant and, as Sir Edward Appleton, Secretary of the DSIR, wrote to Lady Unwin in 1940, shortly after her husband's death: 'it may in the years to come, be seen to rival his more widely known work in its far reaching effects' (Atkinson, 1971, p. 48).

10
The Green Background – Shaping the Greater London Region

Developing a Metropolitan viewpoint

In November 1928 Raymond Unwin speculated on life after retirement:

> I have much to be thankful for, even the uncertainty as to what will be the next move . . . is a path along which I stroll with good on either side! If they want me to plan London it will be very interesting but a heavy job.[158]

He accepted Chamberlain's offer and on 1 January 1929 became Technical Adviser to the Greater London Regional Planning Committee (GLRPC) (Miller, 1989).

Unwin's Metropolitan perspective had been shaped by Morris and Howard. *News from Nowhere* (Morris, 1891) pictured the transformation of post-industrial London into federated villages, a vision Unwin developed on the basis of his continuum from home to city region. Howard also set out his prescription for restructuring the Metropolitan region (Howard, 1898, Chap. XII), developed by Unwin as 'The Garden City Principle applied to Existing Towns'. *Nothing Gained by Overcrowding* (1912) quantified its implications for the decentralization and expansion of Greater London. The articulation of suburban development by open space also drew inspiration from Octavia Hill's Commons Registration campaign, itself mirrored by Henrietta Barnett's determination to preserve the Hampstead Heath Extension as the nucleus for the Hampstead Garden Suburb. At the turn of the century, Lord Meath, Chairman of the LCC Parks and Open Spaces Committee, and William Bull, proposed the reservation of a 'green girdle', a tree-lined circumferential parkway encircling the capital, a concept that figured in Greater London regional planning for many years (Meath, 1901; Bull, 1901).

The planning of London was a major theme at the 1910 RIBA Town Planning Conference. At the opening, John Burns referred to the challenge of the capital and the notable precedent of the development of Bloomsbury by the Duchy of Bedford (RIBA, 1911, pp. 62–76). At a sectional meeting, Pepler described a 'great girdle', a quarter of a mile wide, 10 miles from the centre (RIBA, 1911, pp. 611–20), linking the radial routes and providing the nucleus for a continuous garden suburb. Arthur Crow, District Surveyor for Whitechapel, proposed that an overall Traffic Authority, with executive town-planning powers, should promote 10 'cities of health', 14 miles from the centre, separated by a forest belt (RIBA, 1911, pp. 407–26). This developed Howard's 'Social City' into a foretaste of the Greater London regional strategy proposed by Unwin and Abercrombie.

Unwin's strategic perspective given at the 1910 conference referred to the expansion of a great city by supplementary satellites, articulated by defining belts of parkland, woodland and countryside (Unwin, 1911b, pp. 247–65). His Berlin and Chicago visits had enabled him to visualize the interdependence of neighbourhood units at the local level and an encompassing green girdle at the regional scale, both agents of 'crystallization' of the suburban sprawl. The diagram of 'The Garden City Principle applied to Suburbs', which appeared in 1912, illustrated the concept. Geddes' Civic Survey also stressed the roles of urban centre and rural hinterland.

There was little action to promote Metropolitan planning. Statutory town-planning under the 1909 Act was too narrowly defined to solve problems such as regional transportation. In 1905 the Royal Commission on London Traffic had recommended the creation of a powerful Traffic Board, but the London Traffic Branch within the Board of Trade was an inadequate response. In July 1913 a deputation from the professional bodies and the newly formed London Society pressed the Prime Minister, Herbert Asquith, for a coordinated approach. Asquith suggested the convening of local-authority conferences. That November John Burns presided over the first, held at Caxton Hall, Westminster, attended by 115 local authorities, 12 professional bodies, the Board of Trade and the Road Board.[159] It was hoped that coordination of statutory-planning schemes would enable the safeguarding of lines of major new arteries, including the North and South Circular roads. Burns commended Birmingham's broad-brush approach to planning. Speaking for the RIBA, Aston Webb stressed that the scale of London demanded a central authority. The Chairman of Finchley Urban District Council, who had engaged Unwin to plan their suburban expansion north of Hampstead Garden Suburb, stated that the proposals were in danger of being split apart by the proposed North Junction Railway, then being promoted through Parliament. Unwin himself reiterated the need to consider London as a whole, with 'some final power not only to provide the big ideas but to put them into effect'.[160]

The London Society and its 'development plan'

The London Society, formed in February 1912, was publicly launched in January 1913 at the Mansion House. Membership included London MP's, City, LCC and Borough Councillors, representatives of the professions and middle-class residents. The Society's professional nucleus, led by (Sir) Aston Webb,[161] began the preparation of a Greater London Survey and Plan with a clear commitment to containment:

> London is an immense octopus and its tentacles spread further afield, north, south, east and west, with no one to guide them. It is the endeavour of our Society to insist on some plan which shall govern the movements of the octopus. (London Society, 1913, p. 59)

The survey was subdivided into a Geddesian trinity of 'London Past', 'London Present' and 'London Future'. Six divisional committees and over forty architects assisted. Unwin coordinated a comprehensive survey of existing public and private open spaces and prepared a schedule of those that merited preservation – river banks, marshes, hillsides, vantage points and beauty spots.

In November 1913, Unwin lectured on 'Roads and Streets' (Unwin, 1914b), a topic linked to the Greater London Arterial Roads Conference held that month. He emphasized the links between highway development and regional planning, urging the creation of a central authority with responsibility for strategic routes. A complementary body would:

> plan the main lines of London as a whole and co-ordinate the town planning schemes which are made from the point of view of an individual local authority. (Unwin, 1914b, p. 16)

Existing, fragmentary control was ineffective: it was imperative to:

> take our arterial roads seriously as highways for inter-communication, and [to] preserve through routes from being blocked, to provide for considerable development of through traffic.

The work of the London Society was disrupted by the First World War. The Committee decided to prepare a map of Greater London within a 15-mile radius, showing agreed proposals for arterial roads, existing planning schemes and the Society's proposals for enhancing the outskirts by parkways and open spaces (*A Development Plan of Greater London*, 1914, pp. 1–4). Adshead, Crow, Davidge, Lanchester and the architect Albert Richardson (1880–1964) were involved; the latter supervised preparation of the maps over two years. Early in 1918 Webb told the Royal Geographical Society that the maps would be publicly exhibited:

> as the Society's war contribution towards the better ordered development of Greater London in the future. (The London Society's Map, 1918, p. 280)

Unwin's notes for a London Society meeting in March 1918 indicated his advocacy of broad strategic planning:

> The effect of the war has been to make us think on broader lines and the fact that such a large number of houses will be built immediately after . . . makes

> it the more important to think out on general lines the planning of . . . . such areas as Greater London, the Black Country, the West Riding and South Lancashire. The general lines of development should be laid down, residential and industrial areas mapped out and the building lines of arterial roads etc. indicated . . . We require a general plan for Greater London as a whole. The slums and plague spots of Inner London cannot be cleared until more houses are built on the outskirts and care should be taken to ensure that this is . . . on the best of town-planning lines . . . with due regard to transit facilities and the location of industry . . . The survey made by the London Society should prove of enormous value in considering the development of Greater London.[162]

The maps were published in April 1919 as a *Development Plan of Greater London* (London Society, 1919). They were not concerned with land allocation, but presented a vision of the outskirts beautified, with tree-lined roads, and at Stanmore–Aldenham on the Middlesex fringe a 2,000-acre [800-hectare] regional park with formal avenues on the scale of Versailles. Elsewhere, planned layouts such as Hampstead and Ruislip–Northwood stood out in relief against the disorderly sprawl of uncontrolled development.

Planning the future of London

The London Society redoubled its efforts through its postwar lectures. Early in 1920, Unwin presented his views on the development of London (Unwin, 1920b, p. 117; 1920e, pp. 8–10), published in 1921 in *The Future of London*, edited by Sir Aston Webb. Unwin's paper indicated growing interest in planning from a 'top down' perspective; his more abstract theme suggested rationalizing the distribution of population, resources and opportunities. His initial presentation predated the examination of Greater London by the Unhealthy Areas Committee.

Unwin introduced a characteristic analogy: substitution of the orderly queue for the disorderly scramble to possess coveted central city land. Urban management was to play a key role:

> we can henceforth regard the development of our city as we should regard any other great enterprise, as one needing to be organised and diverted towards producing the best results for the whole. (Unwin, 1921d, p. 180)

His recommended strategy was subsequently urged by the Unhealthy Areas Committee and developed through his work for the GLRPC from 1929–33. Overall development control was to be secured by:

> a green belt . . . preserved around London to protect its inhabitants from disease, by providing fresh air, fresh fruit and vegetables, space for recreation . . . If the vast population of London is to have reasonable access to open spaces in natural conditions, such areas should as quickly as possible be reserved, and to a generous extent, to form a green belt about the present London. (Unwin, 1921d, pp. 181, 187)

The Society's survey formed a logical basis for designation. Preservation of a green belt would require the selection of sites for:

> the development of satellite towns, largely self-supporting, having their own industries, garden cities, and perhaps also, detached dormitory suburbs. (Unwin, 1921d, p. 182)

This use of the country to counteract urban spread reiterated Howard's Social City concept, with more than passing reference to the New Towns group of the Garden Cities and Town Planning Association and to Crow's 'ten cities of health'. In relating development to transport, Unwin stressed that distance was 'more effectively measured in minutes than by miles', which would favour satellites with good transportation, as exemplified by the newly founded Welwyn Garden City, to which, oddly, he did not refer. While recent London growth had been uncontrolled, 'it has in fact escaped the general adoption of the tall tenement building [which] would seem to disprove any necessity for that type of housing' (Unwin, 1921d, p. 185). This rejection of a form of development, which was to be the mainspring of the modern movement in architecture and was ultimately adopted for slum redevelopment in inner London, remained fundamental.

In conclusion Unwin dealt with land acquisition, finance, betterment and compensation. His analysis of the relationship between development, planning and land values had appeared in *Nothing Gained by Overcrowding*. He stated that planning increased the total of land values by designating appropriate uses, altered the apportionment to individual sites and removed the peaks created by uncontrolled overdevelopment. Development value removed by green belt reservation would be reallocated and would raise the value of adjoining land. This redistribution based on expectation of development would be of little consequence under unitary ownership, as at Letchworth, but the multiple ownerships around a Metropolitan conurbation presented required equitable balancing of the resultant gains and losses. Nationalization or municipalization of land, or at least development values created by planning, was the most radical solution. A more modest alternative lay in the purchase of open space, with taxation or rate increases on adjoining sites to reflect their enhanced amenity value. With skilful adjustment, this would balance with the cost of acquisition (Unwin, 1921d, pp. 188–92). This concept underlay a 'special assessment' levied in Kansas City, an example widely cited by Unwin.

Unwin had encapsulated many of the elements that dominated Greater London regional planning over the next quarter of a century. The *Interim* and *Final Reports* of the Unhealthy Areas Committee appeared to herald official endorsement of an overall strategy (Ministry of Health, 1920, 1921). The committee had examined two alternatives: to expand London vertically through high-rise development or to redistribute the population horizontally through decentralization. While the latter required the state development of Garden Cities, it represented 'the only way of escape from the vicious circle' of inner congestion exacerbated by uncontrolled peripheral sprawl (Ministry of Health, 1920, p. 3). Reiss added that a comprehensive plan for London and the Home Counties was essential, involving:

> the delineation of residential, industrial and commercial zones in the existing built-up area, as well as the maintenance of a permanent agricultural belt around the outskirts. (Ministry of Health, 1920, Addendum)

In 1921, the *Final Report* advocated Garden-City development through loans from the Public Works Local Commissioners and the creation of a Greater London planning authority. This initiative was lost after Addison's resignation, though Chamberlain remained sympathetic to the conclusions of his committee.

In 1923 the Royal Commission on London Government (Ullswater Commission) recommended the formation of a single, non-elected body to coordinate town-planning, traffic and housing of the capital city and its region.[163] In 1924 the London and Home Counties Traffic Area was designated, covering an area of 1,846 sq. miles [4,781 sq.km.] within a 25 mile [40 km.] radius of Charing Cross, the traditional 'centre point'. This region was to be the concern of the GLRPC The LCC debated the creation of a London green belt but took no positive action. Growth of statutory planning was slow and sporadic but joint informal regional schemes were begun in the early 1920s. The West Middlesex regional plan, for which Adams was responsible, the North-East Surrey and West Kent, and Thames Valley joint schemes were under way. In the Home Counties, Hertfordshire commissioned a plan from Davidge, following a March 1925 conference at which Chamberlain urged the county to plan for Garden Cities and decentralization.[164] However, all the joint and regional schemes lacked the overall co-ordination required for a consistent strategy for the development of the Greater London Region.

The convening of the Greater London Regional Planning Committee

The year 1926 was a key one for Greater London regional planning. In January, Adams and other eminent planners published letters in *The Times* looking for 'more scientific treatment of the problems of Greater London'. Davidge wrote about the:

> paramount need for concentration . . . on what the future of London is to be. Side by side with the demand for adequate traffic facilities and for more and more open spaces . . . for an ever growing population come constant threats against one or other of our open spaces or against the most treasured of our ancient buildings.[165]

In February, Topham Forrest, the LCC Architect, lectured on 'London 100 years hence', visualizing a regional city stretching east–west from

Romford to Uxbridge and north–south from Watford to Dartford. Swift action by an 'open spaces trust' could secure a recreation belt within 9 miles of Charing Cross. On 1 March the LCC discussed the linkage of Garden Cities and the decentralization of industry, but took no positive steps to assist either. On 23 March, a deputation met Neville Chamberlain, Minister of Health. Patrick Abercrombie represented the TPI and Guy Dawber the RIBA. F. M. Elgood and Lord Harmsworth spoke for the National Housing and Town Planning Council and the Garden Cities and Town Planning Association respectively. Rees Jeffreys, one of the most planning-minded officers of the Road Board, appeared for the Road Improvement Association. Their statement stressed their unanimity of purpose:

> In the opinion of the institutes and societies it is imperative that a regional policy with regard to development and zoning should be formulated for London and the Home Counties and that an outline plan be prepared . . . the Unhealthy Areas Committee had reported that this problem could only be solved by decentralisation based upon a regional plan . . . a piecemeal approach . . . without the guidance of a general and agreed plan, is likely to be ineffective . . . Great extensions of building are taking place in all parts of the metropolis, which do but add to the congestion and confusion in the centre; while owing to sporadic and unregulated development on the outskirts, the amenities of the countryside are being seriously impaired.[166]

Chamberlain replied that they were preaching to the converted, but he could not underestimate the practical difficulties:

> The problem was to lay down the main lines of the metropolis. Colossal operations were involved . . . the transference of industries, and the imposition of restriction on owners in the development of their properties . . . to allow one to develop as a building area and to insist on the other being preserved as part of an agricultural belt . . . before a plan could be prepared, and he did not gather . . . that these difficulties had been faced . . . He agreed, however, that a plan prepared by . . . impartial experts might be made generally acceptable. The willing assent of local authorities was essential and he would make unofficial inquiries as to the prospects of success . . . If the result . . . was satisfactory, he would see whether a conference [of local authorities] could be convened.[167]

It took place on 6 December 1926.[168] Chamberlain presided. Three hundred representatives from 154 local authorities attended, from the City of London, Metropolitan boroughs and surrounding district and county councils. It is uncertain whether Unwin met the deputation or attended the conference. He was in a key position within the Ministry and may well have been involved from the inception of moves towards the formation of the GLRPC. Addressing the conference, Chamberlain pointed to the current work of 11 regional committees:

> It showed there was recognition of the interconnexion between one authority and another . . . the formation of a Greater London Planning Committee

would inevitably have to be followed by the appointment of sub-committees . . . [the existence of regional committees] . . . would help by coordinating their work and increasing their confidence.[169]

Chamberlain believed that the problems of traffic and population distribution should be approached together. He saw no reason to delay pending legislation for replanning built-up areas. He hoped the technical work would be undertaken at the Ministry of Health with assistance from the Ministry of Transport:

The Committee would have to consider questions of a very large policy [*sic*]. For instance they would have to consider how far it was desirable and practicable to control the future development of this or that area of Greater London, and how far it was desirable or practicable to limit the growth of continuous building, and how far they could provide for open spaces which could serve more local authorities than the area in which they were situated. The Committee's labours would be immense but the goal at which they were aiming would be worth all their efforts, however exacting . . . no less than the transformation of Greater London from a formless collection of buildings, vehicles and human beings, without organisation, into a carefully ordered system . . . in which every improvement would be guided so as to satisfy not only their commercial interest but their highest social aspirations.[170]

The speech brought forth cheers. It was unusually broad in its approach and one senses the draughtsmanship of Unwin behind the scenes. A resolution was passed to bury petty jealousies and for the local authorities to work together to secure the greatest good for the greatest number.

The first meeting of the Greater London Regional Planning Committee was convened in November 1927. Chamberlain presided over local authority representatives from within the London and Home Counties Traffic Area. Unwin, Pepler, Montagu-Harris and I. G. Gibbon were a strong Ministry of Health team. Chamberlain's statement echoed his conference speech. The Ministry was anxious to assist and the increasing congestion of London had made action urgent. Outward expansion might continue: 'because forces which tend towards the growth of a great city are so strong . . . it is difficult, if not impossible to dam them up'. At the least they might prevent the situation from getting worse. Satellite towns might be a key to the solution but:

if such towns were merely dormitories they would not solve the whole of the problem – they had to aim at decentralization . . . by the shifting of industries along with the people who were engaged in them . . . It would be a proper subject of investigation as to what had been the experience of Garden Cities, what were the difficulties they encountered, and in what way [they] . . . could be obviated in the future.[171]

Chamberlain expected such settlements to be privately developed. He requested the Committee to consider the question of an agricultural belt, its financial implications and how it might be combined with playing fields and hospital grounds. Land-use zoning powers were to remain local responsibilities and he advised against replanning the built-up area.

The Committee was purely advisory. Its 45 members represented the LCC, the City Corporation, six county councils, the Standing Joint Committee of Metropolitan Boroughs and 126 local authorities from county boroughs to rural districts. The Chairman was Sir Banister Fletcher (1866–1953), an eminent architect and a representative of the City Corporation (GLRPC, 1929, pp. 1–3). Despite its broad representation, the Committee was a cumbersome organization. Progress was tentative. Montagu-Harris was part-time secretary, with an assistant and three draughtsmen. Unwin attended all their meetings and offered informal advice. There was cooperation with Adshead, Davidge and Longstreth Thompson, all of whom were preparing sub-regional schemes. Four subcommittees were formed – General Purposes, Decentralization, Open Spaces and Traffic. Expenses of £3,000 per annum were met through local-authority contributions proportional to their rateable value. Outgoings were initially minute with a mere £129 19s 4d spent between November 1927 and March 1928, and £1,500 for the following full financial year.[172] Although the Ministry carried many of the day-to-day costs, the declared figures scarcely indicated that the work was high priority.

The technical adviser and his *First Report*

Upon appointment, Unwin rented offices in Westminster opposite the Ministry of Health. An interview with *The Times* appeared on 2 January 1929. He explained that all regional spaces had been mapped, with a correlation of proposed highways and industrial development. The Decentralization Sub-Committee had visited industrial estates and had begun to analyse journey-to-work patterns to assess whether industrial decentralization might reduce unneccessary journeys and congestion. The GLRPC intended to propose reservation of a chain of open spaces surrounding London and were also to proceed in mapping-out directions of development of residential and industrial London (*Town Planning in London*, 1929, p. 9).

Unwin was assisted by his son, Edward (1894–1936),[173] who had qualified as an architect and town-planner after the war. By February, both were hard at work formulating policies. The terms of reference had requested consideration of the reservation of additional recreation areas, allotments, areas of natural beauty and historic interest, together with the formation of an agricultural belt: work which Unwin had originally undertaken for the London Society. In 1926, Chamberlain had obtained updated information from the LCC Valuer, Frank Hunt. Edward drove his father around the Metropolitan fringe.[174] They paused to photograph ribbon development, the shacklands of the North Downs, the spreading glasshouses of the Colne Valley and unsightly filling-stations, which pockmarked the countryside before it was overwhelmed by speculative development – for the most part a caricature of Hampstead Garden Suburb. Visits to Letchworth, Welwyn and the Slough Industrial Estate were arranged. The possibility of creating a parkway of the proposed North Orbital Road was discussed.[175]

In mid-1929, Unwin drafted memoranda (Unwin, 1929b, 1929c, 1929d)[176] and collaborated with Montagu-Harris over an outline constitution for a Regional Planning Authority. By August a decision had been taken to request the Ministry of Health to strengthen planning powers for schemes of regional importance, to enable zoning to include power to 'reserve from building', to extend planning schemes to built-up areas and to enable highway authorities to limit frontage development. Unwin also referred to his overall strategic approach:

> The securing of a more adequate distribution of population and industry throughout the Greater London Region is really the basic problem of the plan. Its solution . . . underlies all efforts to prevent sporadic building . . . and to preserve the amenities of lands not already spoiled by such indiscriminate development. More fundamentally, on this must depend the convenient centralization of those national and civic functions which are of a central character: and the complementary decentralization of many industries and other activities which can be better located in subsidiary centres . . . The next point is to secure the best means of reserving an adequate proportion of open space . . . it is hoped that the provision . . . may take the form of a green girdle or chain of open spaces which would set limits to the solidly built up areas of London . . . The problem of regional planning is primarily one of design. It consists of the laying down of an appropriate plan for urban growth, and the plan or pattern should be naturally laid out on a background of fields or open lands. The difficulty at present is that no such background . . . is available. All lands are potentially building lands . . . town planners have been driven to try to design meagre patterns of open spaces on a background of potential building land . . . Little progress will be made until it is possible to allocate building to relatively compact areas where all necessary services and transport facilities can be economically provided. (*Additional Powers Sought*, 1929, p. 9a)

This strategy appeared in the *First Report*. Unwin also sought control over land values, claiming that 'regional planning seeks to do for an area what would be done by a single enlightened owner, but what a multitude of owners are powerless to accomplish unaided'. Those who had profited through development should surely be able to compensate those who had been prevented.

While preparing the work for publication, Unwin drily remarked to his cousin: 'I have had to write most of it in order to get it to the printers . . . now we are working hard on the illustrations'.[177] On 26 November a GLRPC Deputation presented the conclusion to the Minister of Health, Arthur Greenwood. Unwin must have hoped that a Labour Minister would back the strategy, but the reception was non-committal. Ribbon development, which destroyed the amenity of an area ten times the amount developed, and green belts were key issues. The Committee also pressed for the creation of a regional planning authority which could hold and manage land. Greenwood was sympathetic but stated that county councils would acquire powers of frontage control under the forthcoming Highways Act. The proposed regional authority was received with caution. Although 'much attracted by the idea of a green belt round London . . . we must have this belt and get it in the most economical way', he remained uncommitted over its achievement (GLRPC, 1929, p. 7).

The slim, hastily written *Report* (GLRPC, 1929) appeared in January 1930. It nevertheless established a strategic frame of reference for the Greater London Region, and moreover presented two contrasting options, the stronger of which, based upon a strict green belt linked to decentralization to planned self-contained settlements was elaborated by Abercrombie in the *Greater London Plan* of 1944. Its four sections were originally separate memoranda – 'Open Spaces', 'Ribbon Development and Sporadic Buildings', 'Additional Town Planning Powers Required', and 'A Regional Planning Authority for Greater London'. Unwin's memorandum on 'Open Spaces' (Unwin, 1929b, pp. 8–26) took its lead from Chamberlain's initial statement to the Committee in 1927:

> How far and in what direction is it possible to direct the enormous growth of London? . . . How far [would there] be advantage in trying to concentrate the development in particular spots by the establishment of deliberately planned new towns? . . . Should London be provided with . . . an agricultural belt . . . [to] form a dividing line between Greater London as it is, and the satellites? (Unwin, 1929b, p. 8)

This paraphrased the conclusions of the Unhealthy Areas Committee and Unwin's contribution to *The Future of London*.

The overriding problem concerned coordination and balance:

> On the one hand the task . . . is so complex that it can be comprehended only if attention be concentrated on one subject at a time; on the other hand the various aspects . . . are so interdependent that they cannot safely be studied or handled separately; for the main purpose of the plan is to establish harmonious relations among them. In the case of a city as great as London, these considerations are specially insistent. (Unwin, 1929b, p. 8)

Unwin drew four concentric rings outwards from the LCC area to the boundary of the London and Home Counties Traffic Area, analysing demographic trends from 1911–28 within each (Unwin, 1929b, Illustration 7, 10, Table No. 1). Natural decentralization had gathered momentum underlining the urgency of articulating the overall urban form. Open space would simultaneously fulfil physical and social needs for amenity and recreational land. Unwin assigned open space as concentric rings in widths proportional to their population. He generated alternative strategies to articulate the urban area, presenting balanced opposites in terms of 'pattern' and 'background' (Unwin, 1929b, Illustrations 13–16, pp. 16–17) (*see* Figure 62).

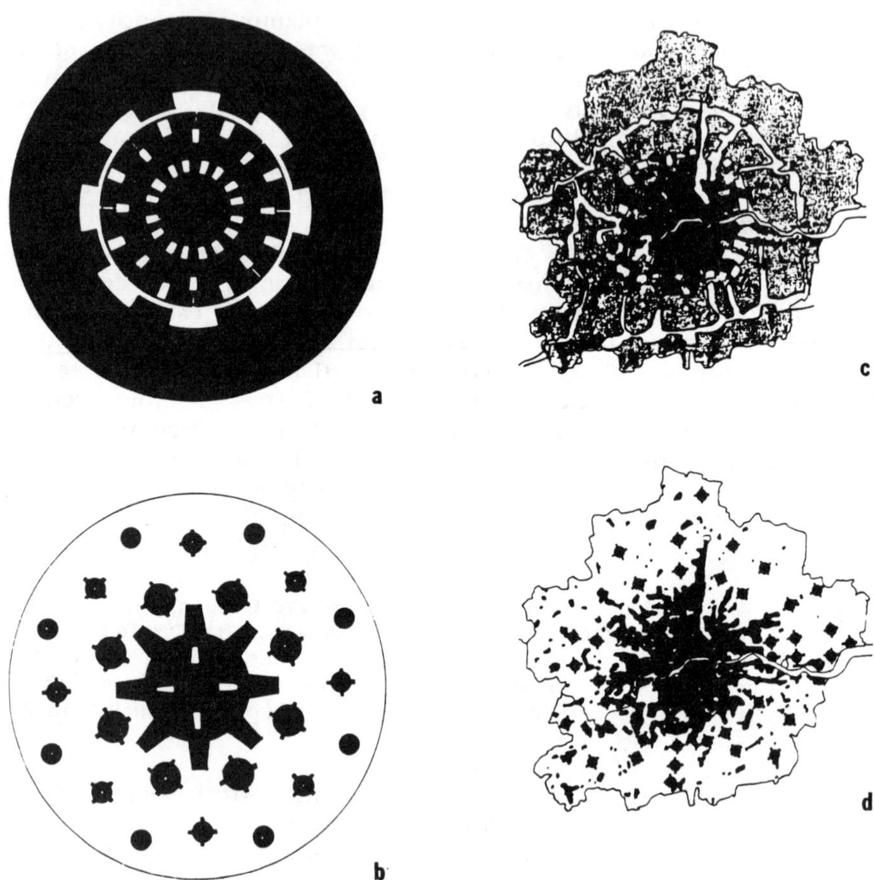

Figure 62 The strategic alternatives from the Greater London Regional Planning Committee *First Report*, 1929. Unwin's twin concepts, characterized as 'The pattern and the background' showed: a) Open spaces on a background of potential building land; b) Building areas designed on a background of open land; c) Green Girdle reserved on a background of land with unlimited development potential; d) Diagram of satellites and development areas on a background of development land. Unwin encapsulated a dual strategy for the Greater London Region; Abercrombie subsequently developed the more radical alternative in his *Greater London Plans*, 1944

In his January 1930 RIBA lecture (Unwin, 1930d, pp. 183–98), Unwin described the alternatives in terms of his homely analogies: 'crystallization' was extended to describe the evolution of 'land planning and harmonious relations between [it and] building' from Bedford Park onwards. Planning was the means of substituting the 'orderly queue' for the 'disorderly crowd' and, he argued, would ultimately, increase the effective liberty for both the individual and society:

> This general principle must be kept in mind, for it determines the legitimate limits of planning . . . If the site plan, having secured to the individual . . . space, prospect, and harmonious relations with the surrounding environment, needlessly restricts the initiatives of the owner in detail or design, then it has exceeded its proper functions. In like manner, the town plan, whilst securing harmony of surroundings and convenience of communications . . . should leave plenty of scope for the exercise of freedom in site planning . . . If Regional Planning is to serve its proper purpose, that too must be made effective for solving the larger problems of distribution and inter-communication, without depriving the present town planning authorities of the opportunity to plan their areas . . . provided they respect the framework of the Regional Scheme. (Unwin, 1930d, pp. 184)

Unwin was a pioneer on advocating strategic guidance. Forty years before he had written of the power of the mature artist to evoke the character of a scene with broad brush strokes. Now he concentrated upon the relationship between the parts, leaving others to fill out the detail, for which his earlier work provided ample precedent. Consistent design principles operated at each level:

> Imagination must be applied first to appreciate, and then to create, those special values whether of use or beauty, which arise from bringing the various parts into right relations and proportions to one another. In this way is unity of design given to the larger whole. The principle applies to parts of a pattern traced on a flat background; to the groupings of walls, roofs and windows into a façade; to the disposition of buildings and openings around a civic centre, or to the laying down of a pattern for distributing urban development over the undulating background of hill and dale, field and forest forming the region. The main purpose of the plan is to secure the best distribution of the dwellings, the work and the play places of the people. The method should be to lay out this distribution in a convenient pattern on a protected background of open land. Only in this way can a right relation or good proportion be maintained between the developed areas and the open land. Here another serious obstacle to proper regional planning must be recognised. For no such secure background . . . is in fact available. All land is potentially building land, and the poor planner has to fall back on scraps of background, in the shape of open spaces, such as he can see some hope of purchasing. He must . . . be content with these oases in a limitless desert of building sites. (Unwin, 1930d, pp. 185–6)

In the *Report* Unwin presented both the ideal and the compromise. He recognized that natural decentralization had already eased central area congestion. In 1912 he had advocated planned decentralization in *Nothing Gained by Overcrowding*, in which his circular diagrams prefigured his analysis in the GLRPC *Report*. The provision of building land to accommodate decentralized population did not inhibit the provision of open space. Conceptual diagrams illustrated the open space required: 63 sq.miles [163 sq.km.] of playing fields and 143 sq. miles [370 sq.km.] of open space, grouped into green wedges and a variable-width green girdle were indicated on a background of building land (Unwin, 1929b. Illustration 13). The ideal strategy reversed the situation to protect the background of open land beyond urban limits, upon which building would be allowed as a pattern of self-contained satellites (Unwin, 1929b, Illustration 14). He also superimposed diagrammatic alternatives on the regional map. The green girdle, about 15 miles [24 km.] from the centre of London, linked by wedges along river valleys (Unwin, 1929b, Illustration 15), contrasted with urban 'rounding off' with a scatter of satellites beyond (Unwin, 1929b, Illustration 16). Acquisition of open space for the lesser strategy would cost £12.8 million. Its unequal distribution among the local-authority areas raised difficulties in equitably spreading the cost.

If 'Open Spaces' contained the strategic concepts, 'Ribbon Development and Sporadic Building' (Unwin, 1929c, pp. 27–33) presented a serious development-control issue. The efficiency of the new arterial radial routes and the partially constructed North Circular Road was already seriously impaired. Unwin's perception of traffic capacity as a function of the potential for unobstructed movement and the distance between road junctions had a distinctly modern ring. He also costed the congestion caused by obstructions through roadside parking and individual access driveways and recognized the inherent danger and erosion of visual amenity. As always, Unwin stressed that functional solutions would be aesthetically pleasing. The 1920s exemplar was the parkway, already integral in Pepler's 1910 green-girdle proposal: later highly developed in the United States. Thomas Adams and Barry Parker were enthusiastic advocates. In his October 1929 TPI Presidential Address (Parker, 1929, pp. 1–10), Parker spoke about traffic problems and ribbon development. The audience included Unwin. Slides were shown of the Westchester County parkways, New York, illustrating their potential to solve interrelated problems: the provision of fast, safe motor roads; the protection of amenity and land values; the protection of pedestrians and the prevention of ribbon development. Unwin's memorandum, prepared shortly afterwards, reflected his brother-in-law's presentation.

'Additional Powers Required' (Unwin, 1929d, pp. 34–9) posed but did not answer political questions. Unwin advocated creation of a new *ad hoc* authority, empowered to acquire and manage land and open space and to coordinate local-authority town-planning schemes. Alternatives would involve the local authorities themselves acquiring unbuilt land in their area, following the model of the Garden City companies. Compensation raised enormous problems, particularly for values created or removed by the planning process operated by the local authorities themselves. Unwin recognized that the 'creation of monopoly through public ownership' would go far beyond the immediate concern with open space, and concluded that for the present 'so drastic a change is not called for in connection with a purpose which can be effected without it'. Fuller use of the land-acquisition powers of county councils was desirable, although the LCC would need to purchase outside its area. This was ultimately sanctioned under the Green Belt (London and Home Counties) Act 1938 (Sharp, 1980). Unwin felt that this needed additional protection for land where purchase could not be contemplated, although much could be achieved by a voluntary pooling of the interests of landowners and local authorities.

Major impediments to a workable green-belt policy were lack of statutory regional planning, continued limitation of action to unbuilt land with imminent development potential and failure to introduce adequate controls over layout and design. Unwin suggested that joint regional authorities should be empowered to make provisional plans, without depriving the individual local authorities of detailed planning powers conforming to the regional scheme. The two-tier development-planning process of 'structure' and 'local' plans introduced through the 1968 Town and Country Planning Act was clearly anticipated. Unwin also pressed for the extension of planning to all land, with the possibility of rearranging individual holdings following the *Lex Adickes*. He looked to the Ministry of Health to certify that the reservation of green-belt land was 'reasonable', thus removing entitlement to compensation for loss of development rights. The Ministry might also adjudicate over betterment payable where amenity value had been enhanced by the proximity of open spaces, and over compensation where 'legitimate expectation of building increment' had been removed (Unwin, 1929d, pp. 38–9). The final section, not written by Unwin, sketched out in greater detail the minimum executive powers required for a new, joint regional-planning authority: considerably less than he had suggested, indicative of the gap between his aspirations and the corporate caution of the GLRPC.

'The public spirit of Sir Raymond Unwin'

Publication of the *First Report* did not provoke widespread comment. In March 1930 *The Times* reviewed the document,[178] endorsing its major strategy but giving the impression of a Committee hamstrung by lack of executive powers. Unwin tirelessly pressed the cause. His January 1930 RIBA lecture has already been noted: as a personal view it was in some respects clearer than the *First Report*, particularly in his reference to Radburn, New Jersey, with its planned separation of pedestrian and vehicular movement and its implications for greatly increasing the use of private cars:

> The rapid growth of motor transport removed the limitation previously set by the need to be within reasonable distance of a railway station. Any part of the [Greater London] region is now accessible for those who drive motor cars; and patches of sporadic building are breaking out all over the region, which damage the amenities over areas . . . out of all proportion to that actually used for building purposes. (Unwin, 1930d, pp. 188–9)

Unwin always maintained that it was land wasted by haphazard development, rather than low-density development itself, that was the fundamental cause of sprawl.

His efforts came to little. Implementation was rejected by all county councils, with the exception of Hertfordshire. The Committee had only been constituted for three years. In November 1930, Unwin was doubtful about its future but felt it was:

> fairly likely that we shall get an extra year or two on our present advisory lines, by which time some more permanent organization may be fixed up to take over the work.[179]

Provision was made in Sir Hilton Young's Rural Amenities Bill 1930 for strengthening regional-planning powers. These were eventually enacted in the Town and Country Planning Act 1932. Unwin's appointment was initially extended until 31 March 1931, and then annually, to terminate with the original Committee on 31 March 1933.

Unwin prepared two further *Interim Reports* for publication in January 1931 (Unwin, 1931d, 1931e). The first, 'Open Spaces' (GLRPC, 1933, Appendix I, pp. 86–92) updated the LCC survey of 1926, revealing that by July 1930, 5,420 acres [2,168 hectares] or 8.5 sq. miles had been developed. He recommended immediate action to secure 20,000 acres [8,000 hectares], 31.25 sq. miles, within 8–12 miles of Charing Cross to form an 'inner chain' or girdle. The Committee approved the concept and requested the LCC to convene a conference of local authorities to seek agreement to act. The second *Interim Report*, 'Decentralization' (GLRPC, 1933, Appendix II, pp. 93–109), noted growing industrial mobility both into and within the region. Since 1919, factories employing 173,834 people had been developed. There was an estimated population increase close to 500,000. Unwin represented this as 16 towns of 30,000 population, 10 of 50,000 or 5 cities of 100,000. He had conducted a survey on industrial and labour mobility. He advocated coordinated decentralization, with a hierarchy of planned communities based on further industrial relocation up to 15 miles [24 km.] from the centre of London, planned suburban units, satellites up to 12 miles [19 km.] from the centre and a series of industrial Garden Cities within the belt 12–25 miles [19–40 km.] from the centre. Although these communities would ultimately prove financially viable, they should be developed by an expert board and financed by government and local authorities who would provide services and infrastructure. He examined this further through membership of the Marley Committee on Garden Cities.

In the spring of 1931, the Ministry of Health *Annual Report* anticipated that the GLRPC would complete its work within a year by allocating major building areas and satellites, a permanent and a provisional green belt and recommendations for main highways and parkways (Ministry of Health, 1931, p. 141). That June, the TPI discussed 'London as it ought to be', with contributions from Adams,

Adshead, Davidge and Lanchester. Adams, having recently completed work on the privately funded New York Regional Plan, looked askance at the 'partial answers' provided by Unwin and called for a comprehensive survey of physical, social and economic conditions. He looked towards replanning built-up London, transformed by 1970, yet 'not Haussmannized – or planned into monotonous regularity . . . still a city of individuals who are allowed to express themselves in their homes and places of business' (*London as it ought to be*, 1931, p. 189). Although Unwin envied the New Yorkers their plan, he hoped that 'before long London would overtake them', stating:

> gentlemen who come back with American experience might not always realize some of the semi-political or strategic attitudes that had to be taken at home . . . but their suggestions are welcome. (*London as it ought to be*, 1931, p. 190)

Unwin saw hopeful signs in the Town Planning Bill, which incorporated Hilton Young's recommendations for strengthening regional planning. The financial crisis of 1931 brought a national government and economic stringency. The Town and Country Planning Bill was withdrawn and the work of the Marley Committee was seriously curtailed. By November 1931 Unwin was deeply depressed over the future of the GLRPC:

> My chance of a Green Belt has gone . . . and I expect our Regional work to be cut down by ⅓ or ¼ this year.[180]

Retrenchment affected the allocation of funds for 1932–3. Annual expenditure of the Committee had averaged around £3,900–£4,000. The LCC paid a major share, with remaining local authorities contributing in proportion. Late in 1931 it was announced that the LCC contribution had been cut to £500 and the remainder sharply reduced:

> This compelled the Committee to relinquish their offices and to dismiss their draughtsmen. It was owing solely to the public spirit of Sir Raymond Unwin that the work done up to that time was not wasted. He undertook to accept a greatly reduced fee, to keep the records and plans up to date, and to provide an office for the purpose. (Ministry of Health, 1932, p 130)

Unwin was determined to keep the Committee alive. In a *Times* interview he referred to his efforts to keep the work up-to-date and the dangers resulting from its being curtailed. His personal optimism and tenacity were stretched to their limits. Steen Eiler Rasmussen, who visited Unwin at this period, did not witness any frustration. However, it appeared to F. Blaise Gillie, a young officer in the Ministry of Health, that Unwin was a comparatively forgotten man, working in an obscure office for a Committee that met infrequently and were indecisive, with a small staff untrained in research methodology, and, Unwin apart, with no one who had a clear analytical approach.[181] This reversal coincided with the height of Unwin's public presence as RIBA President.

The GLRPC published its *Second Report* in March 1933 shortly before disbanding. The *Interim Reports* of 1931 were updated. The availability of 1931 census data enabled Unwin to analyse demographic trends more precisely. Despite the large volume of private-sector building, an overall regional housing shortage was increasing. Family size had fallen significantly between 1921 and 1931. Unwin looked to the 1932 Act to control the distribution of the population and to extend zoning throughout the region. Further expansion of London was to be checked and guided by 'the timely provision of services, to take the form of defined units as self contained as possible . . . by suitably planning ample units . . . and reserving from building an appropriate background of open land' (GLRPC, 1933, p. 48). Industrial and residential development was to be coordinated.

More detail on highways reflected traffic growth. Unwin updated his work on site-planning to minimize the conflict between vehicles and residential development. He noted that sections of the recent Hendon–Watford Bypass were completely built-up, with 11 crossroads, 31 side turnings and two shopping centres within 4 miles (GLRPC, 1933, p. 62). He redefined the road hierarchy to include those fenced against frontage development and those with frontage development from parallel service roads, which became a general solution under the Restriction of Ribbon Development Act of 1935. Roads for industrial traffic were to be free from frontage development, with few junctions and pedestrian crossings by underpass or overbridge. In areas of high amenity value USA-style parkways which excluded heavy traffic (*see* Figure 63), might be developed. Finally, he recommended the functional separation of roads, anticipating Tripp's precinct theory of the 1940s. He advocated grade-separated interchanges, including flyovers (GLRPC, 1933, pp. 62–9). The *Report* included all officially proposed road improvements. Unwin also included the Radburn plan, commending it for its safe pedestrian access from dwellings to schools and shopping centre.

Open space was still regarded as the key to strategic planning. Unwin presented a more detailed green girdle 'to provide as complete a break as possible in the continuous building expansion around the metropolis' (GLRPC, 1933, pp. 78–80, 83). Recent surburban development had forced the girdle too far out to provide playing fields, which required separate reservation closer in. Beyond lay an area of 'white land', not specifically designated as green belt but with diagrammatic sites for satellites. He urged full use of the 1932-Act powers to reserve land, and the right to claim betterment for any land values improved by planning or the reservation of open space.

LCC ascendant

In February 1933 it was announced that the GLRPC would be reconstituted under the 1932 Town and Country Planning Act. It would remain advisory, studying the needs of the region assisting the

PARKWAY TREATMENT OF HIGHWAY

Figure 63 Parkway treatment of highway, 1930. To both Parker and Unwin the parkway symbolized the synthesis of functional and aesthetic aspects of highway design individual authorities. In truth there was little change and the introduction to the *Second Report* emphasized that there was no intention of acquiring executive powers, which Unwin had stressed as extremely desirable. The new Committee had 30 members; greater weight was given to the county councils, including the LCC with 6 representatives (Thomas, 1970, p. 55). Major R. Hardy-Syms, who had worked for Parker and had become interested in the green-belt cause, was Unwin's successor as technical adviser.

Concern was expressed at continued inaction. *The Times* warmly reviewed the *Second Report*, but its leader of 19 May 1933 declared that Unwin 'makes it quite plain what the ultimate aim of the Committee is and how far it is as yet from accomplishment' (*The muddle of a large London*, 1933, p. 15c). The old Committee had paid lip service to Unwin's 'services to it and to the cause of Regional Planning in Greater London . . . through the zeal and enthusiasm he has so generously contributed to the work of the Committee', but the first meeting of its successor in June 1933 seemed to ignore the six years of its predecessor by acting as if nothing had happened. In introducing the area of work, Sir Hilton Young, Minister of Health, reiterated the necessity of considering the development of the Garden Cities, or satellite towns, and early acquisition of open space on the outskirts before land values rose. The reconstituted body remained in being until 1936; and it was subsequently reorganized into the Standing Conference on London Regional Planning, which later commissioned Abercrombie's Greater London Plan.

Of far greater significance was Labour gaining control of the LCC in March 1934 under the leadership of Herbert Morrison, a sympathizer of the green-belt objective. A resolution to prepare a county plan reversed a situation where a mere 20 acres in one of the London boroughs had been brought under planning control. Major landowners opposed the proposals at the first of the long running Public Inquiries which were to become a feature of Greater London planning, but in May 1935 approval was granted. The LCC now began to assume the role of leading authority, tactically willing to cooperate with adjoining authorities, and the GLRPC proposed central authority was quietly shelved. A green-belt scheme was adopted in January 1935, not blanket-zoning but an amalgam of the girdle and playing fields proposed in the *Second Report*. £2 million was allocated over a three-year period for grants up to 50 per cent towards the purchase of agricultural land to secure it against development. By December 1936, 28,500 acres [11,400 hectares], 44 sq. miles [114 sq.km.] had been agreed (Loftus Hare, 1937, pp. 684–5), and was codified under the Green Belt (London and Home Counties) Act, 1938. Unwin enthusiastically commended progress.

The 'tentacles of the octopus' had continued to grow virtually unchecked since the launch of the London Society in 1912. In 1937, W. Loftus Hare regretted the LCC's omission of 'the doctrine of green land studded with satellite units':

> The scheme warns off buildings from 45 sq. miles at a price of about two million pounds . . . but does not guide them into the best places; it is prohibitive and not positive. In rounds of popular applause it leaves the major task for London still unperformed. (Loftus Hare, 1937, pp. 684)

The interwar period was marked by the frustration of attempts to introduce a comprehensive metropolitan development strategy. Unwin's labours on behalf of the GLRPC must be counted as an honourable defeat, but they paved the way for the *County of London Plan* (Forshaw and Abercrombie, 1943) and *Greater London Plan 1944* (Abercrombie, 1945). These were prepared with the support and encouragement of Sir John Reith, the wartime Minister of Works and Buildings. Abercrombie readily acknowledged 'the valuable contribution of Sir Raymond Unwin, on which if action had been taken, the planning problems of Greater London would be far more measurable today' (Abercrombie, 1945, para. 3) and he 'unhesitatingly adopted the second alternative [the strategy of defined satellites on a green-belt background] for the two outer rings [of the Greater London area]' (Abercrombie, 1945, para. 37). Decentralization, however, was now to be linked to the redevelopment of Inner London to retain a working population and industry, which required a density standard of 136 persons per acre [54 to the hectare] and high-rise flats, compared to 50–60 for cottage estates. The outer edge of London was halted by a strictly controlled Metropolitan Green Belt, given statutory effect in 1955,[182] and public corporation development of eight 'first generation' New Towns was promoted by the New Towns Act of 1946. While Unwin would undoubtedly have expressed serious reservations over the treatment of Inner London, he would surely have endorsed the Green Belt and New Towns policies (Osborn and Whittick, 1963, 1969, 1977), which gave government-backing to the strategic concept on which he had tirelessly worked and kept alive through the difficulties of the early 1930's.

11

The Natural Order of Planning

Unwin's earliest writing had dealt extensively with the shortcomings of free-market capitalism as the distribution of wealth, goods and opportunities. His view of the market as a determinant of the form and location of urban development was equally critical following the Ruskin–Morris line. Planning emerged as a control mechanism over market forces in land development; Unwin was among the earliest to realize and project the strategic implications of this in *Nothing Gained by Overcrowding*. Limiting the density of development or preventing it altogether would distort the pattern of land values created by the market, giving rise to the still-unresolved issues of compensation for the removal of the expectation of development, or the imposition of betterment to recoup enhanced values. The solutions, ranging from taxation and rating to municipal or national ownership, were discussed in Unwin's papers but avoided in interwar legislation. They were considered by the Scott and Uthwatt Committees during the Second World War and the nationalization of development values was included in the 1947 Town and Country Planning Act.

Accelerating suburban decentralization without adequate concern for the efficiency of the urban system and the distribution of population, resources and opportunities, led Unwin to consider a 'top down' approach to planning, supplementing the community basis of his earlier work. While recognizing the continuing importance of 'local units of autonomy', he sought their integration into the total system. He began to formulate an 'ideal' size for a city, which would balance individual and communal aspects and be large enough to provide wide-ranging employment and social opportunities, yet small enough to avoid the congestion costs and degraded environment of the existing Metropolitan conurbations. Howard had based his 'Social City' cluster of 250,000 population upon such considerations. Unwin's work led from the 'strategic' aspects of *Nothing Gained by Overcrowding* to his contribution to Purdom's post-1919 symposium of Garden City theory (Purdom, 1921, pp. 80–102), and to interwar conference papers for the International Garden Cities and Town Planning Federation (IGCTPF).

Pioneering management studies, notably Taylor's *Principles of Scientific Management*, applied to the production problems of munitions during the First World War, suggested that a similar approach to urban development might bring the dividends in the form of greater efficiency and better resource distribution. By 1917 Unwin already considered that planning should encompass 'the whole organization and disposition of the services, and other provisions for aggregations of the population'.[183] This led towards consideration of national physical and resource planning. His involvement with the Chelmsford and Marley Committees in the early 1930's influenced moves towards the appointment, in 1937, of the Barlow Commission to consider the 'Distribution of the Industrial Population', to which he presented evidence. The economic and industrial crisis of the early 1930's appeared to demand intervention. Unwin was impressed by the New Deal initiatives in the United States under the Roosevelt administration. By comparison, British measures appeared to be half-hearted.

Notwithstanding his Socialist League apprenticeship, Unwin regarded planning as an adjunct to, rather than a substitute for, the market. Public policy might supplement private enterprise and planning delineate a controlling framework within which the market might operate. Pragmatism rather than doctrine was reflected in Unwin's concept of the abortive proposal for a National Housing Corporation. It would have functioned to ensure that housing and employment could be linked to the goal of providing decent housing for the poorest families, leaving the private sector relatively free to cater for the construction of houses for sale to the expanding middle classes, particularly in the south-east. While Unwin took definition of the scope of planning much further than contemporaries such as Adams and Abercrombie, he stopped short of advocating the centralized allocation of commodities and services.

This is, in a sense, an unfinished chapter. Unwin died in 1940 and played no part in formulating the second great postwar reconstruction in which his concept of planning was to play such a vital and positive role.

Planning and land values

The interface between planning and land values has proved to be an enduring shibboleth. Until the advent of statutory controls over the use or development of land, freehold ownership carried a presumption that the owner might act as he wished, maximizing the financial return. Although the imposition of bye-laws modified this, they did not remove the principle of development itself. Land was a prime target for socialism, one of the commanding heights of the economy and natural resources to be brought under state ownership. Unwin was familiar with such arguments from the 1880s, when he and his father attended the first meeting of the Land Nationalisation Society. He was among the first to realize that the rudimentary development controls of the 1909 Act would distort the pattern of land development values. *Nothing Gained by Overcrowding* (1912) discussed the implications of density restriction on both land value and land take for suburban expansion. Shortly afterwards the government began to consider the question of land and Seebohm Rowntree was commissioned to investigate the matter, including tenure and ownership.

Against this background, the newly created planning profession addressed the issues of ownership and development values. In 1913, Unwin participated in a symposium on the municipal ownership of land. He advocated the creation of municipal-land banks to acquire and hold land for public purposes. He also perceived the difficult position of the public body over valuation when seeking to purchase land to remain open, when the owner had expectations of the price reflecting the land's development value. Action by individual authorities might prove to be a lottery:

> It would seem therefore that any wholesale public purchase would be better carried out as a national movement, in which case local gains and losses would balance one another, and only a decline in the land values of the whole country, an unlikely contingency, would lead to a national loss. (Unwin, 1913d)

Unwin emphasized that he did not necessarily advocate nationalization, which was a separate and larger question. But in referring to compensation and betterment, he separated development value from ownership. He declared that:

> the building value being added to that new area of land purely by the action of the local authority can in no sense be regarded as the rightful property of the owners of the land. If town planning is to have full scope, it must clearly be within the power of the public to decide that certain areas shall be reserved for the purpose of open space, for factories, for future roadways or railways, and it should be possible for them to recover towards the cost of this reservation, the whole of the building value which would be transferred to other land by their action . . . The conditions which have arisen in both rural and urban areas have proved that in modern life the individual interest in land does not coincide with the public interest, even in small matters. (Unwin, 1913d)

Unwin instanced the ability of continental cities to deal with the matter in their extension plans. The following year he presented a more detailed account at a TPI meeting. Here he adopted an econometric approach. Thus:

> the site value in a town may therefore be said to be the true value of any site by virtue of its situation and of the sum of conveniences attached to this situation over and above the value of agricultural land for agricultural purposes. (Unwin, 1914c, p. 107)

Through restrictions on development type, planning would redistribute the values; by removing them from some, it might increase the value of adjoining land. A process of adjustment should ensure that the public was compensated for the purchase of land at building value for open space reservation, by recouping part of the enhanced value of adjoining sites. Unwin referred to the 'Special Assessment' of Kansas City, Missouri, where a comprehensive park system had been created between 1896 and 1913 at no cost to the city authority (Unwin, 1914c, p. 113). He was ever fond of 'robbing Peter to pay Paul' and through manipulation of development values he saw a means of turning private gain to communal benefit.

Perhaps conscious of the political implications, he did not speak specifically on land values until after his retirement. The issue was seldom absent from his more general present IGCTPF papers given in the 1920s and it figured extensively in the GLRPC *Reports*. The presentation of the 1931 Town Planning Bill, with its proposals to recoup betterment, provided the stimulus for a paper on land values, which he presented to the Economics Section of the British Association in September 1931 (Unwin, 1932c, pp. 459–67). The material was updated from his prewar papers, but he also indicated how the purchase of 10,000 acres of land, at building values, for Greater London playing fields, could be recouped from the enhanced amenity value of adjoining sites.

The Committee stage of the 1931 Bill had focused on individual compensation and betterment. Unwin felt that a general tax assessment on all realized increment from the sale or development of land would be preferable to create a national fund from which compensation could be paid in cases where land values were depressed through planning. The economic dimension of planning was assuming significance:

> and those mainly connected with planning are confidently looking to the economists to help in the solution of many problems, but particularly those to do with the better distribution of population and industry and the preservation of adequate open spaces for the health, convenience and enjoyment of urban populations. (Unwin, 1932e)

Town Theory and Practice

The strategic implications of *Nothing Gained by Overcrowding* appeared to be open-ended acceptance of low-density surburban development as an inevitable consequence of the application of Garden-City principles to the suburbs. Unwin provided a corrective in 'Some thoughts on the Development of London', already discussed in Chapter Ten. In the 1920s he began to formulate city-population limits. In 'The City Practical', published in *Housing* in 1920, he tentatively suggested the minima and maxima of 50,000 and 100,000 for a nucleus, which might be enlarged through self-contained satellites (Unwin, 1920, p. 67). The following year Purdom edited *Town Theory and Practice*, which included contributions by Lethaby, Pepler, Unwin and Reiss (Purdom, 1921). Each developed a component phrase from the 'official' Garden City definition.

Unwin's text was 'The town and the best size for good social life' (Purdom, 1921, pp. 80–102). Despite his awareness of the problem of urban congestion, he presented neither rigorous empirical observation nor a strong theoretical basis for his essay. The great city had become uneconomical through increasing costs but the 'increased size of the unit . . . very greatly enhances the opportunities of gain to the fortunate . . . and this is no doubt the reason why . . . our great cities continue to grow' (Purdom, 1921, p. 86). Unwin speculated that 'to some extent at least, the general population is probably bearing the cost of increase of size beyond the most economic unit, while the advantages . . . are going mainly to a limited number of successful traders'. Strikingly he postulated that 'life in the overgrown towns results in sacrificing the welfare of the majority . . . to increase the winnings of those who are fortunate in the city sweepstake' (Purdom, 1921, pp. 87–8). He called for urgent, detailed research into city size, with the proviso that the quality of life should receive priority over economic efficiency.

Unwin had proposed an ideal city-community of 50,000–75,000 inhabitants, comparable with cathedral cities such as Chester, Exeter, Lincoln or York. These traditionally provided a high-quality environment, good educational and social facilities, but might be too small to support specialized higher education, opera or a professional symphony orchestra. This might be made good through an updated 'Social City' cluster:

> a group of towns from 50,000 to 100,000 population, having good means of communication . . . and recognising one capital . . . the centre of those highly specialised activities which must draw from a large population . . . At the same time the limitation of size of each of these units, and their proper arrangement so that every citizen would be in walking distance of open country, would give opportunities of quiet and peaceful contemplation. (Purdom, 1921, pp. 97–8)

Purdom's frontispiece illustrated a belt of satellites around London, predating both Unwin's and Abercrombie's work in this respect. Unwin himself prepared a cluster diagram in 1922. Clearly based on Howard's concept diagrams, the central settlement was divided into defined wards with linked suburbs and an outer-satellite ring. Purdom included it and other cluster concepts in *Garden Cities and Satellite Towns* (Purdom, 1925, chap. 1). In the mid-1920s, Charles Edouard Jeannerat (Le Corbusier) (1887–1965) published his concept of *La cité contemporaine* as conscious anti-Garden City iconoclasticism. Despite high-technology imagery, particularly the central city for the élite, the concept was a cluster of interrelated settlements, in direct lineage from Howard's pioneering work. In Germany, too, the master plan for Frankfurt by Ernst May (1886–1970) represented the classic application of Garden-City principles to town development. Although a modernist, May respected Unwin's contributions to the discussion on planned urban expansion.

Urban efficiency was a major analytical parameter of the 1920s. Unwin's 1921–3 papers on 'Distribution' (Unwin, 1921c, pp. 37–52), 'The overgrown city' (Unwin, 1922b, pp. 85–6) and 'The Garden City and the overgrown town' (Unwin, 1923b, pp. 39–49), focused on the unsatisfactory quality of Metropolitan life. He used the terms 'crowd', 'pressure' and 'congestion' to evoke 'the artificiality of life', increasingly to be sustained by costly technological advance. He saw the Garden-City strategy as the only viable alternative, not as regression to a lost Utopia but a forward move towards the Social City:

> Our criticism of the modern town is not that it is modern, nor that it takes advantage of modern means of locomotion, of large scale production or wholesale commerce, but that it is inefficient, that in fact the advantages which might be derived from modern opportunities are sacrificed wholesale by the unregulated and haphazard character which marks its growth. (Unwin, 1923b, p. 41)

The solution lay in matching the distribution of population and land uses throughout the city region, eliminating the 'prodigious waste . . . which results from endless moving of people and goods from places where they never ought to have been placed, to places where they ought not to require to go' (Unwin, 1923b, p. 41). The solution was, of course, the expanded Garden-City concept of 'definitely planned self-contained and limited suburbs or satellite towns separated from the existing town and from each other by belts of open ground'. This message was reiterated at IGCTPF meetings, the GLRPC and Marley Committee *Reports* and in evidence to the Barlow Commission. This overall view required the creation of a higher-level executive authority to secure the overall pattern of the coherent distribution of development. A 'top down' process of implementation was essential, somehow to be integrated with the community-based approach which had characterized Unwin's earlier work. His proposals for this were made public in the early 1930s.

Town and country planning

The rural cause in planning assumed primacy in the 1920s. It was effectively lobbied by Patrick Abercrombie, who founded the Council for the Preservation of Rural England (CPRE) in 1926. Despoilation through uncontrolled sporadic building had long been Unwin's concern and, shortly before his retirement, he was involved with initiatives to improve rural planning and housing, notably the Ministry's 1927 *Housing Manual*. The Ministry's *Annual Report* for 1926–7 hinted at policy formulation by suggesting control of scattered development, not through very low-density zoning, which exacerbated matters, but by schemes to distribute and group development. These:

> would specify the permissible building centres in the area selected on a review of the suitability of the land for building as compared with other development . . . and would preclude or limit development elsewhere subject to provision to meet special needs or circumstances. (*Ministry of Health*, 1927, pp. 70–1)

Further advice was given on the reservation of regional agricultural belts; but the lack of statutory backing, particularly in the Greater London context, took the matter little further than pious hope.

In 1929 the incoming Labour Government, under Ramsay MacDonald, appointed a Committee of Inquiry into National Parks under Christopher Addison, then Minister of Agriculture. The Rural Amenities Bill, tabled by Sir Edward Hilton Young, a Conservative MP, proposed the introduction of rural planning; its importance lay in extending planning to all land (Sheail, 1981, Chap. V; Ward, 1974, pp. 85–9). A Town and Country Planning Bill was presented by the Labour Minister of Health, Arthur Greenwood, in March 1931, which incorporated the substance of Hilton Young's private initiative. The feature that surprisingly gained all-party support in principle concerned betterment. It was proposed that local authorities should be empowered to recoup 100 per cent and although the Conservatives felt that 50 per cent was more than sufficient, a 75 per cent limit was retained even after Standing Committee scrutiny.

Unwin became personally involved with the Bill's progress. He informed Greenwood that it 'would be highly appreciated by all those who are interested in the improvement of towns or the preservation of the countryside irrespective of whether they belong to our party or not'.[184] He reported on its progress to his cousin, Christy Booth, then resident in Canada. Shortly after its introduction he was 'working hard to get it generally supported and keep it out of the political scrum as far as possible'. By the Second Reading he felt 'our work will have a real chance'. The Bill fell with the Labour administration in the 1931 financial crisis.

In the subsequent National Government, Hilton Young became Minister of Health. He reintroduced the Bill in January 1932. Consensus had evaporated. In Committee, the betterment provisions became inextricably complicated and it became doubtful whether planning would be extended to all land. The TPI and NHTPC lobbied hard to save the situation. Unwin was a principal speaker at a conference organized by the latter and prominent in the delegation that met the Minister on 16 March 1932 (NHTPC, 1932, p. 2). Together with Leslie Scott, who later won distinction for his wartime report on *Land Utilization in Rural Areas*, Unwin stressed that an emasculated Act 'might destroy the efficacy of planning' (NHTPC, 1932, p. 13). Royal assent was granted the following July. Extension of planning to all land was possible but required Ministerial sanction. The duty to plan, a requirement of the 1919 Act, was dropped. The cumbersome procedure of laying schemes before Parliament was revived. Few schemes progressed beyond the early 'interim development control' stage (Ward, 1974, pp. 685–9). However, this enabled some sanction on land use and development over

73 per cent of land in England and 36 per cent in Wales, by 1942, compared with a dismal 5 per cent and 1 per cent under finalized schemes. Permissive suburban development, aptly characterized by Osbert Lancaster as 'bypass variegated', continued unabated.

In 1931 a Town and Country Planning Advisory Committee was convened to monitor statutory planning. In 1937 Unwin participated in the Committee's review of progress under the 1932 Act (Sheail, 1981, pp. 83–93). Visits were made to three sample areas, revealing patchy, inconsistent use of the legislation. After viewing the situation on the Cornish coast, Unwin demanded radical action on compensation and betterment and stricter development control. Although overruled by Sir John Maude, Chairman of the Committee, Unwin's viewpoint was reflected in the recommendations in *The Preservation of the Countryside* (Town and Country Planning Advisory Committee, 1938), which described the concept of a 'rural zone' where development unrelated to agriculture would be strictly controlled, without incurring an automatic right to compensation. This was incorporated into the model clauses of MOH *Circular 1750*, which also emphasized the desirability of coastal preservation. The full impact was not felt until the introduction of the development-plan framework under the 1947 Act; this enabled county councils to restrain development in rural areas, buttressed by a circular on *Green Belts* from 1955.

Towards a national perspective

In 1931 Pepler reviewed twenty-one years of statutory planning. He noted its patchy and haphazard adoption, especially alongside the broader coverage of *ad hoc* joint and regional schemes (Pepler, 1931, pp. 49–72). The map of England and Wales still contained vast areas of uncharted territory. There was little hope of coordinating and interlocking the plans to give a consistent picture of the planned development of resources or infrastructure at a national level. Attention turned to the national level for a synoptic approach to the distribution of population, land-uses and industry. This was a major theme of *Decentralisation of Population and Industry*, a 1930 anthology to which Unwin contributed a foreword (Warren and Davidge, 1930).

In 1931 Unwin addressed the TPI on 'The relation between town and regional planning'. He held that 'the natural order of planning is from the larger area and main lines, down to the smaller area and details'. It was:

> desirable to settle the main regional distribution, the main areas for development, or for reservation as open land, the main locations of industry and the main lines of intercommunication. When those larger matters . . . are determined, it becomes possible to plan sections of that area in true relation with the main outlines; and finally to follow these with more detailed plans of sites as they become ripe for development. (Unwin, 1931f, p. 106)

It was evident that regional plans required to be meshed in with the national level and this required a higher-level authority. This brought a warning from Adams about 'overcentralisation' (Unwin, 1931f, p. 112). Adams accepted the concept of a national plan as 'a skeleton system of the means of communication and perhaps power transmission' but remained adamant that:

> it was not possible to prepare a comprehensive national plan to cover the same ground as a regional plan. No planner could intelligently comprehend the physical problems of a country as a coherent whole. (Adams, 1932, p. 138)

During the 1930s this was the level at which Unwin aimed.

Deepening economic depression provoked the government to examine the regional–national interface. In January 1931 Arthur Greenwood appointed a committee chaired by Viscount Chelmsford to examine regional plans for infrastructure projects that might relieve unemployment. Unwin, Davidge, Alwyn Lloyd and Reiss were involved. The *Interim Report* of June 1931, however, found little potential in existing plans but urged the development of satellite towns, particularly as adjuncts to new industrial or mining areas (*Ministry of Health*, 1931).

In July 1931 Greenwood appointed a committee, under Lord Marley, to examine Garden Cities and satellites and to recommend:

> what further measures . . . should be taken for securing that in the extension of existing towns, industrial, residential and other development are properly correlated. (*Ministry of Health*, 1935, p. 4)

The August financial crisis prevented the commencement of the work for over a year. Twenty meetings were held, with visits to Letchworth, Welwyn and Wythenshawe. Unwin's natural ally was Sir Theodore Chambers (1871–1957), Chairman of Welwyn Garden City Ltd. Their joint memorandum of July 1933 contained working definitions of Garden Cities and satellite towns and the seeds of a policy of regional decentralization in the south.[185] The MP, J. Chuter Ede, felt that this was a premature conclusion, but the draft *Report* incorporated much of this material.[186] In January 1934 Unwin further developed the satellite-cluster concept.

The Marley *Report*, 'Garden Cities and Satellite Towns', finally appeared in 1935, by which time there was little prospect of immediate action. Unwin's influence was strongly evident; the concept of 'Satellites . . . in definite connection with the parent town, though separated from it and from each other by adequate areas of open land to serve the needs of both' (*Ministry of Health*, 1935, p. 26) was, after all, the enduring formula both of Howard and Unwin. Also recommended was the appointment of a Planning Board by the Minister of Health, to undertake a detailed study of industrial problems:

> with a view particularly to determining by what broad distribution of population and industry the resources of the country could be most fully utilised, and how the inconvenience and waste which result both nationally and locally from a haphazard distribution could be avoided. (*Ministry of Health*, 1935, pp. 10–11)

The Board, with executive powers, would guide development to secure a balanced distribution of population and industry. It would also administer a fund into which betterment levy, collected under the 1932 Act, would be paid. Local authorities were urged to emulate the examples of the Garden-City movement and of Manchester, by developing satellites.

The slender Marley *Report* kept the case for a national approach before the government but its enforced sloth was indicative of its low priority. An unidentified civil servant concluded that 'Sir Theodore Chambers and Sir Raymond Unwin ran away with it' and claimed that 'the recommendations were hopelessly unpractical'.[187] Yet its themes were deveoped in greater detail two years later by the Barlow Commission.

The Barlow Commission

The planning profession was more than willing to embrace 'positive planning', which Unwin and others described in a composite paper edited by John Dower for the 1935 London meeting of the International Housing and Town Planning Federation (Dower, 1935). Planning was to identify and achieve optimal goals, embracing social and economic policy as it guided the distribution of new communities and industries: a foretaste of its supremacy in postwar reconstruction after 1945. Unwin played a key role in fostering acceptance of this synoptic view. He was sharply critical of the consequences of existing legislation:

> Apart from the improvement of the accommodation in individual dwellings, what has been the effect . . . of this enormous volume of post-war building? Has it not, by general consent, destroyed the amenities over areas of country from ten to one hundred times those of the land actually occupied? Moreover the efficiency of our main roads has been seriously diminished . . . by lining hundreds of miles . . . with ribbons of villas . . . Had this vast building enterprise been based on some general conception [*sic*] of improved general conditions and distribution; had it been planned in fact, its volume would have been enough to work a beneficial transformation . . . the injury is due to the absence of planning and the consequent scatter of building . . . convenience, cost of service, efficiency of industry, commerce and transport, have all suffered from this want of planning in their development. (Unwin, 1936b, p. 170)

The culmination of Unwin's public career *should* have been membership of the Royal Commission on the Distribution of the Industrial Population, under Sir Montague Barlow. In March 1937, the Minister of

Labour, Sir Malcolm Stewart, announced the terms of reference, closely related to comments made in the Marley *Report*. In April 1937, Unwin pressed the case for a national overview in his speech accepting the Royal Gold Medal in Architecture. Having recently returned from the United States he cited the Tennessee Valley Authority and the proposed National Resources Board as models for emulation, referring to the Minister's statement as evidence that 'the old country' would shortly take a national viewpoint. Unwin hoped that planning would be 'extended . . . to the neighbourhood, to the suburb or the town, and thence still further to the region, the state or nation'.

> Physical planning is, however, only a part of life planning; and though limitation of any one man's powers must require that separate individuals . . . shall chiefly deal with the physical and with the economic and other branches . . ., a clear understanding by each of the aims and methods of the others will alone lead to effective work by either. (Unwin, 1937d, p. 585)

Unwin concluded:

> Of our government I venture to ask that they will, without delay, set up a National Planning body capable of studying the many needs and resources of our people, of creating an ordered pattern of relations between them, and of planning a convenient setting for them, in a beautiful form of environment for which our land offers opportunities both rich and varied. (Unwin, 1937d, p. 587)

In May 1937 Neville Chamberlain became Prime Minister. He had nominated both Unwin and Chambers for membership of the Barlow Commission (Sheail, 1981, p. 1938), but was opposed by Sir John Maude of the Ministry of Health, who asserted that neither would work 'with an open mind'. Maude nominated Patrick Abercrombie, who was duly appointed.[188] Chamberlain did not intervene and the Commission began its work:

> to inquire into . . . the present geographical distribution of the industrial population of Great Britain and the probable direction of any change . . . to consider what social, economic or strategical [*sic*] disadvantages arise from the concentration of industries or of the industrial population in large towns, or in particular areas of the country; and to report what remedial measures, if any, should be taken in the national interest. (*Royal Commission on the distribution of the industrial population*, 1940)

The Ministries of Labour, Transport, Health, Agriculture, the Board of Trade, and public-utility undertakers were all involved. Early in 1938 Sir John Maude pessimistically reported that 'the Commission is making very little headway and there is every likelihood of its report being a fiasco'.[189]

This was far from the truth. The planning process was thoroughly investigated, with Pepler compiling a digest of international practice. Evidence was taken from local authorities, professional bodies and individuals: Leslie Roseveare, Harding Thompson, E. G. Allen and John Dower appeared for the TPI; Osborn and Cecil Harmsworth for the Garden Cities and Town Planning Association. In June 1938, Unwin gave personal testimony. His evidence was summarized under three main headings:

I That population and industry could be located and distributed to greater advantage under comprehensive planning;
II That a national planning agency was urgently required to give coherence to the current patchwork of local plans;
III That measures were required to overcome the problems of compensation and betterment.[190]

Unwin reiterated the GLRPC and Marley Committee strategies. He emphasized the need for positive planning, discussing the desirability and practicability of industrial-location policy. The Commission expressed interest in the US National Resources Board and the proposed National Planning agency. They took comments on Unwin's proposals from I. G. Gibbon, a former Ministry colleague. The next day Unwin's proposals for compensation and betterment, a regional fund and possible land nationalization were discussed. Unwin also collaborated with Osborn in briefing Harmsworth on the possible locations for Greater London satellites.[191] Osborn virtually camped-out on the Commission's doorstep to press the case for Garden Cities at every opportunity.[192] He agreed with Unwin on the need for a strong executive body and was perturbed by 'strong rumours that the Royal Commission is going to let us down . . . they are snatching at the plans the TPI most unfortunately threw them in the shape of an advisory shadow of a planning authority'.[193] Unwin was less dogmatic, having conceded that there was a case for voluntary cooperation during the formulation of the national plan, enabling the central agency to build up its information base and expertise before acquiring executive powers.

It was this point that divided the Commission. The majority opted for an advisory body but Abercrombie and two colleagues pressed for an executive body. Overall there was agreement that the organization should formulate policies to assist the redevelopment of congested areas and that there should be decentralization of population and industry, attaining balanced development and economic diversification through Garden Cities, satellite towns and trading estates. The new super-authority did not materialize but the substantive recommendations, similar to the 'hopelessly impractical' conclusions of the Marley Committee, formed the basis for post-1945 reconstruction. Further examination of the problems of compensation and betterment was recommended. This was achieved by the Committee appointed in 1941 under Mr Justice Uthwatt. The Barlow *Report* was completed in August 1939 but the outbreak of the Second World War in September delayed its publication until January 1940.

It is doubtful whether Unwin saw the *Report*, though he must have been aware of its general conclusions. He was stranded in the United States, having combined a visit to his daughter in Connecticut with early arrival for an international planning forum in Washington. He had worked on an agenda, developing the theme 'Can Planning raise the general standard of living?'. His notes were unhesitatingly affirmative:

1 Planning improves home life by providing better living places in pleasanter surroundings with increased security for their amenity values.
2 It enlarges the economic basis of life by affording more adequate opportunities for the fishing industry and agriculture.
3 It enhances the effective value of all production by promoting rapid and convenient means of transport for persons and food and thus aiding efficient end economical distribution, both wholesale and retail.
4 It adds to the enjoyment of life by increasing the opportunities for every kind of healthy recreation and culture for all.
5 It adds to the richness and quality of life by preserving the natural beauty of the country and by securing orderly and comely urban development, thus satisfying the natural aesthetic hunger of mankind.[194]

In February 1940 a London meeting of planners to discuss wartime social and economic problems was interrupted as a cablegram from the United States was read out:

> Planning now for post-war national development urgent if short war, increasingly important if war prolonged. Emphatically support! Raymond Unwin.[195]

Unwin would have rejoiced to see the proposals of the Barlow Commission, with many of which he had been personally involved, enacted by the 1945 Labour government, and the central role accorded to planning in postwar reconstruction.

12
The Patriarch of Planning

Unwin soon achieved recognition as one of the founding fathers of town-planning, both in Britain and internationally.[196] Links with Germany and the United States were most fruitful. In 1911 the German publication of *Town Planning in Practice* (*Grundlagen des Stadtebaus*) was indicative of his standing.[197] Unwin had personal contacts with A. E. Brinckmann (1881–1958), Ernst May (1886–1970) and Werner Hegemann (1882–1936) among others. In 1913 Unwin invited Hegemann to lecture to the London Society on the *Grosses Berlin* competition and in 1922 he reviewed Hegemann's *American Vitruvius*, a comprehensive manual of civic design prepared in collaboration with Elbert Peets (Unwin, 1923, pp. 416–7). The American edition of *The Art of Building a Home* introduced Parker and Unwin to a transatlantic readership in 1901, the year when F. L. Ackerman met Unwin at Bournville (*Garden City Association*, 1901, pp. 19–20). The book was noticed by the Arts and Crafts entrepreneur, Gustave Stickley (1857–1942), presaging an enthusiastic review of *Town Planning in Practice*[198] and a long series of articles on Parker's domestic design in *The Craftsman*. Unwin was well-known when he, Adams and Thomas Mawson (1861–1933) formed the British delegation to the 1911 Third National City Planning Conference at Philadelphia (*Proceedings*, 1911). There Unwin met John Nolen (1869–1937), one of the most influential American planning pioneers. Nolen illustrated Letchworth and Hampstead in his book, *City Planning*, while his 1916 plan for Kingport, Tennessee, blended formal and irregular elements as in Unwin's work. Nolen's Boston Park system was admired by Unwin. Both were involved with the International Garden Cities and Town Planning Federation in the 1920s.

The War and What After?

Internationalism in planning was rudely shattered by the outbreak of war in August 1914. Delegates hastily fled from the London University Summer School of town-planning, programmed for 3–15 August.[199] Unwin became deeply involved with internationalism. His interest developed in the concept of a League of Nations, with international reconciliation to prevent future hostilities based upon nationalism. More immediately he was concerned with the plight of Belgian refugees[200] and subsequently played a leading role in promoting the postwar replanning of Belgium (Smets, 1977, p. 92).

Early in 1915, Unwin became involved with refugee Belgian architects, assisted with RIBA hospitality and with a conference by the Garden Cities and Town Planning Association on Belgian reconstruction, held 11–15 February. He urged nationally based, planned reconstruction. In May, with Abercrombie, Adshead, Davidge and Lanchester, he lectured at the Belgian Town Planning Exhibition, held at University College, London. He chaired the Belgium Town Planning Committee, held under Bryce's Presidency. In September 1919, a joint reconstruction conference was sponsored by *L'Union des Villes et Communes Belges* and the International Garden Cities and Town Planning Federation. Unwin, Parker, Lanchester, Aldridge and Purdom headed the British delegation. Unwin spoke on planning methodology, land values and transport. In the 1920s Belgian planning was strikingly influenced by Unwin, in schemes by Adrian Blomme and housing promoted by the *Société Nationale des Habitations à Bon Marché*, designed by Van der Swaelman, J. Eggericx and R. Moenaert (Smets, 1977, p. 108ff.).

Early in the war Unwin joined a group led by Viscount Bryce, Lowes Dickenson, E. R. Cross and John Hobson,[201] who sought an analysis of the cause of hostilities and a means of reconciliation. Unwin's privately printed booklet, *The War and What After?* (Unwin, 1915a), emphasized the link between town-planning and broader internationalism:

> because I have profited much by the study of what other nations, including our present enemies, have contributed to the common stock of knowledge and achievement in connection with civics and city building, and have been impressed by the benefit derived from the varied individuality of nations, I ask consideration for a few thoughts on the conditions under which nations may live and prosper side by side without drifting periodically into war in order to settle their differences. (Unwin, 1915a, p. 1)

Unwin differentiated between negotiation on a mutually agreed basis and conciliation where no such basis existed. His tactic lay in analysing the essential points on either side, then trying 'to frame that settlement which will go furthest to satisfy each party and induce each to forego the points to which they attach least importance' (Unwin, 1915a, pp. 39–40). In addition to legal skills, he felt that 'quick insight and keen sympathy' combined with 'a ready tact and broad knowledge of men and affairs' (Unwin, 1915a, p. 43), characteristics that he possessed in abundance, would carry most weight in framing a settlement. He proposed the formation of an International Union to frame international law, to promote the just settlement of disputes and to guarantee peace. This led from his early attempts to define 'the third course' to socialism in the 1880s. It also underlay his work in Dublin, recounted in Chapter Eight. His commitment to German colleagues was evident in the winter after the 1918 Armistice. Geoffrey Barry Parker recalled the family shivering at 'Wyldes' because his uncle had sent coal to Germany to aid his ailing friend, Berlepsch Valendas.

The British League of Nations Society was formed in May 1915 under the Chairmanship of Lord Robert Cecil. Unwin was a keen participant. His daughter Peggy occasionally acted as group secretary. In July Geddes organized a three-week conference, 'The War: its social tasks and problems', to examine the problems of Belgian and French reconstruction (Boardman, 1978, pp. 168–71). Discussions were led by Herbert Hoover, later President of the United States; lectures were given by Unwin, Lanchester, the sociologist L. T. Hobhouse, and the geographer H. J. Mackinder. After the Armistice, the covenant for an International League of Nations was part of President Woodrow Wilson's fourteen point plan, appended to the Treaty of Versailles, reflecting the hard work of Lord Cecil, the South African politician Jan Smuts and, not least, Unwin and Geddes.

Transatlantic journeys

Following his daughter's marriage in 1920 to Curtice Hitchcock, a member of Woodrow Wilson's Peace Delegation, Unwin became a frequent visitor to the United States. The crossings provided agreeable holidays, usually by the slower 'ten-day boats'. Occasionally aboard a faster, more fashionable ship, Unwin would complain about elaborate menus, dressing for dinner and the frivolity of shipboard movies. Each day he prepared papers or lectures and read aloud on quiet corners of the deck. His letters to his cousin, Christy Booth, recall the Whitmanesque pantheism of his youthful association with Edward Carpenter:

> There is no rest cure like . . . a voyage . . . All the cares belonging to one shore are left behind and those of the other can well wait till it is in sight . . . no excuse whatever for worrying over one side or the other, the past or the future. Nothing to do but drink in the invigorating air and the feasts of lovely sky and water all about; watch the birds, how they fly and glide and how by a most subtle adjustment and with infinite skill, they follow day after day, beating whenever they want the speed of the boat seemingly without effort.[202]

In 1920 Unwin invited Lewis Mumford (1895–1989) to tea. Mumford was editing Victor Brandford's *Sociological Review* but on his return to the United States, he became a founder member of the Regional Planning Association of America (RPAA), which developed the regional Garden-City context (Sussman, 1976). Unwin developed fruitful contact with Mumford, Henry Wright (1878–1936), Clarence Stein (1882–1975), Catherine Bauer (1905–64) and Edith Elmer Wood (1871–1945). It was, however, the Russell Sage Foundation that brought Unwin to the United States as a potential consultant planner for the New York Regional Plan. In October 1922 Unwin spent a week in New York, analysing the

Metropolitan problem and lecturing on 'The Overgrown City' (Unwin, 1922b, pp. 85–6). He reiterated the necessity of dividing the city into identifiable communities and physical units, aiming for the equitable distribution of employment opportunities to reduce transportation and congestion costs. For Unwin the celebrated Lower Manhattan skyline represented the consequences of untrammelled *laissez-faire*, which did not endear him to the business community. Thomas Adams was appointed consultant in September 1923 and the plan was completed and published between 1929 and 1931 (Simpson, 1985, Chaps. 6 and 7). The Wall Street crash of October 1929 altered the perspective of accommodating urban growth fired by a fast-expanding economy. Mumford and the RPAA felt that the *Regional Plan for New York and its Environs* ignored the provision of counter attractions to the congested, central business district and failed to apply broader aspects of Garden-City theory (Sussman, 1976, pp. 224–59).

In 1923 Wright and Stein visited Letchworth, Hampstead and Gretna. They developed Garden-City layout principles for the American context. Sunnyside Gardens in New York (1924) was an urban version of the housing block of *Nothing Gained by Overcrowding* (Stein, 1949–50). In 1925 the New York meeting of the International Garden Cities and Town Planning Federation brought Unwin, Parker and Howard to the USA. Mumford recalled Unwin as 'politically gifted, dispassionate, reasoned, always a bit of a Quaker, a sound practical man due to his apprenticeship as an engineer'.[203] Unwin collaborated informally with Wright and Stein over the evolution of the housing superblock. It emerged in 1928, with perimeter culs-de-sac following the precedent of Reynolds Close, Hampstead, combined with the central open space from *Nothing Gained by Overcrowding*. A layout was prepared for a garden suburb at Radburn, New Jersey, in 1928. The neighbourhood blocks were increased to 30–50 acres [12–20 hectares] to support a primary school (Stein, 1949–50, pp. 219–29). Unwin relished his involvement with the project, writing excitedly to Christy Booth in September 1928: 'I am deep in planning their new Garden Suburb'. He tramped the site, as when he had planned Letchworth a quarter of a century before, scrambling up a hillock to proclaim it a splendid site for the high school (Feiss, 1963, p. 424). The depression halted the growth of Radburn but Unwin included its plan in the GLRPC *Second Report*.

Unwin's fascination with the skyscraper continued. He analysed the consequences of building upwards in 'Higher Building in relation to town planning' (Unwin, 1924a, pp. 125–49). Such development, he felt, epitomized the artificial concentration of land values, institutionalized during the 1920s by the uniform zoning of building intensity. He graphically analysed the impact of teeming hordes of clerical employees on the transportation system and the generation of demand for roadside parking.[204] In 1928 he urged a ban on further speculative development in Lower Manhattan, allied to office decentralization.[205]

At the end of his life, in 1939–40, Unwin turned to the problem of the increasing dereliction fringing the central business districts. Citing

Chicago and New York, he described the blighting effect of the expectation of artificially high returns and urged redevelopment for low-density housing that would provide a speedy, more certain, if lower return, spread over a greater area.[206] He familiarized himself with Homer Hoyt's analysis of the distribution of land uses and land values (Hoyt, 1933). In advocating housing redevelopment, he brought *Nothing Gained by Overcrowding* to the inner city as the basis for physical and social reconstruction (Unwin, 1941, pp. 1–9). A staunch supporter of planned decentralization, he perceived inner city regeneration as a corollary of the Garden City, as had Howard and Morris before him.

The International Garden Cities and Town Planning Federation

The International Garden Cities and Town Planning Federation (IGCTPF) was an influential town-planning forum during the 1920s, inaugurated in Paris in 1913.[207] It was not until 1923 that a fully representative postwar conference was held, in Gothenburg, Sweden: a city regarded as a showpiece for Scandinavian planning and civic design. The City Architect, W. Lilienborg, had attended the 1910 RIBA International Congress. The Gothenburg conference exhibition was organized by Hegemann and included recent Scandinavian projects, the revised Grosses Berlin and Ruhr plans, material from the New York Regional Plan and many postwar British housing schemes.[208] As RIBA delegate, Unwin reported that the veteran Joseph Stübben was keen and active as ever at the age of 78, and that John Nolen and Charles Eliot had brought new ideas from the United States. Unwin sensed the integration of the Garden-City movement with town-planning, so that 'the distinction between the propagandist Garden City and practising town planning movements will no longer be required' (Unwin, 1923c, p. 622). The Federation later reflected this by changing its name to The International *Housing and Town Planning* Federation. Unwin's paper was one of his 'Overgrown City' series (Unwin, 1923b, pp. 39–40).

The next conference at Amsterdam in 1924 brought renewed contact between Unwin and the Dutch architect-planner, H. P. Berlage (1856–1934), who subsequently received the RIBA Royal Gold Medal in 1932. Parker and Unwin studied recent housing by Gerrit Rietveld (1888–1964), J. J. P. Oud (1890–1963) and Willem Dudok (1884–1974). Unwin's paper, 'The need for a regional plan' (Unwin, 1924b, pp. 15–30), complemented Abercrombie's on 'The preliminary survey of a region'. Motions on green belts and satellite towns, the preparation of regional plans and the development of park systems were approved. In 1925 New York was an ideal venue to experience the archetypal twentieth-century Metropolis. Unwin spoke on 'Methods of decentralisation' (Unwin, 1925b, pp. 150–65), warning that high-rise building was 'even more shortsighted than horizontal overcrowding'.

In 1926, under the banner of the International Housing and Town

Planning Federation, the organization met in Vienna. Delegates examimed the problems of land tenure and 'the rational distribution of cottages and tenements'. The City's new tenement schemes symbolized a radical new proletarian urban lifestyle. Alongside this, Unwin's call 'to give the individual a place in which he can . . . retire from the bustle of life and live what I call a human life'[209] must have seemed perversely out of step with the rise of the modern architecture. Nevertheless, the conference agreed that houses were preferable to tenements if the difficulties of land acquisition and tenure could be overcome.

Following Howard's death in May 1928, Unwin was elected President of the Federation by an overwhelming majority. He did not present papers at Paris (1928), Rome (1929) or Berlin (1931) but contributed pithy comments: as in Rome, where he called for the study 'of the science as well as the art of town-planning to find natural units of size'.[210] The IHTPF *Bulletin* was multilingual; the December 1930 issue, for example, carried Unwin's summary of the GLRPC *First Report*, with French and German translations (Unwin, 1930c, pp. 4–10). The Federation's 17 national Vice-Presidents included Chamberlain, with Elgood, Pepler, Purdom and Unwin ensuring a strong British presence on the executive committee. A note of weariness occasionally crept into the proceedings, as in September 1930 when Unwin reported to his cousin:

> We had our [IHTPF] Council meeting this weekend. A very rude Prussian Minister, and about 15 other foreign delegates, reception by the Mayor of Westminster, Friday; Federation meeting all Saturday morning; a tour of housing schemes in London in the afternoon and a trip to Welwyn and Letchworth on Sunday. There are a lot of such meetings now.[211]

Was all the effort worthwhile? The Berlin conference in 1931 was linked to three other meetings in Germany.[212] The themes of 'Town planning in relation to traffic' and 'Slum clearance' provoked lively debate, particularly over the issue of the municipalization of urban transit-systems. John Nolen described the parkway concept, and Clarence Stein illustrated Radburn, which Edward Unwin, following his father's enthusiasm over its planning, hailed as 'the basis of future planning both in Europe and America'. The Unwins visited newly developed suburban housing *siedlungen* at Zehlendorf and Siemensstadt. Hegemann explained that land costs were between three and six times greater than in London. The Unwins admired the communal facilities, though they had reservations about the architectural expression. At the end of the Berlin meeting Unwin retired as Federation President, to be succeeded by Nolen.

At the London meeting in 1935 Unwin contributed to the collaborative British paper on 'Positive planning' (Dower et al., 1935, pp. 117–22), reinforcing the progression towards the national level. Abercrombie, Adams, Theodore Chambers of Welwyn Garden City, Davidge, Hardy-Syms of the reconstituted GLRPC, and Longstreth Thompson all contributed, under the editorship of John Dower. The final prewar meeting in Paris in 1937 was an adjunct to the International Exhibition. Unwin assumed the role of elder statesman as he traced the roots of planning back to Howard and Geddes (Unwin, 1937b, pp. 95–6).

Unwin and modernism

By the late 1920s the IHTPF seemed a conservative body alongside the rise of modernism in architecture and planning. The startling images presented by Tony Garnier (1869–1948) in his *Cité Industrielle* (1901–4) (although not published until 1917) (Wiebenson, n.d.), and the Italian Futurist, Antonio Sant'Elia (1880–1916) in his *Citta Nuova* of 1914 prepared the way for Le Corbusier's *La Cité Contemporaine* published in 1922. This presented a high-rise city for three million inhabitants, with apartment towers grouped around a central transportation interchange (Fishman, 1977, pp. 163–277). Yet it initially retained a cluster of industrial housing satellites. The clarity of the plan presented a crisp pattern on a green background in the manner advocated by Unwin; the overall concept owed much to Howard's Social City cluster and the development strategy advocated by Unwin in 'The Garden City Principle applied to existing towns'.

Far from wanting a refuge from the bustle of the city, the modernists gloried in apartment life. In 1928 the *Congrès Internationaux d'Architecture Moderne* (CIAM) was formed, a challenge to the orthodoxy of the IHTPF. By 1933 a manifesto for the modern city had been drawn up and was endorsed as the Athens Charter (Hatje, 1964, pp. 70–3; Tafuri and Dal Co, 1980).

Unwin took no part in CIAM. Although he conceded that 'functionalism' was 'not quite so frightening as it sounds' and perceived 'a good deal of honesty behind these people who want us to build structurally . . . and functionally' (Unwin, 1932, p. 695), he continued to warn against extremes. He was essentially conservative in his appraisal of architecture and town-planning. Politically radical, his personal philosophy cleaved to the visual expression of revitalized traditionalism, inherited from Ruskin and Morris. In a 1930 lecture he characteristically attempted to accommodate both viewpoints, claiming that tradition and innovation represented 'theme and variations' of an overall harmony built upon the judicious counterpoint of old and new.[213] Yet its imagery was entirely traditional – the rich townscape of Oxford High Street, where the startling contrast of the classical-style buildings of the seventeenth and eighteenth centuries with their mediaeval neighbours had been mellowed by the 'kindly hand of time' over two centuries and more. In the early 1930s the aesthetic issue became so polarized as to exclude the middle ground sought by Unwin.

His pronouncements as RIBA President from 1931–3 drew approval from those with whom he certainly would not have agreed politically, as in 1932, when he 'drew the line' on modernists who suggested 'that it is part of the duty of an architect to expose structure' (Unwin, 1932a, p. 695). Most often it was over housing that his criticism was sharpest:

> There is a great deal of talk about housing families in vast steel and concrete warehouses, and of the great economy, and increased urban benefits . . . to follow from so doing . . . It may be that the modern family will like living in a few cells in a vast pile of biscuit boxes . . . That has never appealed to me as an attractive idea of a home . . . If people do want to be housed in big masses in the centre of a town, by all means let them . . . but I do want us to be serious and careful about it; because it is easier to allow these piles to be put up than to get them removed. (Unwin, 1933e, pp. 659–60)

Unwin kept faith with the cottage estate and observed that at 1933 prices, flats cost £300 more per dwelling (Unwin, 1933e, p. 660). He was alarmed by the shift in the LCC programme under the 1930 Housing Act, with its emphasis on slum clearance and redevelopment flats. In 1934 he prophesied that:

> England will rue the day . . . if the housing movement of half a century is sacrificed for the makeshift expedience of congestion, the futility of which has been proved whenever it has been adopted. (Unwin, 1934c, p. vii)

In 1934, Unwin opened an exhibition of the work of Walter Gropius (1883–1969), which included the Bauhaus buildings at Dessau and the Berlin–Siemesstadt *siedlung*. Unwin guardedly related the modernist-design approach to a Germanic predilection for the total application of theoretical constructs, as compared to British pragmatism. This had enabled the Bauhaus to evolve as a logical extension of the Arts and Crafts movement. While he appreciated Gropius' 'Athenian quality of appreciative curiosity', he concluded that:

> It was neither desirable, nor to be expected that all England should go wildly enthusiastic about a movement of building and design which is so clearly foreign to a great part of the architects and the public in this country. (Unwin, 1934, p. 668)

In reply, Gropius stated that 'England's contribution [to the modern movement] has been limited to housing and town planning', but he generously recognized that 'Sir Raymond Unwin's ideas and English Garden Cities have influenced the whole housing movement'. To set Unwin's views in context, it should be recalled that in the early 1930s the pioneer modern houses by Connell, Ward and Lucas were extensively publicized and that F. R. S. Yorke (1906–62) published the first edition of *The Modern House* in 1934. E. Maxwell Fry (1899–1987) would shortly collaborate with Gropius on the design for Impington College, Cambridge, and the first phase of the concrete high rise flats at Highpoint, Highgate, designed by a team led by Berthold Lubetkin (1901–90) had recently been completed.

International honours and home values

Academic honours were showered on Unwin from the 1920s. In 1925 after receiving a Technical Doctorate from the University of Prague, he was most moved to receive a gold-nugget fob for his watch chain from Czech miners who had heard of his housing work.[214] Degrees from Toronto University (1934), Trondheim and Manchester (1935) and Harvard (1937) followed. He was highly amused to be accorded a military escort at Trondheim after receiving his degree from the King of Norway.[215] At Harvard, his slight, tweedy figure among the immaculately clad academics suggested a backwoodsman reminding them of the fundamental values both of his personal philosophy and of the American character.

In July 1931, Unwin was the first town-planner to be elected RIBA President. At his inauguration that November, he invited young musicians to play a Beethoven piano concerto.[216] His two-year term was notable for strong advocacy of a national housing programme (Unwin 1931g, 1932c). He authorized the construction of the Institute's Portland Place Headquarters and organized a relief fund that enabled unemployed architects to make surveys of historic buildings in London. Memories of Morris and Ruskin and their enduring value were recalled in talks to students. His highest accolade was a Knighthood in the 1932 Birthday Honours List. Unwin accepted the honour to the cause of housing and town-planning. To the dismay of his family he wore an old frock coat bought for the 1910 Berlin conference. After the investiture he gleefully observed that both he and the King with his naval uniform had worn the same style of coat.[217] In 1937 he received the Royal Gold Medal for Architecture (Unwin, 1937a, pp. 581–90), followed by the award of the Ebenezer Howard Memorial Medal from the Town and Country Planning Association in 1938.

Unwin's lifestyle remained frugal and unassuming. 'Wyldes', his Hampstead home, had links with Dickens and Constable and, more recently, the anarchist Peter Kropotkin. His own guests beyond an international array of planners and architects included the Boer politician, Jan Smuts, and the black actor Paul Robeson. Arthur Geddes viewed 'Wyldes' in terms of his father's 'conservative surgery':

> RU preserved that lovely farmhouse in an almost unspoilable setting with the heath as a playground for his children and friends. Without a doubt a good new house could have been built, as in Letchworth, but why? This was already a home.[218]

Life at 'Wyldes' was intellectually focused. Reading aloud, a nightly ritual, ranged from Dickens to the philosophy of Tagore, supplemented, from 1930, by broadcast concerts and talks. Etty Unwin dressed discerningly in Liberty style, tall and elegant into old age, always with knitting or embroidery to hand. Meals were informal, largely vegetarian: Margaret Bruce Glasier, the daughter-in-law of Unwin's old socialist comrade, wondered how they could stand the cooking! Through Etty Unwin's work for the Society of Friends, refugees were transitory guests in the nooks and crannies of the old house.

Foreign dignitaries sought out Unwin. Freda Whyte, a cousin, acted as *chauffeuse* and interpreter for a Soviet Chief Housing Commissar, embarking on the development of Magnetogorsk:

> The Russian looked in despair at the LCC schemes pointing out that he was planning vast blocks of flats on the basis of one room per family . . . We could offer plenty of East End slums, but, of course, no new building with this.[219]

In 1931, the Danish architect planner, Steen Eiler Rasmussen (1898–1990) visited 'Wyldes' with Danish students. Unwin prepared coffee at the fireplace:

> a protecting enclosure round our little group that listened so eagerly to the spiritual man in the centre . . . as he stirred up the fire . . . he could bring new life to the discussion by means of a Socratic question now and then. (Rassmussen, 1957, p. 283)

Afterwards, 'off we went through shrubberies, climbing hills, running after our sprightly host. And there on the top of Hampstead Heath he showed us the magnificent view' (Rasmussen, 1963, p. 433).

Edward Unwin had married during the First World War but he remained at 'Wyldes'. Study at Cambridge had been prevented by the outbreak of war. His architectural career was overshadowed by his father. During the depression he founded the Production for Use League, a cooperative for the unemployed. He assisted on GLRPC fieldwork. In 1934 he was commissioned by the Trades Union Congress to design the Tolpuddle Martyrs Memorial Cottages. His death in January 1936, at the age of 41, was a bitter blow. Raymond Unwin felt his own life was prolonged at the expense of his son's fulfilment and immersed himself even more intensively in his work, dividing his time between London and the United States.[220]

A New Deal housing strategy

The Wall Street crash of October 1929, and the subsequent depression in the United States brought the need for public intervention to rebuild the nation's economy and infrastructure. This was accomplished through the New Deal upon which President Roosevelt embarked after his inauguration in January 1933. The Secretary of the Interior, Harold Ickes, drafted a substantial public-works housing programme. In November 1933 the National Association of Housing Officials (NAHO) was formed in Chicago, with Ernest Bohn as President and Charles Ascher, a lawyer involved with the development of Radburn, as Executive Director (Scott, 1969, p. 320). That winter Unwin embarked

Figure 64 Raymond Unwin in 1934: elder statesman of planning. Throughout the 1930s Unwin divided his time between Britain and the United States where he influenced the formulation of the New Deal housing policy

upon a tour of North America (Unwin, 1934f, pp. 646–7). His Chicago visit coincided closely with the birth of NAHO, which drew on his long experience of public housing design and administration. In January 1934 he spoke to the American Civic Association in Washington and was eagerly questioned by Eleanor Roosevelt about British housing policy.[221] His knack of being on the spot seemed infallible.

In August 1934, the Rockefeller Foundation financed an International Housing Commission, under the auspices of NAHO, to tour fourteen major cities and prepare a report on public housing (Feiss, 1963, p. 471). Unwin was joined by Ernest Kahn, a Frankfurt economist; Alice

Samuel, the Housing Manager of Bebington, Birkenhead; Ernest Bohn, NAHO President and Henry Wright, the architect–planner. Bohn recorded that:

> Sir Raymond worked tirelessly. We tried to spare him as many after dinner speeches as possible only to find local committees persuading him to remake engagements that we had cancelled. (Feiss, 1963, p. 471)

The Commission met with NAHO in Baltimore early in October 1934 to formulate policy (Feiss, 1963, p. 472; Scott, 1969, p. 325). The proposal for a National Housing Programme (Public Administration Service, 1935) contained many Unwinesque phrases, not least the opening statement urging the objective of 'a standard of living not below the minimum needed for a decent family life . . . for all citizens'. Attainment required the coordination of government agencies, under the direction of a permanent Federal Housing Authority, with room for local autonomy and initiative. This recalled the original regional structure of the Ministry of Health and Unwin's proposal for a National Housing Corporation. The NAHO *Report* advocated 'the satellite town type of development . . . coordinated with regional and city planning so that they form part of and contribute to the building up of the city plan'. The British influence was readily evident.[222]

Unwin, accompanied by his wife, and Ickes met President Roosevelt at the White House. Flustered, Etty dropped the ubiquitous knitting and the discussion was preceded by the aides gathering up and rewinding the wool. The President had reserved fifteen minutes but spent an hour with them (Feiss, 1963, pp. 423–4). Shortly afterwards he urged a nationwide slum-clearance and rehousing initiative. Legislation, introduced in 1935, was enacted two years later as the United States Housing Act (Scott, 1969, pp. 327–9), which enabled public provision of housing for 'those who cannot pay enough to cause private enterprise in their locality . . . to build an adequate supply of decent, safe and sanitary dwellings'. Although the duty was not statutory, the parallel with British precedent was evident.

Unwin's tours of the United States were extensive. Carl Feiss, an architect with whom he was associated at Columbia University, New York, recalled that Unwin:

> was never hesitant with comments or advice. Even when being severely critical he was soft spoken and respected the judgement of others even when in disagreement. Therefore perhaps he was more readily listened to . . . [he] had the great advantage of being English . . . [he] faced no cultural block, his was a more humanitarian viewpoint than was usually found in distinguished British visitors.[223]

In Canada he assisted the foundation of the Toronto Housing Centre in 1936. The verdict on an earlier Canadian visit might well stand for his overall involvement with North American housing and town-planning:

> it is not too much to say that in three days Sir Raymond Unwin did more to advance the cause of town planning than all the rest of us could do in three years . . . he told us what we wanted to know but never suggested what we ought to do.[224]

Unwin learned from America, particularly New Deal projects such as the Tennessee Valley Authority (TVA), with its programme of rural reconstruction, resettlement, electrification and resource management, and new settlements (Unwin, 1935b, p. 262; 1937d, pp. 583–4). The greenbelt satellites of the Washington–Baltimore corridor were also models for emulation. The sparsely populated prairies represented a resource, which through cooperative planned development might yield a universally high standard of living. *Nothing Gained by Overcrowding* was extended to the far horizons by his provocative pronouncement that the 2000-million world population could be accommodated in Kansas at Garden City densities (Unwin, 1936–7, p. 14). This was contemporary with Frank Lloyd Wright's Broadacre City, a ubiquitous low-density prairie development designed to benefit from the freedom of movement resulting from universal car ownership (Fishman, 1977, pp. 122–34).

Communicator and educator

A didactic purpose underlay Unwin's work: education towards enlightenment accompanied his advocacy of new standards in housing. Although his specific role as an educator was limited, *Cottage Plans and Common Sense*, *Town Planning in Practice*, and *Nothing Gained by Overcrowding* all possessed an educational dimension. During 1908–14 he was visiting lecturer in town-planning at the Architectural Association, London and from 1911–14 Cadbury Lecturer in town-planning at the University of Birmingham. His Ministry career circumscribed his activities, but he was involved with professional development in its broadest sense. In 1919 he provided an introduction and commentary to a gala showing of films organized by Howard and the Garden Cities and Town Planning Association, in the presence of Edward, Prince of Wales (Unwin, 1919b, pp. 163–5). In the 1930s he broadcast on housing; in 1937 he made a pioneer television broadcast on Greater London planning. Frederic Osborn, then a director of Murphy Radio in Welwyn, commandeered sets to enable the Garden Cities and Town Planning Association to view the programme.[225]

Summer schools have long been established features of professional education. Before the First World War, Unwin was involved with London University schools on town-planning, held in the Hampstead Garden Suburb Institute. In 1933, Thomas Adams invited Unwin to chair the first Town and Country Planning Summer School, held at Welwyn (*Town and Country Planning Summer School*, 1933, p. 4). Late in 1935, Unwin was offered a Visiting Professorship in Town Planning at the School of Architecture, Columbia University, New York, in succession to Henry Wright. With his enormous collection of lantern slides, he arrived at Avery Hall, the departmental headquarters, the following summer. During 1936–7 he gave fourteen two-hour lectures on housing and town-planning, presenting a synoptic view based on the Birmingham syllabus he had prepared a quarter of a century before (Unwin, 1936–7). The titles of the first and last lectures indicate his planning odyssey: 'The Nature of Man, his life, and the family and society afford the best basis for good housing and planning' and 'Regional and state planning'. The scheme built up from the individual to the community, city, region and nation, mirroring his broadening philosophy. He recalled his early studies of communal life, the balanced symbiosis of the subsistence economy of the mediaeval village. He emphasized the break of the Industrial Revolution. He contrasted 'planned progress' with the 'rugged individualism' of American entrepreneurship. He reiterated that design was the process of bringing harmonious relationships to and between all scales of planning and development. Etty Unwin would sit on the front row knitting, occasionally correcting her husband over a date or fact, afterwards presiding over afternoon tea in the studio. Unwin's lecture outlines were issued as a mimeographed booklet: Steen Eiler Rasmussen wondered whether they merited publication for the enduring topicality of their approach (Rasmussen, 1963, p. 431).

Carl Feiss, Unwin's assistant, stressed the value of the studio:

> Unwin always spent hours in the studio . . . lecture day or not. Students liked him right away. He was always genial and friendly and relaxed, whatever the age group. Mumford, Stein, Ascher, Churchill, Mayer and Arthur Holden would walk into the drafting room and would have several hours of informal discussions . . . the debate was always lively and memorable. Unknowingly the students were being exposed to a unique assembly of geniuses devoted to the public interest.[226]

In the spring of 1938, during a field trip to the flooded Connecticut River Valley, the whole party succumbed to chills and colds. The Unwins kept going on hot, sweet tea. Unwin was involved with each session to 1939–40. He also lectured at Harvard, Princeton and Cornell Universities, the Massachusetts Institute of Technology, and shared lectures with Catherine Bauer, the housing sociologist, at the Pennsylvania School of Social Work.[227]

Envoi

In the uneasy summer of 1939, Unwin returned to England for what was to be his last visit. He discussed with Frank Pick, the Chief Executive of the London Passenger Transport Board, and with Pepler, the foundation of a School of Planning and Research for National Development and drafted a syllabus.[228] Early in July he spoke at Millthorpe on the tenth anniversary of the death of Edward Carpenter:

> Among the men – Evangelists, Artists, poets, whom the Socialist movement inspired . . . Edward Carpenter holds a unique place . . . at once most penetrating in thought, most delicate in feeling, most lucid in expression and most intimate in his personal relations and affections.[229]

Carpenter's gift of *Towards Democracy* had opened the door of perception and laid foundations for Unwin's quest for harmony between society and environment. He stayed with his cousin, Christy Booth, at her Ashover farmhouse, its rugged walls and well-proportioned façade evoking the vernacular tradition he had always valued.

The Unwins arrived in New York on 3 September 1939, a few days before the outbreak of the Second World War. Unwin had been appointed British delegate to the XV International Congress of Architects, scheduled for 24–30 September, taking the theme of low-density, low-rise housing for his paper.[230] The event was cancelled but he conferred with Rexford Tugwell and Robert Moses about a possible US National Planning Forum. He cabled the Ministry of Health that he would return if there was work for him to do. He attended the NAHO meeting in Cincinatti and joined the Housing Committee of the Twentieth Century Fund in New York.

In the spring of 1940 Unwin fell ill. He died, aged 76, on June 28, in a weatherboarded cottage in Old Lyme, Connecticut, near his daughter's country home. Shortly before, he had received a letter from Eleanor Roosevelt, accompanied by red roses. 'I am deeply grateful,' she wrote, 'for the fine work you have done in public housing, and want to express my appreciation for the help you have given the program in this country' (Thompson, 1940, p. 187). Professional institutes on both sides of the Atlantic added their tributes and endorsed his philosophy as the basis for postwar reconstruction:

> Ruthlessly destroyed cities all over the world must be rebuilt . . . never before have circumstances – the vulnerability of great and congested cities, and the rapid spread of urban blight – given so much point to Sir Raymond's contention that 'Nothing is gained by overcrowding'. The need and opportunity of spreading that gospel are here now. The opposing forces are those of tradition, shrinkage from change, ignorance and greed. (Black, 1940, p. 12)

In 1943, Etty Unwin finally succeeded in obtaining a passage home. Christy Booth took Raymond Unwin's ashes to Crosthwaite Churchyard on the slopes of Skiddaw, near Keswick, in the English Lake District.[231] Etty Unwin died in 1949, having witnessed the beginnings of the second postwar reconstruction in which the central role of planning, at which her husband had aimed, was officially endorsed.[232]

13
The Man and the Planner

Professional tributes and personal memoirs

> He could take great interest in creating pleasant conditions and surroundings for individuals, but to do this for communities interested him more . . . To Unwin the wider appeal was always the greater inspiration . . . The power to benefit humanity in the [town planning] movement was what appealed to him . . . all his energies were directed to widening and deepening that power. His aim was . . . to carry it into the realms of real constructive planning, applied not only to towns, but to regions, and ultimately, to a country as a whole . . . Unwin had vision and high ideals, and the secret of his accomplishing so much was that he promoted everything that *led* to [their] fulfilment . . . and was prepared to go a step at a time. (Parker, 1940a, p. 162)

Though the spirit of *nil nisi bonum* rules over obituaries, they form convenient starting points for evaluation. Two of the most perceptive and personal memoirs of Unwin were provided by Barry Parker (Parker, 1940a, 1940b), in the TPI and RIBA *Journals*, the former providing the quotation above. Parker linked the person to his professional accomplishments. Extensive obituaries on both sides of the Atlantic testified to Unwin's international stature. The *New York Times* (30 June 1940) referred to 'the internationally known dean of town planners'. Its London counterpart (30 June 1940) dwelt on Unwin's 'command of the subject . . . firmly grounded in his sociological interests', concluding that 'in everything he designed it was the social plan he had in mind'. The professional journals noted his ability to surmount parochialism and to resolve conflict 'with tact, dignity and assurance' (Thompson, 1940, p. 187). This personal characteristic had been evident since his Socialist League apprenticeship.

To the TPI, Unwin's death marked the close of the pioneer era for the profession. Howard, Geddes and now Unwin were recalled as founding fathers. Unwin would be remembered for 'his supreme ability in expressing ideals and linking them to practice'. He had:

> lived to carry forward to the new generation of planners the ideals both of Geddes and the late Sir Ebenezer Howard: and it is not a little tragic that the doyen of planners . . . did not live to witness the results of his efforts in the vast work of reconstruction . . . after the termination of the present conflict. (Thompson, 1940, p. 187)

Unwin's death occurred when the outcome of the war was, to say the least, uncertain. Yet the profession was confident of the future and Unwin had cabled home to that effect a few weeks before his death. The Institute saw him promoting a growing awareness and acceptance of planning and developing its scope. Alongside Unwin's personal goal of a transformed society and environment, he elevated the role of the professional as an agent of social and environmental change, but was content to proceed incrementally. His 'third course', education towards enlightenment, and the interaction between his personal traits and professional attitude, represent the key to understanding his achievements and his continued significance. Rasmussen recalled that:

> with all his openness and friendliness this fine old man had an unusual authority, the authority of age and wisdom . . . When Sir Raymond explained town planning problems they seemed so simple that every man could grasp them. (Rasmussen, 1963, p. 431)

Pepler (1940, p. 48), Ernst May (1963, pp. 427–8) and Carl Feiss (1963, pp. 422–7; 471–3) all confirmed this: Purdom (1963b, pp. 428–9) alone left a dissenting view, having encountered 'unexpected coldness and indifference'.

Parker (1940b) identified 'singleness of purpose and the strength of that purpose, selflessness, the absence of personal ambition, disinterestedness, hopefulness, buoyancy and courage' as essential characteristics. The first accorded with Unwin's 'vision and high ideals' inherited from Morris and Carpenter and to his rejected religious vocation. The vision of a new society was never far away: to sympathetic audiences he would advocate planning as 'the basis for social reconstruction'. He had rejected revolutionary change in the late 1880s. Logic and sweet reason enabled him successfully to advocate the statutory adoption of low-density Garden City housing, a radical environmental advance whatever its limitations in achieving the grand social vision.

Parker (1940b) perceived 'everything making for justice, friendship, sympathy and equality of opportunity' as tactical ancillaries. Concern for justice and equality of opportunity were inherited from Unwin's Socialist League days. They were not abstract ideals, but expressed through his insistence that every family should attain a decent minimum standard of housing. Friendship and sympathy were essential adjuncts to constructively gain middle-ground. Unwin's 'sympathy for everyone in trouble and with the underdog' arose from early experience, expressed with Pre-Raphaelite intensity through his anguish at witnessing the unemployed hand turned brusquely away from the Staveley factory gates (Unwin, 1889b, p. 132). In later life he was apt to draw attention to losers when called upon to acclaim winners (Unwin, 1932d, p. 208). Dissatisfaction with the 'Darwinist' basis of capitalism, or *laissez-faire* as the catalyst for urban development, underlay his advocacy of intervention to protect and to advance communal interests.

Unwin's sense of balance, proportion and harmony were drawn from

Ruskin, Morris and Carpenter. Perception of communal identity and the potential of cooperation were drawn through his socialist apprenticeship. Technical skills were painstakingly acquired at Staveley. Unwin's socialist commitment preceded his aesthetic education and enabled him, more positively than most of his contemporaries, to appreciate their interrelationship. His quest for balance was reflected in Carpenter's oft-quoted aphorism that 'everything matters, but nothing overmuch'.[233] Communal identity and cooperation underlay his early designs for cooperative housing and led to his progression from home to community and beyond.

> Co-operation . . . based on mutual knowledge and understanding among individuals . . . sets a limit to the best size of a single unit; and . . . gives rise to . . . the establishment of relations on a federated basis between them, or between regional groups . . . The recognised importance of the interplay between men and their environment suggests that this general scheme of society should find its echo in the best type pattern for urban development . . . which will promote the cooperation of individuals in units while maintaining adequate variety in their individuality. (Unwin, 1935b, p. 261)

'Selflessness, the absence of personal ambition, hopefulness, buoyancy and courage' should not be taken at face value. Unwin was always ambitious and highly motivated. He succeeded despite the lack of formal architectural training and indifference to social convention. He swiftly emerged from provincial obscurity to acceptance as an international authority on housing and town-planning. Walter Creese saw him as a determined leader from the 1880s (Creese, 1966, p. 165). Peggy Hitchcock perceived her father's early experience as a quest for personal satisfaction. She contended that it was the discovery of town-planning as a medium through which his personal aims could be most effectively expressed, which was the crucial spur to his success.[234] His 'selflessness' was ambivalent. Unwin may have cared little for the honours he received. Yet he accepted them and the personal tributes and ceremonial. There was no reason why he should not. It would, however, be misleading to accept uncritically the image of self-effacement. As with Howard, Unwin's inconspicuous appearance concealed an astute intellect and an innate capacity to convert opponents.

Unwin's ability to analyse and resolve complex problems impartially is well-attested, notably in his involvement with the Dublin reconstruction issue. Patient service on RIBA, TPI, IGCTP committees, the Tudor Walters committee and the GLRPC, validates Parker's contention that Unwin 'could bring harmony into the most discordant gathering and find wise and hopeful solutions for any difficulty' (Parker, 1940b). Unwin was an optimist. His faith in human progress led from Darwinism through socialism towards 'the dawn of a happier day'.[235]

Unwin was sustained by this inner belief after his rejection of orthodox religion. The international cataclysm of the First World War did not undermine his optimism. He was stimulated to make positive contributions towards planning for reconstruction through the Tudor

Walters *Report*. Planning was simply the most appropriate medium for harnessing collective human progress. His Royal Gold Medal speech of 1937 affirmed the potential of 'the great movement' of planning, upon 'the wise guidance of which', he averred, 'largely depends the future of human life in society':

> Whether our present social system can develop into something more completely satisfying to the whole nature of man; or whether the great wave of progress on which our civilisation has been carried forward so far must be broken against the rocks of difficulty . . . will depend . . . on whether men can learn to apply the art of orderly planning to their lives, and to the environment in which that life finds its setting. (Unwin, 1937d, pp. 582–3)

Late in 1939, stranded in the USA after the outbreak of war, Unwin still expressed his optimism:

> I have to be content with a less defined and focused faith, which nonetheless, does keep one on the whole happy and hopeful in spite of the mess the world is in . . . I try to hope that the whole position has become so preposterous that the ordinary folk will just come to their senses suddenly.[236]

Unwin's faith in humanity, his extrapolation of optimism and his confidence in the ability of the planner to guide and control human activities towards the fulfilment of optimal goals may now seem simplistic, deterministic and naïve. Yet it was shared by professional and public alike as the basis of the great postwar reconstruction after 1945.

Influences, contemporaries and context

Many of Unwin's contemporaries regarded him as *the* central figure in planning. A pioneer, he yet lived long enough to develop a comprehensive overview of the potential for environmental management. His life and career spanned the turn of the nineteenth and twentieth centuries and paralleled the broadening out from public health improvements and private housing trusts to acceptance of housing and social welfare as public responsibilities. Unwin played a significant role in the defining of the scope of town-planning. His role variously combined the skills of architect, economist, engineer, surveyor and sociologist. Comparisons must thus be widely drawn, but this underlines his centrality and skill in building links between allied areas of concern. According to one of the centenary memoirs, he was 'one of the few progenitors of town planning who were rounded men' (Lyon, 1963, p. 356) – actually a noteworthy characteristic of many pioneers but particularly apposite in Unwin's case. His breadth of vision drew on Howard and Geddes as well as Morris' prescription for 'decency of surroundings'. It became manifest through his combination of Sitte's spatial intimacy, with the broad perspectives of the City Beautiful and the verdure of the Garden City.

Working from the level of the individual, 'visualising and expressing the solutions of the limited problems posed by single buildings and their sites', he extended the realm of planning to encompass generalist coordination.

> To this art of planning, specialists must contribute the scientific facts related to the several parts on which the whole must be based: these no single brain could contain, and no wise planner will attempt to acquire [them]. No mere assembly of the specialised knowledge, and of the partial points of view of many experts, will, however, of itself contribute a clear conception [*sic*] of the whole. There must be one brain, one imagination, to join the conception which will fuse these into a coherent whole. (Unwin, 1937d, p. 586)

In his commentary on Hinton's work, Unwin had referred to the ability of the mature artist to work in broad-brush terms. By the 1930s he was urging the planner to do likewise, resolving the broad relationships between competing uses into orderly design upon the land.

Unwin developed this comprehensive vision from Geddes and Howard.

> Sir Patrick Geddes taught us . . . the essential social influences which go to make up the pattern of life. To Sir Ebenezer Howard, . . . we owe two great conceptions [*sic*]: that of the garden city method of planning, and that of the satellite pattern which provides for city growth in a manner consistent with that method . . . Both Geddes and Howard, each in their own way, based their contributions on the social structure of human society . . . it is the unique achievement of man that he has been able to develop highly civilised communities not through the suppression of individuality . . . but through the utilisation of the enormous power which comes from the cooperation of individuals. (Unwin, 1937b, pp. 95–6)

Unwin drew heavily upon Howard's Social City cluster, gradually broadening it to the Metropolitan scale which had been Howard's point of departure. Unwin was as freely eclectic as Howard and both were effective communicators. They had triumphed over early doubts and it was not surprising that Howard endorsed Unwin as the form-giver to the Garden City, albeit realized very differently from his own diagrammatic concept. The two were closely associated over the IHTPF, with Unwin succeeding Howard as President in 1928.

Contact with Geddes dated from a 1905 Letchworth summer school. Both had studied anthropology – Geddes as a trained scientist, Unwin as a committed amateur seeking to understand the communal organization of primitive society. Geddes conceptualized a symbiotic relationship between society and environment expressed by the interacting trinity of 'Folk, Work and Place'. The civic survey enabled analysis and recording, which Unwin readily assimilated into *Town Planning in Practice*. Geddes and Unwin jointly approached John Burns to advocate a broadening of the 1909 Housing and Town Planning Act and they collaborated over the 1910 RIBA Town Planning Exhibition. In 1914 Geddes provided the *entrée* for Unwin's involvement with Dublin planning. Both were committed internationalists. Geddes brought an historical and regional perspective: he was a true polymath with a capacity for original thought that outstripped Howard or Unwin. But he was a weak communicator, a prolific but disorganized writer and as a lecturer apt to be simultaneously inspiring and incomprehensible. Both Unwin and Abercrombie assisted the recognition and practical application of Geddes' work.

Sitte's influence was crucial but less understood. It was gained second-hand, initially through the corrupt French text. Even this provided Unwin with a technique for ordering outdoor space as a corollary to house design. Following the self-conscious informality of the first Hampstead plan, Unwin applied Sittesque priciples rationally. Later, through his 'new synthesis' of formal and informal elements, he formulated a two-tier process with a formal framework allied to informal neighbourhoods, their individuality derived from an organic relationship with topography.

Howard, Geddes and Sitte provided Unwin with a richly varied theoretical basis for his comprehensive approach to planning. One of his most significant accomplishments lay in his integration of them to form his own 'unique combination of proposals'.

Unwin demands comparison with a wide range of contemporaries. Parker rightly observed that his brother-in-law was most highly motivated by the broader vision, initially expressed in corporate-housing designs. Unwin was conscious of his own aesthetic limitations and acknowledged Parker's role in his education. The Arts and Crafts movement, particularly individual houses by Voysey and Baillie Scott (Kornwolf, 1972; Davey, 1980), provided models for the partners' early work and was developed to a corporate level. For this, Parker and Unwin drew heavily upon Port Sunlight (Hubbard and Shippobottom, 1988) and Bournville. At the latter, Alexander Harvey had evolved simplified Voysey designs before 1900 (Harvey, 1906), preceding any significant work by Parker and Unwin. By 1900, too, the LCC architects under W. E. Riley were adopting a similar design approach for their earliest cottage estates (Beattie, 1980). The significance of Parker and Unwin as housing architects arose not from originality, but from integration of design theory and practice. And Unwin was almost wholly responsible for this, building upon *The Art of Building a Home* and *Cottage Plans and Common Sense* (Unwin, 1902). In the latter he formulated accommodation standards from his analysis of family lifestyle. His rationalization of layouts, backed up by extensive empirical experience, led him to postulate *Nothing Gained by Overcrowding* (Unwin, 1912b), which he skilfully promoted as a general layout and planning theory.

This drew him towards a civil-service career, culminating in membership of the Tudor Walters Committee which set the seal upon acceptance of the new housing standards (Tudor Walters, 1918). Through insistence that professionally designed housing should not be restricted to those who could commission an architect directly, Unwin 'democratized' architecture. He encouraged the profession to recognize a social responsibility. Housing became almost synonymous with town-planning in the 1920s. Technological advance in construction required research and development and improved education. Unwin's lasting contribution to architecture lay in assisting the reshaping of the profession to serve twentieth-century needs, initially in partnership with Parker and later through his Ministry career.

Unwin and Parker were very different but complementary personalities. The division of labour suggested by Parker in 1891 into 'the artistic' (himself) and 'the practical' (Unwin) is helpful but should not be taken too literally. Unwin was essentially a technician with an overwhelming social conscience who acquired a heightened aesthetic sense from his partner; Parker was an artist–architect who developed a social concern. Their major projects attained striking visual characteristics through the attention to detail of the skilled architect, reflecting Parker's influence. Yet Parker was not so preoccupied as to exclude broader matters and he wrote a number of papers on planning. His *Craftsman* articles of 1910–12 contained interesting concepts for housing layout (Hawkes, 1986, pp. 124–48), while 'Horizontality and Verticality in the treatment of Town Planning schemes', given at the TPI in 1916 (Parker, 1916, pp. 45–8), developed Unwin's 'formal versus irregular' dichotomy and possibly assisted his formulation of the design policy for the Dublin Reconstruction legislation. In 1928, 'Economy in Estate Development' (Parker, 1928), a background paper for the Wythenshawe plan, updated *Nothing Gained by Overcrowding* to the motor age and analysed one of the first Radburn superblock proposals. Similarly, Parker's enthusiasm for the parkway (Parker, 1929) influenced Unwin's GLRPC *First Report*.

Parker's proposals for remodelling the Oporto civic centre (1915–16) ingeniously combined the formal City Beautiful with more intimate Sittesque subsidiary spaces. He also developed Unwin's layout for Jardim America, Sao Paulo. Parker's post-1919 housing designs and layouts reflected Tudor Walters' prescription at its best. It helped him to gain the commission for the Wythenshawe satellite in 1927, which incorporated such innovative features as neighbourhood planning and parkways (Creese, 1966; Day 1973), but also represented a classic demonstration of Unwin's 'Garden City Principle applied to existing towns'.

Apart from Parker, Unwin gave two architects special mention in his Royal Gold Medal speech – Lutyens and Aston Webb. He had little in common with Lutyens, either personally or professionally. He may have resented the former's appointment to design the Central Square at Hampstead; Lutyens' description of his first meeting with Unwin suggested the affected humility of an Uriah Heep. Nevertheless the Central Square revealed the benefits of formal design, and was warmly praised by Unwin in *Town Planning in Practice*. It palpably influenced the layout for the New Suburb at Hampstead and the Town Square complex at Letchworth. Aston Webb was one of the first British architects to encompass civic design. Thirteen years Unwin's senior, renowned for his design of The Mall, the Victoria Memorial and Buckingham Palace, the two probably came into contact over the RIBA Conference and Exhibition of 1910. They were subsequently involved with the Ruislip–Northwood competition, the London Society and the Tudor Walters Committee. As with Lutyens, Webb fostered Unwin's enthusiasm for formal civic design.

Among planners, Thomas Adams was probably Unwin's most immediate rival (Hulchanski, 1978; Simpson, 1985). Their careers converged several times. Their contrasting political beliefs – Adams a Liberal–Radical, Unwin a Fabian–Socialist – were brought out in their work. At Letchworth, as Estate Manager, Adams pressed for simple controls to avoid inhibiting developers and industrialists whose participation was vital to the success of the project, while Unwin was determined not to compromise ideals. Adams preceded Unwin at the Local Government Board and initially blocked the aesthetic-control provisions of the Ruislip–Northwood scheme, causing Unwin to appeal directly to Burns for approval. Together they visited the United States in 1911, developing transatlantic connections. Both were approached by the Canadian High Commission in 1913, with Adams appointed. In the 1920s the pattern repeated itself, with both shortlisted by the Russell Sage Foundation. Adams' appointment as consultant to prepare the New York Regional Plan reflected his greater responsiveness to the business community, contrasting with Unwin's strictures on the environmental consequences of untrammelled *laissez-faire*.

During the 1930s both Unwin and Adams advocated an enhanced economic role for planning in the wake of a world depression. Adams was wary of accepting centralist national and regional planning, which Unwin increasingly advocated. Both held important educational appointments in the United States – Adams at Harvard and Unwin at Columbia. And Unwin's interventionist philospphy came into its own in his work with the Roosevelt administration and NAHO to formulate a national public-housing strategy. Both contributed significantly to the foundation and development of planning, in Britain and the United States.

Patrick Abercrombie was a virtuoso technician of planning in the interwar period (Dix, 1981, pp. 103–30). Like Unwin, he assimilated the contributions of Howard and Geddes and added an historical perpective of civic design. His contributions to *Town Planning Review* were broadly comparable with Unwin's *Town Planning in Practice*. The winning plan by Abercrombie and the Kellys for the Dublin Competition bore a close resemblance to Unwin's seminal 'Garden City Principle applied to existing towns', and his Doncaster Regional Plan confirmed the robustness of the Howard–Unwin satellite cluster. Abercrombie's comment that 'town and country planning seeks to proffer a guiding hand to the trend of natural evolution, as a result of careful study of the place itself and its external relationships' (Abercrombie, 1943, p. 27), owed much both to Unwin and Geddes. In leading the deputation to Chamberlain in 1926, Abercrombie played a significant role in promoting Greater London planning; and he built upon Unwin's GLRPC groundwork. As a member of the Barlow Commission, he carried forward Unwin's Marley Committee work. Yet Abercrombie and Unwin had contrasting personalities. Abercrombie was adept at providing comprehensive, elegant plans – albeit that he overworked the satellite-cluster models, presenting them with professional detachment. He felt no need to introduce the overtones of idealism rarely absent from Unwin's work.

There were indeed few major figures in planning during 1900–40 with whom Unwin did not have personal contact. Chapter Twelve has indicated the depth of his international involvement, particularly with Germany and the USA. He became a major communicator – idealist, theorist, propagandist, educator and evangalist in turn. He could present his ideas with inspiring breadth, but could also leave doubt as to how limited and incremental statutory powers might be used to achieve optional goals. Other pioneers, notably Horsfall, Nettlefold, Thompson and Aldridge were closer to local government. Always serious-minded, Unwin did not have the facility of Pepler to decamp from Whitehall to cajole district clerks and surveyors into preparing schemes. This perhaps explains comments by Mumford that Unwin was 'a bit of a Quaker'[237] and by Osborn that Unwin became 'long haired' in his pronouncements (Hughes, 1971, p. 63).

Writer

Unwin was a fluent and prolific writer for over half a century. His early *Commonweal* articles were frankly polemic. His style, which owed much to Morris and Carpenter, avoided the turgid density of many contemporaries. *The Art of Building a Home* (Parker and Unwin, 1901) linked the concept of cooperation to aesthetic and environmental objectives. Like Morris, he harkened back to an imagined golden age of vernacular building, honest craftsmanship and self-contained, self-sufficient communities, seeking to recreate these qualities though housing and town-planning. 'Looking back and forth' became his hallmark: it was evident both in *Cottage Plans and Common Sense* (Unwin, 1902) and *Town Planning in Practice* (Unwin, 1909).

This last, Unwin's major contribution to town-planning literature, ranged beyond the legislative framework and presented town-planning in terms of the 'self-evident truths' revealed by his own work, particularly at Hampstead. Notwithstanding initial misgivings over Unwin's apparent dalliance between formal and irregular town design, the book was enormously influential. It was widely translated, the last of eight editions appearing in 1932. Surprisingly, and perhaps significantly, Unwin never made a revision, apart from a new foreword to the second edition in which he praised formal planning and presented a preview of *Nothing Gained by Overcrowding* (Unwin, 1911c, pp. ix–xviii). Material from his 1911 Birmingham lectures, which chronicled his broadening of the scope of planning, would have been appropriate. In the early 1930s a major revision was contemplated but apparently unfulfilled.[238]

Nothing Gained by Overcrowding (Unwin, 1912b) combined theory with Unwin's practical work and was best-known through the 1912 leaflet. The catchphrase title became as influential as the content, which incorporated suspect assumptions on land and road costs relative to density limitation. The implication for strategic planning contained in the second part of the text, particularly the seminal 'Garden City Principles applied to existing towns' diagram, was widely influential.

Unwin's post-1914 writing appeared anonymously in government reports, as with the Tudor Walters and Marley *Reports*, or was drawn from TPI, RIBA and IGCTPF papers. Noteworthy were 'Distribution' (Unwin, 1921c pp. 37–52), one of the earliest that hinted at the importance of national planning; 'Higher Building in relation to town planning' (Unwin, 1924a, pp. 125–48), his critique of American skyscraper development; 'Regional Planning with special reference to the Greater London Regional Plan' (Unwin 1930d, pp. 183–99), in some respects a clearer presentation than the contemporary GLRPC *First Report*; and 'Urban Development; the pattern and the background' (Unwin, 1935b, pp. 253–66), which returned to the theoretical fundamentals of Howard's satellite cluster. Unwin's contributions to collections, notably 'Some thoughts on the development of London' (Unwin, 1921d, pp. 177–92), published in *London of the Future*, contained the essence of the later GLRPC strategy. 'The town and the best size for good social life' (Unwin, 1921c, pp. 80–102) in Purdom's *Town Theory and Practice*, was 'work in progress' which would have merited more rigorous development. Unwin's constant commitments clearly prevented his following through many of the ideas in his interwar papers.

The limited circulation of much of Unwin's post-1914 writing inevitably restricts appreciation of his significance to the early landmarks of *Cottage Plans and Common Sense*, *Town Planning in Practice* and *Nothing Gained by Overcrowding*. Great achievements as they are, they are largely concerned with physical layout and housing design: in which field they were widely influential. Appraisal of Unwin's later writing and lecture outlines is necessary to reveal his broad synoptic vision of the scope of planning (Creese, 1967).

Unwin's contribution to the evolution of planning

Unwin's substantive achievements have been extensively reviewed in previous chapters. New Earswick, Letchworth and Hampstead Garden Suburb each represented a community paradigm in which he applied design principles that extended outward from his initial concern for the individual family home. The constituent elements were neither sophisticated nor original; Unwin's contribution lay in their assembly in accord with an overall sense of design and spatial relationships to reflect the pattern of his community ideal. Insistence on consistent design principles for all types of housing gave an overall visual and, he hoped, social harmony, with elements such as culs-de-sac and greens fostering neighbourliness. Unwin was guided not by an arbitrary egalitarian concept, but rather by perception of a common thread in society. The marginal but essential element of beauty was brought out in group cottage design, with bays thrust out to capture a distant prospect, or a stepped building line to create visual accents, without disruption of the corporate design. They reflected the social artist at work.

New Earswick represented continuity with the reformist tradition of model industrial communities; it provided a prototype for co-partnership developments and housing estates. Letchworth created the physical and administrative prototype for the twentieth-century, planned, self-contained new town, with uniform ownership of land. Through its planning Unwin introduced primary land-use zoning and development control. The succession ran through Gretna–Eastriggs, Welwyn Garden City and Wythenshawe to the post-1945 first-generation New Towns. Even in the 1960s, it was still accepted that:

> in the interval between 1903, when Letchworth was designed, and today [1963] little or no convincing demonstration has been made of any profound rethinking in town design or housing layout on a large scale. (Lyon, 1963, p. 356)

Hampstead Garden Suburb was Unwin's most complete achievement, in one sense a unique demonstration of Garden City principles applied to suburban development. Even Unwin could not repeat its success for all the efforts he made to incorporate detailed design control in the Ruislip–Northwood scheme. It was the latter which, through the 1909 Act, created the generalized low-density suburb, ubiquitous in the inter-war period and an easy option for 'interim development control', or the stereotype application of the simpler designs from the 1919 housing *Manual*. It was the spread of such suburbs that required action at the regional strategic level. Through its very success in demonstrating 'The Garden City principle applied to existing towns', Hampstead became a dangerous precedent, as Unwin and others realized in the interwar period.

Purdom sensed a hiatus in Unwin's career after 1914:

> An early and convinced advocate of the Garden City, his main activities after the making of the Letchworth plan were directed towards improving the quality of suburban housing; and while his talents seemed to be in town planning, and he wrote the first English work on the subject in 1909, he carried out little such work. (Purdom, 1963, p. 429)

The Ministry of Health, even in the early period when detailed design was vetted, did not give Unwin the opportunity for direct design work. After his retirement, his GLRPC consultancy was generalized to strategy formulation. It was left to Parker to demonstrate at Wythenshawe that the design principles of the three prewar communities could be updated to serve a new social and technological context.

Unwin's influence can be summarized with reference to key projects of planning. He assisted the development of a set of techniques and practice; definition of the qualitative context; and the differentiation of a hierarchy of operational levels with their appropriate institutional agencies. Moreover he elevated the role of the professional, making a significant contribution to the British hegemony of the international housing- and town-planning movement between the wars.

In the early 1900s, Unwin had pushed construction regulation beyond the public health bye-law approach towards the formulation of standards that could promote a radical change in the design of the housing environment. Maxwell Fry, one of the pioneer modernists in British architecture, held that 'Unwin more than any other single man, turned the soulless English byelaw street towards light, air, trees and flowers. And this was no mean thing to have done' (Fry, 1940, p. 65). *Cottage Plans and Common Sense*, the Letchworth *Building Regulations* and *Nothing Gained by Overcrowding* were landmarks, followed up by the Tudor Walters *Report* and the 1919 *Housing Manual*. Before 1914 Unwin was already writing of functional zoning, the differentiation of residential density and reservation of open space and making road widths proportional to anticipated traffic levels. These concepts were demonstrated at Letchworth and Hampstead and were soon assimilated into planning practice.

Beyond lay the vision of an environment transformed. Quality of life, a concept derived from Morris, was exemplified in Unwin's work by attention to the design of the home, including a marginal element of beauty beyond the new standards, radical as these were. Concern for amenity revealed to Unwin the potential for open space as a means of articulating expansion and suggested satellite development on the green background beyond. Beauty was indispensable to the solution of planning problems. Unwin's approach to highway design exemplified this. Roads were to be more than functional arteries, built to uniform standards and lined with serried ranks of buildings. They were to be designed as generators of composed architectural spaces, locally intimate and enclosed, or broad and purposefully integrating town and country at the city or regional scale. Their size would reflect anticipated traffic levels. The cul-de-sac, often banished on public-health grounds in the nineteenth century, was revived, excluding through-traffic and giving visual and social unity to housing grouped around. The highway hierarchy, the basis of modern highway design and traffic management, was anticipated, but with an integrated design process extending to the surrounding buildings.

Unwin defined a series of operational levels. Preparation of the Letchworth plan assisted the formulation of a two-tier approach, with a broad overall framework, within which detail could be adjusted as necessary. This process was discussed in *Town Planning in Practice* and still forms the basis for physical planning where a district framework may be supplemented with local design briefs. Through the influence of Geddes, Unwin added a regional strategic level, the basis of his GLRPC work; his consideration of the distribution of population and resources led him towards national planning.

Each broader level brought increasing importance of the public authority as initiator and administrator of planning. It has been tellingly observed that private landowners had planned and managed estate development for many years before town-planning was defined as a public institutional concern. New Earswick, Letchworth and Hampstead Garden Suburb were all created by landowner process, though this does not diminish their significance as prototypes for statutory practice. The real importance of the 1909 Act lay in the imposition of land-use controls independent of ownership, but with the local authority as the elected representative of the public interest. Apart from Ruislip–Northwood, where he acted for the principal landowner, Unwin had little experience of local-authority planning. His recruitment to the Local Government Board indicated his growing interest in the centralized administration of planning. Wartime experience convinced him of the potential benefits of state-led housing initiatives, with a partnership with local government to maintain the local units of autonomy. The central authority would set major objectives and direct the local authorities towards fulfilment. Lack of overall direction and executive powers undermined the GLRPC and Unwin subsequently advocated the creation of national bodies to undertake comprehensive physical, social and economic planning. He had thus assisted the transformation of environmental regulation from a permissive, limited, specific and localized activity to a statutory, generalized and inclusive process, an essential adjunct to good government.

Unwin reversed his method of working from the particular to the general. He assumed that the planner was a rational technician who could impartially present reasoned choices and that this would be publicly acceptable:

> The public must realise that the planning scheme is made for their advantage and that it is executed with their authority. They must accept it as an expression of their desires and of their corporate sense of duty or ambition. (Unwin, 1913f, p. 106)

Although he insisted that the plan be 'harmonised with the need for close accord between the work of the planner and the people affected', the process was weighted in favour of the institution. In taking the key strategic decisions at the top level, the range of options available below was progressively reduced. Issues of accountability were left unresolved. The concept of cooperatively based planning, Unwin's original point of departure, faded long before his death. He emphasized that comprehensive planning required the guidance of a single mind, although he also recognized that depth of knowledge in all of component fields was beyond individual capability. His faith in the ability of the technician to transform society and its environment may now seem over-optimistic and politically naïve. Yet it influenced the ascendency of planning in the years immediately following his death.

Definition of the profession and its ideology owed much to the varied accomplishments of the pioneers. Unwin followed Adams in uniting the land-based professions in an institute in which experience might be pooled and from which the planner might develop a coordinating role. Like Howard, Geddes and Abercrombie, Unwin viewed internationalism as a valuable means of securing peaceful cooperation between nations, despite two world wars in his lifetime. His central concern with housing accorded him a key role in promoting British hegemony over the movement, underscored by his numerous conference appearances. International acceptance of the Howard–Unwin model of planned dispersal through garden suburbs and satellite clusters owed much to his persuasive advocacy.

The rise of modernism and CIAM, inevitably modified the situation. One of the most influential British members of CIAM, Maxwell Fry, recognized that Unwin's death had 'severed one of the strongest links between the philosophy of William Morris and our own'. Though he considered Letchworth and Hampstead to be romantic retreats, suffused by 'a thinning but still golden mist', Fry praised Unwin as 'an eloquent, untiring and practical reformer', whose work still contained enduring and relevant truths.

> when we take up again the work which the war has stopped, we have to expand Unwin's conception [*sic*] so as to include the machine, but not at the expense of light and verdure'. (Fry, 1940, p. 65)

This was carried through by the 1945 Labour government, with planning as a symbol of reconstruction. The distinctly modified rapture with which planning was later viewed would probably have been seen by Unwin as a reflection of insufficient commitment, allied to human shortcomings. Present-day distrust of the comprehensive view and doubts over its compatibility with environmental identity and quality has redirected attention to the grass roots level. It is arguable that, for all his fine words about the necessity for a national perspective, Unwin's touch was surest, in conjunction with Parker, at the local level: the context of home and community. They matched need with aspiration, aesthetics with economy, tempered idealism with pragmatism, through the revival of deep-rooted traditional values, creating an enduring image reflecting the personal basis of planning.

The strength of Unwin's best work lay in identification with these fundamental values and in setting them in a pragmatic context. He allied himself to the furtherance of successful causes through his ability to be in the right place at the right time, with the technical expertise to assist the translation from ideal to reality. He was able to turn problems to opportunities through his quiet powers of persuasion. Osborn wrote of Unwin as a:

> social reformer who is also a man of intense appreciation of visual beauty . . . a deep sympathiser with deprived humanity who wanted everybody to have the fullest possible life in every way *including* his own aesthetic pleasures. (Hughes, 1971, pp. 404–5)

Osborn had assigned both Ruskin and Morris to that category and 'unquestionably' placed Unwin alongside, awarding him 'higher marks for a sense of the politically practicable, and therefore as a force for actual reform'. Uncritical acceptance of hero-figures induces the danger of over-emphasizing their significance and achievements. Yet each generation has need of figures with whom the ideology of common causes can be identified. To his contemporaries, Unwin appeared to be synonymous with, and inseparable from, planning, an assessment which the half century following his death has strengthened, rather than diminished.

Notes

1 Howard's attribution of his quotation to Ruskin's *Sesame and the Lilies* is incorrect; it has not been possible to trace the origin of the passage among Ruskin's writings.
2 The background information on the Unwin and Parker families is drawn from information provided to the author by Christy Booth (1892–1982), a cousin of Raymond Unwin and a close contemporary of his son, Edward (1894–1936). The family links between the Unwins and the Parkers were researched by Barry Parker's widow, C. Mabel Parker (1882–1974) with the encouragement of Lewis Mumford (1895–1989). They were written up as 'Material available for a memoir of R. B. Parker', typescript, First Garden City Heritage Museum, Letchworth. Additional information was provided by Peggy Curtice Hitchcock (1899–1982), Unwin's daughter.
3 The letters, covering the crucial period 1885–91, were in the possession of Mrs Hitchcock in Lyme, Connecticut, USA, in the late 1970s. Their present whereabouts are unknown. The author has worked from a photocopy. The diary is in the Unwin collection of the Departmental Library of Architecture and Planning at Manchester University.
4 RU to Ethel Parker, 4 May 1883, Hitchcock Collection.
5 RU to Ethel Parker, May 1885, Hitchcock Collection.
6 These are held in the Unwin Collection, Manchester University. The diary, in the form of a letter addressed to Ethel Parker, records:

> August 18 (1887). I have been reading some more of Hinton's life. Do you know Ettie, I sometimes feel as if I might one day have a vocation to interpret Hinton.

The same collection includes the drafts referred to.
7 James Hinton's Ethical work, Unwin Collection, Manchester University.
8 Unwin, R., 1886 (January). The dawn of a happier day, Manchester. Unwin Collection UN15, Royal Institute of British Architects, British Architectural Library, London.
9 Published material on Barrow Hill is scarce. Archival material has been used from the following sources. Sheffield City Reference Library holds a copy of an *Illustrated London News* account, 23 June 1860, a Staveley company capital account book and local obituaries for Barrow and Paxton Markham Snr. and Jnr., Directors' Minutes for the Staveley Company, which was nationalized after the Second World War, were transferred to the British Steel Corporation Archive at Irthlingborough, Northants, where they were consulted by the author in 1979. Some early survey material was then held by the Stanton and Staveley estate department at Barrow Hill.

10 In his diary, 31 April 1887 (Unwin Collection, Manchester University), Unwin noted Markham's choleric nature as he ran into a horse with an engine:

> That's the fellow who is supposed to *manage* the works, and who is responsible for the fellows' lives . . . it's not right for a fellow like that to have such a position just because he is the son of his father.

11 Unwin Collection, Manchester University. As a document recording Unwin's personal feelings, the diary and the surviving letters to Ethel Parker form a moving record of his 'divine discontent'.

12 In contrast to the article, the diary records the evident pride of the young engineer at work; entries for 17 May, 1 June, 5–7 July 1887, Unwin Collection, Manchester University.

13 Barry Parker, typescript, n.d. *c.*1940, Parker Collection, First Garden City Heritage Museum, Letchworth. Possibly a draft for the obituaries written by Parker which appeared in the *Journals* of the Town Planning Institute and Royal Institute of British Architects.

14 RU to Ethel Parker, 9 August 1891, Hitchcock Collection.

15 Unwin's activities have been culled from the Staveley Archives, *vide* 9 *supra*, from information provided by Christy Booth and from general published references such as that by Parker in his Memoir of Sir Raymond Unwin, *Journal of the Royal Institute of British Architects*, 3ss 47(9) 15 July 1940: 209–10.

16 A drawing by Unwin of these cottages, signed and dated 31 July 1893, issued by the Staveley Coal and Iron Co. Engineers Office to the Warsop Urban District Council, is held by the Nottingham County Archivist, DC/WA42. The author is indebted to Mr J. L. Noble who lives in the cottages 'Rhein O' Thorns' Warsop Vale for bringing this to his attention.

17 12 July 1887 entry in Diary, Unwin Collection, Manchester University.

18 RU to Ethel Parker, 10 January 1891, Hitchcock Collection.

19 RU to Ethel Parker, 9 August 1891, Hitchcock Collection.

20 Peggy Curtice Hitchcock, ms commentary on the Unwin letters.

21 RU to Ethel Parker, 9 August 1891, Hitchcock Collection.

22 Parker's biography is outlined in C. Mabel Parker's Notes, *vide supra* 2. These are not entirely accurate and have been supplemented by information from Parker's RIBA Membership Application Forms, F1514, 1913, Royal Institute of British Architects, British Architectural Library.

23 It has not been possible to locate the quotation in Morris' *Collected Works*. However, the tenor of the argument is found in many of the papers in Volumes XXII and XXIII. It is evident that Unwin was heavily indebted to Morris for themes that included art reflecting satisfaction and work.

24 The original drawing is in the Parker Collection, First Garden City Heritage Museum, Letchworth. It was published in *Our Homes*, 1895; *Academy Architecture*, 1896; and in *The Art of Building a Home*, 1901.

25 Joseph Rowntree, An address on the occasion of the opening of the Folk Hall, 5 October 1907. Private offprint, Joseph Rowntree Memorial Trust.

26 *New Earswick, York*, 1913, booklet published by the Joseph Rowntree Village Trust, York.

27 The scheme appears to have been commissioned by W. A. Holmes of Harrogate, for whom Parker and Unwin also designed a large house, 'The Gables', in Cavendish Avenue. Bye-law drawings for both projects are held in the Parker Collection, First Garden City Heritage Museum, Letchworth.

28 Reproduced in Waddilove, 1954, opposite p. 15. The original plan could not be located by the Joseph Rowntree Memorial Trust at the time of the author's research in 1979. A later plan, dated November 24 1904, is reproduced as Figure 22 in Day, 1981.

29 A detailed layout plan of the first, pre-Trust phase was reproduced in Day, M.G., 1973, *Sir Raymond Unwin (1863–1940) and R. Barry Parker (1867–1947): A study and evaluation of their contribution to the development of site-planning theory and practice*, unpub MA Thesis, University of Manchester. This drawing appeared to have been submitted to the Flaxton Rural District Council and was apparently mislaid in the transfer of the records to Ryedale District Council in 1974. It was not available to the author in 1979.

30 Nos. 1 and 2 Western Terrace were shown on Parker and Unwin Drawing No. 1673, held in the Joseph Rowntree Memorial Trust archives. A perspective sketch of the pair in Parker's hand is held in the Parker Collection, First Garden City Museum, Letchworth. Nos. 3–6 Western Terrace were shown on Parker and Unwin Drawing No. 1674, held in Ryedale District Council archives. This is a most attractive ink-and-watercolour drawing on linen, giving a vivid indication of the quality and character of the design.

31 The specific criticism of the designs was not mentioned in Waddilove's account (1954, p.78), but was recorded in the Council Minutes held in the Joseph Rowntree Memorial Trust archives. The same criticism was to be raised at Letchworth.

32 Joseph Rowntree Village Trust Minutes, held by Joseph Rowntree Memorial Trust. The decision was probably brought about by the slow pace of development.

33 Ibid. Although dated 1 July 1907, the Minutes record the meeting that had taken place the previous February.

34 Joseph Rowntree Village Trust Minutes, 5 September 1911, Joseph Rowntree Memorial Trust. There was a fundamental disagreement between Swain and Unwin over the figures. On 19 December Unwin presented revised designs claiming figures giving a saving equal to that of Swain's design.

35 Joseph Rowntree Village Trust, Minutes of Special Meeting, 20 November 1918, Joseph Rowntree Memorial Trust, York.

36 Unidentified Unwin quote cited in Johnson, B., 1977, pp. 18–19. The sentiments are similar to those expressed by Unwin in *Town Planning in Practice*, Chapter XI, of cooperation in site-planning (Unwin, 1909).

37 Typescript, First Garden City Heritage Museum, Letchworth.

38 *Tomorrow: A peaceful path to real reform* (Howard 1898) was republished by Swan Sonnenschein in 1902 in revised form as *Garden Cities of Tomorrow* (Howard, 1902), a title that has become part of the lore of community design in the twentieth century. In 1946 the book was republished, edited by F. J. Osborn, with an Introductory Essay by Lewis Mumford. Faber and Faber, London (Howard, 1946).

39 Hertfordshire County Record Office, Hertford, Howard papers, HCC D/EHo/F3. Early drafts of the material are dated 1892. 'The Master Key' was originally intended as Howard's overall title.

40 The comprehensive press books covering 1900–10 compiled by Adams, held by First Garden City Heritage Museum, Letchworth, are a rich source of information on the formative years of the Garden City movement. Adams' dispute with Burns was conducted through the columns of the

Morning Leader; the latter's rejoinder appeared on 23 January 1902.

41 The full account has been pieced together from Minutes of the Garden City Pioneer Company and correspondence from the chief participants, Letchworth Garden City Corporation Archives. The same sources were used for the account published in Miller, 1989, pp. 22–4.

42 The following account is largely based upon the events recorded in the Engineering Committee Minute Book, Letchworth Garden City Corporation Archives. The Committee remained in operation and reported to the newly formed First Garden City Ltd., after 1 September 1903.

43 A copy of Humphreys' Report is held by First Garden City Heritage Museum, Letchworth.

44 Engineering Committee Resolution 5, 29 October 1903, Minute Book, Letchworth Garden City Corporation.

45 Moffat, B. B., Membership File No. 1464 (L), Royal Institute of British Architects, British Architectural Library.

46 First Garden City Ltd., Directors Minutes, Letchworth Garden City Corporation. Resolution 106 began 'That the modified plan being prepared by Messrs Parker and Unwin be adopted as the plan for the development of the estate, subject to any further modification which may be necessary'. This was followed by the more definitive statement quoted in the text.

47 The 'original' plan presented to the Board by Unwin is not readily identifiable. A fragmentary photoprint crudely labelled 'Mr Unwin's plan' (*sic*) survives in First Garden City Heritage Museum, Letchworth, together with a modified version drawn on linen, which was used as the basis for the first published version.

48 The Lucas–Cranfield plan is represented by a photoprint in the FGC Museum Letchworth. The Lethaby–Ricardo plan was illustrated in Purdom, 1963, but is not held by the First Garden City Heritage Museum. Its present whereabouts is unknown. Adams' letter to Ricardo, dated 29 November 1909, praising the plan, is held by the First Garden City Heritage Museum, as is the Report by Lethaby and Ricardo from which the quotations are taken.

49 RU to Adams, 22 February 1904, Letchworth Garden City Corporation.

50 RU to Adams, First Garden City Ltd. Correspondence files, Letchworth Garden City Corporation.

51 A copy of Unwin's draft is held by the Royal Institute of British Architects, British Architectural Library, UN 12 (Unwin papers). Purdom (1913) includes both the early 'General suggestions' from Unwin's draft (pp. 66–7) and the fuller ***Building Regulations issued by First Garden City Ltd*** (Appendix K)

52 The roads were shown straight on the 'Authorised original' plan published in April 1904, the linen base map for which is held by the First Garden City Heritage Museum at Letchworth, as are the following. An undated, unnumbered, incomplete drawing shows the curved lines for the roads ultimately named Leys Avenue and Gernon Road. The latest numbered Parker and Unwin drawing showing the straight lines is No. 3207 (late 1904) and the 'definitive' curved lines appear on No. 3654 (early 1905).

53 Parker and Unwin Drawing No.7444, dated 18 June 1907, First Garden City Heritage Museum, Letchworth.

54 The drawing, held by the First Garden City Heritage Museum, Letchworth, is titled 'First Garden City Ltd. Suggested layout of Sollershott and Broadway Circus', Parker and Unwin Drawing No. 7923, (July 1908). It appears

to have originated in Unwin's Hampstead office and is the earliest so far located that shows a true 'circus' with a central roundabout. Unwin had met Henard at the VII International Congress of Architects, held at the RIBA in 1906. The *carrefour à giration* was illustrated in *Town Planning in Practice* (Unwin, 1909, Illustration 175).

55 The original research into the architecture of Letchworth was carried out using the original Letchworth Urban District Council bye-law records, summarized in *Letchworth Buildings Index*, an unpublished working paper prepared for the North Hertfordshire District Council Planning Department, 1976.

56 In view of the destruction of most of Unwin's papers stored at 'Wyldes' in 1940, the chronological evolution of the Hampstead plan is more difficult to establish than that of Letchworth. The following sequence relates to the next section of text.

1) Parker and Unwin drawing No. 3471, dated 22 February 1905, is the well-known preliminary plan, widely reproduced. There are copies in the Hampstead Garden Suburb archives and First Garden City Heritage Museum, Letchworth.
2) A minor 1906 revision concerning the roads at the south end of the Heath Extension is held by the Hampstead Garden Suburb archives.
3) A more radical revision in which the road lines were straightened and the Central Square took a more formal layout, undated but *c.*1906–7, possibly showing the influence of Lutyens, is held by First Garden City Heritage Museum at Letchworth. This was published on at least two occasions:
   a Nettlefold, J. S., 1908, *Practical Housing*, Garden City Press, Letchworth, plan D. p. 100.
   b Berlepsch Valendas, H. E. von, 1908, 'Die erste englische gartenstadt und ihr verwandte grundungen', *Kunst und Kunsthandwerk*, X1 Jahr Heft 3.

   There are minor differences, with the latter showing buildings within the Central Square. Both show the Artisans' Quarter as it appeared in *Cottages with Gardens for Londoners*.
4) Fold Map VI, *Town Planning in Practice* (Unwin, 1909), showed the 'definitive' layout of the Artizans' Quarter, but nothing much of Willifield Way. The Central Square had many differences in detail, including housing framing the approaches to both churches and a long, narrow Institute along the whole of the eastern frontage of Central Square. No date is visible but it corresponds to drawing No. 7805 (a mid-1907 number), dated April 1908.
5) An updated version of this was included on Fold Map VI in the second edition of *Town Planning in Practice* (Unwin, 1911). The reproduction includes the drawing No. 7805 (*vide* 4 *supra*, but there have clearly been radical undated revisions for it now shows the area north of Willified Road in detail. The Central Square layout includes the churches in their detached locations; the Institute shows the first phase of construction around the open courtyard.

57 The plan is held by the Hampstead Garden Suburb Archives.

58 Barry Parker and Raymond Unwin, 1907, *Regulations as to buildings issued by the company's architects*, Hampstead Garden Suburb Trust Ltd., Wyldes, London.

59 Hampstead Garden Suburb Trust Ltd., Board Minute 74, 28 May 1906, HGS Archives. A typewritten copy, 'Mr. Unwin's appointment', is held by the Unwin Collection, Manchester University.

60 The Corringham Road quadrangles, the Homesfield cul-de-sac and Temple Fortune Court, Temple Fortune Lane are the most specific examples of this.

61 This is the arrangement shown on the Parker and Unwin drawing held by First Garden City Heritage Museum at Letchworth, *vide* 56 *supra*. However, circumstantial evidence, particularly the resemblance to the concept for the village centre of the Rossall Beach Scheme of 1901, suggests that the author was Lutyens. There are a number of alternative designs for the Central Square buildings in the Lutyens drawings held by the Royal Institute of British Architects Drawings Collection.

62 There are differences between the layouts for Central Square shown on Fold Map VI, and Illustration 166 in *Town Planning in Practice* (Unwin, 1909). The former shows compact church outlines. The housing terraces were taken along to frame the setback churches. However the latter shows longer church outlines, with the halls attached at the (liturgical) west ends and the vicarage and manse projecting at the extreme outer corners of the (liturgical) east ends. Both churches were later reduced in length.

63 The alternative designs for St Jude's were reproduced with their common plans in *The British Architect*, 7 January 1910. Later that year the church rooms were eliminated and the plans shortened – the Free Church was published in *The Building News* in this form on 4 November 1910.

64 The two churches, the exterior of the uncompleted Institute, Vicarage, Manse, Nos. 1–8 North Square and Nos. 1–7 Erskine Hill, are original Lutyens designs.

65 The plain interiors of 'Wyldes' were published in 'The homes of well-known architects' – 3, 1923, *Architects' Journal*, LVII (1476), pp. 682–6.

66 An interviewing correspondent wrote in *The Record* (Hampstead Garden Suburb, 1914, II (VII) Feb: 87, 'something of the mediaeval conditions are thus realised at 'Wyldes', the master craftsman having his apprentices or pupils and assistants within the shadow of his own roof'. The information about the staff was culled from membership records of the Royal Institute of British Architects, and an interview with John Stone, a former 'Wyldes' assistant cited in Jackson, F., 1976, *The sources and planning influences of Sir Raymond Unwin (1863–1940)*, Unpub. Ph.D. thesis, University of Nottingham.

67 From extracts provided by Brigid Grafton Green, the Hampstead Garden Suburb Archivist, in 1979.

68 Taylor, 1971, p. 131, detected the stone-framed arcades from St John's Institute, Westminster and the wrought-iron balconies from Tigbourne Court.

69 Garden City expert here, *Boston Herald*, 10 May 1911, press cutting, Unwin Collection, University of Manchester.

70 Illustrated in *Town Planning Review*, 1918, VII (3–4) March: 251–2.

71 Indeed, in 1908 he introduced the Town Planning Bill in Parliament with the following panegyric:

> It seeks to secure the home healthy, the house beautiful, the town pleasant, the city dignified and the suburb salubrious. It seeks and hopes to secure more houses, better houses, prettier streets . . . it seeks to diminish what have been called byelaw stress with little law and much monotony. (*Parliamentary Debates*, 1908, 188 col. 944, HMSO, London)

72 The dilution of the Co-Partnerships' ideals was already evident during the First World War according to a report by Bryce Leicester, *Public Utility Socities and Housing*, RECO 1/482, Public Record Office, p. 42, which stated of Hampstead Tenants 'No society has had such a unique opportunity for success . . . the results must be deemed as distinctly poor . . . rents and tenancy are a barrier against working class residents for very few of whom it provides housing.'

73 *Town Planning in Practice* was published in Germany in 1910 as *Grundlagen des stadtebau* (*Foundations of town building*). The book was reissued in 1922. Although it was widely circulated in France, particularly during the First World War, the 'official' French edition did not appear until 1922, *L'etude practique des plans de villes: introduction a l'art de dessiner les plans d'amenagement et d'extension par Raymond Unwin*, Libraire Central des Beaux-arts, Paris. A Russian translation cited in Collins, 1965, is more problematical. The German edition was reviewed in *The Architect* (Journal of the Imperial Petersburg Society) in 1910 by P. Bergnard, urging its translation. Catherine Cooke believes that this was not done and that the nucleus of the work was incorporated by Vladimir Semionov into his *Public Servicing of Towns*, 1912. Ms Cooke told the author that none of the detailed Soviet bibliographies on architecture and town-planning record a Russian edition.

74 A letter with the illustration proofs in the Unwin Collection, University of Manchester, indicates the original title. 'Town Planning in Practice' was the title of a report of the National Housing and Town Planning Council report on a continental tour during 1909 for which Unwin was one of the organizers.

75 This conclusion was reached on the basis of Geddes' 1905 report, Visit of the Scottish party to Letchworth, *The Garden City* I (5), November: 86.

76 Unwin was invited to undertake the lectureship by the eminent scientist Sir Oliver Lodge. The precedent of the Cadbury Lectureship was clearly Lever's creation of a Department of Civic Design at Liverpool University two years before. Unwin received £400 p.a. for a day's teaching, involving two lectures, in the Civil Engineering department. A copy of Unwin's syllabus is held in the Unwin Collection, University of Manchester. The letter from Sir Oliver Lodge, together with a copy of Unwin's acceptance, are in file UN 2, Unwin Papers, Royal Institute of British Architects, British Architectural Library.

77 Related to the author by Christy Booth (1892–1982), Unwin's cousin.

78 City Planning: The improvement and laying out of towns. Lecture at Cambridge by the architect of Garden City (*sic*), 1906, *Cambridge Independent Press*, 16 February. Press cutting, Unwin Collection, University of Manchester.

79 Ibid.

80 *Architectural Review*, 1909, XXVI, December: 303.

81 *Journal of the Royal Institute of British Architects*, 1909–10, XVII, 6 November: 11.

82 Built-up churches with associated squares are shown in Unwin's illustration 126. Three, the Duomo, Pistoia (Sitte, 1965, Fig. 23); the Domplatz, Regensburg (Sitte, Fig. 60); and Santa Maria Novella, Florence (Sitte, Fig. 35) were contrasted with three modern equivalents of railway termini and their associated *places*.

Unwin also illustrated Sitte's proposals for visual closure of the Votivkirche Platz in Vienna and described it as if carried out, illustration 163F,

p. 225 in Unwin, 1909.

83 Irregular *places* were one of Sitte's cardinal principles – his chapter five was entitled 'The irregularities of old plazas'. Unwin reproduced and possibly even traced several, included in his illustration 127 – the Piazza San Marco, Venice (Sitte, Fig. 46); the Piazza del Duomo, Verona (Sitte, Fig. 11); the Piazza Erbe, Verona (Sitte Fig.34); the Piazzo del Signoria, Florence (Sitte, Fig. 27). Unwin's remaining examples were modern *places* in Munich which did not have Sitte equivalents.

84 The 'turbine plaza' was the most celebrated of Sitte's proposed road junctions. It was illustrated here by Unwin – illustrations 160c and 187 1a in Unwin, 1909.

85 It seems to have been drawn secondhand from a German source. *Vide* Unwin. R., 1909, Buttstedt (translated from an article by Woenerle, R., and Schwertfeger, R. in *Der Stadtebau*, December 1908). Papers collected by the RIBA Town Planning Committee, *Journal of the Royal Institute of British Architects* 3ss. XVII, November 20: pp. 70–3.

86 The block quadrangle layouts illustrated in Plates 6–11 of *The Art of Building a Home* (Parker and Unwin, 1901) originated in a scheme prepared for an unspecified site in Bradford, West Yorkshire in 1898–9. Some of the original drawings are in the Parker Collection, First Garden City Heritage Museum, Letchworth.

87 Osborn to Parker, 31 October 1946, Osborn Papers, Welwyn Garden City Library.

88 Parker to Osborn, 7 December 1946, Parker Collection, First Garden City Heritage Museum, Letchworth.

89 City Planning, *vide supra* Note 78.

90 It had also been included at the Gothenburg Exhibition organized by the International Garden Cities and Town Planning Federation. The Wembley exhibit was quite elaborate and contrasted a mediaeval town without planning with the layout based on the drawing. Chimneys smoked to demonstrate the polluting effects of mixing housing and industry, *vide* Williams Ellis *c.*1924, *The pleasures of architecture*, Jonathan Cape, London, pp. 231–4, 275.

91 Osborn to Parker, 31 October 1946, Osborn Papers, Welwyn Garden City Library.

92 Unwin was a member of the Executive Committee and Hon Secretary of the Exhibition. The RIBA President, Leonard Stokes, acknowledged that 'labour in connection with it (exhibition and catalogue) had fallen almost entirely on Mr Unwin's shoulders' (RIBA, 1911, p. 733). Unwin and H. V. Lanchester (1863–1953) described the principal exhibits (RIBA, 1911, pp. 734–812).

93 Editorial, *Local Government Officer*, 1910, 9, (7), 15 October: pp. 131–2. The tone of irony reflected the perceived lack of involvement of the other land-based professions, notably the municipal engineer.

94 A retrospect of the town-planning conference, 1910, *Architectural Review*, XXVII, December: 131–2.

95 His paper was a further version of 'The town extension plan', 1913, *Première Congres, international et exposition comparées des villes*, Union Internationale des villes, Ghent, pp. 211–15. See also Smets, M., *19th L'avenement de la cité-jardin en Belgique*, Pierre Mardaga, Brussels, p. 69.

96 *Town Planning Review*, 1914, V (2) July: 174. The school had been held

in Hampstead Garden Suburb the year before. *The Record (Hampstead Garden Suburb)* 1913, I (X), May.

97 This connection resulted in Unwin's being retained as consultant. Many useful papers on the early planning and development of Ruislip-Northwood are held in the King's College Muniment Room, University of Cambridge.

98 The winning plan was published in *The Builder*, 1911, 6 January: 17; Garden Cities and Town Planning Review, 1911, I (4) January: 334.

99 Adams' reports as Local Government Board Inspector are held in the Public Record Office, Kew, London, file PRO HLG 4-1871.

100 The documents are in the Public Record Office, *vide* 99 *supra* and the King's College Muniment Room, Cambridge. For example, see Unwin to Withers, 22 and 27 July 1912; Notes of Conference, King's College and Ruislip–Northwood UDC, 13 November 1912. PRO File HLG 4–1871 contains a printed schedule of objections by King's College and Ruislip Manor Ltd.

101 Unwin had weighed up the difficulties over aesthetic control in *Town Planning in Practice* (Unwin, 1909) and had concluded, p. 367, 'The difficulties of such public control are undoubtedly very great, but the evils which result from absolute lack of control are even greater'. PRO HLG 4–1871, Note 9, February 1914 records that 'Mr. Unwin saw the President (Burns) about this and other matters and it was arranged that I should discuss the matter . . . I discussed it with Mr. Unwin on Saturday morning and he was disposed to regard it as quite satisfactory.'

102 Munro (Local Government Board) sending file to Burns, January 1914, PRO HLG 4–1871.

103 Aldridge, 1015, p. 591. The clause became a *cause celebre* in the early 1930s after it had been used to reject a modern design by Connell, Ward and Lucas. *Vide* Jackson, A. (1972) *The Politics of Architecture*, Architectural Press, London.

104 The Parker and Unwin plans were closely based upon a 1906 design for 'inexpensive cottages' (plan XXIVB in *Report*) and a type from New Earswick (plan XXVI in *Report*). In both cases the exterior was 'rationalised'.

105 Unwin had come near to creating this type at New Earswick, particularly in Ivy Place and at Addison Way, Hampstead. Parker in a 1912 scheme at Goslaw Green, Selkirk, created semi-detached cottages with hip roofs and sash windows, as 'Georgian' as anything by their contemporaries. These examples were apparently unknown to Pepper and Swenarton (1980), 'Neo-Georgian Maison *type*', *Architectectural Review* CLXVIII (1002) August: 87–92.

106 The circumstances of the Bills and the Rosyth development were written up by Witham, D. (1979), 'Like honey from the carcase of the lion: State Housing and the Great War', unpub. paper presented at the Planning History Group Seminar, University of Liverpool, March 1977.

107 The Rosyth layout plans are held by the Scottish Record Office, Edinburgh. It is worth recording that in 1911, Barry Parker had been commissioned by a local landowner, Henry Beveridge of Pitreavie, to lay-out an estate village immediately north of Rosyth. C. M. Parker typescript, First Garden City Heritage Museum, Letchworth.

108 Peggy Curtice Hitchcock, letter to the author.

109 Public Record Office, Kew, London:

HLG series files:
HLG 4/259 (Birmingham)
HLG 4/274 (Birmingham–Stetchford and N. Yardley)
HLG 4/641 (Colne TC)
HLG 4/1084 (Hale UD)
HLG 4/1552 (Mansfield TC)
HLG 4/1690 (Nottingham CB)
HLG 4/3098 (Wrexham UB)

110 A copy was printed in *Report of the Housing Committee, Reports and printed documents of the Corporation of Dublin*, Volume I, 1915.

111 The author acknowledges the work of Fred Aalen in discovering the layout plan and perspective of the preliminary Marino Scheme, and the assistance of the Dublin Corporation Archivist, Mary Clark, in enabling him to study the plans in detail.

112 *Parliamentary Debates, Commons* LXXXV 1916, Col. 1433 (14 August 1916). It is evident from CSORP 1916 14385, one of the Chief Secretary of Ireland files now in the State Paper Office, Dublin Castle, that the term 'King's High Planner' had been gratuitously and cynically used by the Lord Mayor at a Corporation Meeting. The Irish Local Government Board's reaction was to state 'we have never heard of the King's High Planner and we are therefore unable to give any information'.

113 Christy Booth in conversation with the author.

114 Reconstruction of central Dublin, 1916, *Irish Builder and Engineer* LVIII 28 October: 524.

115 *Irish Times*, 1916, 10 November, 3.

116 *Town Planning Review*, 1917 VII (2): p. 105. It is highly likely that 'national' was a misprint for 'rational'.

117 *Statutes*, 6 and 7, Geo.5.

118 *Irish Builder and Engineer*, 1916, LVIII (25) 9 December: 619.

119 South America's First Garden City development, 1916, *Garden Cities and Town Planning* VI (8) August: 130–3.

120 *The Official History of the Ministry of Munitions*, HMSO 1922, ran to 12 volumes. Housing and Welfare were covered in Volumes 5 and 6.

121 *Official History*, V (v), pp. 3–4, notes that Dickenson, Head of Housing at the Local Government Board, offered 'all assistance in his power' at a conference held on 21 July 1915.

122 Peggy Curtice Hitchcock to the author.

123 The author consulted much useful material, including a typescript description of the plant, in the Crickmer Collection, in the possession of his daughter, the late Mrs J. Cruse of Letchworth, at the time of researching this study in 1978–9.

124 Peggy Curtice Hitchcock to the author.

125 Ibid.

126 *Official History*, V (5), p. 70.

127 Gretna and Eastriggs were often published together. Culpin included them in his series of articles for the *Journal of the American Institute of Architects*, 1917, V (10) October: 449–514. The plate illustrations were impounded by the censor and appeared in February: 72–6. The publication of the scheme in Britain was delayed for many months, although Conan Doyle reported on 'Moortown' in *The Times*. In Autumn 1918 publication was extensive: *The Architect*, 27 September; *The Architect and Contract Reporter*, 27 September, *Building News* 2, 16 and 23 October. For

modern assessments see Pepper and Swenarton, 1978; Swenarton, 1981.

128 Culpin, E. G., *Journal of the American Institute of Architects*, 1917, V(12) December: 628.

129 Letter from Unwin to the President of the Local Government Board, Hayes Fisher, 16 June 1918. Public Record Office, Kew, London, File RECO 1/512. Unwin's daughter, however, did not recall that her father visited the United States during the First World War.

130 Public Record Office, Kew, London, File RECO 1/475 contains material relating to several deputations in 1916–17. It is evident that Addison canvassed opinion in November 1917 as to the appropriate standards for postwar housing and that they urged a clear commitment to excellence – 'houses must be so attractive as to secure that they shall be full in demand and be regarded as possibly valuable amenities'.

131 PRO RECO 1/463.

132 Housing in England and Wales, May 1917, PRO RECO 1/477.

133 PRO RECO 1/494; CAB 24/19, GT 1058.

134 The fragmentary papers in the Public Record Office RECO series files do substantiate the degree of collaboration during summer 1917. See particularly RECO 1/556, 14 June, joint draft proposals for the committee which became Tudor Walters; RECO 1/543, 9 July, joint outline for housing and transit; RECO 1/544, 2 August, memo by Unwin discussing county councils as housing authorities; RECO 1/550, 18 August, Unwin to Rowntree discussing county councils; RECO 1/550, 31 August, Kershaw to Rowntree discussing problems of valuation referring to Unwin's work in this respect; RECO 1/573, 24 September, Unwin to Rowntree discussing proposed Department of Scientific and Industrial Research Committee. Briggs, 1961, pp. 141–2, notes that at Unwin's instigation Rowntree served on this.

135 Unwin to Rowntree, 9 July 1917, RECO 1/543.

136 14 July, RECO 1/552.

137 14 June 1917, Minutes of meeting between Rowntree, Unwin and Munro, RECO 1/556.

138 RECO 1/556.

139 What remains is included in the Public Record Office RECO files. The author was informed at the time of research for this study (1978–9) by a spokesman for the Department of the Environment Library that the files of detailed evidence and working papers were destroyed during the Second World War.

140 Housing (Building Construction) Committee, headed in Unwin's hand, 'Draft terms of reference for the Tudor Walters Committees' (*sic*), revised 30/8/17. Not yet adopted, RECO 1/556, 1/576.

141 12 October 1917, RECO 1/471.

142 The conditions are in RECO 1/634 'answers to questions submitted by Dr. Addison to the housing panel'; RECO 1/467 also advocates the holding of a competition 'Proposals for obtaining better house and layout plans, *c.* July 1917; RECO 1/557 appears to be a draft by Unwin. It contains the following paragraph, omitted from the 'answers' (RECO 1/467 above):

> We think it is essential that the local housing commissioners should either themselves have expert knowledge of Garden City planning or should have persons possessing it on their staffs so as to be able to get into touch with the architects in charge of each individual scheme and help them in all questions of layout'.

The competition conditions were published in *Journal of the Royal Institute of British Architects*, 1917, 3ss. XXV(1) November: 11–12, and the results were announced in *JRIBA*, 1918, 3ss XXV(7) May: 178–80.

143 The layout in Illustration No. 1 of Tudor Walters used the block of the Glasgow Garden Suburb from Culpin's *The Garden City Movement up to Date*; Illustration No. 2, repeated Illustrations 246, 247 from *Town Planning in Practice*; Illustrations 3, 3A were taken from the site-layout diagrams of the Rural Labourers Cottage *Report*. Illustration 4 was a development of the principle of *Nothing Gained by Overcrowding* to the cul-de-sac and was a diagram used by Parker as the basis for his interwar layout at New Earswick. Illustration No. 7 used the block from Unwin's London Society Lecture 'Roads and Streets'. Illustrations 10, 11, 11A showed the linking walls in the form developed at Gretna, while illustration 12 showed a cross-section of a steep hillside site related to Unwin's plan for Townshill, Swansea. Among the house-type plans, illustrations 18 and 19 were clearly derived from the 'economical' type designed in 1906 and illustrated in Unwin's article 'Cottage Buildings in the Garden City'; their origin lay in *Cottage Plans and Common Sense*. They were also virtually identical with Plan Nos. I and XXVII in the Smallholding *Report*. Illustrations 24 and 25 were both variants of Hampstead types shown in *Cottages with Gardens for Londoners*. The wide-frontage types, illustrations 34–6, had a precedent in the types designed by Parker for the Howard Cottage Society of Letchworth just before 1914. The bay-windowed parlour house, illustration 38, was based on a type used at Gretna. The absence of types designed by architects outside the immediate circle of Parker and Unwin is significant, as is the omission of the winning designs from the LGB/RIBA Competition, for the delayed appearance of the Report would have given ample time for their inclusion.

144 The study of management as a technique to gain greater productivity was evolved by F. W. Taylor whose *Principles of Scientific Management* was originally published in 1911 (revised by Greenwood, Connecticut, 1972). As noted in Briggs, *op. cit.*, Rowntree was perhaps surprisingly an advocate of Taylor's approach which might be described as entrepreneurial Darwinism and pioneered 'time and motion study' in which the greater part of the benefit of the increased productivity accrued to the employer.

145 Raymond Unwin to Peggy Curtice Hitchcock, December 1920, Hitchcock Collection.

146 Parker, C. M., 'Notes for a memoir', typescript, First Garden City Heritage Museum, Letchworth. The Parker Collection contains representative drawings of his local-authority housing schemes, which paralleled his consultancy for interwar housing at New Earswick.

147 Leslie Watson in conversation with the author.

148 Raymond Unwin to Christy Booth, 4 November 1928.

149 Raymond Unwin to Christy Booth, 7 December 1928.

150 Raymond Unwin to Christy Booth, 20 October 1926, 'I am going to Manchester to hold a Public Inquiry'. A report on the proceedings appeared in the *Manchester Guardian*, 22 October 1926. Regrettably at the time of research in 1978–9 no Public Record Office files for Wythenshawe could be located. The decision appears to have been communicated in a letter from the Ministry of Health, 29 November 1926.

151 Wythenshawe Estate Special Committee, Minutes, 4 August, 1927,

Wythenshawe Library, Manchester. The Minute continued that the Wythenshawe development was 'intended not as a complete garden city but as a satellite to Manchester, containing some local industry for part of the resident population, but being in the main a residential adjunct to Manchester'.

152 Lewis Mumford in conversation with the author, June 1978.

153 It is evident that Parker always began with *Nothing Gained* as the basis for his analytical work on optimal layouts as evident in his *Report to the Housing and Town Planning Committee*, *c.*1929, typescript Parker Coll., FGC Museum, which added culs-de-sac, informal playgrounds and footpaths that anticipated Radburn. The Radburn superblock made its first appearance in Parker's *Report to the Wythenshawe Estate Special Committee*, May 1928. The Radburn site had only lately been purchased, indicating the swiftness of the transatlantic dialogue. Parker's Report subsequently formed the major part of 'Economy in Estate Development', *JTPI*, 14 (8), 1928, pp. 177–86.

154 The 'Through Traffic Roads' of Parker's *Report* appeared on his first plan of 1930. Copies of both are in Parker Coll., FGC Museum. It is evident from the correspondence between Sheena Simon and Parker (Manchester City Archives) that shortly after the presentation of the first plan, he lobbied, with her encouragement, to get agreement to the designation of the roads as parkways. Despite the reservations of the City Surveyor and Chief Constable, and the Ministry of Transport which tartly pointed out that all costs above the minimum highway strip would be borne locally, the first section of the Princess Parkway was opened in February 1932.

155 Parker had been a member of the British delegation to the IHTPF meeting at New York in 1925. He was so impressed by the Westchester County Parkways that he obtained slides which he subsequently showed at his 1929 inauguration as TPI President, *JTPI*, 16 (1), November 1929. For the influence on Unwin's GLRPC *Reports*, *vide infra* Chapter Ten.

156 Parker to Simon, quoting Unwin, 1 January 1932, Simon Papers, Manchester City Library. Other difficulties included the complaint from the City Architect that Wythenshawe was becoming 'an art gallery with all pictures in it by the same architect'.

157 Before his inauguration, Unwin wrote to Christy Booth, 'I hope the position is one that will give me a little extra opportunity to put forward the things I have at heart in town-planning, housing etc.'

158 Raymond Unwin to Christy Booth, 4 November 1928.

159 1913 *Town Planning Review*, IV (iv), January: 287–90.

160 Ibid, p. 290.

161 Sir Aston Webb (1849–1930) was one of the leading Victorian architects and became extensively involved with civic design and planning. The Victoria Memorial (1901), Admiralty Arch (1911), the remodelling of The Mall (1911–13) and the refronting of Buckingham Palace (1913), were his best-known works, giving London a regal splendour with more than a little Beaux Arts influence. In 1914 he was a founder Member of the (Royal) Town Planning Institute.

162 Public Record Office, Kew, London, File RECO 1/593. In a few lines Unwin sketched out the brief for the future Unhealthy Areas Committee of 1920/1.

163 Royal Commission on the Local Government of Greater London, *Report*, cmnd. 1830, 1923, HMSO, London. The commission arose out of an LCC

Report of 1919 contending that the LCC was too restricted in respect of education, electricity supply and housing. The LCC felt that a central authority should be created to cover 'the whole continuous urban area, together with such a surrounding belt as was likely to become an urban character within a short time'. The new authority was to be elected, with 124 members. The proposals generated fierce opposition, particularly from adjoining shire counties. The Commission felt that the LCC procedure had invited maximum criticism and they recommended that the existing local government structure be left intact. Nevertheless they recommended the setting-up of an advisory committee, with not more than 21 members, to advise the appropriate Minister on (a) transport, (b) town planning, (c) housing, and (d) main drainage. The area to be covered was the London and Home Counties Traffic Area, subsequently adopted for the GLRPC.

164 See Hertford County Record File HCC 35/1, Minutes and Papers of Regional Planning General Purposes Sub-Committee. The 'expert shortlist' considered on 8 June 1925 included Abercrombie, Adams and Thompson, Davidge and F. M. Elgood. Davidge's appointment was confirmed on 24 July 1925. See also Davidge, W. F., 1927, *Hertfordshire Regional Planning Report*, Westminister, London.

165 *The Times*, London, 21 January 1926: 10d. The correspondence had begun in response to a letter by Adams, published 2 December 1925.

166 Institute and Societies petition, 19/3/26, *The Times*, London: 11d. This publicized the meeting, set for 23 March.

167 *The Times*, London, 26/3/26: 9d.

168 As is clear from HCC File 35/1, *vide supra* Note 164, the letters were sent out on 5 November, 1926. *The Times*, 15/12/26, reported that the Ministry of Health was considering the coordination of the planning of London and had called a conference of local authorities and regional committees for Monday 6 December. *The Times*, 7/12/26: 11d reported the conference in detail.

169 Mr Chamberlain on town-planning. Joint committee to be constituted, *The Times*, 7/12/26: 11d.

170 Ibid. It should be noted that the phraseology of Chamberlain's statement carried through to his address to the first meeting of the GLRPC, Minutes, GLC Record Office. Unwin paraphrased this in Memorandum No. 1. Open Spaces, Greater London Regional Planning Committee, *First Report*, Knapp and Drewett, London, p. 8.

171 GLRPC Minutes.

172 *First Report*, p. 2. By comparison, the New York Regional Plan under Thomas Adams extended over six years and had a staff of 150 and a budget of one million dollars. Hulchanski, J. D., 1978, 'Thomas Adams; a biographical guide', *Papers on Planning and Design*, No. 15, April, p. 12.

173 Edward Unwin had served articles with Barry Parker and had achieved modest success in practice. He designed a house for Christopher Addison and the Tolpuddle Martyrs Memorial Cottages in Dorset. He died of cancer.

174 Raymond Unwin to Christy Booth, 1 February 1929. Miss Booth confirmed to the author that she took part in some of the sorties that summer.

175 GLRPC Minutes.

176 The Memorandum on Open Spaces was in preparation, in conjunction

with the LCC valuer Frank Hunt, from March 1928; it was completed by July 1929. Sir Banister Fletcher requested him to prepare the Memorandum on Ribbon Development in November 1928; the one on Additional Powers required was considered in July 1929. The proposal for a regional authority, drafted by Montagu-Harris, was considered on 25 November 1929. GLRPC Minutes.

177 Raymond Unwin to Christy Booth, 9 December 1929. On 19 January 1930 he wrote that the report had at last gone to press.

178 *The Times*, 4/3/30: 17f.

179 Raymond Unwin to Christy Booth, Good Friday 1931.

180 Raymond Unwin to Christy Booth, 8 November 1931.

181 F. Blaise Gillie, former Under Secretary at the Welsh Office, in conversation with the author.

182 Although the Green Belt had been implicit in the postwar planning strategy of the 1947 Act, the policy was officially launched by Duncan Sandys MP, Minister of Housing and Local Government, in a Commons statement of 26 April 1955 and with the subsequent issue of MOHLG Circular 42/55, *Green Belt*, dated 3 August 1955. The advice was further elaborated in MOHLG Circular 50/57, dated 19 September 1957.

183 Raymond Unwin to Seebohm Rowntree, 9 July 1917, Public Record Office, Kew, London, File RECO 1/543.

184 Public Record Office File PRO 30/69, 1/38.

185 Public Record Office File HLG 52/726/GLC 23.

186 Public Record Office File HLG 52/728/GLC 31.

187 Public Record Office File HLG 52/741.

188 Public Record Office File HLG 68/50.

189 Public Record Office File HLG 68/50.

190 Public Record Office File HLG 27/69, typed manuscript. Unwin's evidence was printed in *Minutes of Evidence*, Royal Commission on the Geographical Distribution of the Industrial population, HMSO, London. Unwin's evidence was summarized in the *Report*, para. 267, p. 125.

191 Osborn to Unwin, 21 April 1938, Osborn Papers, Welwyn Garden City Library.

192 Osborn to Mumford, 17 October 1941, 8 April 1957, pp. 17, 271–2 in Hughes, M. (ed.) (1971), *The letters of Lewis Mumford and Frederick J. Osborn. A Transatlantic dialogue, 1938–70*, Adams and Dart, Bath. Osborn stated that he redrafted parts of the majority report, Ministry report and dissentient Memorandum 'all very hush-hush and both of us were kept hard at this underground work by Mrs. W. L. Hichens'.

193 Osborn to Unwin, 2 August 1938, Osborn Papers.

194 Sir Raymond Unwin's suggestions for the proposed forum, Unwin–Tugwell–Moses–Heydecker, Lyme, Connecticut, 9 September 1939, UN 16/59, Unwin Papers, Royal Institute of British Architects, British Architectural Library.

195 The cable was quoted in the *Proceedings of the Conference on problems of social environment and the War*, Royal Institute of British Architects, 2 February 1940, Unwin Papers.

196 A comprehensive overview of internationalism in pre-1914 planning was given by Sutcliffe in his paper, 'Urban Planning in Europe before 1914: International aspects of a prophetic movement', given in November 1980 at the Planning History Group Conference, King's College, Cambridge.

197 Among German publications featuring Unwin's work, the following may

be cited: H. E. von Berlepsch Valendas, 'Die erste Englische gartenstadt und ihr verwandter grundungen', 1908, *Kunst und Kunsthandwerk*, Artaria, Wien, XI (3): 117–63; also his 1912, *Die Gartenstadtbewegung in England und ihre jetziger stand*, Oldenburg, Munchen und Berlin; Rudolph Eberstadt, 1909, 'Die neue gartenvorstadt in London – Hampstead', *Der Stadtebau*, Wasmuth, Berlin, 6 (8): 99–103, *Gardenstadt*, Karlsruhe, published from 1906 covered several articles on Letchworth and Hampstead. *See also* Kampffmeyer, B. (ed.) and part author (1910), 'Aus englischen gartenstadten', Deutsche gartenstadt gesellschaft, Renaissance-verlag, Robert Federn, Berlin.

198 'The Editor' (Gustav Stickley), 1910, 'Town Planning in Theory and Practice: the work of Raymond Unwin'; also 'Barry Parker: the architect who designs houses as a whole and according to need rather than precedent', *The Craftsman* XXII (4) January: 391–401; 409–15. Parker's subsequent articles also included some material on site-planning and housing layout, although the major emphasis was placed on individual house designs. *See also* Hawkes, D. (ed.) (1986), *Modern Country Houses in England. The Arts and Crafts architecture of Barry Parker*, Cambridge University Press.

199 *Town Planning Review*, 1914, V (2), July: 174.

200 See *Journal of the Royal Institute of British Architects*, 1915, 23 January: 143; 20 February: 189–90; *The Builder*, 19 February: 182.

The RIBA offered hospitality and the Garden Cities and Town Planning Association organized a conference on the reconstruction of Belgium, 11–15 February 1915. Later, in May, an exhibition of Belgian town-planning was held at University College, London, with lectures by Unwin, Adshead, Davidge, Abercrombie, Lanchester and Elgood. *See The Builder*, 14 May: 471.

201 There were many groups and individuals involved. In his 'Memoir of Sir Raymond Unwin', *Journal of the Royal Institute of British Architects*, 15 July 1940, Barry Parker noted 'we were in constant touch with Sir Edward Grey as members of a group founded to promote the idea of a League of Nations. Quite independently . . . another . . . existed under the leadership of H. G. Wells. Eventually these two groups united as the League of Nations Union . . . and Unwin became one of the most active and constructive members of its executive.'

202 Raymond Unwin to Christy Booth, 3 September 1925, in a letter written to wish her *bon voyage* upon taking up a teaching appointment in Toronto.

203 Lewis Mumford in conversation with the author, June 1978. He described Parker as 'one of the handsomest men I ever saw, the complete artist from head to foot, one of the most lovable men I ever met'. Howard was something else again, a seemingly insignificant man with a knack for doing the unexpected: as when he decided on impulse to journey to Detroit 'to convince Henry Ford of the rightness of the Garden City idea'.

204 His chosen examples were the Woolworth Building, New York and Michigan Avenue, Chicago.

205 Interview with the *New York Times* in which he discussed congestion, 7 October 1928.

206 In discussing an earlier paper, 'Urban Development: the pattern and the background' (Unwin, 1935, pp. 253–6), Harold Buttenheim stated, 'As Sir Raymond, economist, shows signs of overtaking Sir Raymond, planner, hope grows that the Unwin urge against urban overcrowding will

increasingly prevail in effective action. The lessening of the economic lag, in Sir Raymond's pursuit of spaciousness, is a joy to behold'. *The Planner's Journal* (American Institute of Planners) 1935, I (4) November–December: 76.

207 The inauguration of the International Garden Cities and Town Planning Association (*sic*) was described in *Garden Cities and Town Planning*, 1913, NS III (9) September: 224–6. The triumphal progress of the following year was noted in the same periodical which published the itinerary for the summer tour 9–25 July, *GC & TP*, 1914, NS IV (4) April: 78–9. The issue for August NS IV (8): 178–81 recorded that it was only on the date of the declaration of war, 4 August, that the last of the foreign delegates left Britain.

208 The scope of the exhibition rivalled that of London in 1910. A comprehensive *Catalogue* (International Garden Cities and Town Planning Federation, 1923, London) contained an account by Unwin of town planning in the British Empire, pp. 23–6.

209 Papers, Volume I of *Report* of Conference, 1926, International Housing and Town Planning Federation, London, p. 125. F. M. Elgood presented the English viewpoint in 'Houses or Tenements in England', pp. 166–76 in ibid.

210 Volume III, *Report* of Conference 1929, International Housing and Town Planning Federation, London, p. 125.

211 Raymond Unwin to Christy Booth, 24 September 1930.

212 The Berlin Congress attracted 900 delegates. The other events were held by the Frankfurt Housing Association, the German Institute of Architects and the Comité International pour la resolution des problems de l'architecture contemporaire, a CIAM offshoot. Edward Unwin wrote a short account of the Berlin meeting, 'The International Housing and Town Planning Congress, Berlin, 1931', *Journal of the Royal Institute of British Architects*, 1931, 3ss. XXXVIII (17), 11 July: 650–1.

213 Notes for the LCC lecture, 7 February 1930, Unwin Collection, Manchester.

214 Information from Christy Booth.

215 'Presented with a ring as token of Dr. at Trondheim University . . . banquets and speeches by the King . . . later given a young soldier to escort me to my hotel though quite sober', Raymond Unwin to Christy Booth, 18 September 1935.

216 *Journal of the Royal Institute of British Architects*, 1931, 3ss. 39 (1) November 7: 11 note following transcript of Unwin's inaugural address. His choice of Beethoven was probably influenced by memories of Carpenter, who had revered that composer.

217 Peggy Curtice Hitchcock to the author.

218 Undated notes, Unwin Collection, Manchester University.

219 Freda Whyte, n.d., 'Memoir of Sir Raymond Unwin', typescript, Unwin Collection, Manchester University. Peggy Curtice Hitchcock informed the author that these recollections are occasionally embellished and should be treated with caution.

220 Unwin, like Adams, appears to have wished to found a dynasty of town-planners. His letters to Christy Booth of the mid-1930s include references to his hope that one or other of his grandchildren would carry on the family tradition. The author's conversations with Christy Booth, Malcom Bruce Glasier and Paul Mauger, the latter of whom was in partnership

with Unwin for a time, have indicated that notwithstanding his sincerity and loyalty, Edward was temperamentally unsuited to carry on his father's work. However, Unwin felt his death perhaps the more bitterly. On 18 May 1936 he wrote to Christy Booth 'now that Edward has gone I have a feeling that my innings was being prolonged when he ought to have been having his. A good deal of satisfaction has gone out of things.' Shortly afterwards a memorial seat on Hampstead Heath was erected, with teak planking obtained by Malcolm Bruce Glasier and carved by Stanley Parker to a design by Barry Parker.

221 'Unwin questioned by Mrs Roosevelt at Slums Meeting', *The Evening Star*, (Washington), 1934, 16 January. Robert D. Kohn, Deputy Housing Administrator, also spoke.

222 In an introduction to the *Report* (Public Administration Service, 1935), Ascher stated that Unwin had assumed the major drafting burden.

223 Carl Feiss in correspondence with the author, 16 May 1979.

224 Press cutting of visit to Montreal, 1933, UN14, Unwin Papers, Royal Institute of British Architects, British Architectural Library.

225 *Town and Country Planning*, 1937, V (19): 102 noted:

> One pleasant compliment (to the increase of public approbation of the satellite town concept) was the invitation of the BBC to Sir Raymond Unwin and the Secretary of the Garden Cities and Town Planning Association to prepare and stage a television programme on 'The case for a satellite town' on the afternoon and evening of Thursday 6 May 1937 . . . special film was prepared by Mr McAllister showing the expansion of a market town with a hideous conglomeration, and showing Welwyn and Letchworth as a contrast . . . Sir Raymond Unwin illustrated his contribution with plans of American green belt towns as well as Welwyn, Letchworth and Wythenshawe.

226 Carl Feiss in correspondence with the author, 26 May 1979.

227 Unwin Papers, UN 8/28, Royal Institute of British Architects, British Architectural Library.

228 Unwin was Chairman of the Executive Committee. A draft syllabus is included in UN 17, Unwin Papers, Royal Institute of British Architects, British Architectural Library.

229 Notes for Millthorpe address, 3 July 1939. Unwin Collection, Manchester University.

230 Unwin's colleagues were to have been Goodhert Rendel and Curtis Green. Preliminary papers and correspondence are in Unwin Papers, UN 16, Royal Institute of British Architects, British Architectural Library.

231 Christy Booth in conversation with the author.

232 Katharine Bruce Glasier noted after the return of the Labour Government in 1945, 'even Lady Unwin too excited almost to write about "prose" like dishcloths and knitting wool. All sunshine and roses' (Thompson, 1971, p. 242).

233 Christy Booth always emphasized it as the key to his life and work in her conversations with the author, 1976–82.

234 Peggy Curtice Hitchcock commented on the early letters between her father and mother as follows:

> The reaching out through socialism, temperance, religion, living with labourers was trying to put satisfaction into a life that through work didn't interest him much. He was so very different when he felt he was

doing something useful *through* his work.

235 This was the title of one of Unwin's earliest socialist lectures, written in Manchester in January 1886. Unwin Papers, Royal Institute of British Architects, British Architectural Library.

236 Raymond Unwin to Christy Booth, 4 December 1939.

237 In conversation and correspondence with the author, June 1978.

238 Early in 1930 he had written to Christy Booth: 'I am hoping to bring out the old book and try and finish it off', but somehow he never managed it. The eighth edition was published by Benn in 1932 as it stood. In 1946 Batsfords asked Parker to revise the text in collaboration with F. C. Eden of Liverpool University. Parker wrote to Osborn that 'the value of the book was that . . . of the time at which it was written'. Parker Collection First Garden City Heritage Museum Letchworth, and Osborn Papers, Welwyn Garden City Library. This project, too, foundered.

References

1 Documentary sources

Booth Collection:
Correspondence between Raymond Unwin and Christy Booth; family papers.
British Steel Corporation Archives, Irthlingborough:
Material on Staveley Coal and Iron Co.
Department of Town and Country Planning, University of Manchester:
Unwin Papers, photographs and slide collection.
First Garden City Heritage Museum, Letchworth:
Garden City Association pressbooks and correspondence, Parker Collection, plans, photographs and practice records.
Greater London Council Record Office:
Minutes of Greater London Regional Plan Committee; Minutes of London County Council Housing Committee.
Hampstead Garden Suburb Archives:
Minute books of Hampstead Garden Suburb Trust, plans and photographs.
Hertfordshire County Council Record Office:
Ebenezer Howard Papers.
Hitchcock Collection:
Correspondence between Raymond Unwin and Ethel Parker.
Joseph Rowntree Memorial Trust:
Minutes of Joseph Rowntree Village Trust, plans.
King's College, Cambridge:
Papers of the Ruislip Manor Company.
Letchworth Garden City Corporation:
First Garden City Ltd., Minute Books and correspondence.
Letchworth Public Library:
Local History Collection.
Liverpool University Library:
Bruce Glasier Papers.
Manchester City Archivist:
Lady Simon Papers.
Manchester Town Clerk:
Minutes of Housing and Finance Committees, Manchester City Corporation.
National Coal Board:
Survey Material of Staveley Coal and Iron Co.
National Housing and Town Planning Council:
Minute Books and correspondence.

North Hertfordshire District Council:
Bye-law records and plans of the former Letchworth Urban District Council.
Public Record Office:
Bill Papers; Cabinet Papers; Files and Records of Local Government Board; Ministry of Health; Ministry of Munitions; Royal Commission on the Distribution of the Industrial Population; Marley Committee on Garden Cities.
Royal Institute of British Architects, British Architectural Library:
Membership records and Unwin Papers.
Ryedale District Council:
Byelaw records and plans of the former Flaxton Rural District Council.
Salisbury Collection, Hatfield House:
Papers relating to the Reconstruction Committee Housing Panel.
Sheffield City Library:
Local History Collection and material on Staveley Coal and Iron Co.
Town and Country Planning Association:
Minute Books.
Welwyn Garden City Library:
Osborn Papers.
Wythenshawe Public Library:
Minutes and papers of the Wythenshawe Estate Special Committee, Manchester City Corporation.

2 Official publications
(All HMSO London unless otherwise stated)

Advisory Committee on Rural Cottages, 1914, *Report of the Committee appointed by the President of the Board of Agriculture and Fisheries to consider and advise the Board on plans, models, specifications and methods of construction for rural cottages and outbuildings, with appendices and reduced plans.*

Buildings for smallholdings in England and Wales, together with an abstract of the evidence, appendices and a series of plans and specifications, 1913, *Report of the Departmental Committee appointed by the President of the Board of Agriculture and Fisheries*, Cmnd. 6708.

The Design of dwellings, 1944, *Report of a Sub-Committee of the central housing advisory council*, chaired by the Earl of Dudley, (The Dudley Report).

Homes for Today and Tomorrow, 1961, *Report of the Committee under the Chairmanship of Sir Parker Morris*, appointed by the central housing advisory committee to consider the standards of design and equipment applicable to family dwellings and other residential accommodation whether provided by public authorities or private enterprise, and to make recommendations, (The Parker Morris Report).

Housing in England and Wales, 1918, *Memorandum by the advisory housing panel on the emergency programme*, Cmnd. 9087.

The Land, 1913,1914, *Report of the Land Enquiry Committee* (2 Vols.), Hodder and Stoughton, London.

Local Government Board, 1918, *The Housing of the Working Classes Act 1890–1909 Memorandum* for the use of local authorities with respect to the provision and arrangement of houses for the working classes.

———, 1919, *Manual on the preparation of state-aided housing schemes.*

Ministry of Health, 1919, *Manual of unfit houses and unhealthy areas*, I, Policy

and Practice; 1920, II, Legal powers and duties of local authorities.
———, 1920, *Interim Report*, 1921, *Final Report*, of the committee to consider and advise on the principles to be followed in dealing with unhealthy areas.
———, 1920, *First Annual Report*, 1919–20, Part I, housing and town planning, Cmnd. 917.
———, 1920, *Type Plans and elevations of houses designed by the Ministry of Health in connection with state-aided schemes.*
———, 1921, *Second Annual Report*, 1920–1, Cmnd. 1446.
———, 1924, *Sixth Annual Report*, 1923–4, Cmnd. 1450.
———, 1927, *Housing manual on the design, construction and repair of dwellings.*
———, 1927, *Eighth Annual Report*, 1926–7, Cmnd. 2938.
———, 1928, *Ninth Annual Report*, 1927–8, Cmnd. 3185.
———, 1931, *Interim Report of the departmental committee on regional development*, (The Chelmsford Report), Cmnd. 3915.
———, 1931, *Twelfth Annual Report*, 1930–1, Cmnd. 3937.
———, 1932, *Thirteenth Annual Report*, 1931–2, Cmnd. 4113.
———, 1935, *Garden Cities and Satellite Towns, Report of the departmental committee*, (The Marley Report).
Ministry of Reconstruction, 1918 i, ii, Womens Housing Sub-Committee, *First Interim Report*, Cmnd. 9166; *Final Report*, Cmnd. 9232.
Public Administration Service (US), 1935, *A Housing program for the United States*, publication No. 48, Chicago.
Royal Commission on the distribution of the industrial population, 1940, *Report* (The Barlow Report), Cmnd. 6153.
Town and Country Planning Advisory Committee, 1938, *Report on the preservation of the Countryside.*
(Tudor Walters, Sir J.), 1918, *Report of the Committee appointed by the President of the Local Government Board and the Secretary for Scotland to consider questions of building construction in connection with the provision of dwellings for the working classes in England, Wales and Scotland, and to report on the methods of securing economy and despatch in the provision of such dwellings*, Cmnd. 9191, (The Tudor Walters Report).

3 Main bibliography

A national policy for public housing, 1933, *Journal of the Royal Institute of British Architects*, 3ss., XL (7) 11 February: 277–8.
Abbott, E. R. and Elgood, F. M., 1914–15, The Ruislip Northwood Scheme, *Papers and discussions of the Town Planning Institute*, I: 1–14, 15–26.
Abercrombie, L. P., 1910, A comparative review of examples of modern town planning and garden city schemes in England I and II; *Town Planning Review*, I (1): 18–38; I (2): 111–128.
———, 1926, *The preservation of rural England*, Liverpool University Press and Hodder and Stoughton.
———, 1943, *Town and country planning*, Oxford University Press.
———, 1945, *Greater London Plan, 1944*, HMSO London.
Ackerman, F. L., 1917, The significance of England's program of building workmen's houses, *Journal of the American Institute of Architects*, V(11) November: 538–40.
Acton Housing Scheme, 1920, *Housing*, 22 November.

Adams, T., 1911, American Town Planning, *Garden Cities and Town Planning*, I(7) August: 165–73.
———, 1918, Government housing during the War, *Conservation of life* (Journal of the Canadian Commission of Conservation), IV (2) April: 25–33.
———, 1931, London as it ought to be: I. The need of foresight and comprehensive planning, *Journal of the Town Planning Institute*, XVII (8), June 187–91.
———, 1932, *Recent advances in town planning*, Churchill, London.
———, 1934, *Design of residential areas*, Harvard City Planning Series, No. IV, Cambridge, Mass.
———, 1935, *Outline of town and city planning*, Churchill, London.
Addison, C., 1925, *Politics from within*, (2 Vols), Herbert Jenkins, London.
———, 1934, *Four and a half years*, (2 Vols), Hutchinson, London.
Additional powers sought, 1929, *The Times*, August 12: 9a.
Adshead, S.D., 1910, The town planning conference of the Royal Institute of British Architects, *Town Planning Review*, I (3) October: 183.
Aldridge, H.R., n.d., *c.*1915, *The case for town planning*. A practical manual for the use of councillors, officers and others engaged in the preparation of town planning schemes, with an Appendix by Elgood, F. M. and Abbott, E. R., National Housing and Town Planning Council, London.
———, 1923, *Housing Manual*, National Housing and Town Planning Council, London.
Allwood, R., 1987, George Faulkner Armitage 1849–1937, *Furniture history* XXIII: 67–87.
Armytage, W. H. G., 1961, *Heavens below. Utopian experiments in England 1560–1960*, Routledge, London.
Ashworth, W. 1954, *The Genesis of modern British town planning. A study in economic and social history of the nineteenth and twentieth centuries*, Routledge, London.
Atkinson, G., 1971, Raymond Unwin; founding father of the BRS, *Journal of the Royal Institute of British Architects*, 36–78(10) October: 446–8.
Aus Englischen Gartenstadten, 1910, Deutsche Gartenstadt Gesellschaft, Berlin, Renaissance-Verlag, Robert Federn, Berlin.
Barnett, H.O., 1905, A garden suburb at Hampstead, *Contemporary Review*, LXXXVII (470) February: 231–7.
———, 1908, The Hampstead Garden Suburb, *Garden cities and town planning*, NS III (26) March: 22.
———, 1918, *Canon Barnett – his life, work and friends* (2 Vols). John Murray, London.
———, 1928, *The story of the growth of the Hampstead Garden Suburb*, Hampstead Garden Suburb Trust, London.
Barnett, Canon and Mrs S. A., 1909, *Toward social reform*, T. Fisher Unwin, London.
Beattie, S. 1980, *A revolution in London housing*, Greater London Council, The Architectural Press, London.
Beaufoy, S. L. G., 1950, Well Hall estate, Eltham, *Town planning review*, XXI (3) October: 259–71.
Beevers, R. 1988, *The Garden City Utopia. A critical biography of Ebenezer Howard*, Macmillan, Basingstoke.
Bentley, E. G., and Pointon Taylor, S., 1911, *A practical guide in the preparation of town planning schemes*, George Philip, London.
Berlepsch Valendas, B. D. A., 1912, *Die Gartenstadtbewegung in England, ihre Entwickelung und ihr jetziger stand*, Munchen und Berlin.

Black, R. van Nest, 1940, Tribute to Sir Raymond Unwin, given at memorial meeting, New York City, November 12 1940, *Planners Journal*, 6(4) Oct-Dec: 112.

Boardman, P., 1978, *The worlds of Patrick Geddes*, Routledge and Kegan Paul, London.

Book of the Cheap Cottages exhibition, 1905, The County Gentleman and Land and Water Ltd., London.

Bowley, M., 1945, *Housing and the State, 1919–44*, George Allen and Unwin, London.

Briggs, A., 1961, *Social thought and social action: a study of Seebohm Rowntree*, Longman, London.

———, 1968, *Victorian cities*, Penguin, London.

Brunt, A.W., n.d., *c.*1942, *Pageant of Letchworth*, Letchworth.

Bull, W.J., 1901, A green girdle round London, *The Sphere*. 5: 128–9.

Bullock, N., 1977, Housing reform and the Garden City Movement in Germany: 1890–1915, pp. 203–223 in *Transactions of the Martin Centre for architectural and urban studies*, I, Woodhead Faulkner, Cambridge.

Carpenter, E., 1916, *My days and dreams*, George Allen and Unwin, London.

Chadwick, G.F., 1961, *The works of Sir Joseph Paxton*, Architectural Press, London.

———, 1966, *The park and the town*, Architectural Press, London.

Cherry, G. E., 1970, *Town Planning in its social context*, Leonard Hill. London.

———, 1974a, *The evolution of British town planning*, Leonard Hill, Leighton Buzzard.

———, 1974b, The Housing, Town Planning etc. Act 1919, *Journal of the Royal Town Planning Institute* (The Planner), 6 (5), May: 681–4.

———, 1975, *Factors in the origins of town planning in Britain. The example of Birmingham, 1905–15*, CURS WP 36, Centre for Urban and Regional Studies, University of Birmingham.

———, 1981, *Pioneers in British planning*, Architectural Press, London.

———, 1988, *Cities and plans*, Edward Arnold, London.

Chubb, P., 1887, The two alternatives, *Today* 8(46): 69–77.

Collins, G. R. and C. C., 1965, *Camillo Sitte and the birth of modern city planning*, Phaidon, London.

Cottages with gardens for Londoners, n.d., *c.*1907, Co-partnership Tenants Ltd., London.

Creese, W. L., 1963, Parker and Unwin: architects of totality, *Journal of the Society of Architecture Historians*, XXII(3) October: 161–70.

———, 1966, *The search for environment: the Garden City before and after*, Yale, New Haven.

———, 1967, *The legacy of Raymond Unwin: a human pattern for planning*, MIT Press, Cambridge (Mass).

Culpin, E. G., 1913, 1914, *The Garden City Movement up to date*, Garden Cities and Town Planning Association, London.

———, 1917, The remarkable application of town planning principles to the war time necessities of England, *Journal of the American Institute of Architects*, V (9) September: 425: 49.

Curl, J.S., 1983, *The life and work of Henry Roberts 1803–1876*, architect, Phillimore. Chichester.

Darley, G., 1975, *Villages of vision*, Architectural Press, London.

Davey, P., 1980, *Arts and crafts architecture*, Architectural Press, London.

Day, M. G., 1973, *Sir Raymond Unwin (1863–1940) and R. Barry Parker*

(1867–1947): a study and evaluation of their contribution to the development of site planning theory and practice, unpub., M.A. Thesis, University of Manchester.

———, 1981, The contribution of Sir Raymond Unwin (1863–1940) and R. Barry Parker (1867–1947) to the development of site-planning theory and practice, c. 1890–1918, pp. 156–199 in Sutcliffe, A. (ed.), *British town planning: the formative years*, Leicester University Press.

Day, M. and Garstang, K., 1975, Socialist theories and Sir Raymond Unwin, *Town and country planning*, 43 (7–8): 346–9.

Deakin, D., (ed.), 1989, *Wythenshawe. The story of a garden city*, Phillimore, Chichester.

A development plan of greater London of the future, 1914, *Journal of the London Society*, (5) October: 1–4.

Dix, G., 1981, Patrick Abercrombie 1879–1959, pp. 103–30 in Cherry G. (ed.), *Pioneers in British planning*, Architectural Press, London.

Dower, J. (et al.), 1935, Positive planning in Great Britain, pp. 117–22 in *Report*, International Housing and Town Planning Federation, London.

Eden, W. A., 1957, Hampstead Garden Suburb, *Journal of the Royal Institute of British Architects*, 3ss. 64 (12): 489–95.

Evans, P., 1976, Raymond Unwin and the municipalisation of the Garden City, pp. 251–74 in Steadman P. and Owers J., 1976, *Transactions of the Martin Centre for Architectural and Urban Studies*, Woodhead Faulkner. Cambridge.

Feiss, C., 1963, Unwin's American journeys (1 and 2), *Town and country planning*, XXXI (II) November: 423–4; XXXI (12) December: 471–3.

First Garden City Ltd., 1905, *Garden city in the making*, Garden City Press, Hitchin.

Fishman, R., 1977, *Urban Utopias in the Twentieth Century: Ebenezer Howard, Frank Lloyd Wright and Le Corbusier*, Basic Books, New York.

Fitzmaurice, R., 1938, *Principles of modern building. Volume I: walls, partitions and chimneys*, HMSO, London.

Forshaw, J. H. and Abercrombie L. P., 1943, *County of London plan. Prepared for the London County Council*, Macmillan, London.

Fry, E., Maxwell, 1940, Sir Raymond Unwin, *Architectural Review*, LXXXVIII, August, p. 65.

Garden Cities and Town Planning Association, 1933, (W. L. Hare, ed.), *Report of the Town and Country Planning Summer School*, (Welwyn Garden City, Sept. 11–17, 1933), London.

Garden City Association, 1901, *The Garden City Conference at Bournville . . . Report of proceedings*, London.

Gaunt, W., 1913, The Town Square at Letchworth, *Garden cities and town planning*, NS III (3) March: 75–9.

Geddes, P., 1949, *Cities in evolution*, Williams and Norgate, London.

Gibberd, F., 1953, *Town design*, Architectural Press, London.

Glasier, J. B., 1921, *William Morris and the early years of the Socialist Movement*, Longmans Green, London.

Glasier, K. B., 1940, The passing of Sir Raymond Unwin, *Labour's Northern voice*, 15(16) August: 2.

GLRPC (Greater London Regional Planning Committee), 1929, *First report*, Knapp and Drewett, Westminster (London).

———, 1933, *Second Report*, Knapp and Drewett, London.

Grafton Green, B. 1977, *Hampstead Garden Suburb 1907–77*, Hampstead Garden Suburb Residents Association, London.

The Hampstead Garden Suburb and its architecture, 1912, *The Builder*, 30 August: 255.

Hampstead Garden Suburb Trust Ltd., 1937, *The Hampstead Garden Suburb: its achievements and significance*, London.

Hardy, D., 1991, *From Garden Cities to New Towns. Campaigning for town and country planning 1899–1946*, Spon, London.

Harvey, W. A., 1906, *The Model village and its cottages: Bournville*, Batsford, London.

Hatje, G. (ed.), 1964, *Encyclopedia of modern architecture*, Abrams, New York.

Hawkes, D., 1976, Garden cities and new methods of construction: Raymond Unwin's influence on English housing practice, 1919–39, pp. 275–296 in Steadman, P. and Owers, J. 1976, *Transactions of the Martin Centre for architectural and urban studies, University of Cambridge*, Woodhead Faulkner, Cambridge.

———, (ed.), 1986, *Modern country homes in England. The arts and crafts architecture of Barry Parker*, Cambridge University Press.

Hawtree, M., 1981, The emergence of the town planning profession, pp. 64–105 in Sutcliffe, A. (ed.), *British town planning: the formative years*, Leicester University Press.

Hebbert, M., 1981, Frederic Osborn, 1885–1978, pp. 177–202 in Cherry, G. E. (ed.), *Pioneers in British planning*, Architectural Press, London.

Henderson, P., 1967, *William Morris, his life, work and friends*, Thames and Hudson, London.

Hinton, J., (ed. Hinton, M.), 1884, *The lawbreaker*, Kegan Paul Trench, London.

Hobson, S. G., 1938, *Pilgrim to the left: Memoirs of a modern revolutionist*, Arnold, London.

The homes of well-known architects. 3. Mr. Raymond Unwin's house, 'Wyldes', Hampstead, 1923, *Architects' Journal*, LVII (1476) 18 April: 682–6.

Horsfall, T. C., 1904, *The Improvement of the dwellings and surroundings of the people: the example of Germany*, Manchester University Press.

Howard, E., 1898, *Tomorrow: a peaceful path to real reform*, Swan Sonnenschein, London.

———, 1902, *Garden cities of tomorrow*, Swan Sonnenschein, London.

———, 1946, (ed. Osborn, F. J., with an introductory essay by Mumford, L.) *Garden cities of tomorrow*, Faber and Faber, London.

Howard Medal Presentation, 1939, *Town and country planning*, VII (26): 44–7.

Hoyt, H., 1933, *One hundred years of land values in Chicago*, University of Chicago Press.

Hubbard, E., and Shippobottom, M., 1988, *A guide to Port Sunlight village*, Liverpool University Press.

Hughes, M. (ed.), 1971, *The letters of Lewis Mumford and Frederic Osborn: a transatlantic dialogue*, Adams and Dart, Bath.

Hulchanski, J. D., 1978, Thomas Adams: A biographical and bibliographical guide; *Papers on planning and design No. 15*, Department of Urban and Regional Planning, University of Toronto, April.

Hussey, C., 1950a, *The architecture of Sir Edwin Lutyens*, Country Life, London.

———, 1950b, *The life of Sir Edwin Lutyens*, Country Life, London.

Ikin, C. W. (in consultation with Grafton Green, B.) 1990, *Hampstead Garden Suburb. Dreams and realities*, New Hampstead Garden Suburb Trust Ltd. and Hampstead Garden Suburb Residents Association, London.

Irving, R. G., 1981, *Indian Summer, Lutyens, Baker and Imperial Delhi*, Yale, New Haven and London.
Jackson, A. A., 1973, *Semi-detached London*, George Allen and Unwin, London.
Jackson, F., 1985, *Sir Raymond Unwin: architect, planner and visionary*, Zwemmer, London.
Johnson, B., 1977, *Brentham: Ealing's garden suburb*, Brentham Society, London.
Johnson, P. B., 1968, *A land fit for heroes: the planning of British reconstruction 1916–1919*, University of Chicago Press.
Joseph Rowntree Village Trust, 1912, *New Earswick*, York.
The Joseph Rowntree Memorial Trust, 1920, *Housing*, 29 March: 254–5.
Journal, 1934, *Journal of the Royal Institute of British Architects*, 3ss. 41 May 19: 668.
Kornwolf, J. D., 1972, *M. H. Baillie Scott and the arts and crafts movement*, Johns Hopkins Press, Baltimore.
Loftus Hare, W., 1937, The green belt - its relation to London's growth, *Journal of the Royal Institute of British Architects*, 3ss. XLIV May: 684–5.
London housing, 1928, 1931, 1938, London County Council.
London Society - notes of their aims, 1913, *Architectural Association Journal*, XXIX (318) August: 59.
———, 1919, *Development plan of Greater London prepared during the Great War 1914–1918*, Stamford, London.
Lyon, T. Finday, 1963, Sir Raymond Unwin, *Journal of the Royal Institute of British Architects*, 3ss. 70 (9) September: 356.
Macfadyen, D., 1933, *Sir Ebenezer Howard and the town planning movement*, Manchester University Press.
Mairet, P., 1957, *Pioneer of sociology: The life and letters of Patrick Geddes*, Lund Humphries, London.
May, E., 1963, Unwin as a planner for social welfare, *Town and country planning* XXI (ii), Nov: 427–8.
Meath, Lord, 1901, The green girdle round London, *The Sphere*, 6: 64.
Meller, H., 1981, Patrick Geddes 1854–1932, pp. 46–71 in Cherry, G. E. (ed.) *Pioneers in British planning*, Architectural Press, London.
———, 1990, *Patrick Geddes: Social evolutionist and city planner*, Routledge, London.
Miller, M., 1978, Letchworth revisited, cheap cottages from 1905, *Housing outlook* (4): 10–14.
———, 1979a, Garden City influence on the evolution of housing policy, *Local government studies*, 5(6) November/December: 5–22.
———, 1979b, The Howard Cottage Society: pioneers of garden city housing, *Housing outlook*, (5): 13–16.
———, 1980, In search of the £150 cottage, *Town and country planning*, 49 (2) February: 48–50.
———, 1983, Letchworth Garden City - eighty years on, *Built Environment*, 9 (3/4): 167–84.
———, 1984, The roots of planning, *The Planner (Journal of the Royal Town Planning Institute)*, 70(9): 11–15.
———, 1985, Raymond Unwin and the planning of Dublin, pp. 263–306 in Bannon, M. J. (ed.), *The emergence of Irish planning 1880–1920* (A hundred years of Irish planning Volume 1), Turoe Press, Dublin.
———, 1989a, The elusive green background: Raymond Unwin and the Greater London Regional Plan, *Planning perspectives*, 4(1) January: 45–78.

———, 1989b, *Letchworth. The First Garden City*, Phillimore, Chichester.
———, 1990, Letchworth Garden City: an architectural view, pp. 48–87 in *Garden Cities and New Towns*, Hertfordshire Publications.
Minett, J., 1974, The Housing Town Planning etc. Act 1909, *The Planner (Journal of the Royal Town Planning Institute)*, 60(5): 676–80.
Morris, W., 1883, art under plutocracy, a lecture delivered at University College, Oxford, 14 November 1883, *Collected works* XXIII, 1905, Longman, London, pp. 164–191.
———, 1884, Art and Socialism: the aims and ideas of the English Socialist of today, a lecture delivered to the Secular Society of Leicester, 23 January 1884, p. 127 in Volume XXII of Morris, M. (ed.), 1910–15, *The collected works of William Morris*, Longman, London.
———, 1891, *News from nowhere or an epoch of rest; being some characters from a Utopian romance*, Reeves and Turner, London.
'Mr Unwin of the L.G.B.', 1914, *Garden cities and town planning*, NS IV (12) December: 268–9.
'The muddle of a larger London', (1933), *The Times*, 19 May: 15c.
Muthesius, H., 1904, *Das Englische Haus*, Ernst Wasmuth, Berlin, 1904–5. English Translation, 1979, ed. Dennis Sharp and a preface by Julian Posener, translated by Janet Seligman, Crosby Lockwood Staples, London.
National Housing and Town Planning Council (NHTPC), 1932, *Thirty-second annual report*, London.
Nettlefold, J. S., 1908, *Practical housing*, Garden City Press, Letchworth.
———, 1914, *Practical town planning*, St Catherine Press, London.
'New townsmen', 1918, *New towns after the War*, Dent, London.
Olmsted, F. L. Jr., 1909, Through American spectacles, *Garden cities and town planning*, NS (4) May: 198–200.
Orbach L. F., 1977, *Homes for heroes: a study of the evolution of British housing 1915–21*, Seeley, London.
Osborn, F. J., 1946, *Green-belt cities: the British contribution*, Faber and Faber, London.
Osborn, F. J. and Whittick, A., 1963, (new eds. 1969, 1977), *The new towns: The answer to megalopolis*, Leonard Hill, London.
Parker, (R.) B., 1895, Our homes, *Building news*, 10, 26 July. (Also reprinted for private circulation, 1895, Buxton).
———, 1907, Town planning, *The Garden City*, NS II (18) July: 366–7.
———, 1916, Horizontality and verticality in the treatment of town planning schemes, *British Architect*, NS. 85 (2), June: 45–8; also *Papers and discussions of the Town Planning Institute*, 1915–16, II: 133–50.
———, 1919, Two years in Brazil, *Garden cities and town planning*, IX (8) August: 143–51.
———, 1922, Zoning to secure amenities, *Papers and discussions of the Town Planning Institute*, VIII: 77–82.
———, 1923, A lecture on Earswick delivered before the Town Planning Institute, 6 October 1923, offprint from *Journal of the Town Planning Institute*, Parker Collection, First Garden City Heritage Museum, Letchworth.
———, 1928, Economy in estate development, *Journal of the Town Planning Institute*, 14(8) July: 177–86.
———, 1929, Presidental address. Where we stand, *Journal of the Town Planning Institute*, (16) 2 December: 1–10.
———, 1933, Highways, parkways and freeways with special reference to Wythenshawe estate Manchester and to Letchworth Garden City, *Town and*

country planning, I(2) February: 38–43.
———, 1937, Site planning as exemplified at New Earswick, *Town planning review*, XVII (2) February: 79–102.
———, 1940a, The life and work of Sir Raymond Unwin, *Journal of the Town Planning Institute*, XXVI (5) August: 161–2.
———, 1940b, Memoir of Sir Raymond Unwin, *Journal of the Royal Institute of British Architects*, 3ss. 47 (19) 15 July: 209–10.
Parker, (R). B. and Unwin, R., 1901, The art of designing small houses and cottages, pp. 109–33 in *The art of building a home*, Longmans Green, London.
———, 1903, Cottages near a town, pp. 34–43 in *Catalogue of the Northern Artworkers Guild Exhibition*, H. C. D. Chorlton, Manchester. (The First Garden City Heritage Museum at Letchworth also holds a private offprint.)
———, 1906, The cheap cottage: What is really needed, *The Garden City*, I (4) July: 55–57.
Pepler, G. L. 1931, Twenty-one years of planning in England and Wales, *Journal of the Town Planning Institute*, XVII(3) January: 49–72.
———, 1940, Sir Raymond Unwin, *Town and country planning*, VIII(31) August: 48.
Pepper, S., and Swenarton, M., 1978, Home front, *Architectural Review*, CLX III (976) June: 366–75.
Percy, C., and Ridley, J., 1985, *The letters of Edwin Lutyens*, Collins, London.
Pevsner, N., 1951, *The buildings of England: Middlesex*, Penguin, London.
———, (revised Cherry, B.) 1977, *The buildings of England: Hertfordshire*, Penguin, London.
Proceedings of the Third National Conference on City Planning, 1911, The University Press, Cambridge, Mass.
Purdom, C. B., 1913, *The Garden City*, Dent, London.
———, (ed.), 1921, *Town theory and practice*, Benn, London.
———, 1925, *Garden cities and satellite towns*, Dent, London.
———, 1951, *Life over again*, Dent, London.
———, 1963a, *The Letchworth Achievement*, Dent, London.
———, 1963b, Unwin and the Garden City Movement, *Town and Country Planning*, XXXI (II) November: 428–33.
Rasmussen, S. E., 1957, A great planning achievement, *Town and country planning*, XXV (7) July: 283–8.
———, 1963, Unwin: the man and the planner, *Town and country planning*, XXI (ii) November: 433.
———, 1967, *London: the unique city*, Massachusetts Institute of Technology Press.
'Raymond Unwin', 1911, *Garden cities and town planning*, NS I(1), February 17.
Reiss, R. L., 1918, *The home I want*, Hodder and Stoughton, London.
Reynolds, J. P., 1952, Thomas Coglan Horsfall and the town planning movement in England, *Town planning review*, XXII: 52–66.
RIBA (Royal Institute of British Architects), 1910a, *Town planning conference members handbook*, London.
———, 1910b, Town Planning Conference London 10–15 October, *Exhibition of drawing and models at the Royal Academy*, London.
———, 1911, Town Planning Conference London, 10–15 October 1910, *Transactions*, London.
Rowntree, B. S., 1901, *Poverty, A study of town life*, Macmillan, London.

——, 1918, Housing after the War, *Journal of the Royal Society of Arts*, LXVII (3448) 20 December: 65–77.

Scott, Mel, 1969, *American city planning since 1890*, University of California Press, Los Angeles and Berkeley.

Sharp, E. G., 1980, The London County Council green belt scheme – a note on some primary sources, *Planning History Bulletin*, 2(2) 1980:14.

Sheail, J., 1981, *Rural conservation in interwar Britain*, Oxford University Press,

Simon, A. P., 1936, *Manchester made over*, King and Son, London.

Simon, Sir E. and Lady S., 1935, *Wythenshawe*, Longmans Green, London.

Simon, Sir E. and Inman, J., 1935, *The rebuilding of Manchester*, Longmans Green, London.

Simpson, M., 1981, Thomas Adams, 1871–1940, pp. 19–45 in Cherry, G. E. (ed.) 1981, *Pioneers in British planning*, Architectural Press, London.

——, 1985, *Thomas Adams and the modern planning movement*, Mansell, London.

Sitte, C. (trans. Collins, G. R. and C. C.), 1965, *City planning according to artistic principles*, Phaidon, London.

Slack, K. M., 1982, *Henrietta's dream. A chronicle of the Hampstead Garden Suburb 1905–1982*, New Hampstead Garden Suburb Trust Ltd., London.

Slater, A. E., 1910, The planning of an industrial suburb (*sic*), *The surveyor and municipal engineer*, 2 December: 736–8.

Smets, M. 1977, *L'Avenement de la Cité-Jardin en Belgique*, Pierre Mardaga, Brussels and Liege.

de Soissons, M., 1988, *Welwyn Garden City: a town designed for healthy living*, Publications for companies, Cambridge.

Special methods of construction, 1919, *Housing*, 10 November.

Stein, C. S., 1949–50, Toward new towns for America, *Town Planning Review*, XX(3), October: 204–82: XX(4) Jan: 319–418.

Suggestions to promoters of town-planning schemes. Report of the town planning committee, 1910, *Journal of the Royal Institute of British Architects*, 3ss. XVIII August: 662–8.

Sussmann, C. (ed.), 1976, *Planning the fourth migration: the neglected vision of the Regional Planning Association of America*, Massachusetts Institute of Technology Press, Cambridge.

Sutcliffe, A. (ed.), 1900, *The Rise of Modern Town Planning 1800–1914*, Mansell, London.

Swenarton, M., 1981, *Homes fit for heroes*, Heinemann Educational Books, London.

——, 1989, *Artisans and architects: The Ruskinian tradition in architectural thought*, Macmillan, Basingstoke.

Tafuri, M., and Dal Co., F., 1980, *Modern architecture*, Academy, London.

Tarn, J. N., 1973, *Five per cent philanthropy. An account of housing in urban areas 1850–1914*, Cambridge University Press.

Taylor, N. 1971, An architectural appraisal of the garden suburb, pp. 117–43 in Shankland Cox and Associates, *Hampstead Garden Suburb. A conservation study*, consultants' report to the New Hampstead Garden Suburb Trust Ltd. London.

——, 1973, *The village in the city*, Temple Smith, London.

Thomas, D., 1970, *London's green belt*, Faber, London.

Thompson, E. P., 1977, *William Morris, Romantic to revolutionary*, (revised edition), Merlin Press, London.

Thompson, L., 1971, *The enthusiastics: A biography of John and Katharine Bruce Glasier*, Gollancz, London.

Thompson, T. F., 1940, Sir Raymond Unwin, *Journal of the Town Planning Institute*, XXVI (5) August: 187.

Town Planning and modern domestic architecture (at the Hampstead Garden Suburb) 1909, Unwin, London.

Town Planning in London: Dr Unwin on decentralisation, 1929, *The Times*, 2 January: 9d.

Town Planning Conference at Liverpool, 1911, *The Builder*, March 3: 265–7.

Tsuzuki, C., 1980, *Edward Carpenter 1844-1929. Prophet of human fellowship*, Cambridge University Press.

Unwin, R. 1886, The Axe is laid unto the root, *Commonweal*, August, 14: 155.

———, 1887a, Broken cisterns, *Commonweal*, November 19: 370–1; November 26: 378–9; December 3: 386–7; December 10: 394–5; December 17: 402; December 24: 411; December 31: 418–19.

———, 1887b, Early communal life and what it teaches, *Commonweal*, April 16: 122–3; April 23: 134–5; April 30: 138–9; May 7: 146–7; May 14: 157.

———, 1887c, Positivism and Socialism, *Commonweal*, July 23: 235; July 30: 243; August 6: 250–1.

———, 1887d, Socialist tactics. A third course, *Today*, 8 (49), December: 180-6.

———, 1887e, 'Social experiments', *Commonweal*, March 5: 76–7.

———, 1888, Socialism and progress, *Commonweal*, April 7: 108–9.

———, 1889a, Sutton Hall, *Commonweal*, June 15: 190.

———, 1889b, A tramp's diary, *Commonweal*, April 27: 132.

———, 1890, Down a coal pit, *Commonweal*, June 7: 177–8; June 14: 188–9.

Unwin, R., 1900–1, Cooperation in building, *The architects' magazine*, I(2) December: 20; I(3) January: 37–8.

———, 1901a, Of art and simplicity, pp. 55–67, in Parker (R.) B. and Unwin, R., *The art of building a home*, Longmans Green, London.

———, 1901b, Building and natural beauty, pp. 83–9 in *The art of building a home*, Longmans Green, London.

———, 1901c, Co-operation in building, pp. 91–108 in Parker (R.) B. and Unwin, R., *The art of building a home*, Longmans Green, London.

———, 1901d, On the building of houses in the garden city, pp. 66–74 in *The Garden City Conference at Bournville*, Garden City Association, London.

———, 1902, *Cottage Plans and Common Sense*, Fabian Tract 109, Fabian Society, London.

———, 1904, *The improvement of towns*, Conference of the National Union of Women Workers of Great Britain and Ireland, November 8, London (offprint in Parker Collection, First Garden City Heritage Museum, Letchworth); 1905, published in *The Craftsman* 8: 809–16.

———, 1906a, Cottage Building in the Garden City, The Garden City, NS.(V) June: 107:11.

———, 1906b, The planning of the residential districts of towns, pp. 417–25 in *Transactions of the VII International Congress of Architects*, Royal Institute of British Architects, London.

———, 1908, Town and street planning, *Journal of the Royal Society Institute*, XXIX (9) September: 471–8.

———, 1909, *Town Planning in Practice*, T. Fisher Unwin, London.

———, (trans. by Maclean, L.), 1910a, *Grundlagen des Stadtebaues: ein anleitung zum entwerfen stadtbaulicher anlagen* (Town Planning in Practice), Baumgartel, O., Berlin.

———, 1910b, The planning of towns and suburbs, Papers collected by the RIBA town planning committee, XII, *Journal of the Royal Institute of British Architects*, 3ss. XVII, March 5: 365–76.

———, 1910c, Town planning, *Journal of the Society of Architects*, NS III (27) January: 88–108.

———, 1910d, Town planning in Berlin, *Architectural Review* XXVII, August, (housing and town planning supplement): 93–102.

———, 1911a, American town planning, *Garden cities and town planning*, NS I (7) August: 162–5.

———, 1911b, The city development plan, pp. 247–65 in *RIBA* (Royal Institute of British Architects) *Town Planning Conference, London, 10–15 October 1910, Transactions*, London.

———, 1911c, Introduction to the second edition, *Town planning in practice*, T. Fisher Unwin, London.

———, 1911d, Town planning and its effect upon the housing problem, *Local government review*, III (19) May: 299–301.

———, 1911e, Town planning at Hampstead I, II, *Garden cities and town planning*, I(I) February: 6–9 I(4) May: 82–5.

———, 1911f, Town Planning: formal or irregular? *Architectural Association Journal*, XXVI (29) November: 265–72.

———, 1912a, The Hampstead Garden Suburb Extension, *The Record*, Hampstead Garden Suburb I(i) August: 6–10.

———, 1912b, *Nothing Gained by Overcrowding. How the Garden City type of development may benefit both the owner and occupier*, Garden Cities and Town Planning Association, London. Also *Garden Cities and Town Planning*, 1912, NS II (9) September: 192–4; NS II 10 October: 219–22; NS II (11) November: 242–7.

———, 1912c, The town extension plan, pp. 33–62 in *Old towns and new needs: also The town extension plan: being the Warburton lectures for 1912*, Manchester University Press.

———, 1912d, What is town planning? Transcript of introductory lecture at Birmingham University October 1911, *Garden Cities and Town Planning*, NS II(I) January: 11–15.

———, 1913a, The planning of Garden City (*sic*), Appendix B. pp. 222–9 in Purdom, C. B. *The Garden City*, Dent, London.

———, 1913b, The future of Finchley, *The Record* (Hampstead Garden Suburb), I (ix) April: 141–2.

———, 1913c, Some points on school design, *The Record*, (Hampstead Garden Suburb), I (vii) February: 109–10; I (viii) March: 125–7.

———, 1913d, A symposium on the municipal ownership of land, (also includes contributions from Nettlefold, J. and Hyder, J.), *Town Planning Review*, IV (I) April: 13–25.

———, 1914a, Canada and town planning, *The Record*, (Hampstead Garden Suburb), II (vii), February: 87–9.

———, 1914b, Roads and streets, *Journal of the London Society*, (2) January: 13–20 (also published 1914, *Town Planning Review*, V(I) April: 31–9).

———, 1914c, Town planning in relation to land values, *Town Planning Review*, V(2) July: 107–14 (also 1914/5 *Town Planning Institute papers and discussions*, I: xii–xvii).

———, 1915a, *The war and what after?*, Garden City Press, Letchworth.

———, 1915b, The work of the Town Planning Institute, *Town Planning Institute papers and discussions*, I(9): 131–3.

——, 1919a, The cost of open development, *Housing* I(II) 8 December, I(12), 20 December: 146–8; 162–3.

——, 1919b, Homes for human beings, *Garden Cities and Town Planning*, IX(9) September: 163–5.

——, 1919c, Housing: the architect's contribution, *Journal of the Royal Institute of British Architects*, 3ss. XXVI (3) January: 49–64.

——, 1919d, *The nation's new houses: pictures and plans*, (with a foreword by the President of the Local Government Board), Nottingham Journal and Express.

——, 1919e, Vacation lectures. Housing and communal planning, *Architectural Association Journal*, XXXV (392), October: 188–9.

——, 1920a, The city practical: the garden city principle applied to the development of towns, *Housing*, April, 12: 267.

——, 1920b, The future development of London, *The Builder*, LXVIII (4016) January 23: 117.

——, 1920c, New problems in town planning, *Garden Cities and Town Planning*, X(5), May: 108–13.

——, 1920d, Site planning: aspects of site planning needing further attention, *Housing* (site planning number), August 30: 41–3.

——, 1920e, Some thoughts on the development of London, *Journal of the London Society*, (26) April: 8–10.

——, 1921a, American architecture and town planning, *Journal of the Royal Institute of British Architects*, 3ss. XXIX (3) 10 December: 76–84.

——, 1921b, The civic survey – a city's control of its growth, *Garden cities and town planning*, XI (3) March: 59–62.

——, 1921c, Distribution, *Town Planning Institute papers and Discussions*, VII (1920–1): 37–52.

——, 1921d, Some thoughts on the development of London, pp. 177–92 in Webb, Sir A. (ed.), *London of the future: essays by the London Society*, Dutton, London (see also Unwin 1920b, 1920e.).

——, 1921e, The town and the best size for good social life, pp. 80–102 in Purdom, C. B. (ed.), *Town theory and practice*, Benn, London.

——, 1922a, L'etude practique des plans de villes: *Introduction a l'art de dessiner les plans d'amenagement et d'extension par Raymond Unwin*. (Town planning in practice), Libraire Centrale des beaux-arts, Paris.

——, 1922b, The overgrown city, *The survey*, 49, 15 October: 85–6.

——, 1922c, Zoning, *Town Planning Institute papers and discussions*, VIII (1921–2): 115–33.

——, 1923a, An architect's handbook of civic art, *Journal of the Royal Institute of British Architects*, 3ss. XXX (13) May 12: 416–7.

——, 1923b, The garden city and the overgrown town, pp. 39–49 in *Report of conference at Gothenburg, 1923*, International Garden Cities and Town Planning Federation, London, 1923.

——, 1923c, The Gothenburg International Town Planning Exhibition and Conference, *Journal of the Royal Institute of British Architects*, 3ss. XXX (19) 22 September: 621–2.

——, 1924a, Higher building in relation to town planning, *Journal of the Royal Institute of British Architects*, 3ss (5) 12 January: 125–49.

——, 1924b, The need for a regional plan, pp. 15–50 in *Report* of Conference, International Garden Cities and Town Planning Federation, London. Summarized in *Garden Cities and Town Planning*, 1924, XIV (7) July: 170–1.

———, 1924c, Town planning in a city like Oxford, *Journal of the Royal Institute of British Architects*, 3ss. XXXI, 16 August 613–8, (also *Journal of the Town Planning Institute* 1924, X (12) October: 36–47).
———, 1925a, The architect and his city, *Journal of the Royal Institute of British Architects*, 3ss. XXXIII (2) November 4: 35–50.
———, 1925b, Methods of decentralisation, pp. 150–65 in *Report* of Conference, International Housing and Town Planning Federation, London.
———, 1929a, Housing, *Encyclopedia Britannica*, Fourteenth edition, London and New York.
———, 1929b, Memorandum No. 1 on Open Spaces, pp. 8–26 in *Greater London Regional Planning Committee. First report, December 1929*, Knapp and Drewett, Westminster, London.
———, 1929c, Memorandum No. 2 on ribbon development and sporadic building, pp. 27–33 in *Greater London Regional Planning Committee. First report December 1929*, Knapp and Drewett, Westminster, London.
———, 1929d, Memorandum No. 3 on the additional town planning powers required, pp. 34–39 in *Greater London Regional Planning Committee. First report, December 1929*, Knapp and Drewett, Westminster, London.
———, 1930a, Introduction. Decentralisation of industry, pp. 1–19 in Warren, H. and Davidge, W. R. (eds.) *Decentralisation of population and industry*, King, London.
———, 1930b, Making the plan of Letchworth, *Garden Cities and Town Planning*, XX(6) June/July: 156–9.
———, 1930c, Regional Planning in Greater London, *International housing and town planning bulletin*, 24 December: 4–10 (followed by translations).
———, 1930d, Regional planning with special reference to the Greater London Regional Plan, *Journal of the Royal Institute of British Architects*, 3ss. XXXVII (6) 25 January: 183–98.
———, 1931a, The architect's contribution. Inaugural Presidential address, 2 November 1931, *Journal of the Royal Institute of British Architects*, 3ss. 39(1) November 7: 5–12.
———, 1931b, Edward Carpenter and Towards Democracy, pp. 234–43 in Beith, G. (ed.), *Edward Carpenter. In appreciation*, George Allen and Unwin, London.
———, 1931c, Housing and the slums, *The Spectator*, 5398 December 12: 804–5.
———, 1931d, *Interim Report. Decentralisation*, Greater London Regional Plan Committee, London.
———, 1931e, *Interim Report. Open spaces*, Greater London Regional Plan Committee, London.
———, 1931f, The relation between town and regional planning, *Journal of the Town Planning Institute*, XVII (3) March: 105–17.
———, 1932a, The conference banquet (Manchester), *Journal of the Royal Institute of British Architects*, 3ss. 39, July 9: 693–5.
———, 1932b, Housing and unemployment, *Labour newsletter* 2(7) December 10: 10–11.
———, 1932c, Housing: The present opportunity. Inaugural address 7 November 1932, *Journal of the Royal Institute of British Architects*, 3ss. (40) 1, 12 November: 5–13.
———, 1932d, Looking back and forth (Presidential address to students), *Journal of the Royal Institute of British Architects*, 3ss. 39(6) January 23: 204–8.
———, 1932e, Town and country planning and land values (paper read at the

Economics section of the British Association, September 1931), *Contemporary Review*, CXI (796), April: 459–67.
———, 1933a, The cost of houses, *Journal of the Royal Institute of British Architects*, 3ss. 40, 9 September: 796–7.
———, 1933b, The housing problem – preliminary outline of a policy, *Journal of the Royal Institute of British Architects*, 3ss. 40, 11 February: 277.
———, 1933c, Memorandum on the housing problem for 1933, *Journal of the Royal Institute of British Architects*, 3ss. 40, January 14: 173–4.
———, 1933d, A national housing corporation, *The New Statesman and Nation*, V (103), February 11: 155–6.
———, 1933e, The President's inaugural address (Cambridge Conference), *Journal of the Royal Institute of British Architects*, 3ss. 40, 8 July: 658–61.
———, 1933f, The proposed national housing boards, *The Listener*, IX (220) 29 March: 433–5.
———, 1934a, The American Housing Corporation, *The Listener*, XII (287), 11 July: 56–9.
———, 1934b, Britain's experience in low-cost housing, *Journal of the American Institute of Architects*, 6 (1), January: 5–8.
———, 1934c, Cottage homes better than flats: congestion and discontent, housing supplement, *Daily Telegraph*, November 26: vii.
———, 1934d, England's housing example, *Architectural Forum*, LX (2), February: 115–20.
———, 1934e, Property and prosperity. An interpretation of the swing in America in terms of real estate, *The Listener*, XI (280), 23 May: 853–4, 888.
———, 1934f, A trip to Canada and the United States, *Journal of The Royal Institute of British Architects*, 3ss. 41, 28 April: 646–7.
———, 1935a, Founders day ceremony. Honorary degrees conferred by Manchester University, *Manchester Guardian*, Manchester, 16 May: 13.
———, 1935b, Urban development. The pattern and the background, *Journal of the Town Planning Institute*, XXI (10) August: 253–66.
———, 1936a, Edward Unwin (obituary). *Journal of the Royal Institute of British Architects*, 3ss. 43, 18 January: 315.
———, 1936b, Housing and planning, *Journal of the Royal Sanitary Institute*, LVII(3), September: 169–76.
———, 1936c, The housing problem. How planned distribution may prevent crowding, *Journal of the Royal Sanitary Institute*, LV1 (10), April: 602–14.
———, 1936–7, *Housing and town planning lectures*, Sub-committee on Research and Statistics, Central Housing Committee, Washington DC.
———, 1937a, The garden city ideal (contribution to Towards a healthy social life, a discussion on town and country planning, with contributions by Raymond Unwin, Thomas Sharp, R. H. Livett), *The Listener*, XVII (4620 17 November: 1069.
———, 1937b, General Report, pp. 94–6 in *Report of Conference, International Housing and Town Planning Federation*, 1937, London.
———, 1937c, Housing and planning: English and American compared, *Journal of the Royal Society of Arts*, LXXXV (4413), June 18: 716–28.
———, 1937d, The Royal Gold Medal presentation to Sir Raymond Unwin, Monday 12 April 1937. *Journal of the Royal Institute of British Architects*, 3ss. 144(12), 24 April: 581–7.
———, 1938a, The housing problem, *Journal of the American Institute of Architects*, 10 (7), July: 14–16.
———, 1938b, Presidential address (as sectional President for Architecture,

town planning and engineering at the Royal Sanitary Institute Conference), *Journal of the Royal Sanitary Institute*, LIX (3), September: 211–17.

———, 1938c, Memorandum of evidence, submitted to the Royal Commission on the distribution of the industrial population, *Minutes of Evidence*, Twenty-fifth day, pp. 845–61; twenty-sixth day, pp. 879–85.

———, 1939, Plan - or perish, *Town and Country Planning*, VII (28) July/September: 112–3.

———, 1940a, Planning problems in the United States, *Town and Country Planning*, VIII (31), August: 49–50.

———, 1940b, The rural region: the ensemble of economic problems of the country pp. 48–53 in *Report* Volume I of the Fifteenth International Congress of Architects, Washington.

———, 1941, Land values in relation to planning and housing in the United States, *Journal of land and public utility economics*, North Western University, Chicago, 17 (1), February: 1–9.'

Vivian, H., 1906, Co-partnership in Housing, pp. 25–33 in *Housing in town and country*, (transactions of) a Conference of the Garden City Association, London, 16 March.

Waddilove, L. E., 1954, *One man's vision. The story of the Joseph Rowntree Village Trust*, George Allen and Unwin, London.

Ward, S., 1974, The Town and Country Planning Act, 1932, *The Planner*, (*Journal of the Royal Town Planning Institute*), 60(5), May: 685–9.

Warren, H., and Davidge, W. R., 1930, *Decentralisation of popoulation and industry*, King, London.

Weaver, L. 1913, *Houses and gardens by Sir Edwin Lutyens*, Country Life, London.

Webb, Sir Aston (ed.), 1921, *London of the future: essays by the London Society*, Dutton, London.

Webb, B., (ed. Cole, M.), 1952, *Diaries 1912–24*, Longman, London.

Whittick, A., 1987, *F.J.O. - practical idealist: A biography of Sir Frederic Osborn*, Town and Country Planning Association, London.

Wiebenson, D., n.d., *c.*1979, *Tony Garnier: The Cite Industrielle*, Studio Vista, London (and Brazilier, New York).

Williams Ellis, C., 1924, *The pleasures of architecture*, Jonathan Cape, London.

———, 1928, *England and the Octopus*, Bles, London.

Index